Data Compression:

Methods and Theory

PRINCIPLES OF COMPUTER SCIENCE SERIES

ISSN 0888-2096

Series Editors

Alfred V. Aho, *Bell Telephone Laboratories, Murray Hill, New Jersey*
Jeffrey D. Ullman, *Stanford University, Stanford, California*

1. *Algorithms for Graphics and Image Processing*[†]
   Theo Pavlidis
2. *Algorithmic Studies in Mass Storage Systems*[†]
   C. K. Wong
3. *Theory of Relational Databases*[†]
   David Maier
4. *Computational Aspects of VLSI*[†]
   Jeffrey D. Ullman
5. *Advanced C: Food for the Educated Palate*[†]
   Narain Gehani
6. *C: An Advanced Introduction*[†]
   Narain Gehani
7. *C for Personal Computers: IBM PC, AT&T PC 6300, and Compatibles*[†]
   Narain Gehani
8. *Principles of Computer Design*[†]
   Leonard R. Marino
9. *The Theory of Database Concurrency Control*[†]
   Christos Papadimitriou
10. *Computer Organization*[†]
    Michael Andrews
11. *Elements of Artificial Intelligence Using LISP*
    Steven Tanimoto
12. *Trends in Theoretical Computer Science*
    Egon Börger, Editor
13. *Data Compression: Methods and Theory*
    James A. Storer

[†] These previously-published books are in the *Principles of Computer Science Series* but they are not numbered within the volume itself. All future volumes in the *Principles of Computer Science Series* will be numbered.

Data Compression:

Methods and Theory

James A. Storer
Computer Science Department
Brandeis University

COMPUTER SCIENCE PRESS

Computer Science Press
1803 Research Boulvard
Rockville, Maryland 20850

1 2 3 4 5 6 Printing   Year 93 92 91 90 89 88

Library of Congress Cataloging-in-Publication Data

Storer, James A. (James Andrew), 1953-
    Data Compression.

    (Principles of computer science series)
    Bibliography: p.
    Includes index.
    1. Data compression (Computer science)

I. Title. II. Series.
QA76.9.D33S76   1988   005.74'6   87-30107
ISBN 0-88175-161-8

TABLE OF CONTENTS

PREFACE

The term *data compression* refers to the process of transforming a body of data to a smaller representation from which the original or some approximation to the original can be computed at a later time. This book is primarily concerned with *lossless* data compression, where data that is compressed and then subsequently decompressed must always be identical to the original. Although lossless data compression can be applied to any type of data, in practice, it is most appropriate for *textual data* (printed English such as this book, programming language source or object code, database information, numerical data, electronic mail, etc.) where it is typically important to preserve the original data exactly. By contrast, *lossy* data compression allows the decompressed data to differ from the original data so long as the decompressed data satisfies some fidelity criterion. For example, with image compression, it may suffice to have an image that looks as good to the human eye as the original. Although lossless data compression may be viewed as a special case of lossy compression, in practice, the techniques used often differ greatly. Hence, it is reasonable to consider lossless compression separately from lossy compression. However, Chapter 3 will consider lossy techniques that arise naturally as generalizations of practical lossless techniques.

The phrase "Methods and Theory" was included in the title of this book to reflect its basic "flavor", which is a blend of theoretical issues with practical algorithms. The six chapters can be grouped in pairs. Chapters 1 and 2 review traditional concepts from information theory, including the well-known method of Huffman coding. Chapters 3 and 4 address *on-line textual substitution techniques*, which are perhaps the most powerful and practical methods currently available for lossless compression. Chapter 3 also discusses how on-line textual substitution techniques can be generalized to practical lossy techniques. Chapters 5 and 6 consider theoretical issues pertaining to lossless compression. All of Chapters 1 through 6 contain bibliographic notes which attempt to put in perspective that vast amount of research on data compression. In addition, the appendices provide for the practitioner both source code and empirical results.

ix

The book assumes that the reader has a reasonable level of mathematical sophistication and a general familiarity with the field of computer science that includes computer hardware, algorithms and data structures, and basic topics in the theory of computation (e.g., NP-completeness, basic automata theory, and undecidability). However, it is possible for the reader that is either unfamiliar or uninterested in some of these areas to concentrate on only subsets of the chapters. All of Chapters 3 through 6 have been written to be reasonably independent. After at least skimming Chapters 1 and 2, it should be possible to read most of any one of these Chapters without reading the others.

Acknowledgements

I would like to thank Tom Szymanski and Jeff Ullman for their support and advice during the writing of my Ph.D. thesis at Princeton University (on which portions of this book are based), and Juris Hartmanis for his inspiration and encouragement at Cornell University that originally lead me to the field of computer science. My appreciation also goes to David Maier for many helpful discussions during the early phases of the writing of this book as well as a careful reading of the final draft, and to Marty Cohn, Ben Cox, and Bob Lindsay for many helpful discussions during the later phases of the writing of this book. Moises Lejter and Stephen Tsang deserve special thanks for help with some of the programming required for the appendices, Finally, I would like to thank Jacques Cohen who, in his capacity as Chairman of the Computer Science Department at Brandeis, provided a research environment conducive to both the writing and the typesetting[†] of this book.

J.A.S.

9/1/87

---

† This book was typeset by the author at Brandeis University, with the *Troff* typesetting language (device-independent version), running under the Berkeley 4.3 *Unix operating system* (Unix is a trademark of the Bell System), on a Digital Equipment Co. *VAX 11/780* computer, connected to an *Imagen* laser printer (with a resolution of 300 points per inch). The *Eqn* preprocessor was used for equations, the *Tbl* preprocessor for tables, and the *Grn* preprocessor for figures. The Berkeley *Gremlin* line-drawing editor was used to enter figures on a SUN work-station.

1

INTRODUCTION

1.1. WHAT IS DATA COMPRESSION?

For this book, the term *data* will mean *digital* data: data that is represented as a sequence of *characters* drawn from some *alphabet*. The most common examples of an alphabet are the binary alphabet {0,1} or the English alphabet (upper and lower case letters, digits, punctuation characters, and possibly a number of special characters such as backspace). Typical examples of digital data are English text, database information, numerical data, digitally sampled images or video, digitally sampled speech or music, programming language source or object code, and electronic mail.

Data compression is the process of *encoding* a body of data D into a smaller body of data $\Delta(D)$. It must be possible for $\Delta(D)$ to be *decoded* back to D or some acceptable approximation to D. Not all data can be compressed. However, most data that arises in practice contains redundancy of which compression algorithms may take advantage. Although data compression has many applications, the two most common are the following:

Data Storage: A body of data is compressed before it is stored on some digital storage device (e.g., a computer disk or tape). This process allows more data to be placed on a given device. When data is retrieved from the device, it is decompressed.

Data Communications: Communication lines that are commonly used to transmit digital data include cables between a computer and storage devices, phone lines, and satellite channels. A sender can compress data before transmitting it and the receiver can decompress the data after receiving it. As a concrete example, consider a business that leases 10 telephone lines between New York and Los Angeles and communicates digitally over these lines via modems. If the data can be compressed by a factor of 2, then the speed of each of these 10 communication links is effectively doubled. The business then has the option of sending and receiving twice the amount of data per day or leasing only 5 lines. Note that this factor of 2 speedup is independent of the speed of the modems used.

Effective algorithms for data compression have been known since the early 1950's. There has traditionally been a tradeoff between the benefits of employing data compression versus the computational costs incurred to perform the encoding and subsequent decoding. However, with the advent of cheap microprocessors and custom chips, data compression is rapidly becoming a standard component of communications and data storage. A data encoding/decoding chip can be placed at the ends of a communication channel with no computational overhead incurred by the communicating processes. Similarly, secondary storage space can be increased by hardware (invisible to the user) that performs data compression.

Lossless data compression is the process of transforming a body of data to a smaller one, from which it is possible to recover exactly the original data at some point later in time. Lossless compression is appropriate for *textual data* (printed English such as this book, programming language source or object code, database information, numerical data, electronic mail, etc.) where it may be unacceptable to lose even a single bit of information. By contrast, *lossy data compression* is the process of transforming a body of data to a smaller body from which an approximation to the original can be constructed. For various types of data, what defines a "close approximation" is an area of research in itself. An important application of lossy compression is the compression of *digitally sampled analog data* (DSAD) such as speech, music, black and white or color images, video, and satellite data. For example, if one sends a digital representation of a photograph over a communication line, it may only be important that the photograph received looks, to the human eye, identical to the original; that is as long as this was true, it is ok if the actually bits received differ from the bits sent.

Although lossless data compression may be viewed as a special case of lossy compression, in practice, textual data and DSAD are two very distinct "flavors" of data and the techniques used for compression (and the amount of compression gained) typically differ greatly between the two classes of data. This book is primarily concerned with *lossless* data compression. However, the last section of Chapter 3 will consider lossy techniques that arise naturally as generalizations of practical lossless techniques.

Throughout this book, except when explicitly noted otherwise, we shall make the following assumptions:

Noiseless Channel: The communication channel or storage device involved is *noiseless*. That is, when a body of data is transmitted over a communication line, we assume that the identical body of data is received. Similarly, when a body of data is stored on some storage device and then retrieved at some later time, we assume that the retrieved data is identical to the original. We make this assumption primarily for convenience. A host of techniques are available in the literature for error detection and correction[†]. Some special-purpose techniques for efficiently dealing with noise with respect to particular compression algorithms will be mentioned at appropriate points in later chapters.

Serial I/O: There exists some constant k such that all input and output is done at most k characters at a time (typically $k=1$), where the term "character" simply refers to the basic unit that makes up data (e.g., single bits, English characters represented by 8 bits, or numerical data represented by 32 bits). Note that we use the term "serial" to refer to the model of input-output and not to the algorithms we derive; in fact, Chapter 4 is devoted to the study of parallel algorithms for data compression.

1.2. ENTROPY

Data compression has long been considered a topic in the field of *information theory*, the study of the representation, storage, transmission, and transformation of data. Fundamental to all of our discussion to follow is the notion of a source. Before defining this notion, we first give a formal definition of an alphabet and a "string over an alphabet".

Definition 1.2.1: An *alphabet* is a finite set containing at least one element. The elements of an alphabet are called *characters*. A *string over an alphabet* is a sequence of characters, each of which is an element of that alphabet. All strings are assumed to be finite unless otherwise stated. ○

---

† Such techniques typically expand the size of the data (by adding redundancy to it in very precise ways) and there is a trade-off between the amount of expansion and the security of the data against errors. See the bibliographic notes of Chapter 2.

The above definition allows alphabets of only one character, called *unary alphabets*, because this notion is useful for a number of technical reasons. However, throughout this book, whenever we refer to an alphabet without specifying its size, we assume that the size is at least 2.

Definition 1.2.2: Let $\Sigma = \{s_1 \cdots s_k\}$, $k \geq 1$, be an alphabet. A *source* is a process that sequentially produces characters of Σ, the *source alphabet*. A source is *first-order* if independent probabilities $p_1 \cdots p_k$, which sum to 1, are associated with the elements of Σ: character s_i is chosen for transmission with probability p_i (that is does not depend on what has been previously transmitted). ◯

A major achievement of information theory is a precise characterization of the information content of a source. To motivate the notion of information content, consider the following examples of first-order sources.

Example 1.2.1 (The Constant K-ary Source): Although the source alphabet has size $k \geq 1$, there is one designated character of the alphabet that is always chosen as the next character to transmit. That is, there is an i such that $p_i = 1$ (and hence for $j \neq i$, $p_j = 0$). ◯

Example 1.2.2 (The Random K-ary Source): The source alphabet has size $k \geq 1$. The next character to transmit is chosen uniformly and independently. That is, $p_i = 1/k$, $1 \leq i \leq k$. ◯

Example 1.2.3 (The Loaded K-ary Source): The source alphabet has size $k \geq 2$. The next character to transmit is chosen by throwing a k-sided die that has been "loaded" so that one of the faces corresponding to the "loaded character", comes up half the time and the other half of the time the remaining $k-1$ faces (corresponding to the remaining $k-1$ characters) come up with equal probability. That is, there is an i such that $p_i = 1/2$ and for $j \neq i$, $p_j = 1/(2(k-1))$. Note that for $k = 2$, the loaded source is the same as the random source. ◯

The constant source is an example of a source that has no information content; that is, since we always know what the next character will be, nothing is learned when it is received. The random source is an example of a source with high information content; that is, since all characters are equally likely to be the next, we learn a full character's worth of information (as much as we could) when a character is received. When $k > 2$, the loaded source has information content that lies somewhere between the constant and random sources. To see this relationship, consider how the constant, random, and loaded sources can be encoded into bits. With the constant source, the transmitter does not need to send any bits; each time the receiver wants a new character, it can simply generate one. Thus, the average number of bits that must be transmitted per character is 0. With the random source, a distinct sequence of $\lceil \log_2(k) \rceil$ bits[†] can be associated with each of the k characters of the source alphabet, and the appropriate sequence of bits can be sent to transmit a character. In addition, since with the random source each character is equally likely (and a distinct code must be assigned to each character), an average of $\log_2(k)$ bits per character is the best we can do. With the loaded source, the following scheme can be used to encode characters. If the character is the loaded character, then a single 0 can be sent. Otherwise, a 1 followed by $\lceil \log_2(k-1) \rceil$ bits can be sent. The average number of bits that is transmitted per character is:

$$\frac{1}{2} *1 + \frac{1}{2} \left(1 + \lceil \log_2(k-1) \rceil \right) = 1 + \lceil \log_2(k-1) \rceil /2$$

As k becomes large, this amount becomes arbitrarily close to half the average number of bits per character needed for the random source. Since (on the average) half of the time the loaded source looks like the random source over $k-1$ characters, it follows that the average number of bits that must be transmitted per character for the loaded source must be at least $(1 + \log_2(k-1))/2 \geq \log_2(k)/2$.

With the examples above, the less random the source, the fewer bits per character that were needed. This relationship holds in general. In information theoretic terms, sequences that are less random (have patterns or structure) require fewer bits to represent and are thus considered to have less information content. In the late 1940's, C. E. Shannon gave a formal definition of the notion of information content or randomness of a source, which he called *entropy*. We now present this definition as it pertains to first-order sources.

Definition 1.2.3: For some integer $k \geq 1$ let S be a first-order source that generates characters from the alphabet

$$\Sigma = \{s_1 \cdots s_k\}$$

---

† Throughout this book, for a real number h, we use the standard "floor" notation of $\lceil h \rceil$ to denote the least integer that is greater than or equal to h and "ceiling" notation of $\lfloor h \rfloor$ to denote the greatest integer that is less than or equal to h.

with independent probabilities $p_1 \cdots p_k$. The *entropy* of S for radix r, $r > 1$, is given by:

$$H_r(S) = \sum_{i=1}^{k} p_i \log_r(1/p_i)$$

When the radix is not specified, we assume $r=2$ in the formula above (information is measured in bits) and abbreviate $H_2(S)$ as $H(S)$. ◯

A fundamental result of information theory, which we henceforth refer to as *the fundamental source-coding theorem*, is the following:

> Let S be a first-order source over an alphabet Σ and let Γ be an alphabet of $r > 1$ characters. Then encoding the characters of S with characters of Γ requires an average of $H_r(s)$ characters of Γ per character of Σ. Furthermore, for any real number $\epsilon > 0$ there exists a coding scheme that uses an average of $H_r(s) + \epsilon$ characters of Γ per character of Σ.

Intuitively, for a first-order source S, the entropy formula $H_r(S)$ sums over the characters of the source alphabet the probability of a character being chosen times the length of an optimal radix-r encoding of that character. For example, a quick calculation shows that for the constant, random, and loaded sources discussed earlier, $H(S)$ is 0, $\log_2(k)$, and $1 + \log_2(k-1)/2$, respectively.

In practice, sources are rarely first-order. Typically, the probability of a character occurring depends on what came before it. For example, with English text, after seeing the characters "elephan", there is a higher probability that "t" will be the next character than first-order probabilities would indicate. This observation leads naturally to the notion of an ith-*order source*, $i \geq 1$, where i denotes the number of characters (including itself) on which the current one depends[†]. The notion of an ith-order source leads naturally to the notion of being in a "state" after some sequence of characters has already been generated; this notion is captured in the following definition.

[†] There is some disagreement in the literature as to the exact definition of i. Some define it as 1 less than our definition. That is, some authors would term what we call a first-order source, a *zero-order* source.

Definition 1.2.4: A *Markov source* consists of a complete directed graph[†] G where each edge (i, j) is labeled by both a probability p_{ij} and a character s_{ij} of Σ. The nodes of G are called *states*. One of the states is designated as the starting state. At the start of time, a "token" is placed on the starting state. From this time on, each time a character is to be generated, if the token is currently on state i, then the token is moved to state j with probability p_{ij}. When the token is moved from a state i to a state j, the character s_{ij} is transmitted. ○

Example 1.2.4: Figure 1.2.1 is an example of a Markov source. The start state is labeled by S. Each edge has a label of the form $c(p)$ where c is a character and p is a probability. This source works by repeatedly leaving the start state, generating a #, generating (with equal probability) one of the strings cat, dog, or aardvark, and returning to the start state. ○

A Markov source is perhaps the most standard model for a source. It is possible to generalize the notion of entropy and the fundamental source coding theorem to apply to Markov sources. In theory, even extremely complex sources such as English text can be be closely approximated by a Markov source. However, in practice, a manageable and accurate model for a particular real-life source is usually unobtainable. Thus, we shall not carry our discussion of entropy further. The importance of entropy for the purposes of this book is that for a source there *exists* an inherent entropy that we cannot "beat". We say that compression algorithms that are guaranteed to achieve the entropy (for sufficiently large inputs) are *optimal in the information theoretic sense*. The notion of entropy provides a foundation for intuitively reasonable facts such as the following:

- Random data cannot be compressed.

- Data that has been compressed by an optimal compressor (one that always achieves the entropy of the source) cannot be compressed further.

- One cannot guarantee that a data compressor will achieve any given performance on all data.

---

† By a complete directed graph, we mean one for which a directed edge exists for every ordered pair of nodes.

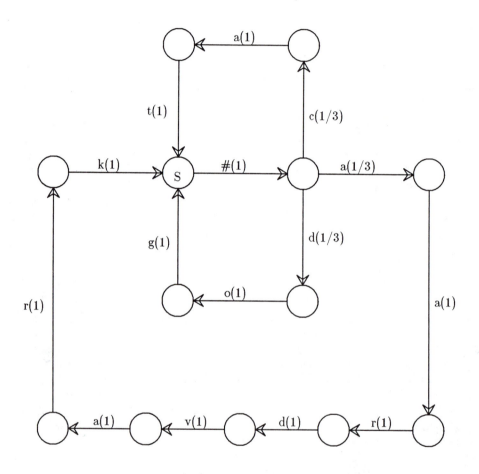

Figure 1.2.1

A technical condition that is often required of a source to prove that a compression algorithm is optimal in the information theoretic sense is that the source be *ergodic*. We shall not address this issue here; references to this condition are contained in the bibliographic notes. However, it should be remembered that a formal proof that a compression algorithm is optimal in the information theoretic sense requires a characterization of the source, which in practice is typically not possible. Thus, the above intuitive "facts" are in reality very good "rules of thumb" or "guidelines". Also, it should be pointed out that these guidelines apply only to the average case. It could be, for example, that a sequence of randomly generated bits just happened to form a pattern that has a very short representation. See Chapter 6 for a discussion of this issue and a discussion of *program size complexity,* which can be viewed as a more general notion of randomness and compressibility[†] than entropy.

The focus of this book is algorithms that attempt to compress data as much as possible, without necessarily knowing in advance anything about the data. Thus, although the notion of entropy (and more general notions considered in Chapter 6) is fundamental to the notion of data compression, it will not be directly relevant to most of the material on practical compression methods to follow in subsequent chapters.

1.3. PRINTED ENGLISH

An important issue for any compression method is how well does it perform in practice? This question is usually hard to answer, especially because the answer depends on the source, which is often hard to model. One way to partially answer such a question is to compare the performance of a given method on a large number of files from the same source. Printed English is one of the most common (and most familiar) sources of text in English speaking countries and we shall use it in examples throughout this book. For this reason it is appropriate to take a close look at the statistical properties of printed English.

In 1950, Shannon published what is now a very well-known paper on the entropy of printed English. In his paper, Shannon provides a convincing calculation of the entropy of English text. His method for the calculation is surprisingly simple. The basic observation is that anyone who speaks English has a great knowledge of the language. In particular, such a person can act as an excellent predictor in the following experiment.

A fragment of English text is selected that is unfamiliar to the subject. He (or she) is then asked to guess the first character. If the guess is correct, he is so informed, and if not, he is told the correct letter. He is then asked to guess the second letter, and so the experiment continues.

---

† Note that the notion of an incompressible string can be used as a definition of a random string.

As one would expect, guesses are more likely to be wrong at places like the beginning of a new word then at places like the end of a word (e.g., consider again trying to guess the next letter in the sequence "elephan"). Shannon observed the following:

> *How predictable data is (how easy it is to predict the next character having seen some number of previous characters) is equivalent to how compressible data is.*

He then constructed a model for computing the entropy of a source based on a series of such experiments that is performed with a perfect predictor (one that makes the best possible prediction based on the text already seen and a perfect knowledge of the language). Using this model in conjunction with experiments with humans (who are very good but not perfect predictors of English), he was able to bound the entropy of English to be between about 1 and 2 bits per character.

The work of Shannon just described is quite useful in that it provides a goal for English text compressors. However, because it assumes certain ideal conditions, such as a very powerful predictor, it does not really shed much light on how much compression might be achieved in practice. Further insights can be gained by experimentally compiling statistics about the language. Such compilations have been done by authors in the past, although often under assumptions that are geared more towards linguistic uses rather than compression (e.g., a limited character set, no distinction between upper and lower case, and ignoring of blanks and special symbols). References to such studies appear in the bibliographic notes at the end of this chapter. In addition, we now summarize some experimental results compiled for this book. The English statistics to be discussed will be most relevant to the "static" compression methods covered Chapters 2 and 3.

Appendix A.1 lists a set of English text files that total approximately one million characters (the manner in which these files were obtained is discussed in Appendix A.1). The files in Appendix A.1 were used to construct a dictionary of approximately 20,000 entries as follows. The dictionary was initialized to be empty and then the files listed in Appendix A.1 were processed one at a time. For each file, all substrings of length 8 or less were added to the dictionary (or their count incremented if the substring was already in the dictionary). Whenever the dictionary became too large (about 30,000 entries), the least frequently occurring entries were successively pruned until the size of the dictionary was brought back down to 20,000 entries. The result of this computation is a dictionary containing what are essentially the 20,000 most common substrings of length 8 or less in the files listed in Appendix A.1. However, due to the periodic pruning, some strings "slipped by" that should not have. For example, a string that occurred only once between each pruning of the dictionary might actually occur more often than a string that occurred several times within a small portion of a file and accumulated a sufficiently high frequency count to never be pruned. In addition, once the dictionary had been pruned to 20,000 entries, it may be that strings with the lowest counts remained in the dictionary while strings of equally low counts had already been removed. Thus, the dictionary obtained should be viewed as only an approximation to the true 20,000 most common substrings of 8 or fewer characters of the files listed in Appendix A.1.

To give the reader a feeling for what this dictionary looks like, Appendices A.1.1 through A.1.8 list the 100 most common 1-grams (single-character substrings) through 8-grams (8-character substrings) respectively in the dictionary and Appendix A.1.9 lists all strings of frequency 1000 or more in the dictionary (about 500 entries); along with each entry in these tables is the frequency of occurrence of that entry. Note that non-printable characters that appear in Appendices A.1.1 through A.1.9 have been replaced with special codes that are listed in Appendix A.1 (e.g., carriage returns are printed as @).

An inspection of Appendix A.1.1 shows that the one-letter frequencies reported there are quite consistent with what one would expect for general English text[†]. However, as one goes from Appendix A.1.1 to Appendix A.1.8, the entries get progressively more specialized. Considering Appendix A.1.8 for example, the strings are clearly not drawn from arbitrary English text; rather, most of them are recognizable pieces of strings such as "algorithm", "pointer", "function", "instruction", etc., which reflects the fact that the English source sampled was primarily technical writing pertaining to computer science. The reader should also note that as one goes from Appendix A.1.1 to A.1.8, the errors introduced due to the dictionary pruning become more evident. For example, "program" appears as one of the 100 most common 7-grams but "progra" does not appear as one of the 100 most common 6-grams. Similarly, "gorith" and "orithm" appear in the 100 most common 6-grams, but "lgorit" does not.

[†] However, even here, the frequencies are somewhat "specialized". Note that the frequency of "(" is not identical to ")"; this difference reflects the special use of "(" in the word-processing language used to type many of the sample files.

"Specialization" of a dictionary may be appropriate when it is used to compress specialized data. However, we should caution the reader to note that all one can really claim about the statistics reported in Appendices A.1.1 through A.1.9 is that they reflect the files listed in Appendix A.1, give some loose indication about technical writing in computer science, and only a slight indication of English writing as a whole. In order to get accurate statistics about a source such as written English, even in a restricted environment such as computer science technical writing, much more data would have to be sampled (i.e., by at least several orders of magnitude over the sample size of 1 million characters used here).

1.4. COMPRESSION BY TEXTUAL SUBSTITUTION

A powerful (and practical) approach to compressing a string of characters is *textual substitution*. A textual substitution data compression method is any compression method that compresses text by identifying repeated substrings and replacing some substrings by references to other copies. We call such a reference a *pointer*[†] and the string to which the pointer refers the *target* of the pointer. Thus, the input to a data compression algorithm employing textual substitution is a sequence of characters over some alphabet Σ and the output is a sequence of characters from Σ interspersed with pointers. We make the distinction between pointers and characters only for convenience. Since any well defined compression algorithm must be able to take as input a string consisting of a single character, it must be possible to represent any single character with whatever coding scheme is used to represent the output from the algorithm. Hence, a character can be viewed as a pointer to a string of exactly one character and the output of the compression algorithm as simply a sequence of pointers, where each pointer specifies some string of ≥ 1 characters of Σ.

---

† In the literature, such references are often called *codewords* or *tokens*.

1.5. OFF-LINE VERSUS ON-LINE ALGORITHMS

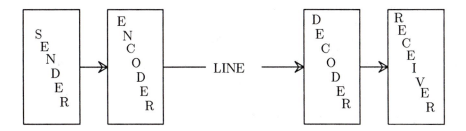

Figure 1.5.1

As depicted by Figure 1.5.1, a practical model for *on-line* data compression by textual substitution is to have an *encoder* and *decoder*, each with a fixed (finite) amount of local memory, which we refer to as a *local dictionary, D*. We assume that the two local dictionaries may be initialized at the beginning of time to contain identical information. The encoder connects the *communication line* to the *sender* and the decoder connects the communication line to the *receiver*. What distinguishes this model from an *off-line* model is that neither the sender nor the receiver can see all of the data at once; data must be constantly passing from the sender through the encoder, through the decoder, and on to the receiver. In theory, if D is large, then the encoder, for example, could read in as many bits of data as D is capable of storing (possibly more if the data is compressible), before having to send any bits to the receiver. However, in practice, the algorithms to be presented in this chapter can easily be implemented to run in real-time.

Definition 1.5.1: A compression-decompression method is *real-time* if there exists a constant k (which does not depend on the data being processed) such that for every k units of time, exactly one new character is read by the encoder and exactly one character is written by the decoder. The only exception to this rule is that we may allow a small "lag" between the encoder and decoder. That is, there is another constant l (that is independent of the data being processed) such that during the first l units of time the decoder may produce no characters and, in the case that the input is finite in length, l

time units may pass between the time that the encoder has finished reading characters and the decoder is finished outputting characters. ◯

In Section 1.1, data storage and data communications were mentioned as the two most common applications of data compression. If compression algorithms are on-line, then data storage can be viewed as the special case of data communications where the sender and receiver are the same and the communication link is the storage device. For example, the "compact" command that is available on the Berkeley UNIX system (used primarily for compressing files contained in secondary storage) employs on-line Huffman coding; this allows it to be used as part of a command pipe. There is a subtle distinction, however, when one considers off-line compression. That is, it is typical with data storage to think of storing files of given sizes whereas with communications, one often does not know in advance how long the transmission will last. Since most of the practical algorithms that we shall consider are on-line, we shall typically focus our examples and informal discussions on data communications. It should be noted, however, that from a theoretical point of view, off-line methods are more powerful than on-line methods for compressing finite length strings under certain models. This issue will be considered in Chapters 5 and 6.

For the purposes of this book, we shall assume that the dictionary D of an on-line data compression algorithm is stored in standard random access memory (RAM memory), that is both readable and writable, and that integer variables used in our algorithms can be large enough to index all memory locations that are used to store D. The major exception to this assumption will be Chapter 4 where direct VLSI implementations of D are considered. Throughout this book, the following notation pertaining to strings and dictionaries will be used: For an integer i, we use the standard notation that $|i|$ denotes the absolute value of i (i if $i \geq 0$ or $-i$ if $i < 0$). However, we also use vertical bars for other purposes. For a string s, $|s|$ denotes its length. For a set S, $|S|$ denotes its cardinality. Thus, $|D|$ refers to the current number of entries that D contains. In addition, $<D>$ refers to the maximum number of entries that D may contain. Note that, in general, entries of D are variable length character strings, and it may be that $|D|$ and $<D>$ are quite different than the amount of memory needed to store D; this issue shall be addressed shortly. From this point on we shall always assume $<D>$ to be a power of 2. Although this assumption is not necessary, it simplifies notation and is almost always the case in practice[†].

---

† Otherwise, $\log_2 <D>$ is not an integer and a number of bits equal to the least integer greater than this value will have to be used to index values of D (at least when D is full); this "round-off error" must necessarily result is some unused bit sequences.

A data structure that allows us to efficiently store a dictionary of strings is the following. Given an alphabet Σ, a *trie* is a tree where edges are labeled by elements of Σ in such a way that children of a given parent are connected via edges that have distinct labels, all leaf nodes are labeled as "marked", and all internal nodes are labeled as either "marked" or "unmarked". The set of *strings represented by a trie* are those that correspond to all root to marked node paths. Although we shall continue to talk about an element of Σ being "associated with an edge of the trie", it is convenient in practice to store the element of Σ that is associated with a given edge in the child attached to that edge.

Example 1.5.1 (A Trie): For the trie in Figure 1.5.2, the marked nodes are indicated by boxes and the unmarked nodes by circles. That is, this trie stores the strings "bear", "beaver", "bee", "bird", "cat", "cattle", "cow", "doe". and "dog". ○

Since leaves of a trie are always marked, a data structure need only associate a mark bit with each non-leaf node of the trie. In addition, there are many practical applications where all or none of the internal nodes are considered in the set of strings represented by the trie; in both of these extremes, mark bits are not needed at all.

There are several standard ways to represent a trie (which have different time-space tradeoffs). One way is to store with each node an array of length $|\Sigma|$ that stores the locations of the children of that node; this representation gives constant access time but can be wasteful of space if the average degree of a node is small with respect to $|\Sigma|$ (often the case in practice). A second way is to store with each node a linked list of its children; this representation is space efficient but can be time consuming if the average degree of a node is large. A third way is to have a global hash table that, when given a node and an element of Σ, returns the corresponding child; this representation is space efficient and gives constant expected access time. The bibliographic notes contain references to introductory material on the trie data structure as well as other tree data structures.

Independent of whether a trie or some other data structure is used to represent a dictionary, $<D>$ may be much different than the actual number of bytes[†] used to represent D. Consider the following two examples:

[†] As is standard in the literature, when discussing amounts of computer memory, we shall use units of *bytes* (8 bits) or *kilo-bytes* (2^{10}=1024 bytes), which we shall abbreviate with a K (e.g., $3K$ bytes = 3,072 bytes).

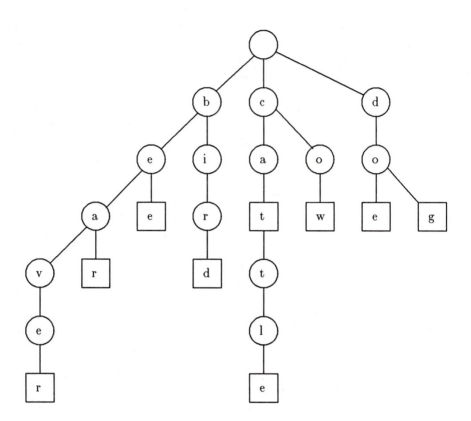

Figure 1.5.2
A Trie

Example 1.5.2: A dictionary of 2^{12}=4,096 entries, each entry being at most 8 characters long is stored as follows. Each character is represented by a byte and each entry is always represented by 9 bytes; the first byte contains the length of the entry. Entries are stored in lexicographic order in a 4,096 element array (9 bytes per element) so binary search can be used to locate entries. This representation uses 9 bytes per entry for a total of $9 \times 4K = 36K$ bytes. ○

Example 1.5.3: A dictionary of 2^{16}=65,536 entries is to be stored. There is no limit (except for the size of D) on how long each entry can be, however, it is the case that whenever an entry is stored, so are all of its prefixes. The entries are stored in a trie data structure where children of a given node are stored in a linked list; each node of the trie contains the fields:

char:	1 byte, character corresponding to this node
lchild:	2 bytes, left-child pointer
rsib:	2 bytes, right-sibling pointer
parent:	2 bytes, parent pointer

Because all prefixes of a given entry must also be in D, each entry of D consumes one new trie node of 7 bytes, for a total of $7\times 64K = 448K$ bytes. ◯

For a given implementation I of a dictionary D, we let $<<D,I>>$ denote the number of bits used to represent D with the implementation I; when I is understood, we simply write $<<D>>$. In practice, the designer is often given a maximum value for $<<D,I>>$ and then asked to produce data compression software or hardware. We shall see in the next section that there can often be tradeoffs between how fast the algorithm runs, how much space it uses, and how well it compresses data. For example, if more memory per dictionary element is needed for a faster algorithm, then the value of $<D>$ must be made smaller (if the total amount of memory used is to remain the same), which in turn could degrade the amount of compression achieved. The size of the program itself must also be counted. However, for the methods that we shall consider, the difference in program size from one implementation to another will not usually be significant. In addition, when hardware is being built, the program can occupy read-only memory (ROM memory), whereas D will require the usual readable and writable random access memory for most of the methods we consider[†].

---

† We have avoided a few small details. In particular, although we shall not consider programs that "cheat" by encoding large amounts of memory into the program code itself, we do allow programs to have a constant number of integer variables (for indexing, to point into data structures, etc.) which we have not formally included in the definition of $<<D,I>>$. In practice, we assume that $<<D,I>>$ is large enough to accommodate a small amount of extra space for such program variables (say 100 extra bytes).

1.6. BIBLIOGRAPHIC NOTES

For introductory and survey material on data compression see Lelewer and Hirschberg [1987], Lynch [1985], Sedgewick [1983], Held [1983], Cooper and Lynch [1982], McEliece [1977], Davisson and Gray [1976], and Lesk [1970].

Bennett [1976] contains an interesting informal introduction to information theory, as does Miller [1951]. For a more thorough introduction to entropy, the reader may refer to a host of publications such as the original paper by Shannon (in Shannon and Weaver [1949]) or the books of Hamming [1980], Ingels [1971], Gallager [1968], Ash [1965], and Abrahamson [1963]. See Gallager [1968] for a discussion of ergodic sources.

There has been much work concerning the application of entropy to more general models of communication. For example, Shannon [1959], Posner and Rodemich [1971], and many others consider channels with an associated fidelity. In addition, Gamal and Orlitsky [1984] consider the exchange data over a two-way communication channel and Wolfowitz [1960] considers the situation when the distribution of error is known by only one of the sender and receiver. The book by Berger [1971] is devoted entirely to rate distortion theory. The book edited by Slepian [1974] is a collection of important early work in information theory. See also Jelinek [1968]. Shannon [1951] estimates the entropy of printed English.

Eichelberger, Rodgers, and Stacy [1968] discuss optimizing the speed of a printer by arrangement and duplication of characters on the print head.

The statistics reported in Appendix A.1 were gathered by Storer and Tsang [1984]. Pike [1981] tabulates word frequencies in English text. Suen [1979] considers n-gram statistics for natural language processing. Yannakoudakis, Goyal, and Huggil [1982] tabulate n-gram frequencies occurring in a large number of bibliographic records; unlike many such tabulations, their statistics do cross word boundaries (but they map upper to lower case). Schwartz and Kleiboemer [1967] has references to studies on the entropy of English. For other statistics on written English, see the book by Kucera and Francis [1967]. Note that the statistics reported in their book are of a different flavor than those reported in Appendix A.1. In Appendix A.1, no attempt is made to attach any meaning to the text, and substring frequencies are reported without any regard to word boundaries, etc. Kucera and Francis [1967] is primarily concerned with the frequencies of basic "pieces" of English, such as word frequencies; their statistics do not take into account upper and lower case letters, punctuation, or the space and newline characters. However, these statistics do provide insights into the structure of English text that are not apparent from Appendix A.1. For example, from the statistics reported in their book, it follows that for technical writing, approximately 45 percent of all text consists of the 100 most common words, distributed roughly as follows:

2 percent	1 letter words
17 percent	2 letter words
17 percent	3 letter words
6 percent	4 letter words
3 percent	5 or more letter words

Miller [1951] claims that the 50 most common English word types make up 45 percent of those written and 60 percent of those spoken. Douchette, Harrison, and Schuegraf [1977] consider compressing French, English, and German.

Zipf's law is a statistical observation about word frequencies in English text. It says that if the frequency of occurrence of each word is plotted against its rank in a list of all words that goes from most common to least common, then a relatively straight line results. That is, if f_i denotes the frequency of the ith word in this list, then f_i is roughly proportional to $1/i$. Chapter 5 of Young [1971] and Chapter 4 of Miller [1951] contain a presentation of Zipf's law. See also Schwartz and Kleiboemer [1967] and Zipf [1935,1949].

Numerical data contained in databases, spread-sheets, etc. is typically non-uniformly distributed. It is somewhat surprising that this is also true of numerical data relating to physical constants arising in nature. For example, the book of Knuth [1969] contains a discussion of why such constants are likely to have small values for the first digit (e.g., for tables of physical constants written in base-10, 1 is the first digit about 30 percent of the time). For other references to this issue see: Raimi [1976, 1969, 1969b], Mardia [1972], Flehinger [1966], Konheim [1965], Pinkham [1961], Furry and Hurwitz [1945], Benford [1938], and Newcomb [1881].

For introductory material on data structures, including graphs and the trie data structure, see Aho, Hopcroft, and Ullman [1983] or Sedgewick [1985].

2

CODING TECHNIQUES

This chapter considers coding techniques that will be useful for data compression methods considered in later chapters. Virtually any data compression method can be viewed as an example of a code, and indeed, some of the codes to be considered in this chapter represent practical compression methods. However, we shall generally view the coding techniques to be presented in this chapter as processes that will occur at a lower level than the compression methods to be presented in the remaining chapters.

Perhaps the most common example of a code is a k-ary *block code* which maps each element of a finite set S of n elements to a $\lceil \log_k(n) \rceil$ long string over an alphabet of size k[†]. For example, the standard ASCII code, shown in Figure 2.0.1, is a binary block code that maps each of the 128 ASCII characters to a unique 8-bit binary string, where the first bit is always 0[††]. Note that Figure 2.0.1 gives decimal values instead of the actual 8-bit sequences. In fact, the mapping of the 128 different 8-bit sequences that start with 0 to the 3-digit decimal sequences 000 through 127 is an example of a block code.

Section 2.1 formally defines the notion of a code and what it means for a code to be *uniquely decipherable*. Section 2.2 considers a general method for converting any code to a uniquely decipherable code. Sections 2.3 and 2.4 develop the notion of prefix codes, a very practical class of uniquely decipherable codes. Sections 2.5 through 2.7 consider *Huffman codes*, which when given ideal computational resources, are the basis of a compression method that is perfect in the information theoretic sense. However, in practice, when given limited computational resources, Huffman codes may not be as effective

---

† We use the term block code here to refer to what is a special case of the notion that is often attached to this term in the literature.

†† In practice, this first bit is often used for either an extended character set or for error correction.

000 nul	001 soh	002 stx	003 etx	004 eot	005 enq	006 ack	007 bel
008 bs	009 ht	010 nl	011 vt	012 np	013 cr	014 so	015 si
016 dle	017 dc1	018 dc2	019 dc3	020 dc4	021 nak	022 syn	023 etb
024 can	025 em	026 sub	027 esc	028 fs	029 gs	030 rs	031 us
032 sp	033 !	034 "	035 #	036 $	037 %	038 &	039 '
040 (	041)	042 *	043 +	044 ,	045 -	046 .	047 /
048 0	049 1	050 2	051 3	052 4	053 5	054 6	055 7
056 8	057 9	058 :	059 ;	060 <	061 =	062 >	063 ?
064 @	065 A	066 B	067 C	068 D	069 E	070 F	071 G
072 H	073 I	074 J	075 K	076 L	077 M	078 N	079 O
080 P	081 Q	082 R	083 S	084 T	085 U	086 V	087 W
088 X	089 Y	090 Z	091 [	092 \	093]	094 ^	095 _
096 `	097 a	098 b	099 c	100 d	101 e	102 f	103 g
104 h	105 i	106 j	107 k	108 l	109 m	110 n	111 o
112 p	113 q	114 r	115 s	116 t	117 u	118 v	119 w
120 x	121 y	122 z	123 {	124		125 }	126 ~	127 del

Figure 2.0.1
The ASCII Code

for data compression as other methods to be considered in later chapters. We consider Huffman codes in this book primarily for the following reasons:

- Huffman codes have been considered extensively in the literature and are, in their own right, the basis for a data compression method.

- The performance of Huffman codes has been well studied and can serve as a useful benchmark on which to judge the effectiveness of more complex methods.

- For several applications, it will be useful to combine more sophisticated techniques with Huffman codes.

Section 2.8 reviews *Tunstall codes,* which encode data in a manner that can be viewed as the reverse to the process of Huffman coding. Sections 2.9 and 2.10 review two other codes, *arithmetic codes* and *Shannon-Fano codes,* that have similar properties to Huffman codes and have historically proved to be popular alternatives to Huffman codes (and can have advantages over Huffman codes in some situations).

Throughout this chapter it will be useful to identify non-negative integers with character strings. The following two functions will be used to perform such identifications:

- Let $\Sigma=\{a_0 \cdots a_{k-1}\}$ be an alphabet. Given a string s over Σ, $INT_\Sigma(s)$ denotes the unique integer that is represented by s in base k notation, assuming that a_0 plays the role of 0, a_1 the role of 1, etc. When Σ is understood, we may drop the subscript Σ from INT.

- Given an alphabet Σ and a non-negative integer i, $STR_\Sigma(i)$ denotes a_0 if i is 0; otherwise, it denotes the unique string s such that $i=INT_\Sigma(s)$ and the first character of s is not a_0. When Σ is understood, we may drop the subscript Σ from STR. In addition, $BIN(i)$ is an abbreviation for $STR_{\{0,1\}}(i)$ (the binary representation of i).

Note that when discussing strings, string concatenation will be denoted by simply writing the two strings together; that is, if s and t are strings, then st denotes the string consisting of s followed by t.

2.1. UNIQUELY DECIPHERABLE CODES

Definition 2.1.1: Given a *source set* S (S may be infinite), and a *codeword alphabet* Σ, a *code* from S to Σ is a function f that maps each element of S to a non-empty string over Σ. The range of f is called the set of *codewords* of f. We say that f is *injective* if it never maps two elements to the same string. Any code f can naturally be extended to apply to any finite list of elements by defining

$$f(s_1, \cdots, s_k) = \prod_{i=1}^{k} f(s_i)$$

where the product above denotes string concatenation. $\bigcirc$

Since we are concerned primarily with lossless data compression, we shall always assume that codes are injective unless otherwise stated and from this point on will not bother to explicitly state this condition when discussing codes. However, even with injective codes, it may still be that there are two lists L_1 and L_2 such that $f(L_1)=f(L_2)$. The following definition provides the terminology for discussing this phenomenon.

Definition 2.1.2: Let f be a code from a set S to an alphabet Σ. A string α over Σ is *uniquely decipherable* with respect to f if there is at most one list L of elements of S such that $f(L)=\alpha$. In addition, we say f is uniquely decipherable if all strings over Σ are uniquely decipherable with respect to f. $\bigcirc$

Example 2.1.1: Let $S = \{a,b,c,d,e\}$, $\Sigma = \{0,1\}$, and f be the following code from S to Σ:

$$f(a) = 00$$
$$f(b) = 01$$
$$f(c) = 10$$
$$f(d) = 11$$
$$f(e) = 100$$

Clearly, $f(a,b,c,d,e) = 00011011100$. In addition, we can verify that the string of bits 00011011100 is uniquely decipherable with respect to f as follows:

a: Since a single 0 is not a code and only the code for a starts with 00, the first two bits (00) correspond to an a.

b: Since a single 0 is not a code and only the code for b starts with 01, the third and fourth bits (01) correspond to a b.

c: Since a single 1 is not a code, only the codes for c and e start with 10, and the seventh bit is a 1, the fifth and sixth bits (10) correspond to a c.

d: Since a single 1 is not a code and only the code for d starts with 11, the seventh and eighth bits (11) correspond to a d.

e: Since no code is one character long, the last three bits must be a code for a single letter. Only the code for e is three bits long. So last three bits (100) correspond to an e.

However, not all binary strings are uniquely decipherable with respect to f. For example, $f(cba) = f(ee) = 100100$. $\bigcirc$

Example 2.1.2: Let $S=\{x_0,x_1,\cdots\}$ be a (possibly infinite) source set, $\Sigma=\{0,1\}$, and f the code from S to Σ defined by:

$$f(x_i) = 0^i 1$$

Then f is uniquely decipherable since any list L of elements from S can be determined uniquely from $f(L)$ by simply reading off the blocks of 0's (which are delimited by the 1's). Note that f is rather "inefficient" because it is simply employing a unary notation[†] for s_i which has length exponential in $|s_i|$.
○

A detail that was not addressed in Definitions 2.1.1 and 2.1.2 is the issue of computability. Consider the following example.

Example 2.1.3: Let $\{T_0, T_1, \cdots\}$ be an enumeration of all Turing machines[††] and let h be the function from the non-negative integers to the non-negative integers that is defined by:

> If $i=0$ then $h(i)$ is the least j such that T_j halts for all inputs. Otherwise, $h(i)$ is the least j such that $j \geq h(i-1)$ and T_j halts for all inputs.

Now let f be a code from the non-negative integers to binary strings that is defined by:

$$f(i) = 1^{h(i)} 0$$

Clearly f is well defined and uniquely decipherable. However, if f were computable, then we could decide if a given Turing machine T_i halts on all inputs as follows:

> Use f to compute $h(0)$, $h(1)$, ... until the first j is found such that $h(j) \geq i$. Then T_i halts for all inputs if $i=j$ and does not halt for all inputs if $i < j$.

[†] Unary notation represents an integer i by repeating a given symbol i times.
[††] As indicated in the preface to this book, we assume that the reader is familiar with basic notions from computability theory. A brief introduction is contained in Chapter 6, which also contains a definition of a Turing machine. However, the reader that is not familiar with these notions will lose very little in the reading of this chapter by simply ignoring this example and the discussion pertaining to it.

Since the problem of whether a Turing machine halts for all inputs is undecidable, it cannot be that f is computable. $\bigcirc$

Although the above example shows that it is possible for a code not
to be computable, we will not be concerned with this phenomenon in this
chapter. For the remainder of this chapter we assume all codes and their
inverses to be computable. However, codes that are either not computable or
not possible to compute in practice will arise naturally in later chapters.

Given a set S and an alphabet Σ, Example 2.1.2 showed that it is always possible to construct a uniquely decipherable code from S to Σ. We
shall see examples of many techniques that are less brute-force than Example
2.1.2 throughout this chapter. However, a natural question for any finite set
S and finite alphabet Σ is, if the lengths of the code words are specified in advance, what are necessary and sufficient conditions on these lengths to ensure
that a uniquely decipherable code from S to Σ exists. The following theorem,
often called the *Kraft/MacMillian inequality*, provides these conditions.

Theorem 2.1.1 (Kraft/MacMillian inequality): Let S be a finite
set and Σ a finite alphabet. If codewords are constrained to have lengths
$l_1, \cdots, l_{|S|}$, then a necessary and sufficient condition for a code from S to Σ
to exist is that:

$$\sum_{i=1}^{|S|} \left(\frac{1}{|\Sigma|^{l_i}} \right) \leq 1 \quad \bigcirc$$

The bibliographic notes to this chapter provide references to a proof
of the Kraft/MacMillian equality. It is easy to check that for any $k \geq 2$, the
Kraft/MacMillian inequality is satisfied by a k-ary block code:

$$\sum_{i=1}^{|S|} \frac{1}{|\Sigma|^{\lceil \log_{|\Sigma|} |S| \rceil}} \leq \sum_{i=1}^{|S|} \frac{1}{|S|} \leq 1$$

The above inequality is an exact equality when n is a power of 2.

2.2. ENCODING COMMAS

Given a code f from a set S to an alphabet $\Sigma = \{a_0 \cdots a_{k-1}\}$, one way to view the problem of decoding is as the process of parsing a sequence of characters over Σ; that is, start with a string of characters over Σ (that has been produced by f) and insert "commas" to delimit the codeword boundaries. One way to guarantee that a code is uniquely decipherable is to explicitly include the commas in the code. For example, in Example 2.1.2, 1's serve as commas. This section presents a construction for converting any code[†] to a uniquely decipherable code by a process that is tantamount to attaching commas to codewords. This construction works even if the size of the set S is not known or is infinite and no bound on the length of codewords produced by f is known.

Before proceeding to the main construction, it is worth noting that there are at least three brute-force approaches to "re-writing" a codeword w (using only the characters of Σ) to effectively add a comma to w.

(1) Example 2.1.2 motivates the following approach. For the case $k=2$, we can proceed exactly as in Example 2.1.2 by replacing w by $INT(1w)$ 0's followed by a 1; which has length exponential in the length of w. However, if $k>2$, we can do much better. Since $INT(1w)$ can be thought of as a 1 followed by $|w|$ digits (each of which is at most k), it follows that:

$$INT(a_1 w) < 2(k^{|w|})$$

Encode w followed by a comma as:

$$STR_{SIGMA - \{a_k\}}(INT(a_1 w)) a_k$$

That is, base $k-1$ notation is used to encode a_1 (which corresponds to the digit 1) followed by w, and the symbol a_k is used for the comma. The length of this representation is:

$$\lceil \log_{k-1}(INT(a_1 w)) \rceil + 1 \ \leq \ \lceil \frac{|w|}{\log_k(k-1)} \rceil + \lceil \frac{\log_k 2}{\log_k(k-1)} \rceil + 1$$

which is always less than

---

† Recall that we are always assuming codes to be injective.

$$\frac{|w|}{\log_3 2} + 2 \; < \; 1.6\,|w| + 2$$

and becomes arbitrarily close to $|w|+1$ as k approaches infinity.

(2) Replace each character c of w by the pair of characters ca_0 if c is not the last character of w and ca_1 if c is the last character of w. Thus, the comma is encoded by whether the second character in a pair is a_0 or a_1. This scheme doubles the length of the representation of w.

(3) Precede w with $|w|-1$ $a_0's$ followed by a a_1. Here, any sequence of codewords can be uniquely decoded from left to right by accepting $a_0's$ until a a_1 is encountered to obtain the length of the actual codeword that is to follow. That is, the comma is encoded by preceding each codeword with its length encoded in unary notation. This scheme doubles the length of of the representation of w.

The three schemes above are very inefficient in comparison to what can be done (with the possible exception of the first scheme for non-binary alphabets). We now present a solution that is much better as the size of S becomes large, although it may be that for small sizes of $|S|$ some variant of one of the schemes above is better.

The idea, which is motivated by scheme (3), is to prepend to each codeword a compact description of its length. However, if this description is simply the base k representation of the length, then we are faced with a new instance of the same problem, how do we identify the end of the characters that describe the length[†]? This line of reasoning does however lead to a well-know method for handling this problem which we shall henceforth refer to as the *cascading lengths technique*. Let s be a (non-empty) string over Σ. The cascading lengths technique works by first prepending a a_1 to s, then prepending $STR(|a_1 s|-2)$ (minus 2 since it is always true that $|a_1 s| \geq 2$), then prepending $STR(|STR(|a_1 s|-2)|-2)$, and so on, until we get down to a single character. We also follow every codeword so constructed with a_0. Thus, in general, the new codewords have the form: a one digit length, followed by a longer length, $\cdots$, followed by a longer length, followed by a_1, followed by the original codeword, followed by a_0. Note that all of the lengths, except possibly for the first one, must have a value that is greater than zero, and hence will start with a digit other than a_0. This will allow us to use the a_0

---

† At least in theory we are faced with this problem. In practice, we may have a bound on the length of a codeword and could simply use $\log_k$ of that length.

that is appended to the right end of the codeword to detect when the right end has been reached.

Algorithm 2.2.1 is the *cascading lengths encoding algorithm and* Algorithm 2.2.2 *cascading lengths decoding algorithm.* Algorithm 2.2.1 works by repeatedly using the current length to decide how many digits to read for the next length. This process stops when the 0 at the end of the codeword is encountered (in which case the current length is the "original" codeword that we are seeking).

Using the cascading lengths method, a binary string of length n is converted to a codeword of length (counting from right to left):

$$1 + (n+1) + \lceil \log_k(n-1) \rceil + \lceil \log_k(\log_k(n-1)-2) \rceil + \cdots + 1$$

$$= n + O(\log_k(n))^\dagger$$

Figure 2.2.1 shows how the cascading lengths technique works for various binary strings; note that this figure uses the notation 0^i to denote a string of i zeros and 1^i to denote a string of i ones. Note also that Figure 2.2.1 uses commas to show the boundaries between the components that make up the codeword; these commas are for illustration purposes only and are not part of the codeword (which consists entirely of 0's and 1's). It is interesting to compare the cascading lengths technique with the three schemes discussed earlier. From inspection of Figure 2.2.1, one can see that for binary alphabets, the cascading lengths technique breaks even with Scheme 1 on strings of length 4 (since Scheme 1 will put out at least 8 zeros followed by a 1 which is at least as long as the 9 bits that are used by the cascading lengths technique) and breaks even with Schemes 2 and 3 on strings of length 6 (since Schemes 2 and 3 double the length to 12 bits which is what the cascading lengths technique uses for strings of length 6).

When n is large, the overhead of using the cascading lengths technique is insignificant. For example, Figure 2.2.1 shows that strings of length 150 are mapped to 164 bits (14 additional bits, a 10 percent increase), strings

---

$\dagger$ As is standard in the literature, for two functions f and g from the non-negative integers to the non-negative integers, we say $f(n)$ is $O(g(n))$ if there exists two constants n_0 and k such that for all $n \geq n_0$, $f(n) \leq kg(n)$. That is, the "big O" notation is used to say when one function grows no faster (ignoring constant factors) than a second function. In addition, we write $O(g(n))$ to denote any function $f(n)$ that is $O(g(n))$.

function CASCADE_ENCODE(s):

   $s := a_1 s$

   $t := s$

   while $(|s|>1)$ **do begin**
      $s := STR(|s|-2)$
      $t := st$
      end

   return (ta_0)

   end

Algorithm 2.2.1
Cascading Lengths Encoding Algorithm

function CASCADE_DECODE(s):

   $t :=$ delete and return the first character of s

   while $(s \neq a_0)$ **do**
      $t :=$ delete and return the first $INT(t)+2$ characters of s

   delete the first character of t

   return (t)

   end

Algorithm 2.2.2
Cascading Lengths Decoding Algorithm

0	0,1,0,0
1	0,1,1,0
00	1,1,00,0
11	1,1,11,0
100	0,10,1,100,0
101	0,10,1,101,0
110	0,10,1,110,0
111	0,10,1,111,0
1000	0,11,1,1000,0
11111	1,100,1,11111,0
000000	1,101,1,000000,0
0^{150}	$1,110,10010110,1,0^{150},0$
0^{1025}	$0,10,1000,10^{10},1,0^{1025},0$
0^{2048}	$0,10,1000,1^{11},1,0^{2048},0$
0^{2049}	$0,10,1001,10^{11},1,0^{2049},0$
0^{131072}	$0,11,1111,1^{17},1,0^{131072},0$
0^{131073}	$0,11,10000,10^{17},1,0^{131073},0$

Figure 2.2.1
Sample Binary Cascading Lengths Codes

of length 1025 are mapped to 1045 bits (20 additional bits, a 2 percent increase), and strings of length 2048 are mapped to 2068 bits (20 additional bits, a 1 percent increase). Note that strings of length 2048 use the same number of additional bits as strings of length 1025. Strings of length 2049, 4097, 8193, 16385, 32769, and 65537 require 21, 22, 23, 24, 25, and 26 additional bits respectively (each require one additional bit in the first length field from the right than the preceding one). Strings of length 131072 require the same number of additional bits as strings of length 65537 (25 additional bits). Strings of length 131073 need another bit in both the first and second length fields from the right for a total of 28 additional bits.

Although the overhead incurred by the cascading lengths technique becomes insignificant as the size of strings gets large, it may not be acceptable for short strings. For example, for binary alphabets about 150 bits are required before the overhead is less than 10 percent and about 2000 bits before the overhead is less than 1 percent. In practice, for encoding short strings, it may be advantageous to modify the cascading lengths technique with something like the step codes to be discussed in the next section.

2.3. STEP CODES

Our only concrete example of a uniquely decipherable code thus far is the block code, where all codewords have the same length. Perhaps the most simple examples of uniquely decipherable codes that have variable length codewords are *step codes*, where codewords may have either of two possible lengths.

Definition 2.3.1: Let k be a positive integer. With the ith *order k-step code*, $1 \leq i \leq k$, each k-bit sequence that does not start with i 1's is a codeword and each $2k$-bit sequence that starts with i 1's is a codeword. $\bigcirc$

Theorem 2.3.1: For an ith order k-step code, the number of distinct codewords is given by:

$$\text{number of } k\text{-bit codewords} = (2^i - 1)2^{k-i}$$

$$\text{number of } 2k\text{-bit codewords} = 2^{2k-i}$$

Proof: Except for the sequence of i ones, all of the 2^i distinct binary sequences can be prefixes of a k-bit code, for which there are 2^{k-i} distinct suffixes. Hence, the stated size for k-bit codes follows. For $2k$-bit codes, there are exactly 2^{2k-i} distinct binary sequences that can be suffixes to the prefix of i ones. Hence, the stated bound for $2k$-bit codes follows. ◯

i	no. of 1-byte codewords	no. of 2-byte codewords
0	0	2^{16}
1	128	2^{15}
2	192	2^{14}
3	224	2^{13}
4	240	2^{12}
5	248	2^{11}
6	252	2^{10}
7	254	2^9
8	255	2^8

Figure 2.3.1
Byte-Step Codes

Block codes are a special case of step codes since a 0th order step code is just the set of distinct $2k$-bit sequences. As a concrete example of a less trivial step code, take $k=8$. Figure 2.3.1 shows the relative number of 1 and 2-byte codes that result for different values of i in the formulas given by Theorem 2.3.1.

For the purposes of this chapter, step codes serve primarily as a simple example. However, they do have practical applications, which are motivated by the following definition.

Definition 2.3.2: Let $k>1$ be an integer. A (noisy) communication line over which characters of some alphabet Σ are transmitted is k-blocking if characters are transmitted in groups of size k and all noise on the line falls into one of the following three categories:

change error: A group is changed to a different group.

delete error A group is lost.

add error A group is inserted.

That is, the communication line preserves group boundaries but may otherwise garble the transmission in an arbitrary fashion. We shall sometimes refer to an 8-blocking communication line as a *byte-oriented* communication line. ○

Example 2.3.1: An example of a noisy byte-oriented communication line is the serial transmission of bytes through a standard serial interface and modem over a telephone line. Here, even though bits are sent one at a time, the hardware detects framing errors, etc., and all that the user (usually) sees are errors of the three types listed in Definition 2.3.2. Note that in this example it is typical that errors come in bursts; that is when a "glitch" occurs in the phone line, it is likely that its duration covers several characters. ○

If a communication line is k-blocking, then we shall see in Chapter 3 that it can be advantageous to transmit codewords with lengths that are multiples of k. For example, the following compression problem will be considered in Chapter 3 when we discuss the static dictionary method for data compression. Suppose a dictionary of strings (e.g., common English words) is to be used to compress a text file; that is, substrings of the text are replaced in some fashion (the exact method is not important for the purposes of this discussion) by indices into the dictionary. A byte-step code allows one to use

2 bytes to represent indices into a dictionary that has fewer than 2^{16} entries. Essentially, the extra bits are traded for the ability to represent some of the entries with 8 bits. This scheme can be useful when insufficient memory is available for 2^{16} dictionary entries. In addition, for some dictionaries, this scheme may yield better compression than could be obtained by using fixed number of bits to represent an index. However, in Chapter 3 we shall see that what is often the most important property of this coding scheme in practice is that it is essentially immune to the problem of loosing synchronization of boundaries (where the bits representing one index end and the bits representing the following index begin) due to noise on the communication line. That is, problems associated with noise on the communication line can be avoided without invoking any additional error detecting/correcting algorithms.

At this point we caution the reader that although we have just digressed with a definition and example concerning of noisy communication lines, and that we will address them again (briefly) in Chapter 3, they are, for the most part, out of the scope of this book, and we will continue to assume that all communication lines are noiseless unless specifically stated otherwise.

It is possible to generalize step codes in many different ways. However, since such codes are typically useful only for special purpose applications we instead turn our attention to *prefix codes*, which can be viewed as a continuous version of step codes.

2.4. PREFIX CODES

Definition 2.4.1: A code from a set S to an alphabet Σ is a *prefix code* if no codeword is a prefix of another codeword. ○

A prefix code must be uniquely decipherable since when reading a string from left to right, the end of a codeword may be determined the instant it is reached (for this reason, prefix codes are often called *instantaneous codes*). However, as the next example shows, the converse is not necessarily true; that is, it is possible to construct codes which are not prefix codes but are uniquely decipherable.

Example 2.4.1: Consider the code f from the set $S=\{a,b,c,d\}$ to $\Sigma=\{0,1\}$ that is defined by:

$$f(a) = 0$$

$$f(b) = 01$$
$$f(c) = 011$$
$$f(d) = 111$$

Clearly f is not a prefix code. However, f is uniquely decipherable. Unfortunately, for a string of the form

$$01^i$$

the only way to decode it is to first scan the entire string to determine the value of i. ○

The example above shows not only that there exist uniquely decipherable codes that are not prefix codes, but that with such codes, an unbounded amount of lookahead may be necessary in order to decode from left to right. Although such lookahead may not be practical in many applications, it is nevertheless natural to ask whether the use of such codes would admit a larger variety of legal codeword sizes that are allowed by the Kraft/MacMillian inequality. It is perhaps somewhat of a surprise that this is not the case.

Theorem 2.4.1: A prefix code exists for any sequence of codeword lengths for which the Kraft/MacMillian inequality holds. ○

Definition 2.4.2: A prefix code over an alphabet Σ is *succinct* if for every string s such that s is a proper prefix of at least one codeword, the following condition holds: For every character a in Σ, sa is a (not necessarily proper) prefix of a codeword. ○

A prefix code can be viewed as a $|\Sigma|$-ary trie (where the root to leaf paths correspond to the codewords). With a succinct prefix code the trie has the added property that every non-leaf node has $|\Sigma|$ children. The following theorem notes that this implies that the trie has a total number of nodes that is proportional to $|S|$.

Theorem 2.4.2: The number of internal nodes in a trie corresponding to a succinct prefix code from a set S to an alphabet Σ is exactly

$$\frac{|S|-1}{|\Sigma|-1}$$

which implies that:

$$\text{leaves + internal nodes} \leq \lfloor \frac{|\Sigma|}{|\Sigma|-1} \ |S| \rfloor \ \bigcirc$$

Proof: The equality follows from a simple proof by induction on the number of internal nodes. The inequality follows by simply summing $|S|$, the number of leaves, with the number of nodes (and simplifying the resulting expression). $\bigcirc$

What most distinguishes succinct prefix codes is that, intuitively, they have no "waste" because once a node of the trie has been "used up" by having a child attached to it, then it is "fully used" by attaching all possible children to it. This intuition is formalized by the following theorem.

Theorem 2.4.3: Succinct prefix codes satisfy the Kraft/MacMillian inequality exactly (make it an equality).

Proof: Let f be a succinct code from a set S to an alphabet Σ. Then each non-leaf node of the trie corresponding to f must have degree exactly $|\Sigma|$. With each leaf of depth i in the trie, associate the cost $1/(|\Sigma|^i)$. Then the sum of the costs of all of the leaves is the left side of the Kraft/MacMillian inequality. Define a *shrinking operation* as starting with a non-leaf node x such that all the children of x are leaves, deleting all the children of x (causing x to become a leaf), and then assigning the weight to x equal to the sum of the weights of the children that were deleted. Clearly, a shrinking operation preserves the sum of the costs of the leaves. In addition, since for $i,k > 1$

$$\sum_{j=1}^{k} \frac{1}{k^i} = \frac{1}{k^{i-1}}$$

it is now easy to show that shrinking the trie down to a single node results in a cost of 1. $\bigcirc$

Given a set S to an alphabet Σ, if $|\Sigma|=2$, then any prefix code can easily be transformed to a succinct one by observing that if the trie leaf corresponding to the codeword is the only child of its parent, then we might as well delete this leaf and associate the codeword with the parent. However, if $|\Sigma|>2$, it may be that $|S|$ is such that a succinct code from S to Σ is not possible (e.g., $|S|=4$ and $|\Sigma|=3$). However, it is always possible to construct a prefix code that is "almost" succinct; that is, a prefix code where the corresponding trie has only one node that has less than $|\Sigma|$ children. One simple approach is to simply associate the elements of S with the leaves of a trie that is a complete Σ-ary tree except that the lowest level of the tree is only partially filled from the left; this construction yields what is essentially a block code. In practice, there are many ways to construct a prefix code that is succinct or almost succinct. We shall be interested in succinct prefix codes, such as the Huffman codes to be considered in the next section, that have desirable properties for data compression.

The interpretation of a prefix code as a trie leads naturally to simple real-time encoding and decoding algorithms. Algorithm 2.4.1 is the *prefix code encoding algorithm* which reads elements from an input stream (via the function READELE) and writes characters of Σ, which are sent to the decoder's algorithm (via the procedure WRITECHAR). This Algorithm works by walking up from the leaf corresponding to the input element (via the PARENT function) to the root to obtain the sequence of characters of Σ that correspond to the input element; since these characters are encountered in reverse order, they are successively pushed onto a stack when going up the trie, and when the root of the trie is reached, the characters are then popped of the stack in the correct order. Algorithm 2.4.2 is the *prefix code decoding algorithm,* which reads characters that have been produced by the encoder's algorithm (via the function READCHAR) and writes elements to an output stream (via the procedure WRITEELE). This algorithm works by walking down from the root (via the CHILD function, which takes a node and a character and returns the corresponding child) to a leaf, and then outputs the element corresponding to that leaf.

Algorithm 2.4.1 works independently of whether the prefix code is succinct or not. The same is true of Algorithm 2.4.2 provided that the input is legal (a stream of characters that forms a sequence of codewords). However, if the input stream is illegal and the prefix code is not succinct, then it is possible that the current trie node at which Algorithm 2.4.2 is located has no child corresponding to the current input character. For simplicity, we shall simply assume that in this case, the *CHILD* function causes Algorithm 2.4.2 to halt and signal an error condition. In practice, some sort of error recovery routine would be called.

forever do begin

  element := READELE

  place := the leaf corresponding to *element*

  while *place* is not the root **do begin**
    PUSH(the character of Σ that connects *place* to its parent)
    place := PARENT(*place*)
    end

  while stack is not empty **do begin**
    char := POP
    WRITECHAR(*char*)
    end

  end

Algorithm 2.4.1
Prefix Code Encoding Algorithm

forever do begin

  place := the root of the trie

  while *place* is not a leaf **do begin**
    char := READCHAR
    place := CHILD(*place*,*char*)
    end

  WRITEELE(the element corresponding to the leaf *place*)

  end

Algorithm 2.4.2
Prefix Code Decoding Algorithm

2.5. HUFFMAN CODES: THE BASIC ALGORITHM

Huffman coding is perhaps the most-well known technique for data compression. In this section, we review the classic construction that was introduced in 1952 by D. A. Huffman.

For a given source set S, suppose that we know its first-order probabilities; that is, suppose that we know for each element x in S the value of p_x, the probability that x will be the next element in the input stream (given no previous knowledge of the input stream). Then, instead of assigning a code of $\lceil \log_{|\Sigma|} |S| \rceil$ bits to each element of S (as would be done with a block code), space may be saved by assigning shorter codes to highly probable elements and longer codes to less probable elements. To simplify our presentation, we shall assume that $\Sigma = \{0,1\}$ (by far the most common case in practice); It is straightforward to generalize the following material to the case $|\Sigma| > 2$; references to the generalized algorithm are contained in the bibliographic notes.

(1) Initialize *FOREST* to have a 1-node trie T_x for each element x of S. Set $weight(T_x) = p_x$.

(2) **while** $|FOREST| > 1$ **do begin**
      Let Y and Z be the two tries in *FOREST* of lowest weight (resolve ties arbitrarily). Combine Y and Z by creating a new root r with weight $weight(Y) + weight(Z)$ that is attached to one of Y and Z via a 0 and to the other via a 1 (the order doesn't matter).
      end

Algorithm 2.5.1
Static Huffman Trie Construction Algorithm

Algorithm 2.5.1 is the (first order) *static Huffman trie construction algorithm* which is a simple greedy algorithm to construct a trie representing variable length codewords for S. Later in this chapter we shall consider Huffman codes based on higher-order probabilities. Also, note that Algorithm

2.5.1 is called "static" because the probabilities are given in advance. In the next section, we shall consider a version of the algorithm that estimates these probabilities dynamically.

Since the codes produced by the static Huffman trie construction algorithm correspond to the leaves of a trie where all internal nodes have degree $|\Sigma|$, which for the purposes of this presentation is 2, they must be succinct prefix codes. Hence, the static Huffman encoding and decoding algorithms are simply the prefix code encoding and decoding algorithms. Thus, the static Huffman encoding and decoding algorithms can be easily implemented in practice.

The static Huffman encoding and decoding algorithms assume that a common Huffman trie is available to both. This assumption may be reasonable for some practical situations (e.g., if only English text is to be compressed, use an agreed upon trie for English characters). However, if the Huffman trie is known in advance to the decoder, the encoder can first transmit a representation of the Huffman trie to the decoder before starting to process its input stream. Since the size of the Huffman trie is proportional to $|S|$, which is a constant, this initial overhead will not be significant when the input stream becomes sufficiently long.

Although the trie produced by the static Huffman trie construction algorithm is clearly not unique (since the order of children is arbitrary and ties among nodes of equal probability are resolved arbitrarily), it is not hard to show that it is always optimal in the sense that no other trie (with its leaves labeled by the elements of S) will produce better compression on the average. In addition, if it is the case that the probability of occurrence of characters in the source are independent, then as the length of the input stream goes to infinity, the compression produced by this algorithm must approach the entropy of the (first-order) source. References to a proof of this limit are indicated in the bibliographic notes to this chapter.

2.6. DYNAMIC HUFFMAN CODES

Often in practice, little is know in advance about the input stream and the character probabilities are not available. One solution is for the encoder to process the input stream twice, the first time to gather statistics on character frequencies and the second time to do the actual encoding. However, this strategy is no longer an on-line process. The naive solution to this problem is to modify the encoder and decoder algorithms as follows. Start with a trie representing the case when all elements of S are equal-probable. Both the encoder and decoder keep track of element frequencies; that is, each time the encoder receives an element x, it increments its count for x and each time the decoder decodes a codeword to obtain an element x it increments its count for x. Each time the encoder transmits a codeword it builds a new trie based on the current element frequencies. Similarly, each time the decoder finishes decoding a codeword, it builds a new trie. The encoder and decoder employ the same (deterministic) trie construction algorithm so that all arbitrary choices, tie breaking, etc. is done identically. Thus, the encoder and decoder maintain identical tries in lock-step.

The approach above will yield optimal compression (assuming that the character probabilities are independent) as the length of the input stream approaches infinity. However, it is rather inefficient if $|S|$ is large, since both the encoder and decoder must reconstruct the entire trie once for each character of the input stream. Fortunately, a much more efficient algorithm exists, which makes use of the following definition and fact:

Definition 2.6.1: The *weight* of a leaf in a Huffman trie for a source set S is the probability of the corresponding element in S; the weight of an internal node is the sum of the weights of its children. A Huffman trie has the *sibling property* if:

(1) Each node, except the root, has a sibling.

(2) The nodes of the trie can be listed in order of non-increasing weight in such a way that each node is adjacent in the list to its sibling. ○

Fact: A binary trie with weights associated with its nodes is a Huffman trie if and only if it has the sibling property. ○

The bibliographic notes contain references to a proof of the above fact. Given this fact, an efficient Dynamic Huffman coding algorithm is now relatively straightforward. Let us start by considering the workings of the encoder. In addition to the trie, a list can be maintained of the nodes in increasing order of weight; for the sake of this discussion, we view this list as going from left (smallest weight) to right (largest weight). Each time a new element x of S is read the encoder starts at the leaf corresponding to x and walks up the trie as with the static case, with one new addition. Each time a node v is visited, its weight is incremented and a check is made if its weight is now greater than the node to its right on the list. If so, then v is exchanged with the rightmost element on the list that has a smaller weight than v; note that to find this element, there may be a number of nodes with weight equal to the old weight of v that must be skipped over. With the exception of skipping over nodes of equal weight, this algorithm consumes only a constant amount of time to advance one level up the tree. Since advancing a level up the tree corresponds to generating an output bit, this algorithm runs in linear time provided the skipping over nodes of equal weight can be done in constant time. To do this, a second (doubly-linked) list can be maintained that has one entry for each distinct weight that currently is the label of some trie node. Such an entry points to the position of the node in the node list that is the rightmost node with that weight. This second list can be used to skip over nodes with equal weight in constant time and can easily be updated in constant time when necessary.

One detail that has not been addressed is what happens when a weight of a node becomes too large to be stored in an integer variable on the machine in question. A simple approach to this problem is to simply rescale all the weights when an integer reaches its maximum value by dividing all weights by some constant[†]. Such rescaling will cause the algorithm to "pause", however, the algorithm is still linear since this extra time can be amortized against the time between rescalings. In fact, real-time performance can still be achieved with sufficient buffering.

The bibliographic note contain references to improved versions of the basic dynamic Huffman coding algorithm described above. However, there is one improvement that we shall discuss now. For dynamic Huffman coding, it does not matter how the Huffman trie is initialized; the initialization of the trie only provides an initial bias that will change to reflect the true probabilities of the elements of S after the input stream becomes sufficiently long. In fact, it is not even necessary to initialize the Huffman trie to contain all of the elements of S. It suffices to initialize the Huffman tree to contain only one node, which we shall call the *unseen leaf*, which always has zero probability. Each time the encoder sees a new element x that is not in the trie, it does the following:

(1) Transmit the code for the unseen leaf followed by $\lceil \log_2 |S| \rceil$ bits that describe x.

---

† In fact, rescaling a periodic intervals can be used as a method of fine tuning how fast the algorithms "forgets" old data. See the bibliographic notes

(2) If the trie has $|S|$ leaves, then associate x with the unseen leaf; otherwise, add two new children to the unseen leaf, a new unseen leaf on the 0-branch (with zero probability) and a leaf corresponding to x on the 1-branch[†].

There are other ways of implementing the unseen leaf than that described above. For example, we could initially give the unseen leaf a high count such as $|S|$ (reflecting the fact that initially, its code is likely to be transmitted), and then lower its count each time it is visited. Dynamic Huffman coding can easily be modified to accommodate most reasonable implementations of the unseen leaf. However, such variations should only be viewed as "fine tuning", since the exact choice only affects compression of the initial portion of the input stream.

An additional benefit of using the unseen leaf is that the encoder and decoder need only use space proportional to the current number of leaves in the trie[††], even if this number is much smaller than $|S|$; that is, instead of having an array of size $|S|$ to map elements of S to leaves of the trie, a standard dictionary look-up data structure can be used (e.g. hashing, binary search tree, etc.). This approach can be useful when S is very large (e.g. encoding 4-tuples of English characters) and it is likely that not all elements of S will be encountered.

For some applications, not only are the element probabilities unknown in advance, but we do not even know $|S|$. One example is when the Huffman coding algorithm is to be used as a "second stage" to some other coding algorithm (i.e., the elements of the set S are in fact codewords produced by some other coding algorithm); it might be that the algorithm producing the codes periodically decides to increase the size of the tokens it transmits. Presumably, there is some method for determining when one token stops and another token begins, but we may not be able to make any assumptions about how many bits comprise each token that arrives to the Huffman encoder. The key observation is that dynamic Huffman coding with the unseen leaf method of initializing the dictionary works for this situation with the exception of one somewhat annoying detail: When the decoder receives a code for the unseen leaf, how does it know how many bits to now ac-

---

† The choice of putting the unseen leaf on the 0-branch and the leaf for x on the 1-branch is, of course, arbitrary (but must be the same for both the encoder and decoder).
†† Since Huffman codes are succinct prefix codes, the total number of nodes in the trie is at most twice the number of leaves.

cept for the new symbol that is to follow? To solve this problem, we can encode the next symbol by using the technique cascading lengths that was discussed earlier in this chapter.

2.7. HIGHER-ORDER HUFFMAN CODES

By *higher order* Huffman codes we mean Huffman codes that are based on higher-order statistics. A simple way to construct such codes is to simply view k-tuples of elements from the source set S as a new alphabet of size $|S|^k$. Each block of k elements from the source set can then be assigned a Huffman code (with either the static or dynamic algorithm) based on the statistics of the k-tuples. A drawback of this approach is that when encoding a sequence of elements from S, no advantage is taken of correlations between elements that "straddle" boundaries between blocks. A more elegant way to employ higher order statistics is to consider the probability of an element occurring given that the $k-1$ elements that preceded it are known; this is what we shall refer to as k^{th}-*order* statistics. Huffman codes for k^{th}-order statistics, $K > 1$, can be constructed by simply maintaining $|S|^{k-1}$ separate Huffman tries (static or dynamic).

Unfortunately, independent of whether the statistics of k-tuples or k^{th}-order statistics are employed, the resulting data structure requires $O(|S|^k)$ space. Even for the case $k=2$, for byte-oriented data, this bound implies storage of size 2^{16} times a constant factor representing the pointer fields employed, etc. A simple heuristic for reducing the space for higher-order Huffman codes is to store only the portions of the data structure that pertain to frequently occurring items. We illustrate this approach for dynamic Huffman codes based on second-order probabilities; however, these ideas can easily be extended for k-tuple and k^{th}-order probabilities, $k > 2$, for both the static and dynamic cases.

As indicated above, the straightforward implementation of static Huffman codes for second-order probabilities is to simply have $|S|$ first-order Huffman codes. In this case, to reduce space, for some integer $m > 1$, one can simply keep the $m-1$ most common codewords of each of the Huffman codes and make the mth most common codeword the *unseen codeword* (analogous to the unseen leaf as discussed in the last section); that is, each time an element of S is encountered that does not correspond to one of the $m-1$ most common codewords, the unseen codeword is transmitted, followed by a "raw" $\lceil \log_2 |S| \rceil$-bit code for the element. This scheme reduces the space for second-order Huffman coding to $O(|S|m)$, which is a substantial savings if $|S|$ is large (e.g., $|S|=256$) and choosing m to be a small constant (e.g., $m=16$) yields an acceptable approximation to the amount of compression achieved by the full data structure.

The same scheme as above can be used in the dynamic case, provided some scheme is adopted for dynamic updating of the code assignments. We now describe two approaches. In both of these descriptions, we restrict our attention to the implementation of one of the $|S|$ first-order Huffman codes that comprise the second-order algorithm.

One method for adjusting code assignments is to employ the dynamic Huffman coding algorithm of the last section with some convention for "seeding" the set of the $m-1$ most common entries with new elements. That is, a convention for deleting the least common element among the $m-1$ most common elements in favour of a new element that is encountered.

A simpler method for dynamic adjustment of codeword assignments is to adopt for each value of m, a "standard" codeword set. For example, for $m=2$, 4, 8, and 16, one might use the sets:

1	1	10	10
0	00	11	11
	010	000	000
	011	001	0010
		0100	0011
		0101	01000
		0110	01001
		0111	01010
			01011
			01100
			01101
			011011
			011100
			011101
			011110
			011111

The last codeword in a set is used for the unseen node. The first $m-1$ codewords can be viewed as labeling positions in a list of $m-1$ elements of S. Assignments of the first $m-1$ codewords to elements of $|S|$ can be adjusted with a simple "transposition" heuristic that, each time an element of S is used, exchanges it with the element above it on the list[†]. Again, some convention must be adopted for "seeding" this list with new elements. One such convention is, when the unseen codeword is transmitted followed by a new element of S, to replace the $m-1^{th}$ element on the list with this new element.

The above approach can be implemented very efficiently. All that is needed is an array of size $m-1$ to store the elements of S (no pointer fields are needed). The standard codeword sets for each value of i, $2 \leq i \leq m$ can be stored in one place and used for all of the $|S|$ copies of the algorithm. Note that if for a given copy of the algorithm, if only i distinct elements of S have been see thus far, $i < m$, then the ith codeword set is used.

2.8. TUNSTALL CODES

In the most simple form, Huffman codes mapped an element from a source set S to variable length strings over an alphabet Σ (we took $|\Sigma|$ to be 2 for the purposes of presentation in the last two sections). It is interesting to consider the dual process; that is, the process of mapping variable length segments of an input stream of elements from S to fixed length strings of characters over Σ. Note that such a process does not fall under the definition of a code as we have defined it in this chapter. Our definition of a code is often referred to as a *fixed-to-variable rate code* to distinguish it from *variable-to-fixed rate* codes *and variable-to-variable* rate codes. In fact, if we wished to classify data compression techniques to be considered in later chapters as codes, we would need the latter two notions.

This section complements our presentation of Huffman coding by considering *Tunstall codes*, which are a variable-to-fixed length codes that can be viewed as the inverse to the process of Huffman coding. Like Huffman codes, for the basic static algorithm, we assume that along with each element x of S we are given a probability p_x. Since Tunstall codes correspond to "reverse Huffman coding", it is typical for $|S|$ to be small compared to $|\Sigma|$. To simplify our presentation, we shall simply assume that $S=\{x,y\}$ (but $|\Sigma|$ may be arbitrarily large); all of what is to be presented can be easily generalized for $|S| > 2$.

[†] This heuristic and the move-to-front heuristic are standard methods for maintaining ordered lists. See the bibliographic notes.

(1) **initialize** the root to have weight 1.

(2) while there are less than $|\Sigma|$ leaves **do begin**

        Let l be the leaf with largest weight. Create a child with weight $p_x * weight(l)$ and connect it to l via an edge labeled by x. Create a child with weight $p_y * weight(l)$ and connect it to l via an edge labeled by y.

        end

Algorithm 2.8.1
Static Tunstall Trie Construction Algorithm

Algorithm 2.8.1 is the static Tunstall trie construction algorithm which like the static Huffman trie construction algorithm uses a greedy approach to construct the trie. In the spirit of "reverse Huffman coding", we can use the succinct prefix decoding algorithm for Tunstall encoding and the succinct prefix encoding algorithm for Tunstall decoding.

We close this section by noting that like Huffman coding, Tunstall coding can be generalized to higher-order sources and can be shown to be perfect in the information-theoretic sense. In addition, there is an efficient algorithm for dynamic maintenance of the dictionary.

2.9. ARITHMETIC CODES

There are other coding techniques which, like Huffman coding, are perfect in the information theoretic sense. Perhaps the most notable are *arithmetic codes*. The basic idea is the following. Suppose that we know that in any given input string, the elements of the source set S appear with probabilities $p_1 \cdots p_{|S|}$. Then we can imagine the real line between 0 and 1 as being recursively sub-divided according to these probabilities so that every string of elements from S corresponds to some sub-interval.

Example 2.9.1: Suppose that:

$$S=\{A,B,C\}$$

$$p_A = .2$$
$$p_B = .3$$
$$p_C = .5$$

The following are examples of the correspondence between strings of elements of S and intervals:

> A corresponds to $(0,.2)$
> B corresponds to $(.2,.5)$
> C corresponds to $(.5,1)$
> AC corresponds to $(.1,.2)$
> CA corresponds to $(.5,.6)$
> BC corresponds to $(.35,.5)$
> CAC corresponds to $(.55,.6)$ ○

As the encoder consumes characters of S and narrows the interval, each time corresponding digits of the beginning and end of the interval become the same, that digit can be transmitted, since it cannot be affected by further narrowing of the interval[†]. As the decoder receives digits, it can reconstruct the interval being constructed by the encoder. Each time a digit is transmitted or received, both the encoder and decoder can rescale the corresponding interval to be $(0,1)$ (thus allowing all computations to be carried out with limited precision arithmetic).

A nice aspect of arithmetic coding is that both the encoder and decoder can work on line. For example, suppose that the codeword alphabet is $\{0,1\}$. Then, referring to Example 2.9.1, if the receiver receives a string beginning with a 1, it can output a C before processing any additional digits; similarly, if the receiver receives 01, it can output a B before processing additional digits. Another nice aspect of arithmetic coding is that there is no round-off in assigning an integral number of bits to a codeword (as there is with Huffman codes). Like Huffman codes, arithmetic codes have a dynamic version and can be generalized to higher-order statistics.

In practice, the amount of compression achieved by arithmetic codes and Huffman codes is comparable. For the purposes of this book, arithmetic codes can be viewed as an alternative to Huffman codes; that is, in most cases

---

[†] For finite transmission, a special character (agreed upon by both encoder and decoder) that is not otherwise used can be encoded as the last character of the transmission, and all remaining digits of the beginning of the interval can be transmitted.

that we use Huffman codes, arithmetic codes could be used instead.

2.10. SHANNON-FANO CODES

A code that was discovered independently in the late 1940's by both C. E. Shannon and R. M. Fano, which is usually referred to as a *Shannon-Fano code,* is similar in flavour to Huffman coding except that the trie construction algorithm works "top-down" instead of "bottom-up" as the Huffman trie construction algorithm does. The idea is the following. Let S be the source set (where each element is given with a first-order probability) and assume for simplicity that the codeword alphabet is $\Sigma=\{0,1\}$; the algorithm is easily generalized to the case $|\Sigma|>2$. Arrange the elements of S in order of decreasing probability. Divide this sequence into two groups so that the sum of the probabilities in each group is as nearly equal as possible; make the first codeword character of all members of the first group 0 and the first codeword character of all members of the second group 1. Now apply this process recursively to each group; the recursion stops when a group has only one member.

Algorithm 2.10.1 is the (first-order) static Shannon-Fano trie construction algorithm, a non-recursive version of the idea just described where a queue of nodes that need to be expanded is maintained. There are two places that Algorithm 2.10.1 makes arbitrary choices. One is when the partitioning is done and one is when 0 and 1 are associated with children. Hence, like Huffman codes, for a given set S, a Shannon-Fano code is not unique.

With the exception of Step 3B, it is straightforward to implement Algorithm 2.10.1 in time linear in $|S|$. Unfortunately, Step 3B presents a problem since optimal partitioning is NP-hard. However, in practice, an approximation algorithm for partitioning may be acceptable (see the bibliographic notes).

Like Huffman codes, Shannon-Fano codes are succinct prefix codes. Hence, the prefix code encoding and decoding algorithms may be employed.

Shannon-Fano codes are not perfect in the information theoretic sense, but can be shown to always be close. Like Huffman codes, the simplified version presented here can be generalized to be dynamic, for higher-order statistics, etc.

(1) Create a root vertex r and associate S with it.

(2) Initialize $QUEUE$ to contain r.

(3) **while** $QUEUE$ is not empty **do begin**

   (A) **dequeue** a vertex v and let V be the subset of S that is associated with v.

   (B) Partition V into two sets V_1 and V_2 so that the sum of probabilities of the elements in each set is as nearly equal as possible.

   (C) Create the two new vertices v_1 (with the set V_1 associated with it) and v_2 (with the set V_2 associated with it).

   (D) Attach v_1 and v_2 to v via edges labeled 0 and 1 (which gets 0 and which gets 1 is arbitrary).

   (E) **if** $|V_1|>1$ then **enqueue** v_1
       if $|V_2|>1$ then **enqueue** v_2

   end

Algorithm 2.10.1
Static Shannon-Fano Trie Construction Algorithm

2.11. BIBLIOGRAPHIC NOTES

The Kraft/MacMillian inequality as applied to prefix codes is due to Kraft [1949]. MacMillian [1956] presented a proof that this inequality also applies to uniquely decipherable codes; this proof was subsequently simplified by Karush [1961]. For a clear presentation of a proof of the Kraft/MacMillian inequality, the reader may refer to an introductory text on information theory such as Hamming [1980] or Abramson [1963].

The cascading lengths technique is described by Even and Rodeh [1978] and also by Rodeh, Pratt, and Even [1981]. Similar schemes are described in Bentley and Yao [1976], Elias [1975], and Levenshtein [1968]. See also Apostolico and Fraenkel [1985] for a discussion of techniques based on a Fibonacci system of enumeration that are not asymptotically optimal but have better properties with respect to errors; early work concerning Fibonacci fixed-length codes is contained in Kautz [1965].

The error-resilient property of step-codes that was alluded to in this chapter is discussed further in Chapter 3, which also contains references to self-synchronizing codes. There is a great volume of past work that pertains to the detection and correction of errors occurring within codewords. Introductory textbooks on error-correcting codes (e.g., Hamming codes, Reed-Solomon codes) include Peterson and Weldon [1972], MacWilliams and Sloane [1977], McEliece [1977], and Blahut [1983].

The static version of Huffman coding is due to Huffman [1952]; the proof of its optimality appears in his paper as well as in many texts in both information theory and computer science. Hufffman's original paper also contains the generalized version of the trie construction algorithm for $|\Sigma| > 2$. Karp [1961], Krause [1962], Cot [1977], and Mehlhorn [1980] consider the case when the characters of the code alphabet have non-equal cost. Gilbert [1971] considers the construction of Huffman codes based on inaccurate source probabilities. Weyland and Puckett [1986] consider the dynamic construction of Huffman-like trees for the compression of a Gaussian source of fixed and floating-point numbers. Dynamic Huffman codes are due to Faller [1973] and Gallager [1978]. Vitter [1987], Knuth [1985], and Cormack and Horspool [1984] consider improvements and generalizations to this algorithm. Lelewer and Hirschberg [1987] summarize the improvements proposed by Vitter [1987]. Mukherjee and Bassiouni [1987] consider VLSI implementations of Huffman encoding and decoding. Teng [1987] presents a $O(log(n)^2)$ parallel algorithm for constructing a Huffman trie with n leaves. Larmore and Hirschberg [1987] consider the off-line construction of Huffman tries where the depth of leaves (the maximum length of a codeword) is limited; see also Larmore [1987], Wessner [1976], Garey [1974], and Hu and Tan [1972]. For other work pertaining to Huffman codes see: McIntyre and Pechura [1985], Knuth [1983], Cormack [1985], Hu [1982], Guazzo [1980], Johnsen [1980], Jacobsson [1978], Parker [1978,1978b], Brown and Elias [1976], Gallager and Voorhis [1975], Perl, Garey, and Even [1975], Garey [1972], Wells [1972] Hu and Tucker [1971], Varn [1971], Schwartz [1963,1964], and Schwartz and Kallick [1964].

The use of fixed codeword sets in conjunction with the transposition heuristic is due to Bacon and Houde [1986]. Rivest [1976] compares performance of the transposition heuristic to the move-to-front heuristic for self-organizing linear lists. For further references on both of these heuristics, see the bibliographic notes to Chapter 3.

For a discussion of Tunstall codes see Rissanen [1982] and Tunstall [1968].

The book of Abramson [1963] (in a note on pages 61-62) gives credit for the idea of arithmetic codes to Elias. More recently, Rissanen [1983], Rissanen and Langdon [1981], Langdon [1981b], and Rissanen [1976] have studied this notion and generalizations of it in great detail. Witten, Neal, and Cleary [1987] is a brief introduction to the subject which includes source code for encoding and decoding algorithms. Cleary and Witten [1984] discuss dynamic arithmetic coding and compare it to the static version. Blumer [1988] considers non-Markov sources. Miller and Wegman [1985] employ arithmetic codes to further compress streams of codewords that are produced by textual substitution schemes.

Shannon-Fano codes were discovered independently by both Shannon and Weaver [1949] and Fano [1949,1952,1961]. Hamming [1980] contains a presentation of Shannon-Fano codes and includes a proof that these codes are close to perfect in the information-theoretic sense. See Garey and Johnson [1979] for a discussion of NP-hardness, the partitioning problem, and approximation algorithms for NP-hard problems.

A classic group of codes that we have not discussed in this chapter are *run-length* codes. As the name indicates, the idea is to replace long runs of repeated characters by counts. An informal introduction to this method is contained in Sedgewick [1983]. A more formal introduction is contained in Hamming [1980]. Blumer [1985] considers a generalization of run-length encoding that attempts to extend arbitrary patterns at each stage. Fraenkel and Klein [1985] consider numeration systems for encoding blocks of zeros to which Huffman codes can be assigned. See also Gonzalez and Wintz [1977], Liao [1977], and Golomb [1966].

Cover [1973], Goldberg and Sipser [1985] consider enumerative codes.

For discussion of other codes with universal properties see Blumer and McEliece [1988], Blumer [1987], Llewellyn [1987], Horspool and Cormack [1984,1986], Davisson [1983], Davisson, McEliece, Pursley, and Wallace [1981],

Jones [1981], Guazzo [1980]. Pasco [1976], Elias [1975], Cover [1973], Davisson [1973], Schalkwijk [1972], Golomb [1966], and Karp [1961].

The texts by Stallings [1985], Halsall [1985] and Techo [1980] provide an introduction to current computer communications and networking technology; see also the book edited by Chou [1983]. The text by Proakis [1983] addresses mathematical aspects of digital communications.

3

ON-LINE
TEXTUAL SUBSTITUTION:
PRACTICAL METHODS

Chapter 1 introduced both the notion of data compression by textual substitution and the on-line model of computation. This chapter examines textual substitution methods for the on-line model that perform well in practice. In addition, these methods employ real-time, serial algorithms that can be easily implemented to run efficiently with minimal computational resources (e.g., a micro-processor together with a few thousand bytes of random access memory). We first introduce general purpose encoding and decoding algorithms that can be tailored to yield specific methods by supplying the update and deletion heuristics to be applied to the local dictionaries. Next, we consider several practical choices for these heuristics, discuss their implementations, and summarize some empirical results. We then consider how these heuristics can be augmented with lookahead. Finally, we discuss how these techniques can easily be generalized to perform on-line dynamic lossy compression.

3.1. THE BASIC MODEL

Algorithm 3.1.1 is an *on-line encoding algorithm*, which reads a stream of characters over Σ and writes a stream of bits, and Algorithm 3.1.2 is an *on-line decoding algorithm*, which receives a stream of bits and outputs a stream of characters over Σ. Note that for both the presentation of these algorithms and for the discussion to follow we shall use the notation pertaining to local dictionaries that was developed in Section 1.4. In particular, recall that we shall refer to indices into a dictionary of strings as *pointers*.

(1) Initialize the local dictionary D with the set *INIT*.

(2) **repeat forever**

    (a) Get the current match:
    $t := MH(inputstream)$
    Advance the input stream forward by $|t|$ characters.
    Transmit $\lceil \log_2 |D| \rceil$ bits corresponding to t.

    (b) Update the local dictionary D:
    $X := UH(D)$
    while $X \neq \{\}$ and (D is not full or $DH(D) \neq \{\}$) **do begin**
        Delete an element x from X.
        if x is not in D **then begin**
            if D is full **then** Delete $DH(D)$ from D.
            Add x to D.
        end
    end

Algorithm 3.1.1
(Encoding Algorithm)

(1) Initialize the local dictionary D by performing Step 1 of the encoding algorithm.

(2) **repeat forever**

    (a) Get the current match:
    Receive $\lceil \log_2 |D| \rceil$ bits.
    Obtain the current match t by a dictionary lookup.
    Output the characters of t.

    (b) Update the local dictionary D by performing Step 2b of the encoding algorithm.

Algorithm 3.1.2
(Decoding Algorithm)

Like the dynamic Huffman coding algorithm in Chapter 2, the key idea behind the methods we shall discuss is to have the encoder and decoder work in lock-step to maintain identical local dictionaries (which may be dynamically changing). The encoder repeatedly finds a match between the incoming characters of the input stream and the dictionary, deletes these characters from the input stream, transmits the index of the corresponding dictionary entry, and updates the dictionary with some method that depends on the current contents of the dictionary and the match that was just found; if there is not enough room left in the dictionary, some deletion heuristic must be performed. Similarly, the decoder repeatedly receives an index, retrieves the corresponding dictionary entry as the "current match", and then performs the same algorithm as the encoder to update its dictionary.

It can be seen that left out of Algorithms 3.1.1 and 3.1.2 is the specification of the following:

The initialization heuristic, INIT: A set of strings that are to be used to initialize the local dictionary; it must be that Σ is a subset of $INIT$ and $|INIT| \leq <D>$.

The match heuristic, MH: A function that removes from the input stream a string t that is in D.

The update heuristic, UH: A function that takes the local dictionary D and returns a set of strings that should be added to the dictionary if space can be found for them.

The deletion heuristic, DH: A function that takes the local dictionary D and returns a set that is either empty (in which case there is no string that can be deleted from D) or consists of a single string of D that is not a member of $INIT^\dagger$ (which may legally be deleted from D).

---

† It is only necessary that characters of Σ not be deleted. Whether or not the strings in the set $INIT-\Sigma$ (or some portion of these strings) are allowed to be deleted is just a variation of Algorithms 3.1.1 and 3.1.2. One could add the parameter $INIT\_DYNAMIC$ to specify a set of strings that are to initially be placed in the dictionary but can be deleted later. In practice, such strings only affect the "start up" phase of the algorithms when the dictionary is not full. We have left out $INIT\_DYNAMIC$ to simplify our presentation.

The choice of the above heuristics is the primary subject of the subsequent sections of this chapter. However, for the moment let us consider the basic structure of Algorithms 3.1.1 and 3.1.2 that is independent of these heuristics. The reader should convince himself or herself that these algorithms are inverses of each other; that is, the input to the encoding algorithm is always the same as the output from the decoding algorithm. The key observations are:

- D is initialized to contain at least the characters of Σ (since Σ must be a subset of *INIT*) and these characters can never be deleted.

- Since D always contains Σ, *MH* is always well defined. Hence, any input string to the encoding algorithm can always be encoded (at worst at a character at a time).

- Encoding is unique (since MH must return a unique value).

- The local dictionaries of the encoder and decoder must always remain identical (since Step 2b of the decoding algorithm is identical to Step 2b of the encoding algorithm).

Another important observation is that these algorithms will pass variable length pointers if:

$$\log_2 \lceil |INIT| \rceil \quad < \quad \log_2 \lceil <D> \rceil$$

That is, it is possible that initially, $|D|$ is smaller than $<D>$, and so pointers shorter than $\log_2 \lceil <D> \rceil$ bits can be transmitted. The size of pointers increases by one bit every time $|D|$ reaches a power of 2 until $|D|$ reaches $<D>$. Presumably, D fills up quickly, and as long as Algorithms 3.1.1 and 3.1.2 are run for a time that is long compared to this start up phase, the savings obtained by transmitting these shorter lengths is not significant. In practice, it is often simpler to transmit pointers of length $\lceil \log_2 <D> \rceil$ no matter what the value of $|D|$. A more significant use of such variable length pointers is to dynamically choose the size of $<D>$ or even to let D grow and shrink. A heuristic can be used to decide whether to increase or decrease the size of D. If sufficient memory is available, one simple heuristic is to maintain two additional dictionaries, one half as large as D and one twice as large, and keep track of not only the current compression ratio but also the compression ratios that would be achieved by these other two dictionaries. At periodic intervals, if one or both of the alternate dictionaries are performing better, the pointer size can be changed by one bit (corresponding to halving or doubling the size of D). This sort of dynamic growth and shrinkage can be useful if the source varies greatly over time. However, in practice, sources usually do not vary enough for this strategy to give significant improvement over a fixed value of $<D>$. Also, the size of D is often limited by memory constraints. Such constraints together with the implementation of efficient error correction and detection algorithms for the communication line and the use of byte-oriented hardware often lead naturally to a choice of pointer size such as one and a half or two bytes. For simplicity, we shall not consider dynamic dictionary growth heuristics further; however, all of what is discussed in this chapter can be generalized to accommodate such heuristics.

Because our definition of the deletion heuristic specifies that elements of *INIT* may not be deleted, we refer to the portion of the dictionary that contains *INIT* as the *static portion of the dictionary*. The condition that *INIT* must include Σ implies that Step 1 of the encoding and decoding algorithms guarantees that each character of Σ is initially present in D. Furthermore, since *DH* is never allowed to return a character of Σ, the characters of Σ must always be present in D. This condition guarantees that Step 2a must always find a match that is at least one character long. Because the existence of the current match has been guaranteed by the existence of Σ in the dictionary, we say that Algorithms 3.1.1 and 3.1.2 have *dictionary guaranteed progress*. Another way to guarantee progress is to relax the conditions that Σ be a subset of *INIT* and *DH* cannot return a character of Σ, and modify Step 2a of the encoding algorithm to transmit $\lceil \log_2 |D| \rceil + \lceil \log_2 |\Sigma| \rceil$ bits that represent the pointer to t and the character of Σ that appears immediately after t in the input stream (and then advance the input stream forward by $|t|+1$ characters). Step 2a of the decoding algorithm is similarly modified to receive a pointer and a character of Σ. Methods that guarantee progress in this fashion have *pointer guaranteed progress*. A compromise between dictionary guaranteed progress and pointer guaranteed progress is *on-the-fly dictionary guaranteed progress*. Here, we again relax the conditions that Σ be a subset of *INIT* and *DH* cannot return a character of Σ. Instead, we reserve one pointer value as the *nil-pointer*. Any rule for what value value is assigned to the nil-pointer suffices so long as it is consistent between the encoder and decoder; for convenience, we always assume that the nil-pointer is $|D|+1$ (one more than the largest current legal pointer value); that is the nil-pointer starts off as 0 and increases by one each time $|D|$ increases by one until the nil-pointer value reaches $<D>$. Hence, one entry of D is in some sense "wasted" since D can never have more than $<D>-1$ entries; in practice, assuming that D is reasonably large (e.g., more than 100 entries), this waste is insignificant. Given that a nil-pointer is available, each time no match can be found, progress can be guaranteed by transmitting the nil-pointer (to signal to the decoder that a new character of Σ is to follow) followed by the next character of the input stream. In addition, the next character of the input stream can be added to the dictionary. On-the-fly dictionary guaranteed progress derives its name from the fact that characters of Σ are added to D (to guarantee progress) only when they are encountered. Hence, it represents a compromise between dictionary and pointer guaranteed progress because unlike dictionary guaranteed progress it does not use space in D for characters of Σ that are not being used but unlike pointer guaranteed progress it does not add overhead to every pointer; overhead is only incurred the first time a character is used (or the first time the character has been used since it has last been deleted from D).

In the limit as D becomes large, it makes little difference which of the above three methods are used to guarantee progress. However, for practical implementations, where D is bounded in size, the overhead of including $|\Sigma|$ bits with each pointer used by pointer guaranteed progress can be substantial; only for special applications where $|\Sigma|$ constitutes a significant fraction of $<D>$ is this overhead warranted[†].

Since for most typical applications, $<D>$ is relatively large compared to $|\Sigma|$ (e.g., $<D>$ is larger that 4096 and $|\Sigma|$ is smaller that 256), unless otherwise explicitly stated, we restrict our attention from this point on to dictionary guaranteed progress, as is used by Algorithms 3.1.1 and 3.1.2. Note that in practice, on-the-fly dictionary progress typically performs equally well; that is, the overhead incurred is typically insignificant so long as the size of the text being compressed is reasonably large (e.g., larger than $<D>$). We have not chosen to use it simply because the standard form of dictionary guaranteed progress is "cleaner" for presentation purposes. However, we will briefly employ on-the-fly dictionary guaranteed progress at the end of this chapter when we generalize Algorithms 3.1.1 and 3.1.2 to lossy compression.

If MH is taken to be the function that returns the longest prefix of the input stream that is in the dictionary, then Step 2a of the encoding algorithm amounts to a greedy algorithm for obtaining the current match. We shall henceforth refer to this heuristic as the *greedy* match heuristic. In terms of worst-case performance, significantly better compression can be achieved

---

[†] Pointer guaranteed progress can be an appropriate model when the data is random or nearly random; see the bibliographic notes for a discussion of this issue. In addition, much of the past work by other authors that we shall mention uses pointer guaranteed progress; particularly information-theoretic work where the primary concern is what happens when D becomes asymptotically large.

by incorporating some amount of lookahead. However, little advantage is gained in practice; we defer further discussion of this issue until later in this chapter. For the sections to follow, unless explicitly otherwise stated, the greedy match heuristic will always be used.

For Step 2b of the encoding (and decoding) algorithm, there are several heuristics that work well in practice. Most of these heuristics are motivated by methods that are perfect in the information-theoretic sense but are computationally intractable to implement directly. The sections to follow can be viewed as successively more general choices for such heuristics.

3.2. STATIC DICTIONARY METHOD

With the *static dictionary* method, Step 2b of the encoder and decoder algorithms is null; that is, $UH(D)=\{\}$. Compression is based only on *INIT*. The static dictionary method is useful when the source is known in advance (e.g., to compress English text, use a dictionary of common English substrings such as the n-gram tables in the appendix). In that case, the static dictionary method offers the advantage of speed and simplicity over the more general purpose methods that comprise the remainder of this section. In particular, for hardware implementations, the static dictionary can be implemented with read-only memory[†]. Another advantage is that there is no danger of the encoder and decoder dictionaries becoming different as a result of noise on the communication line, allowing for much simpler and efficient error detection and recovery.

If the distribution of the entries in the static dictionary is non-uniform in the source text, it can be advantageous to use variable length pointers by assigning shorter codes to more frequently occurring entries. One method is to keep track of the frequency of occurrence of each entry and use a universal coding scheme such as the dynamic Huffman coding discussed in Chapter 2. Another method is for the sender and receiver (in lock-step) to maintain a linear ordering of the dictionary and employ the "move to front heuristic" where each time an entry is used, it is moved to the front of the list. The "cascading lengths" technique for encoding commas discussed in Section 2.1 can then be used to encode the ith entry of the list using

---

† Actually, as was discussed when the notion of a dictionary was introduced in Chapter 1, a small amount of standard random access memory that is both readable and writable (e.g. 100 bytes) is needed for local variables, etc.

$\log_2(i) + O(loglog(i))$ bits[††].

A disadvantage of the two techniques above for variable length coding is that that the association between dictionary entries and codewords is no longer constant. Hence, for hardware implementations, standard random access memory instead of read-only memory must be used. In addition, noise on the communication line could cause the association between entries and codes at each end to be different, which is tantamount to the dictionaries at the two ends becoming different. If some approximation of the distribution of the dictionary entries in the source is known[††], then static versions of the methods above can be used (i.e. static Huffman codes or cascading lengths without the move to front heuristic).

A practical approach that avoids the problems above is to use first-order step codes. Suppose we have the following situation. The static dictionary has 2^{2k-1} entries for some $k > 1$; k-bit pointers, with the first bit 0, are used to point to the first 2^{k-1} dictionary entries (which are presumably chosen to be the entries most likely to occur in the text to be compressed) and $2k$-bit pointers, with the first bit 1, are used to point to the remaining dictionary entries. Suppose further that there is a real number $0 \leq h < 1$ such that the probability of the next block of k bits starting with 1 is $\leq h$. Besides the possibility of saving space over a fixed length encoding, the following theorem shows that we get "for free" what is essentially immunity to noise on a byte-oriented communication line. That is, if a burst of errors occur on the line (bytes are changed, inserted, and/or lost) and the decoder ends up reading the second half of a two byte pointer thinking that it is the first half of a pointer, we are guaranteed to resynchronize quickly. In contrast, with pointers that always have size exactly two bytes, the decoder would never recover from this situation without a compensating error.

---

† As discussed in Section 2.1, for small dictionaries, there may be alternatives to the cascading lengths technique with worse asymptotic performance but better practical performance.
†† We use the term "distribution" very informally here. One must be careful of situations where, for example, the strings "elephan" and "elephant" are both in the dictionary and the first occurs the same number of times as the second but is never used.
††† This scheme is somewhat wasteful since there are two ways two refer to the first 2^{k-1} entries of the dictionary (with either a k or $2k$ bit pointer). In practice, the dictionary can have as many as $2^{2k-1} + 2^{k-1}$ entries. However, as long as k is reasonably large (e.g. $k=8$, which corresponds to 1 or 2 byte pointers), there is little loss of performance in practice and we accept this waste here to simplify our discussion.

Theorem 3.2.1: Suppose that a first order k-step code is used on a k-blocking noisy communication line. Suppose further that at any given point in time, the probability that the first bit of the next block of k bits is 1 is less than h for some $0 \leq h < 1$. If an arbitrary sequence of errors has just occurred, then the probability of not resynchronizing after the next n blocks have been read is less than

$$h^{n-1}(1-h)$$

if no further errors occur.

Proof: Suppose that after an error has occurred, the communication line is left unsynchronized; that is, the decoder is expecting to see the beginning of a pointer but the next incoming block b is the second half of a pointer. There are three cases:

Case 1: The first bit of b is 0. The block b will be (incorrectly) taken as a one-block pointer. The communication line will now be resynchronized. This case occurs with probability $1-h$.

Case 2: The first bit of b is 1 and the first bit of the block c that follows b is 0. The blocks b and c will be (incorrectly) taken as a two-block pointer. The communication line will now be resynchronized. This case occurs with probability $h(1-h)$.

Case 3: The first bit of b is 1 and the first bit of the block c that follows b is also 1. The blocks b and c will be taken as a two-block pointer. The communication line will now remain unsynchronized. This case occurs with probability h^2.

The above argument can be repeated each time Case 3 occurs until the argument terminates with either Case 1 or Case 2. The probability of loosing n blocks and terminating with Case 1 is $h^{n-1}(1-h)$ and the probability of loosing n blocks and terminating with Case 2 is $h^{n-2}h(1-h)$. Either way, the theorem follows. ◯

Corollary 3.2.1: Given the same conditions as stated in Theorem 3.2.1, if an arbitrary sequence of errors has just occurred, then the probability of not resynchronizing after next n pointers have been read is less than $h^{2n-1}MAX(h,1-h)^{\dagger}$.

Proof: Consider the proof of Theorem 3.2.1. Each time Case 1 occurs, no pointers are consumed (we consider the pointer whose second byte is consumed by Case 1 to already be consumed) and each time Cases 2 or 3 occur, one pointers is consumed. Hence, depending on whether resynchronization occurs with Case 1 or Case 2, the probability is less than h^{2n} or $h^{2(n-1)}h(1-h)$; from which the corollary follows. $\bigcirc$

In practice, for sources such as English text, a 2-step code (which employs 1 or 2 byte pointers) is typically no better than a fixed length code (that simply uses 16 bits per pointer). However, it is typically not significantly worse; that is, it is common for the savings achieved by sometimes replacing a string with 1-byte pointer to make up for the "inefficiency" of using two-byte pointers to point into a dictionary that could be accessed with 15-bit pointers. From a theoretical point of view, it is possible to make some rough calculations that bound the ration between the compression achieved with a fixed 16-bit code for a dictionary of 2^{16} entries and a 2-step code for a dictionary of 2^{15} entries that maps the 128 most common entries to one byte and the remaining entries to two bytes. Let:

h = expected fraction of pointers that are 1 byte with a 2-step code
r_{15} = the compression ratio that is achieved with 15 bit pointers
r_{16} = the compression ratio that is achieved with 16 bit pointers

Then given a string s, the expected number of bytes in a compressed form of s using 2-step codes divided by the expected number of bytes in a compressed form of s using fixed size 16-bit pointers is:

$$= \frac{\frac{1}{2}h*r_{15}*|s|+\frac{16}{15}*(1-h)*r_{15}*|s|}{r_{16}*|s|}$$

$$= \frac{r_{15}}{r_{16}}*(\frac{16}{15}-\frac{17}{30}*h)$$

As an example, if we pick $r_{15}/r_{16}=1.02$ and $h=.1$ (typical practical values[††]),

---

† Throughout this book, for real or integer values x and y, we use the standard notation that $MAX(x,y)$ denotes the maximum of x and y and $MIN(x,y)$ denotes the minimum of x and y.
†† The experimental results reported in the Appendix to be discussed later in this chapter support the hypothesis that when pointer sizes are in the range of 12 or more bits, increasing the pointer size by 1 typically yields at most a percent or two improvement in compression (for all of the methods that we consider). However, $h=.1$

then the above formula is 1.03, which is very close to 1.

3.3. SLIDING DICTIONARY METHOD

Conceptually, the sliding dictionary method is perhaps the most simple method that employs a dynamically changing dictionary. The methods discussed later in this chapter usually perform slightly better in practice. However, there are at least four reasons that we consider the sliding dictionary method:

- It and similar methods have received considerable attention in the past.

- It motivates methods to be discussed later.

- Like the static dictionary method, it can be the best method for some special purpose applications.

- As we shall see in Chapter 4, it lends itself to fast and practical parallel implementations.

With the sliding dictionary method, $INIT=\Sigma$ and the remainder of the local dictionary is thought of as a sliding window that passes over the source string; that is, there are two parameters *maxdisplacement* and *maxlength* (determined by the size of the local dictionary), such that the local dictionary consists of all substrings of length $\leq MaxLength$ of the preceding *MaxDisplacement* characters of the input stream. We view a pointer as a pair of integers (m,n) where m is the *displacement* back from the current position to the pointer target and n is the *length* of the pointer target. Step 2b of the encoder and decoder algorithms amounts to sliding a window over the input

---

is more of a "ball park" figure. For dynamic methods, which are the primary subject of the appendix, there is a tendency for entries that are often matched to cause longer entries (that contain them as a prefix) to be added to the dictionary; this point is discussed later in this Chapter when the relationship between dynamic textual substitution techniques to the LZ2 algorithm of Lempel and Ziv is discussed. Hence, it is not necessarily true that there is a non-uniform usage of dictionary entries. However, for static methods, the situation can be much different. For example, in a dictionary of English words that is used to compress written English, it may be that the first 100 entries account for over 40 percent of the words in a text that is being compressed. See the bibliographic notes to Chapter 1 for a discussion of English word frequencies.

stream. That is, if we think of characters entering from the right and leaving to the left, then $UH(D)$ is a set consisting of all substrings of the window of length y or less that overlap with t, when t is concatenated to the right end of the window, and $DH(D)$ is one of the set of substrings of length y that overlap with the leftmost $|t|$ characters of the window[†].

At a given point in time, a pointer consists of two fields: a displacement field of d bits followed by a length field of l bits. In addition, we must allow room for the characters of Σ that are added to the dictionary in Step 1 of Algorithms 3.1.1 and 3.1.2[††]; so it must be that $d+l \geq \lceil \log_2(|\Sigma|) \rceil$. The pointer values 0 through $|\Sigma|-1$ are used to denote the characters of Σ. All pointers numbered $|\Sigma|$ or greater are partitioned into the highest order d bits for the displacement field and the lowest order l bits for the length field. Before decoding such a pointer, $|\Sigma|$ must first be "removed" from the pointer. That is, the length field is ok as is, but if $|\Sigma|>2^l$ (i.e., more than l bits are needed to count up to $|\Sigma|$), then the displacement field must have subtracted from it $|\Sigma|$ divided by 2^l. After $|\Sigma|$ has so removed, we can add 2 to both the displacement and length values since there is no point in having a displacement or length of less than 2 (in both cases, 0 would be meaningless and 1 can only indicate a match of length 1, which can be represented directly as an element of Σ). Thus, the low order l bits (rightmost l bits) of a pointer which lie in the range

$$0 \text{ to } 2^l-1$$

are used to specify a length in the range:

$$2 \text{ to } 2^l+1$$

The high order d bits (leftmost d bits) of a pointer which lie in the range

$$\frac{|\Sigma|}{2^l} \quad \text{to} \quad 2^d-1$$

---

† Note that since a given string may occur more than once within the window, there may be several copies of the same string in the dictionary (which are referenced by distinct pointers). Hence, the local dictionary is not truly a set of strings as we have defined it. This poses no problem from a conceptual point of view; Algorithms 3.1.1 and 3.1.2 can accommodate dictionaries with multiple copies of the same string. In the next section, we shall discuss how to eliminate this "waste".

†† That is, room is needed for Σ so that we may have dictionary guaranteed progress. The encoding of pointers presented here can be easily modified to accommodate on-the-fly dictionary guaranteed progress or pointer guaranteed progress.

are used to specify a displacement in the range:

$$2 \quad \text{to} \quad (2^d-1)-\lfloor |\Sigma|/2^l \rfloor +2$$

A pointer $p=(m,n)$, is decoded as follows:

if $p < |\Sigma|$

    then Output the character corresponding to p.

    else Output the string that starts $m-\lfloor |\Sigma|/2^l \rfloor +2)$ characters back in the window and is $n+2$ characters long.

Example 3.3.1: A typical choice of parameters for compressing sources like English or programming language might be to use 16 bit pointers with a 13 bit displacement field and a 3 bit length field. Assume that Σ is the 128 character ASCII alphabet. Then pointers are constructed as follows. First the pointer values 0 through 127 are used to denote the corresponding ASCII values. Second, all pointers numbered 128 or greater are partitioned as follows. The low order 3 bits (rightmost 3 bits) are used to specify a length in the range 2 to 9. The high order 13 bits (leftmost 13 bits) which must lie in the range

$$\frac{128}{2^3} = 16 \quad \text{to} \quad 2^{13}-1 = 8191$$

are used to specify a displacement in the range 2 to $8191-16+2 = 8177$. Thus, a pointer $p=(m,n)$, is decoded as follows:

if $p < 128$

    then Output the character with ASCII value p.

    else Output the string that starts $m-14$ characters back in the window and is $n+2$ characters long. ◯

The sliding dictionary method will be discussed in Chapter 5 (as the original-pointer macro scheme, restricted to left pointers). Chapter 5 addresses worst-case performance of off-line methods and bounds between the performances of methods. However, probably the best theoretical support for the use of the sliding dictionary method is that it can be viewed as a practical realization of a universal data compression algorithm due to A. Lempel and J.

Ziv. It is the first of two universal data compression algorithms proposed by these authors that we shall discuss in this chapter and we shall henceforth refer to it as LZ1. The LZ1 algorithm, which can be shown to be perfect in the information-theoretic sense, works as follows. At each stage, the longest prefix of the (unread portion of the) input stream that matches a substring of the input already seen is identified as the current match. Then a triple (d,l,c) is transmitted where d is the displacement back to a previous occurrence of this match, l is the length of the match, and c is the next input character following the current match (the transmission of c is pointer guaranteed progress). The input is then advanced past the current match and the character following the current match. Thus, the LZ1 algorithm remembers the entire input string and hence uses a dictionary that is unbounded in size. There is no bound on the number of bits needed to encode the triples that are transmitted and so a variable-length coding scheme is needed (such as one of the techniques for encoding commas that were considered in Chapter 2). The sliding dictionary method can be viewed as the natural practical implementation of LZ1 that uses fixed size pointers; instead of remembering the entire input stream, we remember only a fixed number of characters back, and instead of pointer guaranteed progress, we use dictionary guaranteed progress by reserving codes for the characters of Σ.

3.4. IMPROVED SLIDING DICTIONARY METHOD

As was noted in the last section, the sliding dictionary method is "wasteful" because a given substring may occur more than once within a given window (for example, the previous match is likely to), thus unnecessarily consuming more than one pointer[†]. The *improved* sliding dictionary method modifies the sliding dictionary method to effectively lengthen the window by eliminating redundant pointers. More formally, we can define the encoder and decoder for the improved sliding dictionary method as Algorithms 3.1.1 and 3.1.2 with $INIT=\Sigma$ and the heuristics UH and DH defined as follows. Let d be the number of bits used for the displacement field of a pointer and l be the number of bits used for the length field. The local dictionary D of Algorithms 3.1.1 and 3.1.2 is able to hold a maximum of 2^{d+l} entries (including the characters of $INIT$). To compute UH and DH, we maintain a string variable *extended_window* that contains as a suffix the sliding window of the pure sliding dictionary method. Initially *extended_window* is set to the

---

† In fact, as noted in the last section, such redundancy is not technically allowed by Algorithms 3.1.1 and 3.1.2.

empty string and between Steps 2a and 2b t is concatenated to the right of *extended_window* (we imagine characters entering from the right and leaving to the left). In Step 2b, $UH(D)$ is the set of all suffixes of *extended_window* of length ≥ 2 and $\leq 2^l+1$. For $DH(D)$, we delete from D one of the prefixes of *extended_window* that is in D and has length ≥ 2 and $\leq 2^l+1$ (it doesn't really matter which one, for simplicity, take the shortest one); if there is no such prefix, delete the leftmost character of *extended_window* and try again. The only significant remaining detail is that we associate with each entry of D that is not in *INIT* with a pointer to a substring of *extended_window*; this substring is the rightmost occurrence of that entry in *extended_window* (and must be updated in Step 2b when a string in X is found to already be in D).

There are a number of other possible sources of "waste" with the sliding dictionary method that the improved sliding dictionary method does not address, but which we do digress to mention now.

Pointers with small displacements are another source of waste. For example, a pointer specifying displacement 2 and length 3 cannot possibly occur, even though a pointer is allocated for it. To calculate the number of such wasted pointers, observe that for displacement 2^d+1 or greater no pointers are wasted, for displacement 2^d one pointer is wasted (the pointer with displacement 2^d and length 2^d+1), for displacement 2^d-1 two pointers are wasted, ..., and for displacement two, 2^d-1 pointers are wasted. Thus, the total number of wasted pointers is:

$$\sum_{i=1}^{2^l-1} i = 2^{2l-1}-2^{l-1}$$

Although it is not hard to use these codes to effectively lengthen the window, unless the length field is very large, the number of such wasted pointers is not significant. For example with 16-bit pointers that use 13 bits for the displacement and 3 bits for the length only 28 pointers are wasted out of a total of 65,536.

Another possible source of waste may occur when Σ is large but only a small fraction of the characters in Σ occur frequently. In this case, it may pay to let the length values range from 1 to 2^l so that pointer values do not have to be allocated for those characters that occur in the window. To encode characters that do not appear in the window, on-the-fly dictionary guaranteed progress or pointer guaranteed progress may be employed. This source of waste only applies to rather special situations; either something has to be known about the source in advance, or the sliding dictionary algorithm has to be modified to dynamically change the encoding of pointers as the source changes.

In addition to eliminating waste as discussed above, a natural approach for improving achieved compression of the sliding dictionary method is to place some other on-line compression method between the encoder and decoder, in the hopes of detecting a non-uniform distribution of pointer values, finding correlations between pointer values, etc. An obvious candidate for such a scheme is to treat the space of pointers as a new alphabet and perform some on-line universal coding algorithm (such as Huffman coding). In practice, it is typical for pointers to be close enough to a uniform distribution that the savings achieved are small (e.g., less than 1 percent); intuitively, this is because common matches are more likely to be prefixes of even longer matches. When the input stream is sufficiently long, it may be possible to achieve further compression by Huffman coding of k-tuples of pointers, for $k \geq 2$. However, we shall not address this point further.

3.5. DYNAMIC DICTIONARY METHOD

With the sliding dictionary method, the dictionary is updated in a very restricted fashion: a new match is appended to the right of the window and room is made for it by removing characters from the left of the window. Intuitively, the sliding dictionary method deletes characters at the left end of the window in the hope that substrings there are the least likely to occur again and adds the current match to the right end of the window in the hope that substrings there are the most likely to occur again. In fact, since the right end of the window has the previous match, the hope is that strings formed by the previous match concatenated with some portion of the current match will occur again. This intuition, together with the observations made in the last sub-section about the inherent waste with the sliding dictionary method, lead us to consider more general update and deletion heuristics that maintain a collection of strings that do not, in general, form a contiguous portion of the input stream. *Dynamic dictionary* methods, the subject of this section, are methods where the update heuristic adds the previous match concatenated with some set of strings based on the current match[†]. That is, if *pm* denotes the previous match, *cm* the current match, and *INC* is an "incre-

---

[†] Since we have defined the update function UD of Algorithms 3.1.1 and 3.1.2 as a function of D, to simplify notation, we shall always assume that it is possible to determine from D both the previous and current match.

menting" function that maps a single string to a set of strings, then for some choice of INC:

$$UH(D) = \{pm \text{ concatenated with all strings of } INC(cm)\}$$

The following are three effective choices for INC.

      FC: The *first character* heuristic: $INC(cm)$ is the first character of cm.

      ID: The *identity* heuristic: $INC(cm)$ is cm.

      AP: The *all-prefixes* heuristic: $INC(cm)$ is the set of all (non-empty) prefixes of cm (including cm).

Example 3.5.1: Suppose that the previous match was "THE_" and the current match is "CAT", where we use the underscore to denote a space. Then $UD(D)$ has the following values for the update heuristics discussed above:

      FC: {"THE_C"}

      ID: {"THE_CAT"}

      AP: {"THE_C", "THE_CA", "THE_CAT"}

In general, the FC and ID heuristics always produce exactly one string whereas the AP heuristic always produces a number of strings equal to the length of the current match. In fact, included in the set produced by the AP heuristic are the strings produced by the FC and ID heuristics. Hence, it is illustrative to consider a longer example with respect to the AP heuristic. Consider the phrase:

"THE_CAT_AT_THE_CAR_ATE_THE_RAT"

Assuming that we start with the dictionary containing only the single characters, the following table shows what strings are added to the dictionary as this phrase is processed:

MATCH	STRINGS ADDED
T	
H	TH
E	HE
_	E_
C	_C
A	CA
T	AT
_	T_
AT	_A _AT
_	AT_
TH	_T _TH
E_	THE THE_
CA	E_C E_CA
R	CAR
_AT	R_A R_AT
E_	_ATE _ATE_
THE_	E_T E_TH E_THE E_THE_
R	THE_R
AT	RAT ◯

Two common deletion heuristics are:

FREEZE: The *freeze heuristic:* $DH(D)$ is the empty string, that is, once
the dictionary is full, it remains the same from that point on.

LRU: The *least recently used* heuristic: $DH(D)$ is that string in D
that has been matched least recently.

A third deletion heuristic that can be viewed as a variation of the *LRU*
heuristic is the following:

LFU: The *least frequently used* heuristic: $DH(D)$ is that string in D
which has been matched least frequently. In order to prevent
this heuristic from degenerating into the *FREEZE* heuristic,
some sort of weighting has to be performed when entering a
new match into the dictionary. For example, the new match
can be assigned a frequency equal to the average frequency of
the entries currently in the dictionary. When a match is
found that is already in the dictionary, it may be necessary

to scale down all frequency counts of dictionary entries (making fractional counts 0) if any given count reaches the maximum allowable value for an integer. Alternately, a strategy for periodically rescaling counts can be adopted to prevent the counts from ever becoming too large.

In practice, the LFU deletion heuristic performs comparably to the *LRU* heuristic but is less convenient to implement. We shall not consider this deletion heuristic any further.

A fourth deletion heuristic that can be viewed as as discrete version of the *LRU* heuristic is the following.

SWAP: The *swap* heuristic: When the *primary* dictionary first becomes full, an *auxiliary* dictionary is started, but compression based on the primary dictionary is continued. From this point on, each time the auxiliary dictionary becomes full, the roles of the primary and auxiliary dictionaries are reversed, and the auxiliary dictionary is reset to be empty. Although this heuristic does not fit directly into Algorithms 3.1.1 and 3.1.2, they can be modified to accommodate it.

With the possible exception of rapidly changing data, the *SWAP* deletion heuristic typically performs comparably to the *LRU* heuristic. For this reason, we shall not bother to consider it when we present experimental results later in this chapter. However, this deletion heuristic will provide a useful alternative to *LRU* for some of the parallel implementations in Chapter 4.

A host of data compression methods can be derived from different combinations of the heuristics above. We now list four combinations that we will address in detail in the remainder of this chapter. Except as noted, the computational resources required by these four heuristics are are equivalent in the asymptotic sense, but in practical implementations can differ by significant constant factors for both time and space requirements. The trade-offs between compression performance and these constant factors will be an important concern.

FC-FREEZE: This heuristic is the most simple to implement and, except for the start up phase when the dictionary is not full, runs faster than heuristics that must spend time on updating.

FC-LRU: This heuristic requires more computational resources than

$FC-FREEZE$, but typically yields significantly better compression. It is also more stable than $FC-FREEZE$, in a sense to be discussed later.

AP-LRU: As we shall see, this heuristic requires approximately the same computational resources as $FC-LRU$ but typically yields better compression on text files.

ID-LRU: This heuristic typically yields better compression than the $FC-LRU$ heuristic and sometimes yields better compression than the $AP-LRU$ heuristic. However, although the $ID-LRU$ heuristic may appear at first glance to be simpler or more basic than the $AP-LRU$ heuristic, as we shall see in the next section, the $ID-LRU$ heuristic requires significantly greater computational resources than the $AP-LRU$ heuristic.

For all of the heuristics above, there is an obvious improvement called *pruning*. We say a string s in D is *dead* if for every character c of Σ, the string sc is also in D. Clearly, no dead string can possibly be the next match[†]. If we are using the $FREEZE$ deletion heuristic, the improved strategy is clear: whenever an entry in D becomes dead, it is deleted (creating room for a new entry). The same can be done for the other deletion heuristics. However, when the deletion heuristic removes an entry, there are a variety of strategies for returning prefixes to the dictionary. In practice, pruning is ineffective when $|\Sigma|$ is of any significant size; for example, with $|\Sigma|=256$, is often the case in practice that no entries will ever become dead. For binary alphabets, some savings are typically gained. Such savings are not likely to dramatic. Each dead entry gives rise to at least $|\Sigma|>2$ new entries, so the best we could possibly do (but are unlikely to achieve in practice) is to effectively double the size of the local dictionary (which is tantamount to reducing the length of a pointer by one bit). Because of this, the fact that we shall usually be concerned with larger than binary alphabets (e.g. $|\Sigma|=256$), and the fact that pruning complicates the implementation of some of the update heuristics, we shall not consider pruning further.

---

† This observation assumes that the input stream continues indefinitely. If not, the next match could be a dead string for the special situation when the end of the input stream is reached. There are a variety of ways to handle this detail and we shall not address it further.

Like the sliding dictionary method, another natural approach for improving compression is to place a universal coding algorithm (such as Huffman coding) between the encoder and decoder. However, this addition is unlikely to yield any improvement. The intuition is that the update heuristics considered above all have the property that entries that occur frequently give rise to new entries that contain them as prefixes. Thus, the entries in the local dictionary are constantly adjusted to be equal-probable for becoming the next match (e.g., if x is in the dictionary and xy is added, then x is now less likely to be a longest match). A universal coding algorithm will now be faced with a uniform distribution of pointers, and no further compression will be achieved. As with the sliding dictionary method, it may be possible to achieve further compression by coding of k-tuples of pointers.

Like the sliding dictionary method, probably the best theoretical support for the use of the dynamic dictionary method is that it can be viewed as a practical realization of a second universal data compression algorithm due to A. Lempel and J. Ziv, which we shall henceforth refer to as LZ2. The LZ2 algorithm, which can be shown to be perfect in the information-theoretic sense, works as follows. At each stage, the longest prefix t of the input stream that matches one of the strings in the local dictionary is identified. Then a pair (p,c) is transmitted where p is a pointer to t in the dictionary and c is the next input character following the current match. As with LZ1, the transmission of c is pointer guaranteed progress. The input is then advanced past t and c and the string tc is added to the local dictionary. Thus, the local dictionary used by the LZ2 algorithm is unbounded in size and, like LZ1, a variable length coding scheme must be used to construct pointers.

The particular update and deletion heuristics that we have discussed for the dynamic dictionary method can be viewed as different interpretations of what is a "practical implementation" of LZ2. Like LZ1, since pointers are relatively small in size, we initialize the local dictionary to Σ so that dictionary guaranteed progress can be used. The *FREEZE* deletion heuristic simply truncates the LZ2 growing process once the dictionary becomes full whereas the *LRU* strategy attempts to let the dictionary evolve over time. The *FC* updating heuristic follows most directly from LZ2. The *ID* and *AP* updating heuristics, in some sense, increase the rate of "learning" in an attempt to compensate for the relatively small size of the local dictionary.

3.6. IMPLEMENTATION DETAILS

In this section, we consider the efficient implementation of Algorithms 3.1.1 and 3.1.2 for dynamic dictionary methods. Special purpose data structures are more appropriate for the static and sliding dictionary methods. For the static dictionary method, standard data structures for dictionary look-up can be used (e.g., binary search trees, balanced search trees, or hashing). References to the efficient serial implementation of the sliding dictionary method are cited at the end of this chapter and efficient parallel implementation of the sliding dictionary method is discussed in the next chapter.

We now discuss in detail the efficient implementation of Algorithms 3.1.1 and 3.1.2 for the $AP-LRU$ heuristic. At the end of this section, we discuss how this implementation can be modified to accommodate other heuristics.

To implement the $AP-LRU$ method, both the encoder and decoder use four data structures. We begin by describing these data structures as *abstract data types* (ADT's).[†] That is, we start by specifying only the operations the data structures support. It will then be possible to consider the implementation of the $AP-LRU$ heuristic from a "high-level point of view", where the method for implementing the abstract data structure operations is handled by "low level" routines (which do not have to be seen in order to understand the workings of the high-level code). Later, when we present Pascal code for the $AP-LRU$ heuristic, we will discuss specific low-level implementations of these ADT's.

Before proceeding to these ADT's, we digress briefly with a discussion of how pointers are represented. In the particular implementation that we shall describe when presenting Pascal code, we shall represent linked structures with arrays and it will turn out that the internal representation of a pointer that is used to implement the ADT's is simply an integer identical to the external representation of a pointer (which is an integer corresponding to the bits that are actually sent over the communication line). However, in general, the internal and external representations could be quite different; it is only necessary that there is a way to map between the two representations. Even though we are not using on-the-fly dictionary guaranteed progress, we shall assume that the (external) pointer value $|D|+1$ is reserved as the nil-pointer, just as is done with on-the-fly dictionary guaranteed progress. We also assume that the nil-pointer has an internal representation. The nil-

---

† For a discussion of abstract data types, see Aho, Hopcroft, and Ullman [1983].

pointer has two major uses:

(1) On the communication line (in its external form) it can be used as an escape to signal special conditions. For example, a nil-pointer could signal to the decoder that an agreed upon number of bits to follow are not part of another pointer but are instead some sort of control information (change the line baud rate, perform error recovery, make a change to the dictionary for on-the-fly dictionary guaranteed progress, etc.). In fact, we shall need such a facility when we consider generalizations to lossy compression.

(2) The internal representation of the nil-pointer can by used to terminate linked structures (e.g., the end of a linked list).

As mentioned earlier, a small disadvantage to the nil-pointer is that it in some sense "wastes" one dictionary entry which can no longer be pointed to; but in practice, the loss of a single dictionary entry has an insignificant effect on the amount of compression achieved[†].

The four ADT's are the following:

(1) A map between the external representation of a pointer (an integer) and the internal representation of a pointer used by the algorithm. This map is provided by the following two functions:

INT(integer): Returns the corresponding internal pointer.

EXT(pointer): Returns the integer that corresponds to this pointer.

---

† This waste is actually not necessary for the Pascal code to be presented in this section. All this code really needs is the internal representation of a pointer (which could be an illegal pointer value). However, we will need the external representation of the nil-pointer later when we generalize to lossy compression. Assuming its existence now will add consistency to our presentation. Another reason to assume it is that in many hardware implementations, there may not be enough bits in a word of memory to accommodate an illegal pointer value. For example, if 16-bit pointers are being used on a device that has memory organized into 16-bit words, an extra illegal pointer value to signal the nil-pointer would require using 17 bits for the internal representation of a pointer.

Note that because the implementation we shall use has identical internal and external pointer representations, calls to *INT* and *EXT* will be unnecessary in the Pascal code to be presented later in this section.

(2) A trie that represents the local dictionary with all strings labeling a path from the root to some interior node or leaf (so if a string is in D, then all of its prefixes must be also)[†]. The trie is accessed via the following operations:

CTR(pointer): Returns the character of Σ stored at the trie node associated with *pointer*.

CHILD(pointer,character): Returns the child of the trie node associated with *pointer* that corresponds to *character* (or a nil-pointer if there is no such node).

PARENT(pointer): Returns the parent of the trie node associated with pointer (or a nil-pointer if *pointer* is the root).

DELETELEAF(pointer): Deletes the trie node associated with *pointer* (which is assumed to be a leaf) from the trie.

ADDLEAF(parent_pointer,pointer,character): Adds a new trie leaf that is associated with *pointer* as the child of the trie node associated with *parent_pointer* corresponding to *character* (it is assumed that the trie node associated with *parent_pointer* does not already have a child corresponding to *character*).

(3) A doubly-linked list of all dictionary elements of length greater than 1 to store the *LRU queue;* the *LRU* queue stores dictionary entries (trie nodes) in order of *oldest* (least recently used) to *newest* (most recently used). For convenience, we shall think of nodes getting newer going from left to right. The *LRU* queue is accessed via the following operations:

---

† It could be argued that that for a discussing of an ADT, we should not mention the term *trie*, but just the notion of a local dictionary with the property that if a string is in the dictionary, then so are all of its prefixes. We do not worry about this distinction, and consider the notion of a trie synonymous with that of a dictionary with this property.

NEWER(pointer): Returns the pointer associated with the node that follows (is newer and to the right of) the node associated with *pointer* in the *LRU* queue (or a nil-pointer if *pointer* is associated with the newest node in the *LRU* queue). Note that the function *NEWER* is not used in the implementation we shall discuss, but might be used in alternate implementations.

OLDER(pointer): Returns the pointer associated with the node that precedes (is older and to the left of) the node associated with *pointer* in the *LRU* queue (or a nil-pointer if *pointer* is associated with the oldest node in the *LRU* queue).

DEQUEUE(pointer): Removes the node associated with *pointer* from the *LRU* queue.

ENQUEUE(pointer1,pointer2): Places the node associated with *pointer1* to be the next newer node after the node associated with *pointer2* (to the right of the node associated with *pointer2*) in the *LRU* queue. It is always assumed that the node associated with *pointer2* is currently in the *LRU* queue unless *pointer2* is a nil-pointer; in this case, the node associated with *pointer1* is made the oldest entry of the *LRU* queue.

(4) An array *match* that contains the current match; *match* is indexed from 1 to *maxmatch*, where *maxmatch* is the longest allowable length for a match[†]. The current match is not necessarily stored starting at location *match*[1]. Rather, it is stored starting at location *match*[*mstart*] where *mstart* is a variable that depends on the current match (the reason will become clear shortly).

Let us first consider the encoding and decoding algorithms while ignoring manipulations of the *LRU* queue. Given the abstract operations above, the encoder identifies the current match by reading successive characters of the input stream and walking down the trie from the root (via the *CHILD* operation) until a leaf is reached (that is, until *CHILD* applied to the pointer corresponding to the current trie node and the incoming input character returns the nil-pointer). Similarly, the decoder identifies the current match by receiving a pointer and walking up to the root via the *PARENT*

[†] In their pure form, Algorithms 3.1.1 and 3.1.2 would set *maxmatch* to $<D>$. However, in practice, *maxmatch* might be smaller. This issue will be discussed in the next section.

operation (that is, until the *PARENT* operation returns the nil-pointer). Note that the encoder constructs the current match *cm* from left to right and places it a character at a time in locations 1 up to $|cm|$ of the array *match*, whereas the decoder discovers *cm* from right to left and places it one character at a time in the locations *maxmatch* down to $maxmatch-|cm|+1$ of the array match. After identifying the current match, both the encoder and decoder set the variable *mstart* to the starting location of *cm* in *match* (the variable *curlen* contains the length of the current match) and then execute the same update procedure. The update procedure starts at the node in the trie corresponding to the previous match and walks down the trie as far as possible according to the current match[†]. When a leaf is reached, the remaining characters of the current match are added to the trie via the *ADDLEAF* operation.

Let us now consider the workings of the *LRU* queue. The naive approach is as follows. As both the encoder and decoder identify the current match, each time a trie node is visited, it is moved from where it is in the *LRU* queue to the right end. When the trie becomes full, the update procedure makes room for a new node by deleting the leftmost node in the *LRU* queue (and the new node is added to the right end). The problem with this naive approach is that a node may reach the left end of the *LRU* queue before some of its descendants, so the update procedure might have to delete a node that is not a leaf. Of course, it is possible to handle this problem, but it makes the data structure unnecessarily complicated. The key observation is that whenever a node is moved to the right end of the queue, its ancestors must have just been recently moved there also, so we can simply move a node to the right end of the queue, but after its ancestors. This observation results in the following modifications. When it is time to start constructing a new match, the encoder starts by saving a pointer to the right end of the *LRU* queue and then as it walks down the trie, nodes are always added after this saved location; this causes the current match to be placed at the right end of the LRU queue in reverse order, so that a node is to the left of its ancestors. Since the decoder discovers the current match in reverse order, there is no problem here, as the decoder walks up the trie it can simply move nodes to the right end of the *LRU* queue. The update procedure can remember the po-

---

† Note that it is typical that none of the current match is "hanging below" the previous match (because if it was, we would have taken it as part of the previous match). However, this situation can occur as follows: Let *cm* denote the current match, *pm* denote the previous match, and *ppm* denote the match before the previous match. If *ppm=pm* and a prefix of *cm* is also a prefix of *pm*, then after matching *cm*, when we go to update by adding *pm* concatenated with *cm* to the trie, we will start at *pm* and find the first character of *cm* as one of its children.

sition of the lowest node of the previous match in the *LRU* queue and insert the characters of the current match (in reverse order) at this location.

Example 3.6.1: Consider again the phrase:

"THE_CAT_AT_THE_CAR_ATE_THE_RAT"

Assume, as is typically done in practice, that characters are stored one per byte of memory with the 7-bit ASCII code; that is byte values are always in the range 0 to 127, so $|\Sigma|=128$. In addition, to force the dictionary to "turn over", assume a very small dictionary of size of 144; this size allows it to be initialized with the 128 ASCII values (which are not part of the *LRU* queue) and to have up to 16 additional entries. The following table shows the contents of the *LRU* queue as this string is processed by the *AP−LRU* heuristic.

MATCH	LRU QUEUE
T	
H	TH
E	TH HE
_	TH HE E_
C	TH HE E_ _C
A	TH HE E_ _C CA
T	TH HE E_ _C CA AT
_	TH HE E_ _C CA AT T_
AT	TH HE E_ _C CA T_ AT _AT _A
_	TH HE E_ _C CA T_ AT_ AT _AT _A
TH	HE E_ _C CA T_ AT_ AT _AT _A TH _TH _T
E_	HE _C CA T_ AT_ AT _AT _A THE_ THE TH _TH _T E_
CA	HE _C T_ AT_ AT _AT _A THE_ THE TH _TH _T E_CA E_C E_ CA
R	_C T_ AT_ AT _AT _A THE_ THE TH _TH _T E_CA E_C E_ CAR CA
_AT	AT THE_ THE TH _TH _T E_CA E_C E_ CAR CA _AT _A R_AT R_A R_
E_	THE TH _TH _T E_CA E_C CAR CA _ATE_ _ATE _AT _A R_AT R_A R_ E_
THE	E_C CAR CA _ATE_ _ATE _AT _A R_AT R_A R_ E_THE E_TH E_T E_ THE TH
_	CAR CA _ATE_ _ATE _AT _A R_AT R_A R_ E_THE E_TH E_T E_ THE_ THE TH
R	CA _ATE_ _ATE _AT _A R_AT R_A R_ E_THE E_TH E_T E_ THE_ THE TH _R
A	_ATE_ _ATE _AT _A R_AT R_A R_ E_THE E_TH E_T E_ THE_ THE TH _R RA
T	_ATE _AT _A R_AT R_A R_ E_THE E_TH E_T E_ THE_ THE TH _R RA AT ○

Pascal Code

Appendix A.8 contains a Pascal implementation of the $AP-LRU$ heuristic. The files *squeeze.p* and *unsqueeze.p* are the high-level code for the encoder and decoder. The remaining code is divided into a number of files that are included by both squeeze.p and unsqueeze.p:

Declarations of program parameters and variables:
  declare.i

Data Structures:
  map.i: maps between internal and external pointers
  dictionary.i: trie implementation of the dictionary
  queue.i: doubly linked list implementation of LRU queue

Input/Output routines:
  io_byte.i: routines to read and write bytes
  io_ptr.i: routines to read and write pointers

Initialization Code:
  start.i: initialization of variables and structures

Update code (included by both squeeze.p and unsqueeze.p):
  update_code.i: update (and deletion) heuristics

This code is written in standard Pascal; all input and output has been done using the streams "input" and "output"[†]. It is system independent with the possible exception of the *#include* compiler directives[††] and the operations READBYTE and WRITEBYTE in the file *io_byte.i*[†††]. In addition, it was

---

† These streams are always included in standard Pascal (with the program statement) and have an implicit declaration as of lines of characters. On the Berkeley Unix operating system, these streams are by default identified with the standard input and output; hence, the command "cat *filename1* | squeeze.p | unsqueeze.p > *filename2*" makes a file with name *filename2* that is identical to the file with name *filename1*.

†† The *#include filename* statement is a compiler directive to have the file with this name textually included in place of the #include statement. An equivalent program can be obtained by simply replacing each *#include* statement with the contents of the corresponding file.

††† Unfortunately, standard Pascal does not fully define a correspondence between characters and bytes. Hence, the functions READBYTE and WRITEBYTE may be system dependent because technically, $ord(i)$ should be undefined if $128 \leq i \leq 255$. If a particular compiler is not extended to allow character values in this range, then an explicit file declaration can be made. In the case of the version of Berkeley Unix Pas-

written without using the Pascal pointer facility; that is, arrays are explicitly declared to store the trie and *LRU* queue and pointers are represented by integer variables. This representation makes the translation of this code to a variety of programming languages (including assembly languages) more direct. Another advantage of this representation is that the internal and external representations of a pointer are identical. Hence, the routines *INT* and *EXT* provided by the file *map.i* are simply identity functions. In fact, calls to these routines could be removed from the code presented in Appendix A.8. We have left the calls to emphasize that, in the context of abstract data types, these routines are needed (e.g., *INT* and *EXT* would be needed if the Pascal pointer facility was employed for the internal representations of pointers).

Conceptually, the files *start.i*, *squeeze.p*, *unsqueeze.p*, and *update_code.i* contain all of the logic, stated in terms of a set of abstract operations; these abstract operations are defined by the the remaining files, which can be viewed as "low-level" code. The implementation of this low level code is not central to an understanding of the $AP-LRU$ heuristic, but from a practical standpoint, it can affect greatly the efficiency of the method. For this reason, we digress to discuss the implementation of these low-level files and how it compares to other implementations. The file *io_byte.i* contains the operations *ENDFILE*, *READBYTE*, and *WRITEBYTE*, which, as mentioned earlier, may be system dependent; we shall not discuss them further. The file *io_ptr.i* contains the operation *READPTR* to read a pointer from the standard input stream and *WRITEPTR* to write a pointer to the standard output stream (these routines call on the *READBYTE* and *WRITEBYTE* operations); *io_ptr.i* also contains the procedure *FLUSH* which is used to flush any remaining bits when the encoder encounters the end of the input stream. The operations *READPTR* and *WRITEPTR* must read or write a number of bits that is not necessarily a multiple of 8 and save any leftover bits for the next read or write operations; the variable *leftover* and *losize* are used to save this information[††††]. The code contained in *io_ptr.i* is very inefficient; it con-

---

cal used by the author, although $ord(chr(i))=i$ for $0 \leq i \leq 255$, if the sequence $read(c); b:=ord(c)$ is used to read a byte (where c is declared type char and b is declared type byte), then c is effectively treated as an 8-bit integer in two's-complement form; that is, the two statements above map values of c in the range $128 \leq c \leq 255$ to values of b in the range $-128 \leq b \leq -1$. Hence the test for $b < 0$ in included in the procedure *READBYTE*. See the bibliographic notes for a discussion of two's-complement notation.

[††††] Ideally, *leftover* and *losize* would be declared as "static" local variables to the file buffer.i (i.e., space is permanently allocated for them so their values remain from call to call); however, standard Pascal does not include this feature (although many compilers provide this extension). Since *WRITEPTR* is used only by *squeeze.p* and

structs pointers one bit at a time and and is intended only for instructional purposes. In practice, it is much more efficient to construct pointers by combining blocks of bits at a time using logical operations[††††]. In addition, for any particular dictionary size, more efficient routines can be written. For example, for 16-bit pointers, the procedure *WRITEPTR* could be:

```
procedure WRITEPTR(ptr:integer);
begin
WRITEBYTE(ptr div 256);
WRITEBYTE(ptr mod 256)
end;
```

We leave such modifications to the reader. The code contained in *queue.i* is a straightforward implementation of doubly-linked lists which we do not discuss further. The file *dictionary.i* is an implementation of tries that employs a standard linked-list implementation of trie nodes that works as follows. Each trie node has the following fields:

ctr: The character of Σ associated with the edge connecting this node to its parent.

parent: The parent of the node.

lchild: The leftmost child of the node.

lsib: The left sibling of the node.

rsib: The right sibling of the node.

With this implementation, the *CTR*, *PARENT*, *ADDLEAF*, and *DELETELEAF* operations are all constant time. The space used by each node is also constant. However, the *CHILD* operation must search the linked list of children of a node and can be quite time consuming if Σ is large and many nodes have close to $|\Sigma|$ children. In practice that when Σ becomes large, trie nodes do not often become very full except at the root. As is done

---

READPTR is only used by *unsqueeze.p*, *leftover* and *losize* are global variables that are used by both operations. If for some reason it was desired to use both *READPTR* and *WRITEPTR* at the same time, different names for these variables could be used.

[††††] Unfortunately, arithmetic operations such as logical **and**, logical **or**, logical **xor**, and logical **shift** are not defined for standard Pascal; however, they typically are available as extensions to the language with most Pascal compilers.

in the file *dictionary.i*, the root can be stored as an array of length $|\Sigma|$ so that the first level of the trie can be accessed directly. However, as mentioned in Chapter 1, there are several other standard techniques for implementing tries that may perform better in different applications; such techniques are a standard topics for textbooks on data structures. The most "brute force" alternative to the linked list representation is to store the children of a node as an array of length Σ; this method reduces the time for the *CHILD* operation to constant but when Σ is large uses an enormous amount of space for most practical problems where on the average, nodes have much less than $|\Sigma|$ children. Hashing provides a nice compromise between these two extremes. To compute *CHILD(pointer,character)*, apply a hash function to *EXT(pointer)* and *character* (jointly) to directly index the appropriate child. The *CTR* and *PARENT* functions are essentially unchanged, however, the *ADDLEAF* and *DELETELEAF* functions will now also have to use the hash table. This method yields expected constant time for these operations and constant space per node. In practice, where software is forced to obey certain time and space constraints, the three implementations described above as well as a host of other methods and variations must be examined in order to determine the implementation most suitable for a given application. The linked-list implementation presented here simply provides one example. The code in Appendix A.8 has been presented so that data structure issues of this kind are reasonably independent of the workings of the code contained in *start.i*, *squeeze.p*, *unsqueeze.p*, and *update.i*.

Other Heuristics

Consider now how the code in Appendix A.8 can be modified to yield other heuristics besides *AP−LRU*. At the beginning of the file *declarations.i* some constants are declared; the values of these constants not only determine parameters associated with the *AP* heuristic but also allow the specification of other heuristics. We now list the program parameters in alphabetical order:

FreezeFlag: If set to 1, then once the dictionary becomes full, the update code is prevented from adding any further entries. The default setting of 0 designates a *LRU* queue.

MaxChildren: The update code is prevented from adding an entry that causes a non-root node of the trie to have more than *MaxChildren* children. This parameter can be useful for gathering various statistics. In addition, for some sources it may be possible to limit the number of children per node and still achieve acceptable compression; this can be useful for reducing the size of data structures or reducing worst-case running time. For example, with the implementation presented here, the smaller the value of MaxChildren, the smaller the worst-case running time of the implementation per character of the input stream. The default setting of 256 designates no limit on the number of children per node.

MaxDict: This parameter is $<D>^{\dagger}$.

MaxIncrement: If $MaxIncrement \geq MaxMatch$, then this parameter has no effect. Otherwise, when the update code forms a new dictionary entry, instead of adding the previous match concatenated with all prefixes of the current match, only the previous match concatenated with the first $MaxIncrement$ prefixes are added (all prefixes if the length of the current match is less than or equal to $MaxIncrement$).

MaxMatch: The maximum allowable length for an entry of D. That is, the update code is prevented from adding to the dictionary a string longer than $MaxMatch$.

StaticSize: The size of the alphabet used by the input stream to the encoder. The integers 0 through $StaticSize-1$ are permanently assigned to the pointers to the characters of Σ.

PtrType: If set to 1, then pointers grow in size from log2(StaticSize) to log2(MaxDict), which represents a "pure" implementation of Algorithms 3.1.1 and 3.1.2. However, the default setting of 0 (which runs a little faster) is to have pointers of a fixed size log2(MaxDict), which causes a small loss of performance for the initial portion of the input stream but makes little difference in the long run.

---

† Note that all array declarations pertaining to D in the code of Appendix A.8 are for $0..MaxDict$ even though the maximum possible value for a pointer is $MaxDict-1$. Because standard Pascal does not allow expressions for array bounds, rather than declaring another constant, we simply waste the small amount of additional memory.

Given the above options, it is trivial to change the dictionary or alphabet size or to change to the *FREEZE* deletion heuristic (FreezeFlag=1) or the *FC* update heuristic (MaxIncrement=1). However, the *ID* update heuristic does require some non-trivial modifications, which we address now.

The ID-LRU heuristic

Although the *ID* update heuristic is conceptually simple, in practice it requires a more complex implementation of the trie to store the dictionary. The problem is that when a string is added to the dictionary, it is not necessarily true that all prefixes of it are also in the dictionary. Thus, although all leaves of the trie must correspond to entries, many internal nodes may not. The most straightforward solution to this problem is to simply allow internal *dummy nodes;* a dummy node acts as a place holder but does not get assigned a pointer. The code of Appendix A.8 can be modified to accommodate dummy nodes. The major change is that a new field must be declared for each trie node to either hold the external representation of the pointer associated with it or some other value (e.g. -1) to indicate that the node is a dummy node; note that we would now need the functions *INT* and *EXT* provided by the file *map.i*. The introduction of dummy nodes does not change the time complexity of the code of Appendix A.8. However, when the the source is highly compressible, there can be many more dummy nodes than non-dummy nodes[†]. One possible solution to this problem is to simply put an upper limit on the number of dummy nodes (e.g. no more than 5 times the number of non-dummy nodes) and if ever the quota of dummy nodes gets filled, revert to the *AP* update heuristic until more dummy nodes become available (due to deletions); this approach yields an update heuristic lying somewhere "between" the *AP* and *ID* update heuristics.

The alternative to dummy nodes is to use a compact representation of the trie. We say a node in a trie is a *fork* node if it has at least two children. By a *chain of dummy nodes,* we mean an ancestor to descendant path in the trie that consists entirely of dummy nodes that are not fork nodes (i.e., each has exactly one child). The idea, which is similar to what is done to compact position trees for pattern matching problems, is to not store chains of dummy nodes explicitly. However, for this application, the problem is somewhat more complicated for two reasons:

[†] In theory, it is possible for a dictionary to have exponentially many more dummy nodes than non-dummy nodes; however, this is unlikely to happen in practice.

- We do not assume the entire input stream to be available at any given time, so we cannot represent a chain of nodes in the trie (i.e., a substring if the input stream) by indexing to its starting and ending positions in the input stream.

- For the *LRU* heuristic, we must worry about deletions as well as additions to the trie.

The following scheme can be used to handle these difficulties. In place of the trie with dummy nodes, which we hence forth refer to as the *expanded trie*, two data structures are maintained. One data structure is the *pair forest;* each time two entries of the dictionary are concatenated to form a new entry, a new node of the pair forest is added that points to the two nodes that induced it. The other data structure is the *compact trie*. The compact trie contains one node for each entry of the dictionary. In addition, the compact trie has a node corresponding to every fork node of the expanded trie that does not correspond to a dictionary entry. Each node of the compact trie contains both the length of the associated root-to-leaf path in the expanded trie and a pointer to to a node in the pair forest of which it is a prefix. That is, if the node in the compact trie corresponds to a dictionary entry, then it points to the corresponding node in the pair forest. If the node in the compact trie is a fork node that does not correspond to a dictionary entry, then it points to a node in the pair forest that corresponds to one of its closest descendants that corresponds to a dictionary entry. Thus, in the compact trie, chains of the expanded trie are represented by pointers into the pair forest (together with the length field that designates how large a prefix of the corresponding node in the pair forest is to be used). Due to the non-trivial interaction between these two data structures, it is most simple in practice to place only leaves of the compact trie (which are nodes in the pair forest that do not have ancestors) in the *LRU* queue; when a leaf is deleted from the *LRU* queue, some convention must be adopted for entering its parent (if it becomes a leaf) into the *LRU* queue (e.g., place it at the head of the queue).

The space used by both the compact tree and the pair forest is proportional to the number of entries in the dictionary (and independent of the lengths of the entries), which is the best that can be hoped for to within a constant factor. In practice, however, the constant factor is significantly larger than required by other heuristics that we have discussed. In addition, the worst-case time complexity using this representation is $O(n<D>)$ for processing an input stream of length n. The problem occurs during encoding when matching with the input stream ends along a chain (and the encoder has to back up to the previous node in the compact trie). If the pair forest is not well balanced, it could be that a chain of length $O(<D>)$ must be decoded in order to discover that the first character of this chain does not match the input string.

Fortunately, the worst case time performance of the ID heuristic is unlikely to occur in practice. However, to guarantee better worst-case performance, it is also possible to modify the update code to force the pair forest to remain approximately balanced. By "approximately balanced", we mean that given two integer parameters r (the "ratio" parameter) and d (the "difference" parameter), we can adopt the rule that the previous match pm and the current match cm are concatenated together and added as a new entry to the dictionary only if:

$$|pm| \leq |cm|^* r + d$$
$$|cm| \leq |pm|^* r + d$$

So long as r and d are constants, balancing reduces the worst case performance to $O(n^* log <D>)$ (where the constant that is subsumed by the O notation depends on r and d); this bound is still not linear, but nevertheless represents a great improvement in worst-case performance. From a theoretical point of view, it is possible to construct worst-case examples where balancing greatly degrades the performance of the ID heuristic. However, later in this chapter when we consider experimental results, we shall see that in practice, the running time it not degraded significantly if r and d are not chosen to be too small.

A nice feature of the ID heuristic is that both the space and time problems discussed above apply only to the encoder; that is, only the encoder need store both the compact trie and the pair forest, the decoder needs only the pair forest (and the LRU queue if that deletion heuristic is being used). This situation is ideal for applications where a powerful source (e.g., a mainframe computer) transmits data to a small site (e.g., a personal computer). If, however, the decoder does not maintain the compact trie, there is an important detail that must be addressed. When a new string is to be added to the dictionary, we must first check that it is not already there. Fortunately, as observed by the following lemma, the new string can only be in the dictionary under very special situations.

Lemma 3.6.1: Let cm denote the current match, pm denote the previous match, and ppm denote the match before the previous match. With the ID heuristic, the string $pm+cm$ (where $+$ denotes string concatenation) cannot already be in the dictionary except when $ppm+pm = pm+cm$.

Proof: Consider the point at which we have just found *ppm* and are now looking for *pm*. It cannot be that *pm+cm* was already in the dictionary, otherwise we would have matched it. Thus, after we read *cm* and go to add *pm+cm*, we know that the only way that *pm+cm* can already be in the dictionary is if *ppm+pm* = *pm+cm*[†]. ◯

In light of the lemma above, all that is needed to detect if *pm+cm* is already in the dictionary is a *lastentry array* that stores *ppm+pm*.

Other Heuristics

Making all of the modification discussed above for the *ID−LRU* heuristic to the code presented in Appendix A.8 requires a substantial effort[††]. Later in this chapter we shall discuss the Pascal code presented in Appendix A.9. Although this code performs lossy compression, as a special case it can be set to perform lossless compression. It is intended to be used for experimentation (and runs much slower that the code of Appendix A.9) and takes a host of parameters which can be set to specify many different heuristics (including *ID−LRU* and *ID−FREEZE*). In addition, the code of Appendix A.9 employs data structures that are sufficiently simple so as to allow the user to easily make modifications.

3.7. EXPERIMENTAL RESULTS

The performance of any data compression method is highly dependent on the data being compressed. Sometimes something can be said about the expected compression ratio of a given method on a given source. However, very few practical sources can be precisely characterized; for example, all English text bears basic similarities, but there is a great difference among technical writing, poetry, newspapers, etc. It is difficult to make any precise and meaningful statement about the expected performance of a given method. Instead, our approach is to compare the performance of different methods on the same source files. We choose for our source files, textual data, since as

---

† Note that this condition does not imply that *ppm=pm=cm*; consider the string *aaaaa*.
†† Such code is available from the author but was not included in this book due to its length.

discussed in Chapter 1, textual data must typically be preserved exactly, making lossless compression appropriate. The textual source of most interest to us is printed English, primarily because there has been so much other experimental work with this source with which to make comparisons. In addition, we also look at two contrasting languages: Lisp source code with all English comments removed, and Pascal source code with all English comments left intact. The rationale is that the Lisp source code provides a significantly different language source than English, and the Pascal source code with the English text comments left intact, lies somewhere between English and Lisp. In addition, files written in all three of these source are relatively easily obtained on the Unix system on which this book was written. Appendix A.2 lists the files used for the experiments summarized in subsequent appendices, henceforth referred to as the *sample files*. All of the sample files consist of ASCII characters stored one per byte. All statistics pertaining to the sample files are reported as the *percent compression ratio;* that is:

$$\frac{(number\ of\ bytes\ in\ compressed\ file)}{(number\ of\ bytes\ in\ original\ file)} * 100$$

Before comparing the performance of methods considered in this chapter, as a benchmark, we first look at the performance of dynamic Huffman coding on the sample files.

Huffman Coding

Appendix A.3 shows the compression that is achieved by dynamic Huffman coding on the sample files for 8-bit input codes (1-grams), 16-bit input codes (2-grams), 24-bit input codes (3-grams), and 32-bit input codes (4-grams). For the smaller sample files (under 100,000 characters), the compression achieved for 24-bit codes is worse than that for 16-bit codes; this is because with less than 100,000 characters, not enough 3 character sequences are seen to get a non-trivial distribution of 3-grams. Small additional savings are achieved for the larger files by using 24-bit instead of 16-bit codes. No savings are achieved for 32-bit codes; files an order of magnitude bigger would be needed for such significant savings with 32-bit codes to be observed. For sufficient large files, the Huffman tree will become full or nearly full. Even 24-bit codes will imply a tree of approximately $256^3 = 16$ million nodes, where each node corresponds to several bytes of memory. Although there may be ways to reduce this number (by collapsing nodes with close to zero probability back into the unseen node), it is at least an order of magnitude greater than the resources required for any of the methods evaluated in subsequent appendices. If one wishes to compare the performance of Huffman coding with other statistics reported on the basis of comparable computing resources, the column for 16-bit codes is most appropriate (but still uses greater computational resources than most other statistics reported).

Static Dictionary Method

The static dictionary method is inherently a special-purpose method. Before one can use it, a static dictionary must first be constructed for the source in question. Rather than construct three separate dictionaries for English, Pascal, and Lisp source, we shall restrict ourselves to English text. We use for our static dictionary the dictionary discussed in Section 1.2 that was constructed from the files listed in Appendix A.1. The files listed in Appendix A.1 are different from the English text files listed in Appendix A.2 but were obtained in the same fashion (i.e., they are technical papers that were present on the author's Unix system). It is our intention that the files listed in Appendix A.1 provide a reasonable compromise between being too similar to or too unlike the English text files listed in Appendix A.2. That is, it is intended that the static dictionary that we have constructed be a reasonable model of a "general purpose" dictionary for technical papers that appear on the author's Unix system. For a given pointer size p, the static dictionary that was actually used consisted of all 256 distinct bytes together with the 2^p-256 most common 2 or more character entries of the static dictionary. Statistics are reported for $10 \leq p \leq 14^\dagger$. Appendix A.4 shows the results of compressing the sample files with this dictionary.

---

† The smallest "interesting" pointer size was judged to be $p=10$. The pointer size $p=14$ is the largest that can be accommodated by 20,000 entries; as indicated in Appendix A.1, the number 20,000 was chosen because of limits on the computational resources available to gather statistics used to construct the static dictionary.

Sliding Dictionary Method

Appendix A.5 presents statistics for the sliding dictionary method. Since running all sample files on all possible combinations of displacement and length implies a prohibitively large amount of data, Appendix A.5 restricts the number of possibilities as follows. Appendix A.5.1 shows the result of compressing the sample files on combinations of displacement and length that add to 16 bits; for the purposes of these experiments, the number 16 is somewhat arbitrary, but it is an appropriate choice since in practice, a pointer size that is an integral number of bytes may be desirable. To see what happens with other combinations of displacement and length, Appendix A.5.2 shows what happens for files $e2$, $p2$, and $l2$ for a range of combinations of values for the two parameters. As indicated in Appendix A.5, to maintain consistency with statistics reported by other authors, all of these statistics were gathered using uniform length pointers.

Improved Sliding Dictionary Method

Appendix A.6 presents results for the improved sliding dictionary method in the same format as Appendix A.5.1.

Dynamic Dictionary Method

Appendix A.7 presents statistics for the dynamic dictionary method; Appendix A.7.1 the $FC-FREEZE$ heuristic, Appendix A.7.2 the $FC-LRU$ heuristic, Appendix A.7.3 the $AP-LRU$ heuristic, and Appendix A.7.4.1 the $ID-LRU$ heuristic. Appendices A.7.4.2 and A.7.4.3 present statistics for the $ID-LRU$ heuristic with balancing. Since running all sample files on all possible combinations of difference and ratio is prohibitive, we have reduced the number of possibilities by presenting in Appendix A.7.4.2 the result of compressing the sample files on select combinations of difference and ratio and presenting in Appendix A.7.4.3 a large range of combinations of the two parameters for just the files $e2$, $p2$, and $l2$. Note that as indicated in Appendix A.7, to maintain consistency with statistics reported by other authors, all statistics reported in Appendix A.7 were obtained using uniform length pointers (i.e., with $PtrType=0$ in the code of Appendix A.8). Appendix A.7.4 also reports statistics for the $ID-LRU$ method with lookahead (Appendix A.7.4.4); the lookahead modification and these statistics will be discussed later in this chapter.

Conclusions

We remind the reader that the statistics presented in the appendices are intended only to give an indication of the relative performance of the methods we have considered, and are not intended to represent any sort of thorough statistical test. Neverless, we can reasonably make the following observation.

If given reasonable resources (e.g. sliding dictionary with 12 to 16 bits for displacement and 3 to 6 bits for length or dynamic dictionary method with 12 to 16 bit pointers), then all of

sliding dictionary
improved sliding dictionary
FC−LRU
AP−LRU
ID−LRU

perform equivalently to within a difference of 10 in the percent compression ratio.

In practice, a difference of 10 in the percent compression ratio may be significant; for example, 45 can be viewed as "slightly less than a factor of 2" whereas 35 can be viewed as "nearly a factor of 3". If one considers a difference of 5 to 10 significant, then there are a number of other observations that can be reasonably made. The following are some of these observations as well as some observations that can be made about the methods we have considered but are not in the above list.

- Huffman coding performed significantly worse than all of the other methods reported.

- For all of e1 through e6, the static dictionary method did not perform significantly better than the best ratio obtained with the sliding, improved sliding, or the best of the dynamic dynamic methods; however, in some cases, it performed significantly worse.

- The improved sliding dictionary method consistently reduces the percent compression ration by 1 to to 2 over the sliding dictionary method[†].

- The best performance of the dynamic methods (best choice of method and parameters) is consistently significantly better than the best performance of the sliding dictionary and improved sliding dictionary methods.

- For dynamic methods, the *FREEZE* deletion heuristic may not be "stable". That is, when the dictionary size gets small, its performance can degrade drastically. The cause for this instability appears to be that in practice, the initial portion of an input stream (on which the *FREEZE* heuristic forms the dictionary) is often not typical of the input stream as a whole (e.g., a programming language source file preceded by a large comment or by a large table of numerical data).

- Although the *FC−LRU*, *AP−LRU*, and *ID−LRU* heuristics are roughly equivalent in performance, it appears that

$$ID-LRU \leq AP-LRU \leq ID-LRU$$

where we write $x \leq y$ to mean that y never does significantly worse than x but sometimes does significantly better. The exception to this observation is for pointer sizes 14 and 16 where the *AP−LRU* heuristic typically performs slightly better than *ID−LRU*. However, this exception could be explained by the fact that *AP−LRU* fills its dictionary faster, and so for sufficiently long input streams, ID-LRU will eventually catch up (this happens with e10).

The observations above pertain to the relative performance of different methods. As indicated earlier, meaningful conclusions about absolute performance (on the average, how well will a given method perform for a given source) are difficult to obtain because of both the problem of character-

---

[†] Since percent compression ratios were typically in the 30 to 50 range, an improvement of 2 is tantamount to a 4 to 6 percent improvement in the size of the compressed form.

izing the source and the need for very large sample sizes. The sample files presented in the appendix are at least an order of magnitude smaller than what is really needed. In addition, because files present on the author's Unix system are typically under 100,000 characters each, many of the larger of the sample files are constructed by concatenating smaller files (which may result in files that are somewhat harder to compress). Nevertheless, we can draw a few very general conclusions about absolute performance.

- Not surprisingly, compression gets better as the file and dictionary sizes grow.

- The performance of the textual substitution methods that we have considered (using reasonable parameters) on the sample files is typically between 30 and 50 (between 3-to-1 and 2-to-1) on English text and between 20 and 40 (between 5-to-1 and 2.5-to-1) on programming language text.

- It appears that the sample files are not big enough to accurately demonstrate the compression obtainable with 14 or 16-bit pointers (for this reason and because of limits on computational resources, we have not even attempted experiments with larger size pointers).

We close this section by noting that, with only a few exceptions, all of the sample files with all of the methods reported compressed in the range 2-to-1 to 5-to-1. There are many common types of data that typically do not fall in this range. For example, the author has found that encrypted data is likely to be below 2-to-1 with any of the methods we have considered whereas spread sheet data may compress by a factor of more than 10-to-1 with methods such as $FC-LRU$, $AP-LRU$, or $ID-LRU$. The statistics and conclusions reported in this section may have little or no bearing on data with such "extreme" compression ratios. For example, for spread sheet data, dynamic Huffman coding using first-order statistics only compressed by a factor of 3.5-to-1 the spread sheet data that was compressed by a factor of more than 10-to-1 by $FC-LRU$, $AP-LRU$, and $ID-LRU$. Although the experimental results presented here show Huffman coding to be inferior to these methods, the difference is not nearly as great as with the spread sheet data. We leave the question of what types of textual data are commonly encountered in practice (and should be used for benchmark tests) and "how much compression can be expected" as a subject for future research.

3.8. THE IMPLIED DICTIONARY

The running of a dynamic compression algorithm gives us something "for free" that we have not discussed thus far: the dictionary that is computed in the process of performing the compression. A particular on-line method together with a finite string defines a unique dictionary (the one that remains after the string has been compressed), which we refer to as the *implied dictionary*. The notion of an implied dictionary is useful for several reasons:

- Examination of implied dictionaries can serve as an instructional aid to understanding the workings of different methods.

- Implied dictionaries can be a useful tool for studying particular sources (e.g., gathering common English substrings).

- Implied dictionaries provide a "summary" of the data that may be useful in a variety of applications (e.g., data retrieval).

- Careful study of the structure of implied dictionaries may be useful for future research into better heuristics for on-line methods.

The file *dump.i* of Appendix A.8 contains the procedure DUMPDICT which is a recursive procedure that takes two arguments, a pointer *ptr* and an integer *pathlen* that is equal to the length of the path from the root to the trie node corresponding to *ptr* and prints all dictionary entries that correspond to leaves of the subtree rooted by the trie node corresponding to *ptr*[†]. DUMP-DICT is not called anywhere in the code of Appendix A.8. To print the current contents of the dictionary, the user may insert a call of the form

DUMPDICT(INT(nilptr),0);

at any place in vsqueeze.p or vunsqueeze.p (and re-compile the code).

Appendix A.7.5 shows the implied dictionaries for a variety of methods applied to the same file; this file is described in the introduction to Appendix A.7.5. To reduce the size of the implied dictionaries presented in Appendix A.7.5, dictionaries of only 1024 entries were used. The implied dictionaries for Appendices A.7.5.1 through A.7.5.3 (FC-FREEZE, FC-LRU, and AP-LRU) were obtained with the code of Appendix A.8. The remaining im-

---

† The argument *pathlen* is redundant; it is included simply to shorten the presentation of DUMPDICT.

plied dictionaries presented in Appendix A.7.5 were obtained with software for the *ID* heuristic as described earlier. The reader should also note that additional facilities to dump program statistics are provided by the code in Appendix A.9 (which will be discussed in the last section of this chapter); this code may have its options set to simulate the code of Appendix A.8.

3.9. LOOKAHEAD

Thus far, we have restricted ourselves to the greedy match heuristic for *MH* in Step 2a of the basic encoding algorithm given by Algorithm 3.1.1. However, any choice for the current match (as long as it is in *D*) will work. Running Algorithm 3.1.1 on a string (using any of the update and deletion heuristics that we have discussed) can be viewed as a method for *parsing* the string into a sequence of *phrases* that are each assigned a single pointer. As we shall see in Chapter 5, in terms of worst case performance for a given model of compression, it is possible for the greedy approach to perform significantly worse (produce significantly more phrases) than an optimal parsing. The problem is that by taking the longest possible match as the current match, we may exclude taking a very long match as a subsequent match. Consider the following example.

Example 3.9.1: Suppose that the input alphabet consists of the two characters *a* and *b*, and that the dictionary *D* is only capable of holding 4 strings and currently contains:

$$\{a, b, ab, b^n\}$$

Now consider the input string:

$$ab^n$$

Then, using any of the update and deletion heuristics that we have considered, the greedy algorithm will first match *ab* and then match a *b* $n-1$ times, to produce a parsing of *n* phrases. An optimal parsing will not be so greedy at first, matching just the *a* and then b^n, to produce a parsing with only 2 phrases. ○

The type of worst case performance shown in the example above is not typical of the greedy approach in practice (where it tends to perform near optimally). However, it is still interesting to consider how the greedy approach may be improved upon. Unfortunately, in order to obtain optimal parsings it can be necessary to look arbitrarily far into the future, which amounts to the off-line model to be considered in Chapter 5, where the entire input string may be examined before any pointers are output. A compromise between the on-line model of compression used by Algorithm 3.1.1 and off-line compression is to look only a fixed distance into the future in order to decide on what characters to take as the current match. A *lookahead buffer* of length $k > 1$ in which the next k characters of the input stream are stored supports this approach. As long as the lookahead buffer has a small constant size, it does not violate either the technical definition or the informal notion of an on-line algorithm.

There are several definitions of what it means to have k characters of lookahead. For us it will mean that we can look at as many characters of the incoming input stream as necessary to examine, for each of the next k positions of the input stream, the longest string that starts at that point and is also in the dictionary. Thus, it may be necessary to examine the next $k + maxmatch$ characters of the input stream in order to determine how many characters to take as the current match, where *maxmatch* denotes that maximum number of characters allowed in a match[†]. Note that $k=1$ will correspond to the normal greedy algorithm.

Algorithm 3.9.1 can be used by Step 2a of Algorithm 3.1.1 to find the current match t by making use of lookahead. The lookahead buffer is the array *buffer* which is indexed from 1 to $looksize + maxmatch$. The notation (i, j) denotes the string formed by concatenating the characters contained in $buffer[i]$ through $buffer[i+j-1]$. To simplify the presentation, Algorithm 3.9.1 assumes that the input stream is infinite; the details of what to do when the end of the input stream is reached are left to the reader.

The basic idea of Algorithm 3.9.1 is to use dynamic programming to determine the best compression ratio for the next *looksize* characters plus however far the longest match from the next *looksize* characters takes us. This is done by working from right to left in *buffer*. Once the best parsing of *buffer* is found, the first match in this parsing is taken as the current match t. The array $comp[i]$, $1 \leq i \leq looksize$, records the length (in bits) of the shortest compressed form that starts at position i and extends to or past position *look-*

---

† As discussed earlier in this chapter when we consider implementation details, for the pure form of Algorithms 3.1.1 and 3.1.2, *maxmatch* could be as large as the dictionary, but in practice it suffices to bound matches to the order of 100 characters.

1) shift in enough characters of the input stream to fill up *buffer*

2) **for** $i=looksize$ **down to** 1 **do begin**

        comp[i] := psize
        raw[i] := csize

        for each j such that (i, j) is in D **do begin**

                $top := psize + comp[i+j]$
                $bottom := (j*csize) + raw[i+j]$

                if $top/bottom <$ comp[i]/raw[i] **then begin**
                    $comp[i] := top$
                    $raw[i] := bottom$
                    end

        end

    end

3) $t :=$ the pointer corresponding to $comp[1]$

NOTE: The code above uses the following constants:

    csize   = number of bits per input character
    psize   = number of bits per pointer
    looksize   = number of characters of lookahead
    maxmatch = max number of characters allowed in a match

Algorithm 3.9.1
(lookahead code to find the current match t)

size; $raw[i]$ records the number of bits of the raw form of the data corresponding to $comp[i]$. For simplicity of notation, we assume that the arrays $comp[i]$ and $raw[i]$ are defined and have value 0 for $looksize < i \leq looksize + maxmatch$.

The time for Algorithm 3.9.1 to process n characters is bounded in the worst case by $O(n*looksize*(maxmatch-1))$; note that the -1 appears with the *maxmatch* term because the cost of computing $comp[1]$ and $raw[1]$ can be charged to the characters of t that are actually consumed. Hence, from a theoretical point of view, Algorithm 3.1.1 remains linear with this modification, assuming that *looksize* and *maxmatch* are constants. However, in practice, the size of these constants will greatly affect the running time.

For the ID-LRU algorithm, another factor when considering the practicality of adding lookahead is that with the compact trie and pair forest implementation, the decoder can no longer maintain a *lastentry* array as a means to avoiding storing the compact trie. Consider the following example.

Example 3.9.2: Let s be the string:

$$ad^4bcabcf^8cd^4f^8abcd^4f^8$$

The $ID-LRU$ heuristic as modified by Algorithm 3.9.1 with *looksize*=3 (when started with only the characters of the input alphabet in the local dictionary) parses s up to the second occurrence of abc as:

$$a,d,d,d^2,b,c,a,bc,f,f,f^2,f^4,c,d^4,f^8$$

During this parsing, the following strings are added to the dictionary:

$$ad$$
$$d^2$$
$$d^4$$
$$d^2b$$
$$bc$$
$$ca$$
$$abc$$
$$f^2$$

$$f^4$$
$$f^8$$
$$f^4 c$$
$$c d^4$$
$$d^4 f^8$$

Now, consider what happens when processing the second occurrence of abc. First, ab is taken and $f^8 ab$ is added to the dictionary. Next, c is taken. Now we must decide whether to add abc to the dictionary, but it does not suffice to check only the last two matches to verify that abc is already in the dictionary. $\bigcirc$

The example above shows that starting with an initial dictionary containing only the input alphabet, the $ID{-}LRU$ algorithm with lookahead 3 can construct the same string at points that are far apart in the input stream; furthermore, the two instances do not have to be constructed in the same way. This phenomenon can happen arbitrarily often with any lookahead >1.

To see how much savings may be obtained with lookahead, Appendix A.7.4.4 shows how the $ID{-}LRU$ algorithm performs with various amounts of lookahead. It can be seen from this table that lookahead typically reduced the percent compression ratio by $2^{\dagger}$. This savings is not great, but it is worth noting that all savings were achieved with lookahead values in the range 4 to 16. Appendix 7.5.6 shows a sample implied dictionary using lookahead.

3.10. DYNAMIC LOSSY COMPRESSION

In this section we generalize Algorithms 3.1.1 and 3.1.2 to perform lossy compression. As discussed in Chapter 1, an important application of lossy compression is the compression of *digitally sampled analog data* (DSAD) such as speech, music, black and white or color images, video, and satellite data. In practice, it is typical for such data to be nearly uncompressible (e.g.,

---

† Note that since percent compression ratios were typically in the 30 to 50 range, an improvement of 2 is tantamount to a 4 to 6 percent improvement in the size of the compressed form. For highly compressible sources (e.g., 10-to-1 or more) that are beyond the scope of our experiments, it is not clear if or how the improvement as expressed as a percentage of the size of the compressed form would change.

the compressed size is more than 75 percent of the uncompressed size) with
any of the lossless methods based on Algorithms 3.1.1 and 3.1.2 that we have
discussed. However, with lossy techniques, great amounts of compression may
be possible. For example, with *vector quantization* techniques (to be discussed
shortly), a black and white image stored as a 512 by 512 array of bytes (each
byte being an intensity value) may be compressed by a factor of more than
50-to-1 and still look quite good (to the human eye) compared to the original[†].

Many types of DSAD are multi-dimensional. For example, single
black and white or color images can be viewed as two dimensional and video
as three dimensional. At the end of this section we discuss how the lossy techniques presented here can be further generalized to multi-dimensional data.
For the moment, however, we continue to assume that the input to a
compression algorithm is a stream of characters from and underlying alphabet
Σ. A good example of 1-dimensional DSAD, which may be useful to keep in
mind while reading what is to follow, is digitally sampled speech such as *96
kilo-bit speech* (and industry standard) which consists of 8,000 12-bit samples
per second (where each sample represents the corresponding amplitude of the
signal at that moment). A similar example, but with a much higher data-
rate, is stereo music stored on a compact disc which consists of 44,100 pairs of
16-bit samples per second.

Our approach to generalizing Algorithms 3.1.1 and 3.1.2 is to use a
form of approximate matching that is tantamount to an on-line form of vector quantization, but with *variable size* vectors. We start by briefly describing the traditional off-line form of vector quantization with fixed size vectors.

Vector Quantization

Vector quantization traditionally refers to any method that partitions
the input into blocks of *blocksize* characters and maps each block to one of
the elements in a table of *tablesize* entries, where each entry is a *blocksize*-
tuple of characters from Σ. Compression is achieved by outputting only the
indices into the table. Decompression is just table lookup. To simplify nota-
tion, for the remainder of this section we assume that $|\Sigma|$ and *tablesize* are
powers of two.

---

† See the bibliographic notes for references to image compression.

A nice feature of this approach is that we know in advance that the compression ratio achieved (bits out divided by bits in) will be exactly:

$$\frac{\log_2 |\Sigma| * blocksize}{\log_2(tablesize)}$$

We do not, however, have any guarantees about the quality of the "quantized" image. To discuss methods that attempt to get the best quality possible, we need the notion of a *distance metric*.

We can view the set of all possible *blocksize*-tuples, *blocksize*$\geq$1, of characters from Σ as forming a *blocksize*-dimensional vector space. If V is a vector of *blocksize* characters from Σ, then we let V_1 through $V_{blocksize}$ denote the components of V. A metric for the distance between two vectors V and W, $d(V,W)$, can be defined in many ways. For the purposes of defining such a metric, depending on the particular application, we henceforth assume one (but not both) of the following:

nn characters: To each of the characters of Σ is associated a unique non-negative integer in the range 0 to $|\Sigma|-1$.

tc characters: To each of the characters of Σ is associated a unique integer in the range $-|\Sigma|/2$ to $(|\Sigma|/2)-1$. That is, since we are assuming that $|\Sigma|$ is a power of 2, the set of integers corresponding to the characters of Σ is the set of integers that can be represented in two's complement notation using $\log_2 |\Sigma|$ bits.

In most applications, DSAD is stored in one of the above two forms. For example, with digitally stored black and white images or video, 8-bit *nn* characters are typically used whereas with digitally sampled speech or music, 12 or 16-bit *tc* characters are typically used. Perhaps the three most commonly used metrics are:

$$\text{L1: } d(V,W) = \sum_{i=1}^{blocksize} |V_i - W_i|$$

$$\text{L2: } d(V,W) = \sum_{i=1}^{blocksize} (V_i - W_i)^2$$

$$\text{L-INFINITY: } d(V,W) = \underset{i=1}{\overset{blocksize}{MAX}} |V_i - W_i|$$

A natural way to visualize the above three metrics is to think of them in the context of 3-dimensional Euclidean space[†] (*blocksize*=3). The *L*1 metric corresponds to traveling from *V* to *W* by moving along coordinate axes. The *L*2 metric corresponds to traveling from *V* to *W* in the shortest (Euclidean) distance possible (a straight line segment). The *L−INFINITY* metric simply measures the component on which the two vectors differ the most; it derives its name from the following observation. If for any integer $k > 0$ define the *Lk* metric as

$$d(V,W) = \sum_{i=1}^{blocksize} |V_i - W_i|^k$$

then *L*1 and *L*2 correspond to $k=1$ and $k=2$, and:

$$L-INFINITY(V,W) = \lim_{k \to \infty} Lk(V,W)$$

Although the name *L−INFINITY* arises naturally as indicated above, we shall henceforth refer to it simply as the *MAX* metric; this name is motivated more directly by the way the metric is actually computed (and is also shorter to write).

Example 3.10.1: Suppose that the input is a raster scan[††] of a black and white image where each pixel is stored as a byte. A simple way to achieve 2-to-1 compression is to simply discard the low-order 4 bits of each pixel (i.e., replace them by 0). This is an example of vector quantization where $|\Sigma|=256$, *blocksize*=1, and *tablesize*=16. By performing this quantization using any of the metrics *L*1, *L*2, or *MAX* (which are equivalent when *blocksize*=1), we have replaced 256 distinct intensity levels by 16 levels that are spread uniformly. This loss in precision has been traded for the 2-to-1 compression. ○

[†] Euclidean space refers to the usual physical notion of space and distance; typically 1, 2, or 3-dimensional.

[††] The term "raster scan" refers to a row by row listing of the intensity values, called *pixels*, that represent the image.

Preprocessing for the Lossless Algorithm

As illustrated by Example 3.10.1, a special case of vector quantization is *scalar quantization*, where *blocksize*=1. Scalar quantization provides a very simple method for on-line dynamic lossy compression:

> *Quantize the incoming characters of the input stream before passing them to an on-line dynamic lossless compression algorithm.*

This approach can be viewed as preprocessing the input for the lossless compressor to make characters that are "similar" be identical (so that the lossless compressor can more easily find patterns). This preprocessing step also has the desirable side-effect that compression ratio of the entire algorithm is the product of the ratio obtained by the scalar quantization and the ratio obtained by the lossless algorithm. In practice, this product has a "snowballing" effect; that is, the more compression achieved by the scalar quantization, the more achieved by the lossless compression.

Given that we are viewing scalar quantization as a preprocessing step to lossless compression, if Q is the scalar quantization function, then from the point of view of the lossless compressor, the input alphabet is just the set of distinct values of $Q(a)$ where a is a character of Σ. Hence, from this point on, it will be convenient to view scalar quantization as the *INIT* heuristic. That is, a function that places a set of characters *INIT* in the dictionary with the understanding that if a character of Σ that is not in *INIT* arrives in the input stream, it is mapped to the closest character in *INIT*. Some common scalar quantization methods (dictionary initialization heuristics) are:

ALL: Place all possible characters in the dictionary. No compression is achieved, no information is lost. If we are compressing data by first scalar quantizing and then performing lossless compression, then instructing the scalar quantizer to use *ALL* quantization forces pure lossless compression.

UNIFORM: Example 3.10.1 is an example of *UNIFORM* scalar quantization. In the literature, any technique that spreads values approximately evenly may be referred to as uniform quantization. For our purposes, given an integer parameter $s \geq 1$, which designates the *spacing*, for nn characters $UNIFORM(s)$ places into the dictionary the values

$$0,\ s,\ 2s,\ 3s,\ ...,\ |\Sigma|-1^{\dagger}$$

and for tc characters the values:

$$0,\ s,\ -s,\ 2s,\ -2s,\ ...,\ |\Sigma|/2-1,-\ |\Sigma|/2^{\dagger\dagger}.$$

For example, for 8-bit nn data, $UNIFORM(33)$ produces the nine dictionary entries:

0:	0
1:	33
2:	66
3:	99
4:	132
5:	165
6:	198
7:	231
8:	255

COVER: The $COVER$ heuristic is a variation of $UNIFORM$ where for an integer parameter $d\geq0$, which denotes the *maximum difference*, $COVER(d)$ places a minimal number of entries in the dictionary (symmetric about 0 for tc characters) so that every character of Σ differs by at most d from at least one of these values. $COVER(d)$ is essentially $UNIFORM(2d+1)$ with some "fine tuning". First, the smallest value d such that $COVER(d)$ creates the same number of entries as $COVER(d)$ is determined. Second, the values created are made as small as possible. That is, the largest positive value is set to d less than the largest positive value in Σ, the second largest positive value is set to $2d+1$ less, and so on; similarly for the negative values (for tc characters). This has the effect of putting any "round-off error" near 0. For example, for 8-bit nn data, $COVER(16)$ produces the eight dictionary entries

---

† If $|\Sigma|-1$ is not a multiple of s, then the difference between $|\Sigma|-1$ and the second to largest value on this list will be less than s.
†† A similar comment to that for nn data applies when $|\Sigma|/2$ or $|\Sigma|/2-1$ is not a multiple of s.

0.	8
1.	41
2.	74
3.	107
4.	140
5.	173
6.	206
7.	239

where the last gap (239 to 255) is 16, all gaps but the first are 31, and the first gap (0 to 8) is only 8; the reader should compare $COVER(16)$ to the $UNIFORM(33)$ example mentioned earlier. Note that although values produced for tc data are always symmetric about $0^{\dagger}$, they may or may not include 0, depending on the values of $|\Sigma|$ and $d^{\dagger\dagger}$. For example, for 8-bit tc data, $COVER(16)$ produces the eight dictionary entries

0.	12	1.	-13
2.	45	3.	-46
4.	78	5.	-79
6.	111	7.	-112

whereas both $COVER(14)$ and $COVER(15)$ produce the nine dictionary entries:

0.	0		
1.	26	2.	-27
3.	55	4.	-56
5.	84	6.	-85
7.	113	8.	-114

LOG: For a given integer parameter $i \geq 0$, which denotes the number of *additional bits*, log scalar quantization saves only the position of the leading non-zero bit of the character along with the next i bits that follow it. It is possible to use a cod-

---

† Actually, we allow positive and negative values to differ by 1 in magnitude.
†† In practice, there may be types of data where forcing 0 to be included is desirable, even though it may cause the size of the covering set to be 1 larger than necessary. For example, scalar quantized digital speech tends to sound better when 0 is included than when it is not. However, we will not address this issue further.

ing scheme from which this information can be directly read. For example, 8-bit nn characters can be encoded as 4 bits; the first 3 are an integer between 0 and 7 to denote the position of the leading non-zero bit and the fourth bit is the bit after that. However, this coding scheme wastes some codes (e.g., the code 0001 does not denote anything). As discussed in the bibliographic notes, in the literature there are several methods for constructing such an explicit code without waste. Here, we avoid this problem by defining $LOG(i)$ to be a function which places the actual character values in the dictionary (not descriptions of them). $LOG(i)$ initializes the dictionary by sliding a window that is a 1 followed by all combinations of i bits over each possible bit position of a character. In addition, we always add the largest possible positive value[†]. For example, for nn characters, $LOG(0)$ creates 0, all powers of 2 less than $|\Sigma|-1$, and $|\Sigma|-1$. For tc characters, $LOG(0)$ creates 0, all powers of 2 less than $|\Sigma|/2-1$, $|\Sigma|/2-1$, the negatives of all powers of 2 less than $|\Sigma|/2$, and $-|\Sigma|/2$. As a larger example, $LOG(1)$ for 8-bit tc characters yields the dictionary entries:

0.	0		
1.	1	2.	-1
3.	2	4.	-2
5.	3	6.	-3
7.	4	8.	-4
9.	6	10.	-6
11.	8	12.	-8
13.	12	14.	-12
15.	16	16.	-16
17.	24	18.	-24
19.	32	20.	-32
21.	48	22.	-48
23.	64	24.	-64
25.	96	26.	-96
27.	127	28.	-128

Let b denote the number of bits per character, i the parame-

---

† For tc characters, the smallest possible negative value is always added, even if the window is only 1 bit wide. We have included the largest possible positive value primarily for symmetry.

ter to LOG, and:

$nn(b,i)$ = number of entries generated for nn characters
$tc(b,i)$ = number of entries generated for tc characters

Then

$$nn(b,i) = \begin{cases} (b-i+1)*2^i+1 & \text{if } 0<=i\leq(b-2) \\ 2^b & \text{if } (b-1)\leq i \end{cases}$$

and $tc(b,i)$ can be expressed in terms of $nn(b,i)$:

$$tc(b,i) = \begin{cases} (b-i)*2^{(i+1)}+1 = nn(b,i+1) & \text{if } 0\leq i\leq(b-3) \\ 2^b & \text{if } (b-2)\leq i \end{cases}$$

Figure 3.10.1 is a table of $nn(b,i)$ for $0\leq i\leq 15$ and either $b=8$ or $b=16$. As can be seen from this table, it is possible for both $nn(b,i)$ and $tc(b,i)$ to be slightly more or less than a power of 2. If just scalar quantization is being performed (without subsequent lossless compression), then this is un-desirable (since codewords will be wasted). However, since we are concerned primarily with subsequent lossless compression (where the values placed in the dictionary by scalar quantiza-tion typically comprise only a small portion of the diction-ary), we will not worry about this. In practice, there are a host of techniques for "fine tuning" the LOG algorithm to make the values of $nn(b,i)$ and $tc(b,i)$ have desirable values.

As the degree of scalar quantization becomes greater (as the set $INIT$ gets smaller), the quality of the data (how close it is to the original) goes down. One phenomenon that commonly occurs with such loss of quality is what we shall henceforth refer to as *contouring*. As an example of contouring, imagine a black and white digital image that has been scalar quantized to a high degree (e.g., 8-bit pixels have been mapped to 4 bits with the $COVER(8)$ heuristic), and consider an area of the image that close to (but not quite) uni-form in intensity (e.g., a portion of a person's forehead). As the quantizer moves across such an area, it may periodically jump back and forth between two values because the area being quantized is roughly centered between these two values. In the case of something like a person's forehead, it can be that the effect of this jumping back and forth is that the forehead looks basically

i	b=8	b=16
0	10	18
1	17	33
2	29	61
3	49	113
4	81	209
5	129	385
6	193	705
7	256	1281
8	256	2305
9	256	4097
10	256	7169
11	256	12289
12	256	20481
13	256	32769
14	256	49153
15	256	65536

Figure 3.10.1
nn(b,i)

correct but has an artificial looking checkerboard-like contour boundaries superimposed on it. The problem is that when the quantizer goes from an area with one value to an area with another, it can do so in a very discrete fashion that creates the contouring effect. A technique to soften such transitions is *dithering*. The idea is to start up a random number generator[†] and successively add in a random value to each character before quantizing and then subtract that same random value after quantizing has been completed. A simple example is when the scalar quantization is $UNIFORM(x)$, in which

---

† For our purposes, a random number generator is a function such that each time it is called, it returns a random real value between 0 and 1 (which can then be scaled to lie within a desired range). In practice, it is typical for the values returned to not be truly random, but instead, to be computed by some deterministic "random looking" function of the previous value that was returned; the process is started by providing the function with a *seed* value.

case each random value would be scaled to lie in the range $-x/2$ to $x/2$. In general, however, the random value added to a character is a function that depends on the character. Note that no extra storage is needed for this scheme if a deterministic random number generator is used since the random number generator can be restarted with the same seed after the scalar quantization is completed. The effect of dithering can be to "blend" discrete boundaries. Dithering can be effective for general vector quantization as well, and there are a host of issues that we have not addressed. However, since it comprises a simple pre and post-processing stage that is completely separate from the lossy compression algorithm in question, we shall not consider dithering further. References to dithering are contained in the bibliographic notes.

Generalizing the Lossless Algorithm

Scalar quantization followed by lossless compression is a simple approach that has a lossy component (provided by the scalar quantization) that is completely separate from a pattern matching component (provided by the lossless compression algorithm). We now consider a potentially more powerful approach that combines these two components[†]. The idea is to use Algorithms 3.1.1 and 3.1.2 with just two changes.

The first change is that the definition of the match heuristic is generalized to:

> **The match heuristic, MH:** A function that removes from the input stream a string t that is acceptably close (according to a specified metric) to a string in D.

To define "acceptably close", the algorithm must be supplied a *vector distance metric VM* that takes a single string s as an argument and returns a non-negative integer equal to the "distance" between s and the first $|s|$ incoming characters of the input stream. This function must satisfy two constraints:

- $VM(s)=0$ if and only if the first $|s|$ incoming characters of the input stream are exactly the characters of s.

[†] In practice this approach may be more powerful. In theory, this may not be true. See the bibliographic notes.

- $VM(s){=}\infty$ if there are fewer than $|s|$ characters left in the input stream[†].

Given that such a metric is supplied to the algorithm, "acceptably close" is defined by a single integer parameter *Epsilon*. That is, all dictionary entries s such that $VM(s){<}Epsilon$ are acceptably close. *Epsilon* can either be supplied to the algorithm or the algorithm can dynamically adjust the value of Epsilon to either maintain a fixed data rate (with varying quality) or a fixed quality (with variable data rate). Because of the conditions placed on *VM*, the value *Epsilon*=0 forces pure lossless compression.

As with pure lossless compression, a host of choices can be made for the match heuristic *MH* (e.g., limited lookahead). However, to simplify our discussion, we shall restrict ourselves to the greedy heuristic (remove from the input stream the *longest* string t that is acceptably close).

The second change that we make to Algorithms 3.1.1 and 3.1.2 is to employ on-the-fly dictionary guaranteed progress. The reason for this change is that we no longer wish to force *INIT* to contain all of Σ since in many practical applications (e.g. 16-bit digitally sampled speech), $|\Sigma|$ is very large (possibly larger than $|D|$). Note that even if $|INIT|{<}|\Sigma|$, the on-the-fly mechanism will never be used if *INIT* contains enough characters so that every character of Σ is acceptably close to some character in *INIT*.

Given the two changes discussed above, Algorithms 3.1.1 and 3.1.2 are a general purpose framework for performing on-line dynamic lossy compression, where the tradeoff between the degree of lossiness and the amount of compression can be adjusted (beforehand or dynamically) via a single integer parameter *Epsilon*.

Pascal Code

The generalization of Algorithms 3.1.1 and 3.1.2 to lossy compression as described above is conceptually quite simple but can require non-trivial data structures (which may depend on the distance metric) to run efficiently. Instead of considering a particular implementation, Appendix A.9 contains a Pascal implementation of Algorithms 3.1.1 and 3.1.2 (generalized to lossy compression) that is much more flexible and general purpose than the code of

---

† In practice, some arbitrarily large value (e.g. maxint in Pascal) can be used.

Appendix A.8, at the expense of running much slower. Unlike the code of Appendix A.8, Appendix A.9 has no map routines; the internal representation of a pointer is an integer identical to its external representation. The data structure used to store the dictionary is similar to the pair forest that was discussed earlier for the *ID* heuristic. Each dictionary entry is represented by five fields:

> size field
> left pointer field
> right pointer field
> character field
> references field

The size field contains number of characters in the entry. The entry is the concatenation of the entry corresponding to the left pointer, the entry corresponding to the right pointer, and the character stored in the character field. The data structure uses the nilptr to specify that a field denotes the empty string; legal combinations are:

> left=nilptr   right=nilptr   character present
> left≠nilptr   right=nilptr   character present
> left≠nilptr   right≠nilptr   character not present

Entries consisting of a single character are always combination 1. With the *FC* and *AP* heuristics, all other entries are combination 2, whereas with the *ID* heuristic, all other entries are combination 3.

To fully understand the dictionary data structure, it may help to examine a procedure that uses it. Consider the following procedure $POS(ptr,i)$ which returns the ith character of the dictionary entry corresponding to the pointer *ptr* (*POS* makes no check for illegal arguments).

```
function POS(ptr,i:integer):integer;
begin
if (i=sizefield[ptr]) and (rightfield[ptr]=nilptr) then POS:=elefield[ptr]
else if (i<=sizefield[leftfield[ptr]]) then POS:=POS(leftfield[ptr],i)
else POS:=POS(rightfield[ptr],(i-sizefield[leftfield[ptr]]));
end {POS};
```

Note that the procedure *POS* that is actually used in Appendix A.9 is a non-recursive version of the above procedure so that with most Pascal compilers it will run faster (by a small constant factor).

The references field contains the number of other entries that have this entry as the left or right pointer field. It is used to simplify the operation of the *LRU* queue. Whenever an entry is used it is simply moved to the front of the queue. Whenever it is time to delete an entry, the algorithm starts at the back of the queue and looks for the first entry with a reference count of 0. This differs from the more clever strategy that was used by the Appendix A.8 for the *AP* heuristic, which moved entries to the front of the queue but after their ancestors in the trie; so that the entry at the end of the queue was guaranteed to be a leaf (which is tantamount to a reference count of 0). However, as discussed earlier, which of these two queuing strategies is used in practice has an insignificant effect on the amount of compression achieved.

The files *vsqueeze.p* and *vunsqueeze.p* are the high-level code for the encoder and decoder. They are similar to the files squeeze.p and unsqueeze.p in Appendix A.8 with the addition of the code to handle on-the-fly dictionary guaranteed progress. The remaining code is divided into a number of files that are included by both vsqueeze.p and vunsqueeze.p:

Declarations and utility routines:
> *declare.i*: declarations of parameters and variables
> *utility.i*: system dependent code to read in arguments, etc.

Data Structures:
> *dictionary.i*: dictionary (includes distance metrics)
> *queue.i*: doubly linked list implementation of the *LRU* queue

Dump Routines:
> *dump.i*: routines to dump the dictionary and various statistics

Heuristics:
> *heur_init.i*: initialization heuristics
> *heur_delete.i*: deletion heuristics
> *heur_update.i*: update heuristics

Input/Output routines:
> *io.i*

Initialization and Finish-Up Code:
> *start.i*: initialization of variables and structures
> *finish.i*: code to dump the dictionary and various statistics

As with Appendix A.8, this code is written in standard Pascal with some exceptions pertaining to input and output that are noted at the beginning of Appendix A.9.

The parameters to the program are specified on the command line[†] in one of the following three formats:

>   parameter
>   parameter=value
>   parameter=value_argument

Value and *argument* may be integers or strings depending on the parameter in question; for string values, only the first character is significant. For all of *parameter*, *value*, and *argument*, case is ignored. Legal parameters are the following:

CharBytes: Specifies the number of bytes that comprise a character; *one* specifies 1 byte, *hl* specifies two bytes where the high-order byte precedes the low-order byte, and *lh* specifies two bytes where the low-order byte precedes the high-order byte.

CharDiv: A positive integer; all incoming characters to the encoder are divided by this amount.

CharMult: A positive integer; all outgoing characters from the decoder are multiplied by this amount.

CharForm: The character form; *tc* for two's complement characters, *nn* for non negative characters.

CharInit: A non-negative integer equal to the maximum positive value of a character that can be added by an initialization heuristic (the maximum negative value is minus this minus 1). A value of −1 sets CharInit to the largest possible positive value of a character.

---

† The code to process command line parameters in the file utility.i is written for Berkeley Unix and is system dependent. This code may have to be rewritten for other systems. Alternatively, the code can be removed and replaced with simple assignment statements to the appropriate variables; in this case, the program must be re-compiled each time the parameters are changed.

CharQuant: *Yes* to quantize all characters input to the encoder to the closest entry of length 1 in the static portion of the dictionary; *no* to disable this mechanism.

Epsilon: A non-negative integer equal to the largest allowable distance to form a match; 0 specifies lossless compression.

HeurD: Deletion heuristic - FREEZE, LRU.

HeurI: Initialization heuristic - *EMPTY, ALL, COVER, FILE, LOG, UNIFORM*. The *EMPTY* heuristic places nothing in the dictionary. The *FILE* heuristic simply reads in a list of integers from the file name specified by *value*.

HeurU: Update heuristic - EMPTY, AP, FC, ID. The EMPTY heuristic specifies that no updates are allowed; compression is based only on INIT.

Ignore: A non-negative integer that specifies how many leading characters the encoder should ignore and pass through unchanged to the decoder. This is useful for files that have headers that must be preserved.

MaxMatch: A positive integer equal to the maximum allowable length for a match. Setting MaxMatch=1 and CharQuant=yes specifies pure scalar quantization. In this case, the *LOG* initialization heuristic is slightly modified if $nn(b,i)$ or $tc(b,i)$ is just 1 more than a power of 2. In this case, the largest possible positive value is not added. In addition, for the case $i=0$ where $nn(b,i)$ is 2 greater than b (which is 8 or 16), 0 is not added either.

PtrSize A positive integer equal to the maximum number of bits per pointer.

PtrType: *Fixed* specifies that all pointers are *PtrSize* bits; *variable* specifies that pointers grow from $\log_2\lceil|INIT|+1\rceil$ bits to *PtrSize* bits.

VecMetric: The vector distance metric - 1L, 2L, MAX, SMAX. 1L specifies the $L1$ metric and may be entered as $L1$. 2L specifies the $L2$ metric and may be entered as $L2^{\dagger}$. *SMAX* specifies a variation of the MAX metric which is identical for nn characters but for tc characters requires the signs of corresponding characters to match (or else the distance is set to Pascal maxint).

A number of secondary parameters specify the dumping of statistics, etc. For these secondary parameters, all characters of a string value may be significant.

DumpDict: Set to a file name to dump the final dictionary; set to *off* to disable the dictionary dump.

DumpStats: Set to a file name to dump parameter settings and various statistics; set to *off* to disable the stats dump.

DumpTrace: Set to a file name to dump a trace of the matches made and pointers transmitted; set to *off* to disable the trace dump.

DumpUpdate: *Yes* to include update information in the trace file; *no* to not include this information.

HeurIParam: Can be used to specify separately an integer argument to the *HeurI* parameter.

HeurIString: Can be used to specify separately a string argument to the *HeurI* parameter.

LineLength: Specifies the maximum line length for dump output.

Readable: *Yes* to dump matches in readable form; *no* to dump matches with integer values of characters.

ReadChar: The character used to write unreadable characters when $Readable=yes$.

ReadLow: The smallest character value that is readable.

ReadHigh: The largest character value that is readable.

---

† Even though only the first character of string values is significant, for this special case, $L1$ and $L2$ are recognized.

To reduce the length of command lines, program parameters may be abbreviated with just the upper-case characters in their name (e.g., *hd=lru* instead of *HeurD=lru* or *e=0* instead of *Epsilon=0*). In addition, the following abbreviations may be used:

> *dict* for *DumpDict=dumpdict*
> *stats* for *DumpStats=dumpstats*
> *trace* for *DumpTrace=dumptrace*
> *traceu* for *DumpTrace=dumptrace* and *DumpUpdate=yes*

The default settings of the parameters are for lossless compression and are listed at the beginning of the file *start.i*. At the end of the file *utility.i* are several abbreviations for parameter settings for things like speech, images, and lossless compression of ASCII text. These abbreviations are included primarily as examples of how to use the parameters. The abbreviation *squeeze* is also included which sets the parameters to simulate the code of Appendix A.8[†].

The code of Appendix A.9 is reasonably straightforward. The running time is dominated by the *FIND* procedure in the file *dictionary.i* which finds a longest match between the input stream and the dictionary with a "brute force" linear search that expands each dictionary entry to the string that it represents and then compares it to the appropriate prefix of the input stream using the appropriate distance metric. The time to perform the update heuristic is reduced by not bothering to check if the entries added are already in the dictionary. Although it is possible that duplicate entries could be created (thus wasting dictionary entries), as discussed earlier, this is not a significant problem in practice.

Because the code of Appendix A.9 employs linear search to find the current match, it should be viewed as code for experimentation (for both lossy and lossless compression), not code for an actual implementation. More sophisticated strategies for finding a longest match may depend on the distance metric, may involve additional data structures, and may require some modifications of the update heuristics; such strategies are beyond the scope of this discussion.

---

† The output of the code of Appendix A.9 with the *squeeze* setting will not actually be identical to the output of Appendix A.8 because the *LRU* queue works slightly differently (as discussed earlier) and no check is made if update strings are already present in the dictionary (to be discussed shortly).

Multi-Dimensional Data

We now consider how the lossy generalization of Algorithms 3.1.1 and 3.1.2 discussed above can be further generalized for higher dimensional data. Since this is a relatively new area of research, we only provide a brief overview of basic concepts.

An example of 2-dimensional DSAD is a digitally stored image; in practice, there are a number of common types of digital images:

- A black and white image stored as a two-dimensional array of pixels. For example, a 1024 by 1024 array of bytes.

- A color image stored as three two-dimensional arrays of pixels, one for each of the colors red, green, and blue.

- A color image stored as a single two-dimensional array along with a *palette* that specifies for each pixel value, the corresponding red, green, and blue values that are associated with it.

An example of 3-dimensional DSAD is digitally stored video which consists of a sequence of digital images (e.g., 30 frames per second).

A simple approach to dealing with multi-dimensional data is to reduce it to a one dimensional problem by placing a linear ordering on the data. In Chapter 5, a technique is discussed that has optimal asymptotic properties. In practice, however, correlations between adjacent characters can be lost (resulting is less compression) if the multi-dimensional data is scanned in a some 1-dimensional fashion.

In the case that the multi-dimensional data is highly biased in one dimension, another approach is to divide the problem into a collection of 1-dimensional problems. For example, with video, there is typically a high similarity when traveling along the same horizontal and vertical coordinates from frame to frame. Hence, if the frames are n by n pixels each, one could divide the problem into n^2 separate 1-dimensional problems. A simpler approach is to concatenate all first rows, all second rows, etc. to form n 1-dimensional problems[†].

---

† In practice, for some constant k, one might divide the problem into n/k problems, where each problem is a "band" of pixels.

The alternative to reducing a multi-dimension problem to some form of 1-dimensional problem is to generalize our notion of a dictionary to store multi-dimensional entries. To simplify our discussion, we restrict ourselves to two dimensional entries; however, all of what we discuss can be generalized to higher dimensions.

A simple generalization is to allow only entries that are rectangular in shape. Each dictionary entry can still be stored as a string, which is just the concatenation of the rows of the rectangle. The only additional information needed is to associate with each entry a single integer field that uniquely determines the *aspect ratio* (height divided by width) of the associated rectangle; for example, it suffices to let this integer be the width of the rectangle. Note, however, that although dictionary entries are all simple rectangles, we assume that the vector metric function may compare any two 2-dimensional (possibly disconnected) regions so long as they have the same shape; that is, one can translated (without being rotated) to lie on top of the other. For example, the $L1$, $L2$, MAX, and $SMAX$ metrics discussed earlier can all be so generalized by simply scanning a region in a row by row fashion to form a vector.

Figure 3.10.2 depicts how the 2-dimensional matching is done. Matching begins by finding the largest rectangle in the dictionary which when placed at the upper left corner of the array (i.e., its upper left corner lines up with the upper left corner of the array) matches acceptably closely. At any point in time, the array is partially covered by rectangles (portions of the array that have already been matched). As depicted in Figure 3.10.2, these rectangles may overlap; we shall discuss how the array is reconstructed from overlapping regions shortly. The *growing boarder* is the boundary between the portion of the array that is currently covered by rectangles and the portion that is not. The *growing points* are those points on the growing boarder such that the incident edges to these points on the growing boarder go down and to the right; the growing points in Figure 3.10.2 are circled. A host of heuristics may be used by the match heuristic to select a growing point. For the purposes of this discussion, the exact choice is not important; we only assume that growing points are chosen so that the array is filled up in a wave that progresses (approximately) diagonally from the upper left corner down to the lower right. That is, it is desirable that progress in the horizontal and vertical directions is somewhat balanced.

Given that we have a strategy for selecting growing points, the current match is simply the largest rectangle in the dictionary such that when its upper left corner is placed on the growing point, it matches the array ac-

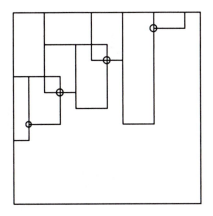

Figure 3.10.2
Growing Points

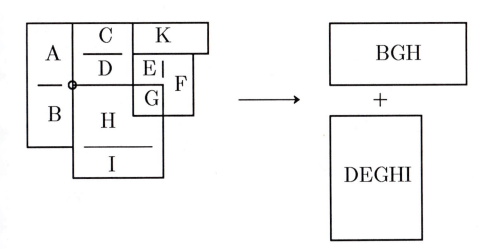

Figure 3.10.3
2D-ID Heuristic

ceptably closely. There are however, some details that should be noted:

- The current match may overlap with already covered regions of the array. In this case, only the characters in non-overlapping regions are used to compute whether the match is acceptably close. When the decoder has to output the array, it will output rectangles in the same order they were matched and only output the portions of a rectangle that do not overlap with rectangles that have been previously outputted.

- When we reach the bottom or right edge, we allow matches to overlap the side of the array. In this case, the distance metric is only applied to those characters that are within the array.

- It is possible to form a match that causes one or more uncovered regions to be closed off. For example, in Figure 3.10.2, if a horizontally long match was found at the second growing point from the left, then a region (associated with the third growing point from the left) would be closed off, forming a "hole". This is not a problem, the hole can simply be treated as a separate sub-problem. Alternately, the match heuristic can be modified to prevent such holes from forming.

Given that a strategy for selecting a growing point and forming the current match has been adopted, all that remains to be specified are the update and deletion heuristics. For the deletion heuristic, the same strategies as used in the 1-dimensional case work. For the update heuristic, a variety of methods based on generalization of the *FC*, *AP*, and *ID* heuristics can be defined. As an example, the *2D−ID heuristic* is depicted in Figure 3.10.3. This heuristic always adds at most two new entries and can be viewed as a simple interpretation of

> *Add the previous match concatenated with the current match*
> *in both the horizontal and vertical directions.*

where the "previous match" is not necessarily the match previously made but rather, the match(s) adjacent to the current match. In order to insure that the new entries added by the *2D−ID* heuristic are simple rectangles, the *2D−ID* heuristic projects the sides of the current match back (the lines of projection are indicated in Figure 3.10.3). In addition, if more than one rectangle abuts the current match in either the horizontal or vertical direction, then the largest rectangle that is contained in these abutting rectangles is used. Referring to Figure 3.10.3, the current growing point is circled, the current match is rectangle *GHI* (the rectangle consisting of regions *G*, *H*, and *I*), the matches previously made are rectangles *AB*, *CD*, *K*, and *EFG*, and the rectangles added to the dictionary by the 2*D*−*ID* heuristic are *BGH* and *DEGHI*.

3.11. BIBLIOGRAPHIC NOTES

The basic notion of the encoder and decoder working in lock-step has been known for many years and has been used extensively by information theorists (e.g., the dynamic Huffman coding algorithm that was discussed in Chapter 2).

The presentation of on-line textual substitution techniques as instances of the basic model of Section 3.1 is due to Storer [1985]. The presentation of the *AP* heuristic is new work by this author. The *AP* heuristic, modifications of the *LRU* strategy discussed in this chapter, limited lookahead, and the use of the MaxChildren parameter are addressed by some of the claims contained in the U.S. Patent of Storer [1987].

For other examples of compressing English text with a static dictionary of common English substrings, see Storer and Tsang [1984], Cooper and Lynch [1982], Yannakoudakis, Goyal, and Huggil [1982], Pike [1981], and White [1968]. Wagner [1973] and Storer [1977b] consider the problem of efficiently storing compiler error messages with the use of a static dictionary. Compression with static dictionaries is often studied in the context of off-line computations. For example, Wagner [1973] gives an algorithm for optimally parsing a string with respect to a static dictionary; this algorithm and related issues are discussed in Chapter 5.

The LZ1 algorithm is presented in Lempel and Ziv [1976] and Ziv and Lempel [1977]. Efficient serial implementation of the sliding dictionary method is discussed in the bibliographic notes to Chapter 5 and efficient parallel implementation is the subject of Chapter 4. Chapter 5 also considers efficient implementations of more general models. For other past work concerning the sliding dictionary method see Storer [1985], Storer and Szymanski [1982], Seery and Ziv [1977] ("Version 4" in their paper is essentially the sliding dictionary method with pointer-guaranteed progress), and Storer [1977].

The LZ2 algorithm is presented in Ziv and Lempel [1978]. Many authors have experimented with the $FC-FREEZE$ heuristic; most notably Seery and Ziv [1978], Lempel and Ziv [1984] (who also have experimented with the $FC-SWAP$ method) and Welch [1984] (who refers to this algorithm as the "LZW algorithm"). Past work concerning the $FC-LRU$ heuristic is contained in Miller and Wegman [1985], Storer [1985], and Storer and Tsang [1984].

Experimentation with the basic mechanism of concatenating pairs of adjacent dictionary entries to form new ones were performed by Seery and Ziv [1978]; More recently Miller and Wegman [1985] introduced the data structure consisting of a compact trie (which they call the "discriminator tree") together with a pair forest for representing the dynamic dictionary for the $ID-LRU$ heuristic, and experimented with the use of this heuristic in the context of a large main-frame computer performing the encoding that was subsequently decoded by a small personal computer. Miller and Wegman [1985] do not discuss the worst-case time complexity of their data structure. The balancing technique for reducing this worst case complexity is due to this author and the experiments with it were performed as part of the writing of this book. For past work pertaining to the applications of compact tries to data compression, see the discussion about pattern matching and the sliding dictionary method in the bibliographic notes to Chapter 5.

Other variations of "learning" heuristics have been considered by Mahaney [1985]. For past work concerning tree pruning see Ziv and Lempel [1978] and Seery and Ziv [1977, 1978].

As discussed earlier, both the LZ1 and LZ2 algorithms employ pointer guaranteed progress. With both schemes, two things must be represented by a pointer, the longest match and the following character, which in the literature are often called the *citation* and the *innovation*. For this reason, some authors refer to dictionary guaranteed progress as *deferred innovation* because one can think of dictionary guaranteed progress as deferring the transmission of the next character to be the first character of the next citation. As discussed in this chapter, in practice, for fixed size dictionaries and fixed size pointers, dictionary guaranteed progress typically out-performs pointer guaranteed progress by avoiding the overhead of explicitly transmitting a character with each pointer. However, these schemes give up the property of being optimal in the information theoretic sense. A nice property of the pure LZ1 and LZ2 algorithms is that they will not expand the size of random (incompressible) data. In contrast, for some common combinations of pointer size and alphabet size (e.g., 8-bit characters and 12-bit pointers) it is typical for the methods discussed in this chapter to expand the size of such data by a factor close to the pointer size divided by the alphabet size. That is, with totally random data, most pointers will represent only one character. This phenomenon may not occur with all combinations of pointer size and character size. For example, with 16 bit pointers and 8 bit characters, the dictionary is large enough to store all pairs of characters and we will transmit an average of two characters per pointer (with the exception of a "start-up" period that occurs during the first 256^2 characters). For a discussion of how pointer size, character size, and the size of the file being compressed relate to how much random data is expanded, see Cohn [1986]. The reader concerned with this issue should note that there are a variety of methods (with low overhead) for adapting the coding schemes used in this chapter so that no significant expansion occurs with random data. For example, one approach is two employ some variation the 2-step codes discussed in Chapter 2.

The technique of *interval coding* proposed in Elias [1985] is similar in flavor to LZ1. The idea is, given a codeword set, which may be finite or countably infinite, a given codeword in an input stream is represented by a variable length coding of the number of codewords since its last occurrence.

A technique presented by Bentley, Sleator, Tarjan, and Wei [1986] (and independently introduced in Elias [1987] as *recency-rank coding)* can be viewed as a method for ordering the entries of a dictionary via a *move-to-front heuristic*. For the case of a static dictionary, their algorithm works as follows. At each stage, the longest match between the input stream and an entry of the dictionary is identified, the index of this entry is transmitted using a variable length encoding (one that uses shorter codes for smaller indices) such as the cascading lengths method, and then the given entry is moved to be the first entry of the dictionary. The motivation is that more frequently occurring entries move to the front of the dictionary and thus get shorter codes. For the dynamic case, they rely on being able to parse the input stream into words; for example, with English text, words can be defined as the character strings that are separated by special characters (blank, carriage return, comma, etc.). Each time a new word is discovered, the index $n+1$ is transmitted (where n is the number of entries in the dictionary), the word itself is transmitted, and then the word is moved to the front. These authors present empirical results that show this technique to be comparable to Huffman coding. Although this scheme allows the dictionary to become potentially unbounded in size, it could be modified to accommodate a *LRU* strategy for dictionary entry deletion. For further work on the use of the move-to-front heuristic and the transposition heuristic (that was considered in Chapter 2) for self-organizing linear lists, see: Rivest [1976], Franasek and

Wagner [1974], Knuth [1973], Burville and Kingman [1973], Hendricks [1972,1973], McCabe [1965], Schay and Dauer [1957].

Tomborson [1987] employs the move-to-front heuristic to reduce pointer size for dynamic methods that employ a LRU queue. The idea is to use the heuristic to keep track of the relative frequencies for which each position of the LRU queue is referenced. Shorter codes are assigned to frequently used positions, longer codes to less frequently used positions.

Williams [1987] employs a predictive method to adaptively extend a tree structure from which Huffman codes can be constructed based on estimated conditional probabilities.

Theorem 3.2.1 is new to this book. The error-resilient property of step codes that is used by this theorem is a probabilistic approach to dealing with the problem of code synchronization. A traditional self-synchronizing code (e.g., Stiffler [1971], Guibas and Odlyzko [1978], Lakshamanan [1981], Apostolico and Fraenkel [1985], Guibas [1985], Odlyzko [1985]) provides a guarantee that input stream can resynchronize after an error has occurred; such a guarantee is tantamount to asserting the existence of at least one synchronizing sequence; that is, a sequence that whenever encountered, always allows the decoder to identify a codeword boundary. The text by Berstel and Perrin contains a theoretical treatment of synchronous codes.

References to error detecting and correcting codes are contained in the bibliographic notes to Chapter 2.

The experimental results summarized in the Appendix A.7 as well as the Pascal code presented in Appendices A.8 and A.9 is new work that was prepared specifically for this book.

The material on limited lookahead is due to this author and is addressed by some of the claims contained in the U.S. Patent of Storer [1987].

See Cavanagh [1984] for a discussion of two's-complement notation.

As mentioned earlier, the version of log scalar quantization used in this chapter is not exactly what is used in practice. For example, two versions of log scalar quantization that are commonly used in practice for speech stored as 12-bit tc characters are the *mu-law* and the *A-law*. Both versions produce an 8-bit code from the original 12-bit tc character. The A-law, copies the sign bit, encodes 11 magnitude bits by locating the highest order digit if any (1 if positive, 0 if negative) among the 7 leading positions (this takes 3 bits), copies the next 4 bits, and OR's in a 1 if the next position is 1; this yields a total of 8 code bits. The Mu-law can encode 11 or 12 magnitude bits. It copies the sign, adds an offset of 16 to the magnitude (to guarantee a high order digit among the top 8), encodes its position in 3 bits, copies the next 4 bits, subtracts or adds back the offset of 16, and OR's in a 1 if the next position is 1. Both the A-law and mu-law are piecewise linear; A-law is identity from 0 to 31 while mu-law is identity from 0 to 15.

Jayant and Noll [1984] is a comprehensive treatment of lossy coding and quantization techniques in general, including log scalar quantization, dithering, etc. The contouring effect is often called *staircasing* in reference to 1-dimensional problems. Rosen [1987] presents software for quantizing color images represented as 3 bytes per pixel (red, green, and blue intensity values) down to a single byte per pixel.

For an introduction to random number generators, see Knuth[1969].

Ziv [1985] shows that under certain assumptions, scalar quantization followed by lossless compression has asymptotically optimal information-theoretic properties.

There has been a large amount of past research relating to vector quantization which we shall not attempt to address here. We mention only a few introductory sources that contain further references. For an introduction to vector spaces, see a text on linear algebra such as Hoffman and Kunze [1971] or Noble and Daniel [1977]. The March 1982 issue of the IEEE Transactions on Information Theory (volume 28:2) is a special two volume issue dedicated to quantization. Gray [1984] is a survey of vector quantization techniques. Makhoul, Roucos, and Gish [1985] is a comprehensive survey of quantization for digitized speech. Lindsay and Chabries [1986] consider vector quantization of color images. Aravind and Gersho [1987] is a recent paper that provides an introduction to vector quantization for image compression and contains experimental results for the widely used "woman in the hat" and "living room" photographs. Recent work by Stockholm [1987] suggests that vector quantization is able to achieve over 50-to-1 compression on single 512 by 512 pixel (8 bits per pixel) black and white images and still retain very good quality. The key to his approach is the computation of distance in a visual domain together with relatively large dictionaries and vectors.

A localized version of vector quantization called *cluster coding* is considered by Hilbert [1977] and Ramapriyan, Tilton, and Seiler [1985].

For an introduction to image processing and reconstruction, the reader may refer to a host of texts such as Bates and McDonnell [1986], Blahut [1985], Pavlidis [1982], and Pratt [1978].

The material on generalizing Algorithms 3.1.1 and 3.1.2 to lossy dynamic on-line compression is new work by this author and is an area of ongoing research. Preliminary experiments with 96 kilo-byte speech have shown that with a simple metric such as the *MAX* metric, more than 25-to-1 compression (1/2 bit per sample) can be achieved and still have speech that is understandable (but very low quality). The *MAX* metric with *Epsilon=x* for some x, however, differs little in practice for speech than scalar quantization with *COVER_x* followed by lossless compression (*Epsilon*=0). Better distance metrics and the question of how this approach compares (in terms of how much compression is achieved) to other methods for compressing speech is an area of current research by this author and M. Cohn [1987].

State of the art vector quantizers for digital images, such as the work of Stockholm [1987] mentioned earlier, can be very time consuming (e.g., hours to compress a single image). The on-line dynamic lossy algorithm consider in this chapter is computationally more tractable, and could be implemented to run in real time with the appropriate hardware and data structures. However, how much compression that can be expected and with what quality is a subject of current research.

As is apparent from inspection of implied dictionaries, textual substitution schemes can be viewed as primitive "learning" algorithms. In fact, any compression method that succeeds in compressing a body of data can be viewed as having learned something about that data. Formal models for learning such as that proposed by Valiant [1984] have been an active area for research (e.g., Kearns, Li, Pitt, and Valiant [1987], Natarajian [1987], Angluin [1986], Blumer, Ehrenfeuct, Haussler, and Warmuth [1986], and Pitt and Valiant [1986]). Rivest [1986] has proposed a formal model for learning that employs data compression for defining the optimality of a representation for a learned concept. Wegeman [1987] has also used compression to study learning.

4

PARALLEL IMPLEMENTATIONS
OF ON-LINE METHODS

The ability to put significant processing power on a single chip makes
sophisticated data compression algorithms truly practical. This chapter considers parallel algorithms for data compression by textual substitution that
are suitable for VLSI implementations. Section 4.1 overviews the notion of a
systolic array, a powerful and practical model for special-purpose VLSI chips.
Section 4.2 considers parallel algorithms for the static dictionary model and
Section 4.3 considers the sliding dictionary model. Section 4.4 considers the
dynamic dictionary model. Section 4.5 addresses VLSI layout issues that arise
in practical implementations.

4.1. THE COMPUTATIONAL MODEL

We implement our algorithms in VLSI with *systolic arrays*, a model
of parallel computation studied by many authors. The idea is to lay out a
regular pattern of processing elements that have a simple interconnection
structure; idealy, each processing element is connected only to adjacent processing elements. Perhaps the simplest example of a systolic array (and the
only kind we use in this chapter) is a *systolic pipeline*, which we henceforth
refer to as simply a *pipe*. For example, an automobile assembly line may produce a new car every 20 minutes even though each car is in the assembly line
for a day. Although each station in the automobile assembly line performs a
different task, the stations are at least conceptually identical, if we view them
all as taking as input a partially built car, performing an elementary operation (such as welding), and then outputting a partially completed car to the
next station.

For both theoretical and practical reasons, we shall be concerned with the resources consumed by an implementation as a function of the number of processing elements. Note that we shall say that a particular resource bound is $O(1)$ if it is bounded by some constant that is independent of the number of processing elements. From the point of view of VLSI, an "ideal" pipe has the following properties:

- There are $O(1)$ basic processing elements from which the entire array is constructed.

- Each processing element is connected only to its two adjacent neighbors in the pipe.

- The structure can be laid out on the plane using an amount of area that is linear in the number of processing elements.

- All connections between processing elements have length $O(1)$ and thus the time for two adjacent elements to communicate is $O(1)^\dagger$.

- The layout strategy is independent of the number of chips used. A larger pipe can be obtained by placing as many processing elements as possible on a chip and then, using the same layout strategy, placing as many chips as possible on a board.

We have intentionally left out of our definition of a systolic array the specification of what constitutes a "processing element". In principle, an computational device, including a main-frame computer, could be used for a processing element. In practice (and in this chapter), processing elements are usually very simple constructs that have only $O(1)$ local memory (perhaps only a single register) and can perform only simple comparisons and arithmetic operations (perhaps only a single operation). From this point on, we shall refer to a processing element as simply a *processor*. But the reader should remember that they are usually much simpler than a typical small general-purpose computer (which is often associated with the term "processor").

---

† There is no general agreement in the literature as to the right model for the time (as a function of the length of the wire) for a signal to propagate along a "wire" in current VLSI technology. However, it is clear that it becomes a significant factor for large chips.

In contrast to the systolic pipe model of computation, one could simply implement a serial data compression algorithm using, for example, a micro-processor chip with some memory. However, a practical advantage of a pipe implementation is speed, making the resulting data compression chip appropriate for a wider range of applications. In addition, the through-put of a pipe is independent of its size; this property is important from both a practical and theoretical standpoint.

4.2. STATIC DICTIONARY METHOD

This section outlines a basic systolic structure for data compression along a communication channel, using the static dictionary model. Recall from Chapter 3 that given a dictionary, data is compressed by replacing substrings of the data by pointers to matching strings in the dictionary. We do not address the dictionary selection in this chapter, but simply assume that a dictionary is available.

In this section we assume a *two-way* communication channel which consists of two one-way communication lines, one going in each direction. Of course, it is always possible to consider compression in each direction as two separate problems. Our motivation here for explicitly considering a two-way channel is that the algorithms that we shall present for static encoding and decoding can share a common data structure "for free". Figure 4.2.1 depicts the basic situation. There is a a communication channel (with one line going in each direction) and at each end of the channel are identical encoding / decoding modules. At the start of a "session", a dictionary is loaded into the modules. From this point on, data is (transparently) compressed, transmitted, and decoded.

Figure 4.2.2 shows the structure of the array of processors that comprises an encoding / decoding module. It is a pipe with 3 processors for each string in the dictionary[†]. Referring to Figure 4.2.1, Figure 4.2.2 is shown as connected to location A on the left and the communication line on the right. For the remainder of this section, we shall assume that the encoding/decoding array is oriented this way, and we use the terms "left" and "right" as they pertain to Figure 4.2.2. The dictionary entries themselves are stored in the middle row, one dictionary entry per processor.

[†] At least from a conceptual point of view. In practice, these processors may be combined into a single circuit.

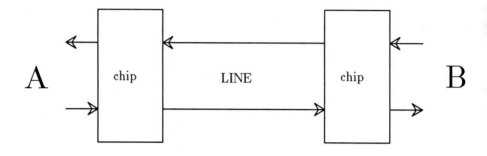

Figure 4.2.1

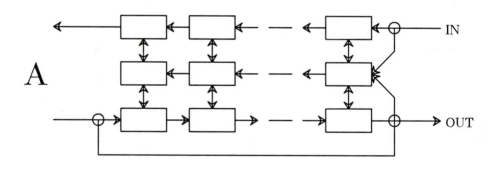

Figure 4.2.2

Pointers within dictionary entries will always point to a dictionary entry (or possibly a substring of a dictionary entry) to the left. Data to be encoded enters from the left, is piped along the bottom row, and encoded as it progresses. Data to be decoded enters from the right, is piped along the top row, and decoded as it progresses. The dictionary may be loaded by either location A or location B sending a control sequence to divert data from the normal path into the dictionary. The circle next to the transmitter for location A indicates a switch to divert data via the bypass line, to the dictionary, and to the output (to the dictionary for location B).

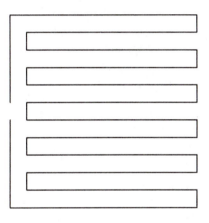

Figure 4.2.3

One advantage of the structure in Figure 4.2.2 is that any number of these can be combined to produce a larger one[†]. Another advantage, both practical and theoretical, is that the array can be laid out so that all connections have length $O(1)$. In Figure 4.2.2, the only edge whose size depends on the length of the pipe is the bypass line. If Figure 4.2.2, less the bypass line, is "folded" as depicted in Figure 4.2.3 (an $O(n)$-node pipe goes to an $O(\sqrt{n})$ by $O(\sqrt{n})$ rectangular region), then the entrance and exit of the structure are

---

† That is, they can be chained together end to end. A technical point: the bypass line would have to be modified to go from the lead chip to the end chip.

next to each other, and a fixed length bypass line can be placed. Thus, from the standpoint of VLSI layout, the array structure depicted by Figure 4.2.2 (and modified as depicted by Figure 4.2.3) is quite desirable:

- There are 3 types of processors from which the entire array is constructed.

- Each processor is connected only to its nearest neighbors in the pipe (except the bypass line).

- The structure has a linear area layout.

- All edges (including the bypass line) have length $O(1)$.

- The layout strategy is independent of the number of chips used.

A nice aspect of the systolic implementation to be presented is that the following generalizations of the basic static dictionary model come "for free":

- Dictionary entries themselves may contain pointers to other entries which in turn may contain pointers, and so on (recall that all pointers must point to the left); so decoding a pointer may involve several dictionary lookups. We refer to the string represented by a pointer, after all such lookups have been performed, as the *expanded target* of that pointer. Pointers in dictionary entries can reduce the space for the dictionary, but the major reason for such pointers is that they allow for the representation of strings longer that the maximum length of a dictionary entry. As we shall see, the ability to reduce the maximum size of a dictionary entry can reduce the size of the VLSI implementation.

- A pointer may point to a substring of a dictionary entry. From a theoretical point of view, the model of Chapter 3 is all that is really needed. The ability to point to substrings can be modeled by simply adding those substrings to the dictionary; that is, the extra bits per pointer that are needed to specify the start and end of a substring can be used instead to point to a larger number of entries. Compression will always be as good or better with this method. However, practical constraints on both the size of an individual processor and the total size of the pipe may be optimized for a particular application by having fewer dictionary entries that may referenced in a more complex way. For example, to allow pointers to indicate any suffix of a dictionary entry, we can let a pointer with integer value i denote the string consisting of the ith character of the dictionary (i.e., the ith character in the string that is the concatenation of all of the dictionary enties) through the end of the dictionary entry containing the ith character.

- Variable size pointers. As discussed in Chapter 3, variable size pointers may be of marginal advantage in practice. However, the implementation to be presented can handle this generality with no significant increase in the size of an individual processor. In addition, for situations where substrings of dictionary entries may be pointer targets, variable size pointers may be useful for encoding substring information.

To discuss more precisely the size and workings of an individual processor (which may include one or more of the generalizations above), for the remainder of this chapter we use the following notation:

b = Number of bits per character.
ρ = Minimum size of a pointer, in units of characters ($\rho > 0$).
p = Maximum size of a pointer, in units of characters ($p \geq \rho$).
d = Maximum length of a dictionary entry, in units of characters.

By using characters as the units for ρ and p, we are restricting the number of bits in a pointer to be an integer multiple of b. None of what we do requires this restriction, but it simplifies our discussion. In particular, a pointer can be viewed as a sequence of *pseudo-characters*, each b bits long. We define an *item* to be either a character or a pseudo-character. Given this definition, a compressed form is simply a sequence of items. For a string S of items, $|S|$ denotes its length (in units of b). If q is a pointer to a target t, it is always assumed that $|q| < |t|$.

Example 4.2.1: Consider a dictionary of $2^{12} = 4096$ entries of at most 8 characters ($d=8$). The input to the encoder is a sequence of 8-bit character codes ($b=8$). The output is a sequence of 8 or 16 bit pointers ($p=2$). A pointer is either a 1 followed by a 7-bit integer pointing to entries 0 through 127 of the dictionary or a 0 followed by a 15-bit integer i pointing to the ith character of the dictionary (where $0 \leq i \leq 2^{15}-1$); that is, long pointers can point to any suffix of any entry. Every character of the source is itself an entry of the dictionary. For example, for English text, the characters "a" through "z" along with common strings such as " the" might be in the first

128 dictionary entries while less common characters such as "#" and less common words such as "aardvark" might be in the locations numbered 128 or greater. ○

Static Decoding

We now present a systolic algorithm for decoding using the static dictionary model; that is, the algorithm to be used by each processor along the top row in Figure 4.2.2. For a given one of these decoding processors, we refer to the corresponding dictionary entry as *dictentry*. The representation of a pointer is not important[†]; we assume only that a pointer uniquely specifies a substring of a dictionary entry (which itself may contain pointers). In addition, there must be some way to distinguish the item starting a pointer from a character, and given the start of a pointer in a stream of items, it must be possible to determine where it ends. It could be, as in Example 4.2.1, that the input stream can contain only pointers (and distinguishing the start of a pointer from a character is a moot question), and in this case, there is a minor technical problem of how to distinguish decoded characters from pointers. This problem is easily handled by, for each input item of b bits, adding an extra bit, initially 0. When characters are substituted for pointers, they are coded as 1 followed by the character; the 1's can be stripped off as the characters leave the decoding pipe. In any case, we henceforth assume that characters (whether part of the input stream or produced while decoding) are always distinguishable from the first item of a pointer, and we make no more mention of these details.

Algorithm 4.2.1 is the basic decoding algorithm for a processor, less the initialization of variables. Each decoding element has a buffer with $p+1$ *cells*, each capable of holding an item. The buffer behaves like a queue, where items enter from the right and leave to the left. We assume two global alternating time intervals called *pulse*1 and *pulse*2. During *pulse*1, the algorithm does the following: First, the contents of the buffer is shifted as far as possible to the left (so that all empty locations are at the right of the buffer). The (local) variable *count* is used to keep track of how much of a pointer has been transmitted. The second step checks if $count=0$ and if there is a complete pointer starting at the left of the buffer. The test $count=0$ insures that if the

---

[†] At least not from a theoretical point of view. The exact representation of a pointer may affect the size of an individual processor by an amount that is significant in practice.

during *pulse*1 **do begin**

    shift buffer to the left (so all empty cells are at the right).

    if (*count*=0 and leftmost item starts a complete pointer *q*)
        then if (*q* points to a substring of *dictentry*)
            then begin
                last = <index of last item of target>
                count = <length of target>
                remove *q* from buffer
            end
          else *count* = − <length of *q*>

    if (buffer has $\geq p$ items and *nextlock*=1 or *count*>0)
        then *lock*=1
        else *lock*=0

end

during *pulse*2 **do begin**

    if (buffer not empty and *nextlock*=0) **then begin**

        if (*count*>0) **then begin**
            count = *count*−1
            transmit the *last*−*count*+1 item of *dictentry*
        end

        else if (*count*<0) **then begin**
            count = *count*+1
            transmit leftmost item
        end

        else if (leftmost item a character) **then transmit** it

    end

    end

Algorithm 4.2.1
Static Processor Decoding Algorithm

leftmost item in the buffer is part of a pointer, then it is the beginning of the pointer. That is, we want to determine the cell containing the end of the pointer, and it may not be possible to make this determination when starting from a cell in the middle of the pointer. Given that $count=0$ and a complete pointer is leftmost in the buffer, there are two possibilities, either the pointer points to a substring of *dictentry* or it is some other pointer. The variable *count* is used differently depending on which of these cases holds. In the first case, *count* is set to the length of the target of the pointer (and the variable *last* is set to the index of its last item), the pointer is deleted, and *count* will be used to count down as the target is transmitted one character at a time. In the second case, *count* is set to minus the length of this pointer and will be used to count up as this pointer is passed down the pipe one item at a time. Thus, the first two cases can be distinguished by testing the sign of *count*[†]. The third and final step of *pulse*1 is to prevent buffer overflow. The problem is that, as we transmit a target of a pointer that was deleted from the buffer, more characters could be coming into the buffer (which has only $p+1$ cells) from the right. To take care of this problem, the decoding processor has a (local) variable *lock* (initially set to 0) which, when set to 1, has the purpose of blocking new characters from entering on the right. The decoding processor is capable of reading the value of *lock* for the processor after it (to the left) in the pipe; we refer to this value as *nextlock*. The last step of *pulse*1 sets *lock*=1 only if the buffer contains p items and either *nextlock*=1 or $count>0$ ($count>0$ means that characters will be transmitted from *dictentry*, not from the buffer). Propagation of *lock*=1 (possibly to the pipe entrance) is an issue that will be discussed shortly.

*Pulse*2 is when characters are transmitted from one processor to another along the decoding pipe. An element transmits at most one item during *pulse*2, and only if *nextlock*=0. Given that *nextlock*=0, there are three cases: First, if $count>0$, then we are part way through transmitting a target from *dictentry*, so we decrement *count* and transmit the appropriate character of *dictentry*. In the second case, $count<0$, so we must be in the process of transmitting the items comprising a pointer (but not a pointer to a substring of *dictentry*), and we increment *count* and transmit the leftmost item of the buffer. The only two possibilities left are that the leftmost cell contains the start of a pointer (but not all the items comprising it are in the buffer yet) or the leftmost cell contains a character. *Phase*2 transmits the leftmost item only if the second possibility holds; it is always possible to distinguish these

---

[†] This sign checking method has been used primarily for convenience. Alternately, *count* could be positive in the second case and a bit could be set to distinguish between these two cases.

two possibilities since an item that is the start of a pointer is always distinguishable from a character (as discussed at the start of this section).

A difficulty with Algorithm 4.2.1 concerns the locking to prevent buffer overflow. The locking works properly since when a buffer contains p items, at most one more item is received before the processor preceding it in the decoding pipe detects that $lock=1$. However, in theory, $lock=1$ could propagate arbitrary distances up the pipe (propagating at most a distance i after i cycles of $pulse1$ and $pulse2$), causing a problem if it should ever reach the entrance to the pipe. Such a global propagation is clearly unavoidable if no assumptions are made concerning the data rate into the decoding circuit versus the amount of decompression that takes place.

In practice, average compression is bounded above by a constant factor. For example, in Chapter 1 we saw that the information content of printed English is slightly over 1 bit per character, which for 8-bit character codes, would bound average compression obtainable for English text by a factor of 8 (although it is unlikely that even this much compression for English text could ever be obtained in practice). It is also typically the case in practice that large deviations from the average compression do not account for a significant portion of the savings achieved. That is, if for the times that it is possible to find a very large match we replace it by two or more smaller matches, then the overall compression is not changed significantly. For example, with the code of Appendix A.8 that was discussed in Chapter 3, if *maxmatch* is set to 16 instead of its default of 100 (which was used for the experimental results) then none of the experimental results reported in the appendix for the dynamic dictionary method are affected by more than 1 percent[†]. Similar observations apply to the experiments reported for the static dictionary and sliding dictionary methods (for the sliding dictionary method, the maximum match length is an explicit parameter in the tables presented in the appendix).

For the static dictionary model, we shall henceforth assume that for a sufficiently large constant l, there is no significant loss of average compression to let:

$$l = \text{Maximum length of an expanded target.}$$

---

† It is interesting to note that decreasing *maxmatch* from its default of 100 down to 16 sometimes improves compression for the sample files considered in the appendix (but not significantly).

Given l, the maximum compression ratio is l/ρ. We also define the two parameters:

> r = Rate of communication channel; i.e. the minimum time between successive characters of input to the decoding circuit.

> s = Speed of decoding circuit; i.e. time for one cycle of $pulse1$ and $pulse2$.

Given the parameters l, ρ, r, and s, we make the basic assumption that the data rate of the communication channel is sufficiently slower than the speed of the chip so that the maximum compression ratio is less than the ratio of r to s:

$$\frac{l}{\rho} < \frac{r}{s}$$

The following theorem shows that this assumption guarantees that the entrance to the pipe can never be held up. The parameter pr/s can be given to a dictionary construction algorithm as a maximum value for l.

Definition 4.2.1: A compressed form S is *blocking* if there exists a dictionary (and corresponding circuit)[†] such that when S is input to the decoding pipe, at some point the first processor of the pipe sets $lock=1$ at a time when an item of S is arriving to the pipe. ○

Theorem 4.2.1: Given that $l/\rho < r/s$, no compressed form can be blocking.

Proof: Before proceeding, we observe that for the purposes of this proof, Algorithm 4.2.1 can be modified by adding the condition

(buffer has $\geq p$ items)

to the first **if** of $pulse1$ and to the last **if** of $pulse2$. This modification does not change the correctness of the algorithm[††] but does insure that every item

---

[†] That is, for some n, there is some dictionary of n elements that can be assigned to a pipe structure (of the type of Figure 2) of length n, subject to the constraints b, p, and d.

[††] There is a minor problem of how to flush out the pipe when the input ends or is suspended. This is irrelevant here, since we will be assuming that the input is blocking.

effectively moves through the pipe one buffer cell at a time[†]. Also, it is clear that if S is blocking using Algorithm 4.2.1, then it is also blocking with Algorithm 4.2.1 modified as described above.

Now, let us assume the contrary to this theorem; that is, assume that S is a shortest blocking compressed form. It must be that S starts with a pointer, since a leading character could never hold up the pipe (and we could delete it to get a shorter blocking compressed form). Thus

$$S = qT$$

where q is a pointer and T a compressed form.

For the remainder of this proof we measure time in units of s[††]. Hence we have:

$$r > l/\rho$$

This inequality insures that an item of S enters the decoding pipe at most once every l/ρ time units. We write q as:

$$q = q_1, \ldots, q_k$$

where the q_i's are items and $\rho \leq k \leq p$. Now imagine a "tag" attached to q_k; we call it $tag1$. The purpose of $tag1$ is to mark the rightmost item generated by q. Although $tag1$ is initially attached to q_k, when q is replaced by its target, $tag1$ moves to the rightmost symbol of the target; and if the rightmost item of the target is part of a pointer, then $tag1$ is moved again when this pointer is expanded, and so on.

A key observation is that $tag1$ must move forward 1 buffer cell at all but at most $l - |q|$ time units. To see this, note that $tag1$ moves forward every time unit except when a pointer is being replaced, and each replacement of a pointer x by a target y adds an effective delay of $|y| - |x|$. Hence, since the expanded target of q has length at most l, the delay is at most $l - |q|$.

---

† Actually, even with this modification, an item can skip over the $p+1^{th}$ cell of the buffer, but we will be concerned only with the leftmost p cells in a buffer.
†† We assume each "tick" of the clock coincides exactly with the start of $pulse1$.

We now consider the first ρ items of T, which we refer to as $i_1,..,i_\rho$. Note that since all pointer must have length at least ρ, i_ρ is the first item in T that could be the rightmost item in a pointer. Since $l < r\rho$, i_ρ enters the pipe at least l time units behind q_k. We attach $tag2$ to i_ρ as it enters the pipe. If i_ρ is a character, then $tag2$ simply moves with i_ρ as it progresses through the pipe. If i_ρ is an item that is part (or all) of a pointer, then when this pointer is first replaced by a target, $tag2$ then begins to move like $tag1$ but marks the leftmost item generated by the pointer containing i_ρ, so that whenever a pointer is replaced, $tag2$ goes to the left of the target.

The second key observation is that $tag2$ can never catch up to $tag1$. This is because $tag1$ and $tag2$ both move forward one buffer cell each time unit with two exceptions. The first is when $tag1$ is held up due to pointer replacement, which accounts for a total delay of at most $l-|q|$. The second occurs only if i_ρ is combined with adjacent items to form a pointer, in which case $tag2$ jumps to the left a distance of at most $|\rho| \leq |q|$. Since q_k enters the pipe l time units ahead of i_ρ, this second observation follows.

Thus, q can have no effect on how T travels through the pipe, and so T is a shorter blocking compressed form than S, a contradiction. $\bigcirc$

Before leaving the subject of the static dictionary decoding algorithm, we digress with a few comments concerning our presentation of Algorithm 4.2.1. It is clear from inspection of Algorithm 4.2.1 that its implementation in VLSI requires a constant amount of area that is independent of the number of processors (but this constant may depend on the values of b, ρ, p, and d). For the purposes of this chapter, which is concerned with the global operation and layout of the pipe, the fact that such a constant exists is all that we need to know. Algorithm 4.2.1 has been written only for the purposes of presentation and does not reflect a particular VLSI implementation. In practice, to achieve the best possible VLSI implementation of an individual processor requires "fine tuning" of a host of details such as the exact choice of the parameters b, ρ, p, d, the coding of pointers, the implementation of the sequencing implied by the local variables $count$ and $last$, and so forth.

Static Encoding

during *pulse*1 **do begin**

>   **if** (buffer full and a suffix matches a legal substring of *dictentry*)
>   **then begin**
>   Let s be the longest such suffix and q a pointer to s
>   and if $|q| < |s|$, replace suffix s of the buffer by q.
>   **end**

>   **shift** right the items in buffer (so that all empty cells are at the left).

>   **end**

during *pulse*2 **do begin**

>   **if** (buffer full) **then transmit** rightmost item.

>   **end**

Algorithm 4.2.2
Static Processor Encoding Algorithm

We now consider the construction of the encoding pipe. Algorithm 4.2.2 is the encoding algorithm. Each encoding processor has a buffer capable of holding d items. Like the buffers used by the decoding processors, the buffer behaves like a queue; however, the it goes in the reverse direction; that is items enter from the left and leave to the right. During *pulse*1, if the largest match between a suffix of the buffer and a legal substring of *dictentry*[†] is

---

[†] What constitutes a legal substring depends on the implementation of pointers that is being used. For example, it could be that the only legal substring is the entire entry (as with the pure algorithm of Chapter 3) or that the legal substrings are the set of all suffixes (as with Example 4.2.1).

bigger than a pointer to the dictionary substring, then it is replaced by the pointer. After this replacement, the characters in the buffer are shifted to the right as far as possible (so that all empty space is to the left in the buffer). During *pulse2*, the rightmost item is transmitted only if the buffer is full; this condition insures that the largest match possible is found. A few details have been left out; in particular, how to "flush out" the pipe when the input stream ends or slows down.

Example 4.2.2: For this example, let us assume that the source consists only of the characters a through z, A through Z, and punctuation, and that pointers are represented by two digit numbers. We make this assumption and use this code to ensure that compressed forms are "readable"; this code would not be used in practice since it has only 100 different pointers of length (exactly) 2 characters (whereas pairs of 8-bit character codes should be able to represent up to 2^{16} different targets). Suppose that we wish to point to any suffix of a dictionary entry, where the dictionary consists of entries of maximum length 8 characters, organized as follows:

```
00  -  07 :  '  p r o g r a m '
08  -  15 :  '  e x t r e m e '
16  -  21 :  '  l a r g e '
22  -  26 :  '  s ome '
27  -  30 :  '  a r e '
31  -  38 :  '  ALGOL00 '      ( '  ALGOL  p r o g r am ' )
39  -  44 :  ' 08 l y 16 '     ( '  e x t r eme l y  l a r g e ' )
45  -  48 :  ' 27 39 '         ( '  a r e  e x t r eme l y  l a r g e ' )
```

Then the sentence "Some ALGOL programs are extremely large." would be transformed by Algorithm 4.2.2 as follows:

```
Some  ALGOL  p r o g r ams  a r e  e x t r eme l y  l a r g e .
Some  ALGOL00 s  a r e  e x t r eme l y  l a r g e .
S 24  ALGOL00 s  a r e  e x t r eme l y  l a r g e .
S 24  ALGOL00 s  a r e 08 l y  l a r g e .
S 24  ALGOL00 s  a r e 08 l y 16 .
S 2431 s  a r e 08 l y 16 .
S 2431 s 2708 l y 16 .
S 2431 s 2739 .
S 2431 s 45 .                                                    ◯
```

Something not discussed thus far is the ordering of dictionary entries. Clearly, if dictionary entry j contains a pointer to a substring of entry i, then it must be that $i < j$; that is, entry i appears earlier that entry j in the pipe. However, beyond this condition, Algorithm 4.2.2 is compatible with Algorithm 4.2.1 for any ordering of the dictionary entries that satisfies this constraint. If we do not allow the generalizations of the static dictionary model introduced in this chapter (pointers within dictionary entries, the ability to point to substrings of an entry, and variable size pointers), then the simple greedy heuristic for parsing the input of the static dictionary model presented in Chapter 3 can be modeled by ordering the entries from largest to smallest. Note that from a theoretical point of view, even with this ordering, the output of Algorithm 4.2.2 could be different from a "pure" version of the greedy heuristic because matches are not necessarily discovered in left to right order. In fact, it is possible that the systolic algorithm could do better. For example, suppose the strings of length ≥ 2 in the dictionary were:

cdefghi
abc
def
ghi
ab

Then Algorithm 4.2.2 would parse the string *abcdefghi* as *ab,cdefghi* and produce an output consisting of two pointers; whereas the static dictionary algorithm of Chapter 3 would produce the parse *abc,def,ghi* for a total of three pointers. It is also possible to construct examples where Algorithm 4.2.2 does worse. Issues such as this one are theoretically interesting (and will be discussed further in Chapter 5) but from a practical standpoint, Algorithm 4.2.2 with the dictionary entries ordered from largest to smallest performs nearly identically to the true static greedy heuristic. Even if generalizations of pointers that have been considered here are allowed, simply strategies for ordering the dictionary work well in practice. For example, if pointer within dictionary entries are allowed, then a topological sort of the pointer dependencies can first be performed[†] and then entries for which the order doesn't matter can be ordered from largest to smallest. We shall not consider this issue further in this section. However, related parsing issues will be considered later in this chapter when we discuss how to implement the static dictionary method and other methods with a number of processors that is less than the

---

† A topological sort orders the dictionary entries so that if entry j contains a pointer to entry i, then $i < j$. A topological sort can be performed in linear time; see the bibliographic notes.

number of dictionary entries.

To accommodate the generalizations of the static dictionary model that were introduced in this chapter, some further modification of the largest to smallest ordering are necessary. If variable size pointers are allowed, then the ordering should be from largest difference between pointer size and target length to smallest difference. If pointers within dictionary entries are allowed, then for the purposes of ordering the dictionary, the length of a dictionary entry should be taken as its expanded length.

4.3. SLIDING DICTIONARY METHOD

Recall from Chapter 3 that with the sliding dictionary method, if S is a string, then a compressed form of S is a string of items T such that pointers in T indicate substrings of S, and S can be obtained by expanding the pointers of T from left to right. We refer to the last n characters of the input stream as the *sliding dictionary* and use the following notation:

p = Pointer size, in units of characters $(p \geq 1)$.
n = Length of the sliding dictionary, in units of characters.

As in the preceding section, the exact representation of a pointer is not important; we only assume that it is possible to distinguish pointers from characters. However unlike the preceding section, in order to simplify our presentation, we shall assume that all pointers have size exactly p (although what is to be presented can be easily generalized to accommodate variable size pointers). As done in Chapter 3 we use the notation (x,y) to denote a pointer at location x with target of length y; however, to further simplify our presentation, x will denote that distance from the start of the sliding window rather than the distance back from the pointer as was the convention in Chapter 3. Note that for most of the discussion to follow which meaning of x is used is irrelevant; for the few places that it is, it is trivial to translate between these two meanings for x and that all that is to be presented could be so modified.

The previous section considered a two-way communication channel. We now return to the simpler model of a single communication line. We shall use some examples with English phrases. Since English is written from left to right, to make these examples readable, we will henceforth assume (unlike some of the preceding portions of this book) that the sender is on the right and the receiver on the left, so that data that flows along the communication line will have earlier characters to the left of later characters. That is, raw data enters the encoder from the sender on the right and leaves to the communication line on the left. Similarly, compressed data enters the decoder from the communication line on the right and leaves to the receiver on the left.

Slide Encoding

This section develops several systolic implementations for encoding with the sliding dictionary model. We store the last n characters processed (the sliding dictionary) in a pipe (one character per processor). The dictionary is updated by sliding old characters left in order to bring in new ones. We can think of this dictionary as a window of width n which is sliding through the input stream. As new characters are read in, we compare them with each of the dictionary entries (the substrings of the preceding n characters) We attach a pair of values [location,length] to each character that indicate the location and length of the longest substring of the dictionary that matches a portion of the input that starts with this character (when the character gets shifted from processor to processor, its [location,length] information accompanies it). The [location,length] information is updated any time a longer match is found. After a character has passed over the n characters preceding it, its [location,length] information is examined to decide whether data compression should take place.

Since the dictionary needs to be constantly updated so that each character can be compared to exactly the n characters preceding it, our implementation uses a pipe of $2n$ processors; that is, instead of just storing the last n characters, we will store the last $2n$ characters, as depicted in Figure 4.3.1a. The top row will serve as the dictionary, consisting of processors numbered 1 through $2n$, from right to left. The bottom row will contain the characters being processed. Each character will be processed by the processor directly above it. Two different kinds of timing pulses will be used, called *pulse*1 and *pulse*2. After every n *pulse*1's a *pulse*2 will occur. Each processor has a counter which tells the processor how many *pulse*1's have occurred since the last *pulse*2. The comparisons are done in blocks of n characters at a time. While these characters are processed, new characters are read in, and characters that have already been processed are transmitted (or pointers to them if compression took place).

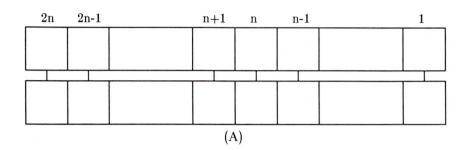

(A)

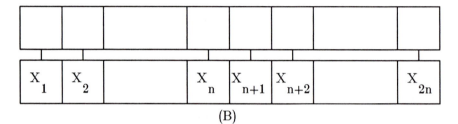

(B)

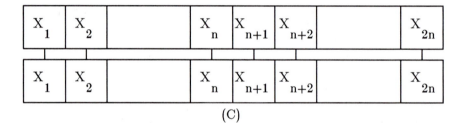

(C)

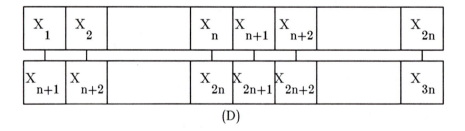

(D)

Figure 4.3.1

We begin with an informal explanation of how the algorithm works. Suppose that characters $x_1, \cdots, x_n$ have already been processed, and while these characters were being processed $x_{n+1}, \cdots, x_{2n}$ were read in. Figure 4.3.1b shows what this situation would look like. Since we have just finished processing a block of n characters, a $pulse2$ would occur. On a $pulse2$, every processor will copy the character below it into some local memory location, call it $char$ (top row of Figure 4.3.1c). Note that we want to compare x_{n+i} with x_i through x_{n+i-1}, which correspond to the n characters preceding x_{n+i}; After a $pulse1$ takes place, all characters are shifted, the leftmost character (or a pointer) is transmitted, the block $x_{n+1}, \cdots, x_{2n}$ is involved in the comparisons, and a new character is read. After the n $pulse1$'s, we have the configuration of Figure 4.3.1d, and a $pulse2$ will occur. This pulse will tell each processor to copy the character below into $char$, and the algorithm is then repeated.

We have not discussed how to obtain the information $[location,length]$ which is attached to each character. This information must be updated after each comparison. We shall present two updating schemes; but for the moment, to simplify the presentation, we are presenting the systolic algorithm without any provisions to update the $[location,length]$ information.

Not all processors do the same thing all the time. For example, Processor 2 will make a comparison right after the first $pulse1$, but after the next $pulse1$'s, it will only be reading characters. For this reason, every processor needs to keep a count of the number of $pulse1$'s. Each processor also needs to know where in the pipe it is located, and so a processor number is assigned to each one. For example, suppose we were starting out with the situation shown in Figure 4.3.1b, and suppose that processor i is in the right half of the pipe ($i \leq n$). Then processor i will process x_{2n} at the $(i-1)^{th}$ $pulse1$. Since x_{2n} is the last character of the block that is being processed, we know that processor i need not make any more comparisons. Similarly, suppose that processor j is in the left half of the pipe ($j > n$). Then x_{n+1} will not reach processor j until the $j-n^{th}$ $pulse1$. For example, if $j=n+2$ then x_{n+1}, will reach this processor at the second $pulse1$. Thus, processor j does not need to make any comparisons until the $j-n^{th}$ $pulse1$.

The leftmost processor (processor $2n$) has the additional special function of deciding what gets transmitted. At $pulse1$, it looks at the $[location,length]$ information of the character it is processing. If $length \leq p$, then it transmits the character. If $length > p$, then it transmits the first character of the pointer ($location,length$). In addition, it sets the local memory lo-

cation *buffercount* to *length*−1, (*buffercount* is initially 0), and places the
remaining $p-1$ characters of the pointer in a local buffer. On the next successive $p-1$ pipe shifts, *buffercount* is decremented, and the character coming
from the right in the pipe is ignored, and instead, the next character of the
buffer is transmitted. On the following successive pipe shifts (until
buffercount becomes 0), *buffercount* is decremented, the character coming
from the right is ignored, and nothing is transmitted. Once *buffercount*
equals zero, this processor will begin transmitting again.

   Algorithm 4.3.1 is the encoding algorithm, less the facility to update
the [*location,length*] information. We now present two schemes updating this
information; that is, an implementation for the procedure *UPDATE* of Algorithm 4.3.1.

   SCHEME 1: We build a binary tree of processors where the leaves are
the processors of the sliding dictionary. For simplicity, we assume that n is a
power of 2. The algorithm works as follows. After each comparison, each
leaf processor for which *char* matched the character below checks to see if it is
at the start or at the end of a match. If the processor at its left did not
match, then this processor sends a left bracket ("[") to its parent processor in
the binary tree. Similarly, if the processor at its right did not match, then it
sends a right bracket ("]") to its parent processor. These left and right
brackets (along with the corresponding processor numbers) are sent up in the
tree until some processor is able to pair them up, calculate the length of the
matching string, and then return this value down the tree to the processor
that sent the left bracket (i.e., to the processor currently processing the first
character of the matching string). This processor will then update the information [*location,length*] information if the length of this matching string is
greater than the current *length* value. If the value is not greater, then it must
be that there exists some other longer string starting with this character that
matched. If the value is greater, then we update by writing the length of this
matching string and by writing this processor number as the location.

   Figure 4.3.2 illustrates an example. The possible inputs to a processor in the binary tree (excluding the leaves) are listed in Figure 4.3.3. If we
were to read the brackets of the sliding dictionary from left to right, we
would find a sequence of the form [][][]...[]. Hence, a processor in the binary
tree will not receive as input two consecutive ['s or]'s, and so the only possible inputs are the ones shown above. Thus, every processor can receive at
most four brackets as input, and can send at most two brackets as output.

during *pulse*1 **do begin**

    if $(processor\# = 2n)$ **then begin**
        if $(buffercount=0)$
            then if $(length \leq p)$
                then transmit character
                else begin
                    transmit first character of the pointer
                    $(location, length)$ and put the remaining
                    characters in a local buffer
                    $buffercount = length - 1$
                end
            else begin
                if (buffer not empty) transmit next char
                $buffercount = buffercount - 1$
                end (*)
        end

    if $(processor\# = 1)$
        then read character from input stream
        else read character from processor to right

    $pulse1count = pulse1count + 1$

    if $(pulse1count < processor\# \leq pulse1count + n)$
        then UPDATE$([location, length])$

    end

during *pulse*2 **do begin**
    Copy character below into *char*
    $pulse1count = 0$
    end

Algorithm 4.3.1
Slide Encoding Algorithm (less UPDATE procedure)

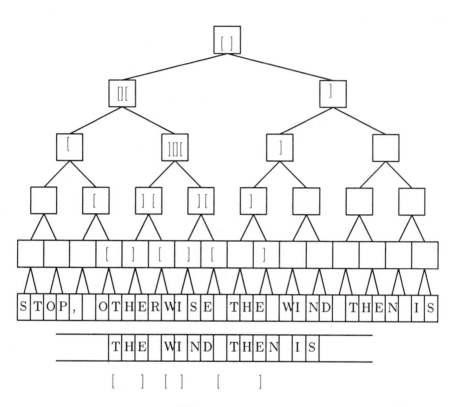

Figure 4.3.2

INPUT   ACTION

1. Nothing   None
2. [Send [to parent
3.]   Send] to parent
4.][Send][to parent
5. []   Compute length and send to processor that sent it
6. [][Handle first two as in 5 and send other [to parent
7.][]   Send first] to parent and handle last two as in 5
8.][][Send first and last to parent and handle as in 5.

Figure 4.3.3

case of brackets received **begin**

    [: **begin**

          send [to parent

          wait = *true*

          end

    ]: send] to parent

    ][: **begin**

          send][to parent

          wait = *true*

          end

    []: **begin**

          newlength = (processor # of [)-(processor # of])+1

          send *newlength* to child which sent the [

          end

    [][: **begin**

          handle [] as is done for case []

          send [to parent

          wait = *true*

          end

    ][]: **begin**

          send] to parent

          handle [] as is done for case []

          end

    ][][: **begin**

          send][to parent

          handle [] as is done for case []

          wait = *true*

          end

    end

if (*wait*=*true*) **then begin**

    wait for parent to transmit *newlength*

    transmit *newlength* to child that sent the [

    wait = *false*

    end

Algorithm 4.3.2
Update Scheme 1 (algorithm for tree processors)

if ($curchar{=}char$) **then begin**

      if (left processor didn't match and right processor did match) **then begin**
          Send to parent processor (processor#, [])
          Wait for parent to respond with *newlength*
          if ($newlength{>}length$) **then begin**
              $length\ =\ newlength$
              $location\ =$ processor#
              end
      end

      if (left processor did match and right processor didn't match)
          then send to parent (processor #,])

    end

Algorithm 4.3.3
(update scheme 1: algorithm for dictionary entries)

if ($length{>}buffercount$ and
        $length{-}1\ >$ (*length* attached to character to right)) **then begin**

    (*length* attached to character to right) $=\ length{-}1$

    (*location* attached to character to right) $=\ location{-}1$

    end

Algorithm 4.3.4
(scheme 1 modification to handle overlapping pointers)

Algorithm 4.3.2 is the algorithm used by the processors of the tree and Algorithm 4.3.3 is the procedure *UPDATE* to be used by Algorithm 4.3.1 to implement Scheme 1. In Algorithm 4.3.3, *curchar* denotes the current character below this processor in the pipe (so the test *curchar=char* checks if this processor has a match). In Algorithm 4.3.2, it is assumed that the processor number is passed along with the bracket.

As we can observe from Algorithm 4.3.2, only the first character of the matching string knows the length of this string. This limitation could be a problem when overlapping pointers can occur. For example, suppose that the input currently being processed is *bcdefgh* and suppose that *bcd* matched at location *i* of the dictionary, and suppose that *defgh* matched at location *j* of the dictionary. In this case, *b* has [*i*,3] and *d* has [*j*,5], but the other characters do not have any information about these matches. So, if *bcd* were compressed, we would like character *e* to know that *efgh* matched at location *j*−1 of the dictionary. In other words, if *e* does not have a match longer than 4, we would like to update by making it [*j*−1,4]. Processor 2*n* (the leftmost processor) can take care of this update. Referring to Algorithm 4.3.1, recall that *buffercount* contains the number of characters that remain to be "ignored" because they are part of the pointer that was last transmitted. Suppose a character *x* is part of the pointer last transmitted, so when it reaches processor 2*n*, *buffercount*≠0. If the value *length* of is greater than *buffercount*, then there are some characters from the matching string represented that are not part of the pointer last transmitted. In this case, its information is transmitted to the character on the right. Hence, to modify the algorithm all we have to do is to execute Algorithm 4.3.4 whenever statement (*) is executed in Algorithm 4.3.1.

Algorithms 4.3.3 and 4.3.2 work by attaching a binary tree to the encoding pipe. This structure violates the basic notion of a systolic array in two ways. Both violations may not be a problem in practice, but at the very least have theoretical significance. The first violation of the systolic model it is that there is a $O(log(n))$ time delay between pipe shifts (for brackets to propagate up and down the tree). The second violation concerns layout. The next section shows the layout of such a structure on a $O(\sqrt{n})$ by $O(\sqrt{n})$ grid so that pipe edges have length bounded above by a constant (independent of *n*) and contain no bends. Unfortunately, as discussed in the next section, it is unavoidable that at least some of the tree edges have long lengths. Scheme 2, to be presented next, eliminates long edges, but introduces a longer logical delay.

SCHEME 2: This scheme requires two additional special pulses: *pulse*3 and *pulse*4. After every pipe shift, there are $2\sqrt{n}$ *pulse*3's followed by $\sqrt{n}$ *pulse*4's. We first describe how the *pulse*3's are used.

The purpose of *pulse*3's is to signal each processor to pass information to the processor on the left about the consecutive matches starting with itself. For instance, suppose that processors i through $i-3$ matched. Then on the first *pulse*3, processor i knows that processor $i-1$ matched, processor $i-1$ knows that processor $i-2$ matched, and processor $i-3$ knows that processor $i-4$ did not match. Since each processor now knows about the processor that follows it, it can now transmit this information on the next *pulse*3. So, after k pulses, each processor can know the number of consecutive matches of length less than or equal to k, starting with itself. We will require each processor to have a memory location, call it *sum*3, where it will count the number of consecutive matches. First, if the processor matched, it will set *sum*3=1. At the first *pulse*3, it will transmit a 1 to the left indicating that it matched. It will also receive information from the right telling if processor to the right matched or not. If it receives a 1, it will increment *sum*3. At the next *pulse*3 it will again transmit a 1, because it last received a 1. This process is repeated until it receives a 0 (non-match), in which case it updates [*location,length*] to [Processor #,*sum*3] if *sum*3>*length* (*sum*3>*length* if this current match is longer than any other encountered). In addition, *sum*3 is set to 0. From then on, it will transmit a 0 to the left and *sum*3 will remain 0 regardless of what information may be received.

We now describe how the *pulse*4's are used. Assume that the pipe is laid out in a simple snake fashion as depicted in Figure 4.3.4. The *pulse*4's are used to transmit the information gathered by the *pulse*3's along vertical wires (not shown) that run up every column of processors. Figure 4.3.4. The treatment of the *pulse*4's is similar to that of the *pulse*3's. As with *pulse*3, we will assume that the processors in row 1 will at *pulse*4 receive 0 indicating 0 more characters matched, and the processors in row $2\sqrt{n}$ will not transmit anything. Each processor has an additional memory location, *sum*4, to count the number of consecutive matches. After all the *pulse*3's, each processor knows how far back it matched (up to $2\sqrt{n}$), and the value of *sum*3 is copied into *sum*4. If *sum*4=$2\sqrt{n}$ at the end of the *pulse*3's, then it is possible that the string that matched is longer. Suppose that processor i has value *sum*4 = $2\sqrt{n}$. Notice that processor $i-2\sqrt{n}$ is exactly two rows above it, and processor $i-4\sqrt{n}$ is two rows above processor $i-2\sqrt{n}$, and so on. Therefore, the *pulse*4's that processor i is interested in are the even numbered ones. At odd numbered *pulse*4's, processor i will simply take the information it receives, store it, and transmit it at the next pulse. On even numbered pulses,

Figure 4.3.4

it takes the value it receives and adds it to *sum4*. If the value it received was $2\sqrt{n}$, then it will wait for the next even pulse, because it is possible that the matching string is longer than the value in *sum4*. However, if the value it received was less than $2\sqrt{n}$, it will update as in the previous algorithm, setting it to [Processor #,*sum4*] if *sum4*>*length*. In addition, *sum4* is set to 0.

Thus, unlike Scheme 1, Scheme 2 has an extremely simple layout (it maps in a simple fashion onto the planar grid) with no long edges. Unfortunately, the logical delay is $O(\sqrt{n})$ instead of $O(log(n))$. However, this delay may not be a problem in practice where it is likely that there is a small bound on the maximum length allowed for a target. For example, in Chapter 3 we saw that 3 to 5 bits for the length field of a pointer sufficed for many common sources such as English text; that is, for many practical implementations it may be that pointer targets are never longer than a small constant in the range 9 to 33. Scheme 2 can be modified to have a logical delay of k, for any $k\geq1$, if one is willing to limit the maximum length of a target to k. Note that since k would (presumably) be less than $\sqrt{n}$, the *pulse4*'s (and the vertical connections) would not be needed.

Slide Decoding

As the compressed data is received by the decoding chip, it gets decoded into the original text and transmitted to the receiving processor; the function of this chip is to expand all the pointers of the encoded data. All pointers point to earlier strings that are at most n characters away (since they were in the sliding dictionary when these strings were being compressed). Assuming the last n characters are stored (after decompression), then the string represented by a pointer $(loc,lgth)$ can be obtained by concatenating the characters from processor loc to processor $loc-lgth+1$.

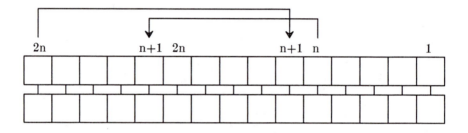

Figure 4.3.5

Like the encoding algorithm, the decoding algorithm employs a sliding dictionary. It uses a pipe of length $3n$ with two extra connections as shown in Figure 4.3.5.

Two different kinds of timing pulses will be used, called *pulseA* and *pulseB*; after every $2n$ *pulseA*'s, there is one *pulseB*. The processors will contain a counter for the *pulseA*'s. Each processor is assigned a processor number such that those processors on the leftmost third will be assigned the same numbers as those on the middle third; that is, the processor which would normally be processor $2n+i$, will be assigned the number $n+i$.

Decoding is done in blocks of n characters. While this decoding is being done, more input is being read in. A pointer $(loc,lgth)$ arriving to the pipe   is   transformed   into   the   sequence   of   integers *loc*, *loc*−1, *loc*−2, ..., *loc*−*lgth*+1. For example, pointer (5,4) would become 5,4,3,2. Each one of these integers represents the location of the pipe at which that character of the original string may be found. These characters need to be marked in some way to distinguish them from integers that are part of the text; to simplify the presentation, these details are left out of the algorithm to be presented. After pointers are expanded into such a sequence of integers, these integers are entered into the pipe on every even *pulseA*[†]. As discussed earlier, unless some assumptions are made regarding the relative speeds of the chip and the data rate of the communication channel, there is no guarantee that another pointer will not arrive before the integers for the current pointer have entered the pipe (and there is no bound on the maximum size of a buffer to hold such pointers).

Let us illustrate the algorithm via an example. Suppose that $n=5$, and suppose that A,B,C,D,E were the last 5 characters processed. In addition, suppose that the next input read was (9,2)x(4,2). Figure 4.3.6a shows what this situation would look like. Since we have just finished processing a block of n characters, a *pulseB* would occur. On a *pulseB* each processor copies the character (or digit) below it into its memory location *char*. Figure 4.3.6b shows this process. Note that the block A,B,C,D,E was transmitted while it was being decoded. So, it can now be erased from the data processors. After each *pulseA* the block 9,8,*x*,4,3 will get shifted one processor to the left. Each processor will look at the item below it. If it is a character, it does not do anything. But if it is a digit, it checks to see if the processor number is equal to this digit. If so, it replaces this digit by the contents of its memory location *char*. There will be $2n$ *pulseA*'s. At every even numbered pulse, a new character will be read in. The new characters that are read in will only get shifted at even numbered pulses so that at the end of all the *pulseA*'s, they will all be underneath the rightmost n processors. The function of the leftmost n processors is the same as that of the middle block. Their functions are exchanged after every block of n characters is processed. So, during the next set of *pulseA*'s, the pointers of the next block will be expanded by using the characters from the leftmost n processors.

Figures 4.3.6c through 4.3.6l illustrates the algorithm by continuing the example that is started by Figures 4.3.6a and 4.3.6b. As can be seen from Figure 4.3.6, it is possible to have pointers to pointers; after the second *pulseA*, processor 4 had a 4 below it, and replaced it with an 8 (the character at

---

[†] Characters enter the pipe only on even *pulseA*'s because every block of n characters that enters the pipe will have to pass by $2n$ processors of the pipe before the next block of n characters enters the pipe.

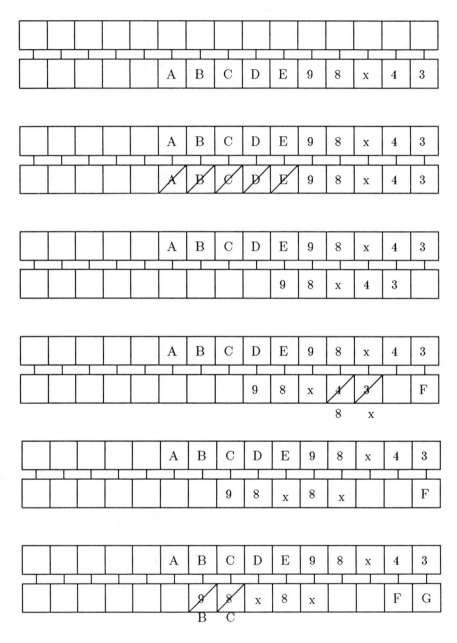

Figure 4.3.6

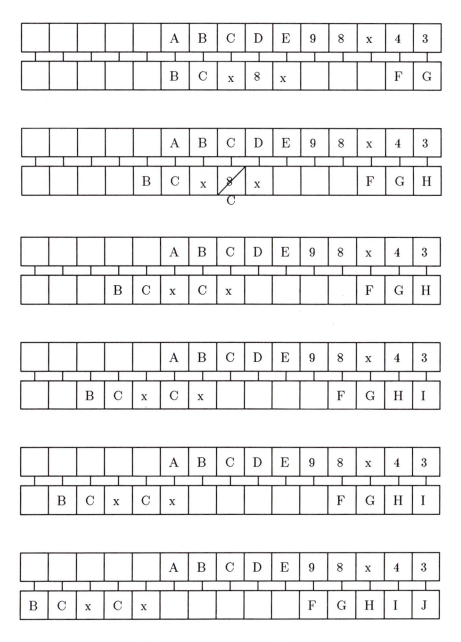

Figure 4.3.6, continued

during *pulseA* **do begin**

　　　pulseAcount $=$ *pulseAcount*$+1$

　　　if (*pulseAcount* is even or processor $\# >$ *pulseAcount*)
　　　　　then shift left

　　　if (processor has a digit below it and (processor $\#$ = digit)
　　　　　then replace digit by *char*

　　　if (processor$\#=2n$)
　　　　　　　then if (odd block and middle or even block and leftmost)
　　　　　　　　　then transmit

　　　end

during *pulseB* **do begin**

　　　copy character below into *char*

　　　if (processor$\# > n$) **then** erase character below

　　　pulseAcount $= 0$

　　　end

Algorithm 4.3.5
Slide Decoding Algorithm

location 4 was compressed with a pointer that pointed to location 8). Notice that after the tenth pulse the block just decoded is underneath the leftmost processors.

Algorithm 4.3.5 is the decoding algorithm. Referring to Algorithm 4.3.5, note that processor n will pass the character (or digit) below it to the middle block if an odd numbered block is being processed or to the leftmost block if an even numbered block is being processed. The leftmost processor will pass to processor $n+1$ in middle block. Note that, as mentioned earlier, Algorithm 4.3.5 assumes that pointers entering the pipe are expanded to a sequence of integers (e.g, a pointer $(i,3)$ is expanded to the three integers i, $i+1$, and $i+2$). Algorithm 4.3.5 also omitted the details of marking these integers to distinguish them from characters.

4.4. DYNAMIC DICTIONARY METHOD

In this section we turn out attention to systolic implementations for the dynamic dictionary model. Our approach is to generalize the implementation used for the static dictionary model that is depicted in Figure 4.2.1. However, unlike Figure 4.2.1 (which depicts a two-way communication channel), we restrict ourselves to a one-way communication line; a two-way communication channel can be implemented with separate compression hardware on two one-way communication lines that go in each direction.

In the serial case, methods employing the FC or AP learning heuristics could use a simply trie data structure and were easier to implement that the ID heuristic which appears to require more complicated data structures. In addition, LRU seemed to be the natural choice for the deletion heuristic since it allowed continuous learning (unlike $FREEZE$) and could easily be implemented with a doubly-linked list. In the parallel environment of a systolic pipe, however, data structures that are efficient for a serial environment may not be the best choice.

The systolic implementation for the static dictionary model that was considered in earlier in this chapter stores the dictionary in an associative memory, implemented as a pipe, that allows a dictionary entry to contain pointers to entries that are earlier in the pipe. Two obvious problems to generalizing this structure to handle dynamic dictionary methods are the following:

(1) How can new entries be dynamically added?

(2) How can existing entries be dynamically deleted?

For problem (2), the use of a LRU queue, which was an important tool for the material discussed in Chapter 3, seems to require global communication (which is slow with a systolic pipe). For Problem (1), even if the least recently used entries could be quickly identified, deleting them could leave many "holes" in the memory which are hard to find and keep track of without global communication.

Many of the methods considered in Chapter 3 were roughly equivalent in terms of how much compression could be expected for typical types of data. The key idea for an efficient systolic implementation is to select among such equivalent alternatives, a method that lends itself well to a systolic implementation.

Dynamic Encoding

We start by describing a systolic pipe implementation for the dynamic dictionary method only as it pertains to encoding. The pipe consists of $<D>$ processors numbered 0 through $<D>-1$ from left to right. We shall view data as leaving the sender, entering the pipe from the left, leaving the pipe to the right, and entering the communication line. That is, if $i<j$, then processor i is to the left of processor j and occurs earlier in the pipe than processor j.

For the update heuristic, we use *ID*. The systolic pipe can be viewed as storing the pair forest representation of the dictionary. However, unlike the serial case, no additional data structures are used. The pipe is always initialized so that the first $|\Sigma|$ processors store one character of Σ each; for simplicity, we henceforth assume that these first $|\Sigma|$ dictionary entries are assigned the pointer values 0 through $|\Sigma|-1$. The remaining $<D>-|\Sigma|$ processors in the pipe are each capable of holding a pair of pointers (corresponding to the left and right pointers into the pair forest), but are initialized to be empty. The *flag* bit is initially 1 for processor $|\Sigma|$ and 0 for all others. It is always the case that at most 1 processor has its *flag* bit set to 1. The processor with *flag*=1 is designated as the *learning processor*. It is always the case that processors to the left of the learning processor contain dictionary entries (either a single pointer representing a character of Σ or a pair of pointers that are left and right pointers into the pair forest representing the dictionary) and processors to the right of the learning processor are empty. As data passes through the processors to the left of the learning processor it is encoded just as with the static dictionary method. Data passes unchanged through the processors to the right of the learning processor. When a pair of pointers enters the learning processor, they represent adjacent substrings of the original data and can be viewed as the "previous" and "current" match. The learning processor can simply adopt this pair of pointers as its entry, set its *flag* to 0, and send a signal to the processor to its right to set its *flag* to 1.

A number of small details have been left out of the description above. In particular, we do not want the learning processor to adopt the same pair of pointers that was adopted by the processor to its left. Hence, when a processor first becomes the learning processor, it must allow one pointer to pass through before proceeding to "learn".

We now turn our attention to the deletion heuristic. When the rightmost processor becomes the learning processor, it adopts a pair of pointers as its entry and then sends a signal to the right to pass on the *flag* bit; this signal indicates that the dictionary is full. It is at this point that a serial algorithm might employ a LRU queue to delete entries of the dictionary so that room can be made for new ones. However, as mentioned earlier, it is not clear how to efficiently maintain an LRU queue in the systolic pipe. Instead, for the deletion heuristic, we use *SWAP*. As discussed in Chapter 3, the *SWAP* heuristic can be viewed as a discrete version of *LRU*, and typically performs equivalently to LRU in practice. The most direct implementation of the *SWAP* heuristic is to simply double the hardware and add a controller to each end of the pipe that switches input/output lines appropriately as the dictionaries turn over.

Dynamic Decoding

Consider now the operation of the decoding pipe. Again, the pipe consists of $<D>$ processors. However, it is convenient to number them 0 through $<D>-1$ from right to left. We now view (compressed) data as leaving the communication line, entering the pipe from the right, leaving the pipe to the left, and entering the receiver. That is, if $i < j$, then processor i is to the right of processor j and occurs earlier in the pipe than processor j. Operation of the decoding pipe is essentially the reverse of the encoding pipe. The first $|\Sigma|$ processors are initialized to contain the characters of Σ, processor $|\Sigma|$ is initially the learning processor, and the remaining processors are empty. Compressed data enters from the left, passes through the empty processors unchanged, and decoding in the non-empty portion of the pipe works as in the static case. The operation of the learning processor is essentially the same as for the encoder (with the same buffering issues that were discussed for static decoding).

Relationship to the ID-SWAP Heuristic

The systolic pipe implementation described above compresses data in a fashion that is similar but not identical to the $ID-SWAP$ heuristic, using the greedy match heuristic, as defined in Chapter 3. The difference is that in Chapter 3, at each point in time the longest match between the dictionary and the input stream is taken as the current match; that is the input stream is parsed into a sequence of longest possible matches to the (dynamically changing) dictionary. By contrast, here the parsing is computed in a "bottom up" fashion where, as the stream of pointers flows through the pipe, larger matches are constructed from pairs of smaller matches. As discussed in Section 4.2, the parallel parsing can be better or worse than the greedy serial parsing, depending on the dictionary and string in question. In the case of the static dictionary of Section 4.2, the difference in practice appears to be insignificant. However, the experimental evidence to support this claim employed static dictionaries where pointers within entries to other entries were used only when the length of an entry exceeded some limit (e.g., 8 characters). Here, we have taken the ability of an entry to point to another entry to the extreme where every entry (except the characters of Σ) is just two pointers to other entries. In addition, the dictionary is dynamically changing. Hence, it is not reasonable to assume that because the parallel parsing had no significant effect on the static dictionary method, it will have no effect here. To get some indication of whether parallel parsing affects the amount of compression achieved, the performance of the algorithm described in this section was compared to a serial implementation of the ID heuristic using the LRU deletion strategy. For all of the sample files in Appendix A.2, the difference was insignificant. This provides some evidence that the systolic pipe implementation described here can be expected to perform equivalently in practice to a serial implementation. However, this issue should be studied carefully for a particular application[†].

---

† It would appear that the fact that the dictionary used for the parallel parsing is dynamically constructed in parallel is important. The following type of experiment

4.5. VLSI LAYOUT ISSUES

The snake layout of Figure 4.2.3 used for a linear pipe of the static and dynamic models is trivial. The snakes used by the Scheme 2 of the slide encoding algorithm and by the slide decoding algorithm are also basically trivial, but there are the details of placing pipe ends and extra connection points physically close together on the chip. After addressing these details, the remainder of this section will consider layout issues pertaining to Scheme 1 for slide encoding.

For Scheme 2 of the slide encoding algorithm, there are no extra connection that require that the pipe ends be physically close together, but there may be additional practical constraints that make this proximity desirable. The layout of Figure 4.2.3 places the pipe ends physically close together; the only problem is that the first $\sqrt{n}/2$ and the last $\sqrt{n}/2$ processors are not $O(1)$ distance from processors $\sqrt{n}$ down the pipe since they are now along the left column of the layout. However, all other processors except theses first $\sqrt{n}/2$ and last $\sqrt{n}/2$ are arranged in a simple snake layout like that of Figure 4.3.4. Hence, by simply running the algorithm for an additional $\sqrt{n}/2$ steps and an additional $\sqrt{n}$ steps at the end, information cat be transmitted between these leading and trailing $\sqrt{n}/2$ processors and the top and bottom rows of the simple snake layout formed by the remaining processors.

The two extra connections of the sliding dictionary decoding algorithm require that the pipe ends and the 1/3 and 2/3 points in the array be physically close together. The following theorem notes that these two extra connections do not cause a problem for the circuit layout.

Theorem 4.5.1: The pipe of Figure 4.3.5 can be laid out on an $O(\sqrt{n})$ by $O(\sqrt{n})$ grid so that all edges, including the two extra connections, have length $O(1)$[††].

---

was performed by the author. First, a static dictionary was constructed using a serial implementation of the *ID* heuristic. This static dictionary was then used to compress files with both a serial static dictionary algorithm and with a parallel simulator. For the parallel simulator, the static dictionary was ordered in an arbitrary fashion that preserved the property that pointers only pointed to entries earlier in the pipe. It turned out that on some of the sample files in Appendix A.2, the difference was significant: the parallel parsing was worse, sometimes by as much as 10 to 15 in percent compression ration. A possible conclusion to be drawn from this experiment is that the dictionary that is learned in parallel is somewhat different that the one learned serially, and that the parallel parsing needs to have the dictionary constructed in parallel in order to perform as well as the serial algorithm. That is, the parallel learning orders the dictionary in a way that works well with the parallel parsing.

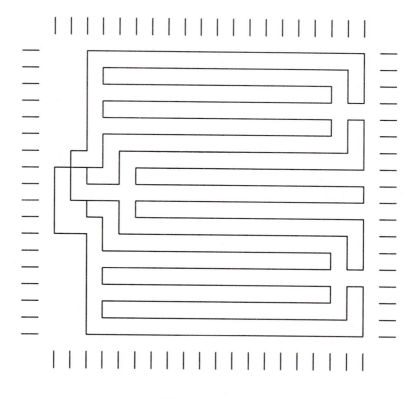

Figure 4.5.1

Proof: If $n = (3k)^2$ for some even integer k, then the pipe can be place on a grid of size exactly $3k$ by $3k$. Figure 4.5.1 shows the layout for $k=6$. The marks around the pipe layout indicate the 18 by 18 grid on which the pipe is embedded; except for the two extra connections shown on the left side of the layout, there is a processor everywhere the pipe intersects a grid point. This construction can be viewed as a generalization of the snake layout of Figure 4.2.3. It is essentially three snake layouts of size k by $3k$. Each of these three layouts has exactly $k(3k-4)$ nodes in columns 3 through $3k-2$. The top and bottom snakes each have $(3k-2)/2$ nodes in each of the first two

---

†† Although it is not directly relevant to the results of this chapter, it should be noted that the construction to be presented can be generalized to any fixed number of extra connections, placed at arbitrary points in the pipe.

columns, whereas the middle snake only has 2 nodes in each of the first two columns. On the other hand, the middle snake has $2k-2$ nodes in each of the last two columns whereas the top and bottom snakes each have only $(k+2)/2$ nodes in each of the last two columns. Hence, each of the three snakes has exactly $3(k^2)$ nodes. In addition, the two extra connections have constant lengths (5 and 7 units respectively). If n is not of the form $(3k)^2$ for some even k, then first the construction can be carried out for the least integer m larger than n which is of this form, and then nodes can be deleted from each of the three snakes (by trimming back from the rightmost columns). Since it must be that

$$m \leq (\sqrt{n}+5)^2 = n+10\sqrt{n}+25$$

it follows that for sufficiently large n, $m<2n$ (in fact, for any $\epsilon>0$, $m<(1+\epsilon)n$ for sufficiently large n). ◯

Scheme 1 used for the sliding dictionary model superimposed a complete binary tree over the pipe. The resulting structure is essentially a linear pipe but periodically needs to perform global communication via the tree. The efficient VLSI layout of this structure is the subject of the remainder of this section.

The linear pipe and the complete binary tree are both common VLSI structures. Both have simple linear area layouts on the planar grid. Figure 4.5.2a depicts how an $O(n)$ node pipe has a "snake" layout on a $O(\sqrt{n})$ by $O(\sqrt{n})$ grid and Figure 4.5.2b depicts the $O(\sqrt{n})$ by $O(\sqrt{n})$ H-tree layout for a complete binary tree with n leaves. Here, we consider the the problem of laying out a pipe connected to the leaves of a complete binary tree; that is, the layout of a graph of the type depicted in Figure 4.5.2c.

Definition 4.5.1: A *closed complete binary tree* is a complete binary tree (we call the edges of this tree *tree edges*) together with a set of *pipe edges* that form a simple path that visits each leaf exactly once. The *implied H-tree* for a closed complete binary tree is the H-tree for the tree edges[†]. ◯

Since a closed complete binary tree has an $O(1)$ separator[††], standard divide and conquer approaches to graph layout yield linear area. However,

---

† To make this correspondence unique, we assume that there is an ordering associated with the tree.
†† That is, only a constant number of edges must be removed from the tree to divide it into two equal size disjoint pieces.

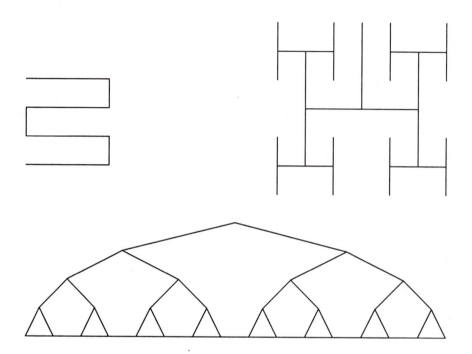

Figure 4.5.2

such a construction may introduce relatively long pipe edges (e.g. $O(\sqrt{n})$).
As discussed in the bibliographic notes, there has been much debate as to the
right model of time for a VLSI signal to propagate along a wire. For our purposes, we only assume that the delay is significant (i.e. not constant), and we
seek layouts that minimize both area and the length of pipe edges. As discussed in the bibliographic notes, it can be shown that if the leaves of a complete binary tree layout must lie on the border of a convex region, then the
layout must consume at least $O(n*log_2(n))$ area (whether or not edges are allowed to cross); this condition rules out many simple approaches. Other approaches such as laying Figure 4.5.2a on top of Figure 4.5.2b give linear area
but the pipe visits the leaves of the tree in a scrambled order. The following
theorem gives a construction that simultaneously achieves linear area and
$O(1)$ length pipe edges. We assume nodes to be points (consuming no area)
and edges to be lines (consuming no area), and view the layout problem as
one of embedding the graph on the planar grid (so that nodes must lie on grid

points and edges must follow grid lines)[†]. In addition, we make the reasonably standard assumptions with regard to legal circuit layout; that is, an edge may cross another edge but not cross over a node, two edges may not lie on top of each other, at most two edges cross at a point, etc.

Figure 4.5.3

Theorem 4.5.2 There is a constant k, depending on the layout design rules but not on n, such that an n-leaf closed complete binary tree can be embedded on a planar grid so that all pipe edges have length at most k and total area is at most $3/2$ the area of the implied H-tree.

Proof: Our approach is to "thread" the pipe edges through the implied H-tree. Some modification of the implied H-tree will be necessary to achieve the $3/2$ bound claimed. We define a *bar* with root r to be a node r together with a point to the left connected via a horizontal line segment and a point to the right connected via a horizontal line segment (see Figure 4.5.3). An H-tree of n leaves with root r can be viewed recursively as either the single root r, a bar with root r, or as a set of four H-trees T_1, T_2, T_3, and T_4 of $n/4$ leaves each, with roots a, b, c, d, connected to the four ends of an H (horizontally oriented) with center r as depicted in Figure 4.5.4b (Figure 4.5.4a shows the tree represented by Figure 4.5.4b). Certain nodes along the top and bottom borders of Figure 4.5.4b have been labeled. The top left corner and top right corner are labeled TLC and TRC respectively and the TRC node of T_1 and TLC node of T_4 are labeled TLM and TRM (M for "middle") respectively. Similarly, the bottom nodes have labels BLC, BLM, BRM, and BRC.

---

† This assumption is rather conservative. We have assumed nodes and edges to have the same width; in practice, it is not unlikely that a node would be wider than an edge (and if this were the case, the bounds stated in the following theorem with regard to area may be improved). Given this assumption, letting this width be 0 only changes the scale of the layout, not its proportions. We have also been conservative in ruling out diagonal edges, which may be acceptable in practice.

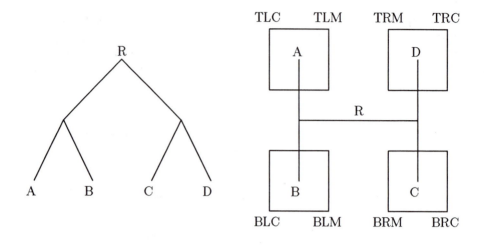

Figure 4.5.4

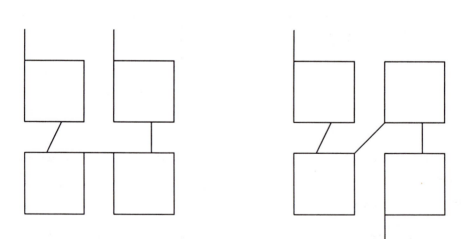

Figure 4.5.5

An (x,y) *traversal* of the leaves of an H-tree is one that has end points x and y. A U *traversal* refers to any one of the four traversals (TLC, TRM), (TLM, TRC), (BLC, BRM), or (BLM, BRC). A Z *traversal* refers to any one of the four traversals (TLC, BRM), (TLM, BRC), (TRM, BLC), or (TRC, BLM).

Figure 4.5.5a depicts how a (TLC, TRM) U traversal can be composed of two U and two Z traversals of T_1, T_2, T_3, and T_4; here, a path can be traced from TLC to BRM_1 (BRM_1 refers to the BRM node of T_1) to TLM_2 to TRC_2 to TLC_3 to TRM_3 to BRM_4 to TRM. Similarly, Figure 4.5.5b depicts how a (TLC, BRM) Z traversal can be composed of two U and two Z traversals by tracing the path TLC, BRM_1, TLM_2, TRC_2, BLC_4, BRM_4, TRM_3, BLM. By considering reflections around both the horizontal and vertical axes, Figure 4.5.5 gives rise to four *standard* U traversals and four standard Z traversals.

For the moment, we ignore layout considerations and assume that pipe edges can be laid on top of the tree in any way. Then, since a standard U or Z traversal is defined in terms of standard U and Z traversals of subtrees, the construction is a well defined traversal of the leaves of the H-tree. Furthermore, since the nearest leaf to a given leaf in an H-tree in a horizontal or vertical direction is at most 2 units away[†], horizontal and vertical edges are at 2 units long and diagonal edges are $2\sqrt{2}$ long. Figure 4.5.6 depicts the construction for a H-tree of 64 leaves. The leaves are traversed in the correct order, provided the appropriate identification of left and right sub-trees is made. For example, the standard U traversal of Figure 4.5.5a visits T_1, T_2, T_3, and T_4 in exactly that order and the standard Z traversal of Figure 4.5.5b visits in the order T_1, T_2, T_4, and T_3; however, T_3 and T_4 can be effectively switched by simply changing the identification of left and right sub-trees in the common parent node of c and d. In subsequent recursive calls, it is true that the H-tree may be rotated 180 degrees (as T_2 and T_3 are in Figure 4.5.5) and that a different one of the four standard U or Z may be used than the ones of Figure 4.5.6. However, the key observation is that a standard U or Z traversal always visits the left half (T_1 and T_2) before the right half (T_3 and T_4) or vice versa; but never, for example, the top half before the bottom half.

---

† This observation follows directly by viewing an H-tree recursively as depicted in Figure 4.5.4b and noting that adjacent T_i's are separated by at most one edge.

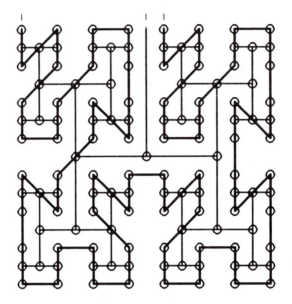

Figure 4.5.6

We now describe how to convert a layout like the one depicted in Figure 4.5.6 to a legal one (i.e., no diagonal edges and no pipe edges on top of tree edges or nodes). To do so, we will stretch the layout of Figure 4.5.6 by a factor of 3/2 in the horizontal direction. We observe that an H-tree of n leaves has bars at the lowest level only if n is an odd power of 2 (and in this case, the H-tree is twice as wide as high). However, if the H-tree is rotated 90 degrees, it is just the left half of the layout for an H-tree of $2n$ leaves. Hence, the first half of a U traversal can be used, and without loss of generality, we assume n to be an even power of 2.

An H-tree can be viewed as an array of 4-leaf H-trees separated by 2 units of space in all directions. Since the 4-leaf H-trees are 2 units high by 2 units wide, the gap to the right and below each 4-leaf H-tree can be "charged" to that tree for a total of 4 units high by 4 units wide[†]. We start

---

[†] This charge is not quite right; the 4-leaf H-trees along the bottom cannot be charged for a lower gap and the 4-leaf H-trees along the right cannot be charged for a right gap.

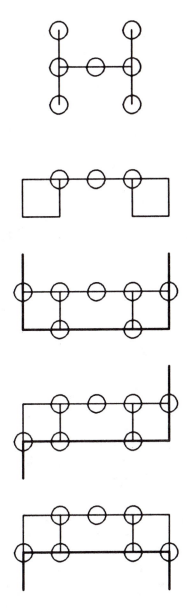

Figure 4.5.7

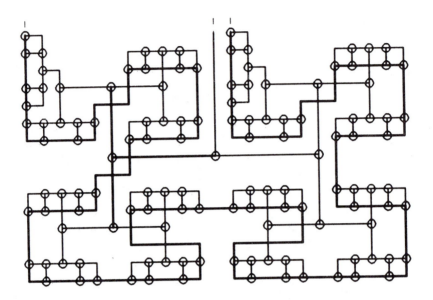

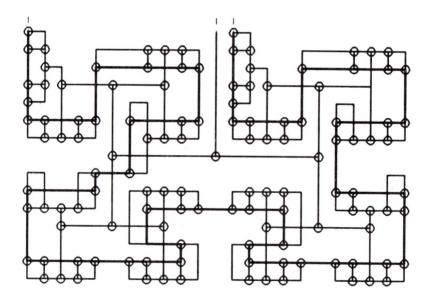

Figure 4.5.8

by replacing each 4-leaf H-tree, shown in Figure 4.5.7a, by the graph 1 unit high and 4 units wide shown in Figure 4.5.7b; this transformation changes the charge for each 4-leaf H-tree from 4 high by 4 wide to 3 high by 6 wide. The entire layout is widened by a factor of 3/2 in the horizontal direction to accommodate the increase in width of 4-leaf H-trees, however, the vertical height of the layout is not decreased. By keeping the vertical dimension, a spare track above each row of 4-leaf H-trees may be reserved, to be used shortly.

Figure 4.5.7b has only the root and its two children of Figure 4.5.7a specified. Two edges (one from each cycle) must be deleted from Figure 4.5.7b in order to get a graph topologically equivalent to Figure 4.5.7a. The edges deleted depend on how the 4-leaf tree is traversed by the pipe, as shown in Figures 4.5.7c, 4.5.7d, 4.5.7e, or reflections of them. With the appropriate choice of Figures 4.5.7c, 4.5.7d, and 4.5.7e, horizontal and vertical edges connecting adjacent 4-leaf trees in Figure 4.5.6 can be placed directly as horizontal or vertical line segments. For diagonal edges there are two possibilities. First, a diagonal edge could leave from the right (left) of a 4-leaf tree up to the right (left). In this case, we can simply route vertically up 1 unit (into the spare track), horizontally 2 units, and vertically up 2 units. The other possibility is that a diagonal edge in Figure 4.5.6 leaves a 4-leaf tree from the right (left) and goes up to the left (right) of the 4-leaf tree above it. Usually, we can route vertically up 1 unit (into the spare track), horizontally 4 units, and vertically up 2 units. However, in the case that the edge is connecting subtrees of 8 leaves, it could be that when we route up 1 into the free track, we will be "knocked-kneed"[†] with a corner of an edge from the first case. To eliminate knock-knees, (although they may be acceptable in a particular application), each time one is encountered, we "tilt" a 4-leaf tree on its side as can be seen in Figure 4.5.8a, which shows the layout described above for 64 leaves. Note that Figure 4.5.8a has the same height but 3/2 the width as Figure 4.5.6. ◯

It can be shown that $O(\sqrt{n}/\log_2(n))$ is a lower bound on maximum edge length in a linear area binary tree layout. Hence, the theorem above is optimal to within a $log(n)$ factor for maximum tree edge length and optimal to within a constant factor for maximum pipe edge length and total area. Another cost measure is the number of bends introduced into edges[††].

---

† Knocked-kneed routing allows a 90 degree bend of an edge (a single point) to lie over a 90 degree bend of another edge.
†† See the bibliographic notes for a discussion of the bend cost measure and its applications.

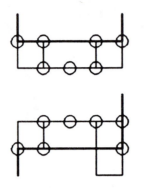

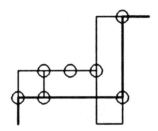

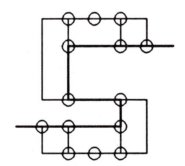

Figure 4.5.9

Corollary 4.5.2: The requirements of the above theorem can be satisfied with no bends in the pipe edges.

Proof: No bends are present in 4-leaf trees configured as in Figure 4.5.7e (or reflections of it). Bends can be removed from the pipe edges of all other 4-leaf trees, which must have the configuration of Figures 4.5.7c or 4.5.7d (or reflections of them), by transforming them to the configurations of Figure 4.5.9a or 4.5.9b, respectively. After this transformation, the only remaining bends in pipe edges occur on diagonal edges from Figure 4.5.6 that are not part of 4-leaf trees. As in the proof of the above theorem, we divide these edges into two classes: first, the diagonal edges leaving a 4-leaf tree from the left (right) and going to the left (right), and second, ones leaving from the left (right) and going to the right (left). In the first case, the exit node can be stretched up or down to the bend; Figure 4.5.9c shows how this stretching is done for Figure 4.5.9b. In the second case, the diagonal edge must connect 4-leaf trees directly above and below each other and a similar stretching to the first case can be done, as shown in Figure 4.5.9d. Figure 4.5.8b shows the construction for 64 leaves. Note that where 4-leaf trees have been tilted on their side, there is a more straightforward method of removing the bends in the associated diagonal edge (the one the 4-leaf tree was tilted to avoid), and this method has been used in Figure 4.5.8b. ○

4.6. BIBLIOGRAPHIC NOTES

There is a great deal of literature on computational issues pertaining to VLSI. For general an introduction (which contains an extensive bibliography) to the theoretical aspects see Ullman [1984]. See also the books edited by Kung, Sproull, and Steele [1981] and Bertolazzi and Luccio [1985]. For a general introduction to more applied aspects see the texts by Mead and Conway [1980], Aryes [1983], Mavor, Jack, and Denyer [1983], and Pucknell and Eshraghian [1985], Glasser and Dobberpuhl [1985]; the text by Weste and Eshraghian [1985] is similar in content to these but is based on CMOS technology rather than NMOS technology. The book edited by Sze [1983] addresses VLSI fabrication. The text by Denyer and Renshaw [1985] considers VLSI architectures for a variety signal processing problems.

Computing structures in the spirit of systolic arrays have have appeared quite early in the literature (e.g., Von Neumann [1951], Hennie [1961], Slotnick [1962], and Cole [1969]) under other names; most notable are *cellular automata;* the text by edited by Burks [1970] contains a variety of work on the subject and the text of Preston and Duff [1984] provides a more recent presentation. Steiglitz, Kamal, and Watson [1988] consider the power of a simple class on one-dimensional cellular automata. The term "systolic array" was first explicitly introduced by the work of Leiserson and Kung that appears in Section 8.3 of Mead and Conway [1980]. The reader may also refer to Culik and Fris [1985], Kung [1982], and Leiserson [1982]. Lipton and Lopresti [1985] present a systolic array for string comparison; such algorithms have applications to lossy data compression. Snyder [1982] considers architectures that can be re-configured into different interconnection patterns. For a recent non-technical introduction to systolic arrays, see the article by Fortes [1987]; the issue of *IEEE Computer* that contains this article is devoted entirely to systolic arrays and contains a number of introductory articles.

Leighton [1983] considers the theoretical aspects of circuit layout and contains an extensive bibliography on the subject. Leiserson [1980] presents a general divide and conquer approach to graph layout; this approach is also presented in Leiserson [1982]; see also Valiant [1979]. Mead and Rem [1979] introduce the notion of an H-tree. Brent and Kung [1980] show that if the leaves of a complete binary tree layout must lie on the border of a convex region, then the layout must consume at least $O(n*log_2(n))$ area (whether or not edges are allowed to cross); Paterson, Ruzzo, and Snyder [1981] show $O(\sqrt{n}/log_2(n))$ is a lower bound on maximum edge length in a linear area binary tree layout; they also present a variety of other results concerning tree layout, as do Ruzzo and Snyder [1981], Fisher [1980], and Gordon, Koren, and Silberman [1984]. Bhatt and Leiserson [1982] consider how to efficiently assemble large tree layouts from smaller components. Gordon [1987] considers alternative layouts to the H-tree that are more efficient under some measures.

Minimizing the number of bends in a layout has a number of applications for VLSI. For example, it can model the problem of minimizing the number of connections between layers when different layers are being used for routing in the horizontal and vertical directions. In addition, some layout systems minimize bends simply because it can make layouts easier to process (e.g., Dunlop [1980]). Another application of bend minimization is for the layout of networks that communicate by light or microwave, where a device is required to turn a corner; related to this application are optical computing devices (e.g., see the December 1987 issue of *IEEE Computer*). A third application is for transportation problems in space where energy is not needed to sustain a velocity but is needed to turn (e.g., Niedringhaus [1979]). A fourth application is to mobile robots that must stop to turn; minimizing bends reduces the traveling time of the robot (e.g., Reif and Storer [1987]). For discussion of knocked-kneed routing, see Pinter [1982]. Storer [1984] considers layout algorithms that minimize the number of bends introduced into edges; see also Tamassia [1985].

The material in Sections 2 and 3 is from Gonzalez and Storer [1985]. Prior work prior, such as Lea [1978], has been primarily concerned with much more limited implementations (e.g., a small static dictionary). Vishkin [1985] and Landau and Vishkin [1986] consider parallel algorithms for string matching, including the case where some number of mismatches are allowed.

For a discussion of topological sort, see a text on algorithms such as Aho, Hopcroft, and Ullman [1974,1983].

The material in Section 4 is from Storer [1982]. The construction of Section 4 uses both the U and Z traversal. Leighton [1982] has observed that a U traversal can be constructed entirely from U traversals. However, in half of the subsequent recursive calls, simple identification of left and right subtrees is not sufficient to produce the proper order in the pipe; rearranging the tree is necessary. The resulting (constant factor) increase in layout area may not be acceptable in practice.

There has been much debate as to the right model of time for a VLSI signal to propagate along a wire and some authors have argued that as much as $O(n^2)$ should be charged to an edge of length n; Bilardi, Pracchi, and Preparata [1981] address this issue.

5

OFF-LINE
TEXTUAL SUBSTITUTION:
THE MACRO MODEL

Recall from Chapter 1 that with *off-line* data compression, the entire input string can be read before any of the output is produced. Off-line models are not only powerful, but are also useful for examining theoretical issues. This chapter considers a general model for off-line data compression called the *macro model.* The term "macro model" is motivated by the notion of a macro in a programming language where the user can enter a macro statement which will be replaced before compilation by the corresponding macro body. This allows a shorthand notation for segments of code that occur frequently in a program. The analogy with data compression should be clear: macro statements correspond to pointers and macro bodies correspond to pointer targets. For the most part the reader can view the terms "macro scheme for data compression" and "textual substitution scheme for data compression" as synonymous. We use the term "macro scheme" in this chapter instead of the term "textual substitution scheme" not only because it specifically refers to off-line computations, but also to emphasize that the macro model, at least in principle, includes more general mechanisms than discussed in earlier chapters. For example, just as with macros in programming languages, a macro scheme may allow pointers to take arguments to control various aspects of the replacement of a pointer by its target.

For convenience, throughout this chapter we view a compressed form of a string as a sequence of pointers interspersed with characters of the input alphabet. As discussed in earlier chapters, a character can be viewed as a pointer to a string of length one, so that all compressed forms are simply a sequence of pointers. However, we distinguish characters from pointers in this chapter for the purposes of presentation; this issue is addressed in detail in the next section. The precise manner in which pointers are encoded into bits is not important for most of the theorems to be discussed in this chapter. We assume only that it is always possible to determine where one pointer ends and the next one begins.

The material in this chapter is more theoretical in nature than that in Chapter 3, although the two chapters have strong interconnections. Clearly, algorithms that run on-line will run off-line; but the converse is not necessarily true. In fact, we shall see that the macro model captures may complexities that are not present with on-line textual substitution. For this reason, it is appropriate to consider complexity issues and theoretical results concerning worst-case performance.

Section 5.1 presents basic definitions and illustrates some of the increased generality that is available with off-line textual substitution. Section 5.2 studies the "power" of the model by examining how well "easy" strings can be compressed. Sections 5.3, 5.4, and 5.5 investigate several key methods and their complexity. Section 5.6 investigates worst-case performance bounds between provably optimal off-line algorithms and on-line greedy heuristics of the type considered in Chapter 3. Sections 5.7 and 5.8 consider generalizations of the macro model.

5.1. DEFINITIONS

We treat the source data as a finite string over some alphabet. With *external macro schemes*, a source string is encoded as a pair of strings, a *dictionary* and a *skeleton*. The skeleton contains characters of the input alphabet interspersed with pointers to substrings of the dictionary. The dictionary is also allowed to contain pointers to substrings of the dictionary. The source string is recovered by substituting dictionary strings for pointers. With *internal macro schemes*, a string is compressed by replacing duplicate instances of substrings with pointers to other occurrences of the same substrings. The result is a single string of characters and pointers.

For the purposes of this section, we let $p \geq 1$ be an integer denoting the implementation dependent size of a pointer. If x is a string containing pointers, the *length* of x, denoted $|x|$, is defined to be the number of characters in x plus p times the number of pointers in x. We shall treat a pointer as an indivisible object that, in some unspecified fashion, uniquely and unambiguously identifies some string which is referred to as the *target* of the pointer. The way a pointer is written is not important; for simplicity, we shall write a pointer as a pair (m,n) where m indicates the position of the first character in the target, n indicates the length of the target, and $|(m,n)|$ is the pointer size p. For simplicity of presentation, we assume that that both m and n are in units of characters and that m specifies an absolute location[†].

Example 5.1.1: Let $p=1$ and consider the string

$$w = \text{aaBccDaacEaccFacac}$$

which might be encoded under the external macro model as

$$x = \text{aacc\#(1,2)B(3,2)D(1,3)E(2,3)F(2,2)(2,2)}$$

where $\#$ separates the dictionary from the skeleton; for simplicity, we assume $|\#|=0$. The compression achieved by the string x (i.e., the ratio $|x|/|w|$) is $14/18$. Using the internal macro model, w could be encoded as

$$y = \text{aaBccD(1,2)cEa(4,2)Fac(13,2)}$$

achieving a compression of $15/18$. $\bigcirc$

At this point, we digress briefly with some comments about our assumptions concerning pointers. As mentioned in the introduction, in practice, the output of a textual substitution compression algorithm can be viewed simply as a sequence of pointers, rather than as a sequence of characters interspersed with pointers. In this context, we have really allowed two pointer sizes: unit size (which can only indicate single characters) or size p. Our motivation for doing so is to simplify theoretical results by having a uniform integer pointer size p (which can be arbitrarily large) together with the ability to represent single characters without a large increase in size. This "2-step" scheme of characters and pointers of size p is already more general than is required to model many practical methods, since $p=1$ models a method that outputs a sequence of uniform size pointers. For example, 12-bit pointers

---

[†] Both of these assumptions do not necessarily reflect what would be done in practice. The first argument m can just as well specify a displacement between the pointer and its target; in fact the displacement representation is crucial for on-line methods (e.g. the sliding dictionary method of Chapter 3) where a fixed number of bits are used for pointers and there is no bound on the magnitude of absolute locations. Using units of characters for m and n can be "wasteful" when pointer targets are substrings of strings of variable length pointers or equivalently, as is the case in this chapter, when pointers are substrings of strings that contain both characters and pointers (where the length of a pointer may be greater than the length of a character). In this case, m and n need only count the number of distinct pointers and characters.

work well for some of the practical methods discussed in Section 3; here, the true length in bits of the output of the compression algorithm is simply 12 times the length as defined in this section. It is possible to generalize the material of this chapter to allow for a continuous range of pointer sizes between 1 and p (including non-integer sizes) and to allow p to be a function of the size of the source string. However, it does not seem to lend significant additional insights; the model of characters interspersed with uniform integer sized pointers seems to be a nice compromise between fixed size pointers and arbitrary variable size pointers for examining theoretical issues pertaining to off-line data compression by substitution.

Implementation considerations motivate us to describe a number of variations on our basic models. A scheme is *recursive* if a pointer target may contain pointers. Two pointers *overlap* if their targets overlap. Whether overlapping pointers are permitted in the external model depends highly on the implementation chosen for the dictionary. In fact, implementation considerations can lead to the placement of various restrictions on the kinds of overlapping permitted. An *original pointer* is one that references a substring of the original source string, whereas a *compressed pointer* references a substring of the compressed representation itself. The string y of the previous example contains compressed pointers. Using original pointers we could encode w as

$$z = \text{aaBccD}(1,2)\text{cEa}(4,2)\text{F}(8,2)(8,2)$$

achieving a compression of 14/18. Original pointers are more natural for one-pass decoding. Compressed pointers allow the recovery of portions of the source string without requiring the implicit decompression of the entire string. A *left* (or *right) pointer* is one that references a substring occurring earlier (respectively, later) in the string. Considering the strings x, y, and z presented above, only x uses overlapping pointers, only z uses recursion, and none of these strings use right pointers. By using both left and right pointers it is possible to save additional space over the use of just one direction. For example, using both right and left pointers, the compressed forms y and z presented above could be replaced by

$$y = (5,2)\text{B}(10,2)\text{DaacEaccF}(6,2)(6,2)$$
$$z = (7,2)\text{B}(12,2)\text{DaacE}(8,2)\text{cF}(8,2)(8,2)$$

achieving a compression of 14/18 and 13/18 respectively. We discuss recursion in relation to original pointers primarily to study the power of various methods. With original pointers, a pointer is recursive if all or part of its target is represented by a pointer.

Cycles cannot occur with compressed pointers but using original pointers, cycles can often make sense. For example, the compressed form

$$ab(5,2)a(1,3)$$

uniquely determines the string $abaaaaba$ even though the two pointers $(5,2)$ and $(1,3)$ form a cycle in the sense that each points to a portion of the string represented by the other. An example of a degenerate cycle is given by the compressed form $a(1,n)$ which uniquely determines the string a^{n+1}. Schemes which allow recursion but that do not allow cycles are said to have *topological recursion*. From the discussion above it should be clear that topological recursion is not necessary for a compressed form to be uniquely decodable. However, it can be useful to consider topological recursion for three reasons: First, authors in the past have made this assumption. Second, study of such schemes leads to a deeper understanding of the power of original pointers. Third, topological recursion may model some practical considerations in the design of efficient original pointer compression methods.

The discussion above leads us to define formally four basic *macro schemes* and three types of *restrictions that may be placed on any of these schemes*. Throughout this section, Σ will denote the underlying alphabet from which the data in question is constructed. For simplicity, as was done in Example 5.1.1:", we assume that $\#$ is a special symbol (not an element of Σ) such that $|\#|=0$; $\#$ will be used for the sole purpose of separating an external dictionary from a skeleton.

Definition 5.1.1: A *compressed form* of a string s using the *external pointer macro* (EPM) *scheme* is any string $t=s_0\#s_1$ satisfying

(1) s_0 and s_1 consist of characters from Σ and pointers to substrings of s_0.

(2) s can be obtained from s_1 by performing the following two steps:

A: Replace each pointer in s_1 with its target.

B: Repeat step A until s_1 contains no pointers. ○

Definition 5.1.2: A *compressed form* of a string s using the *compressed pointer macro* (CPM) *scheme* is any string t satisfying:

(1) t consists of characters from Σ and pointers to substrings of t.

(2) s can be obtained from t by forming the string $t\#t$ and then decoding as with the *EPM* scheme. ◯

Definition 5.1.3: A *compressed form* of a string s using the *original pointer macro* (OPM) *scheme* is any string t satisfying:

(1) t consists of characters from Σ and pointers representing substrings of s.

(2) s can be obtained from t by replacing each pointer (n,m) by the sequence of pointers $(n,1)$, $(n+1,1)$, ..., $(n+m-1,1)$ and then decoding as with the *CPM* scheme with the stipulation that pointers are considered to have length 1. ◯

Definition 5.1.4: A *compressed form* of a string s using the *original external pointer macro* (OEPM) *scheme* is any string $t=s_0\#s_1$ satisfying:

(1) t consists of characters from Σ and pointers.

(2) s_0 may be decoded using the *OPM* scheme to produce a string r. Furthermore, pointers in s_1 point to substrings of r.

(3) s may be obtained by replacing each pointer in s_1 with its target in r. ◯

For a given scheme, a string may have more than one minimal length compressed form. For formal discussions, we assume that there is some lexicographic ordering to distinguish among compressed forms of the same length, and we henceforth refer to *the* minimal length compressed form of a string s for pointer size p according to a given scheme S as $\Delta_{S,p}(s)$; when S or p is understood or not relevant, we will drop one of the subscripts. We shall refer to the process of replacing a string r by a pointer as *factoring out* r, and often refer to a string that is a target or potential target as a *factor*.

Definition 5.1.5: A compressed (original) pointer q_1 *depends on* pointer q_2 if the target of q_1 contains q_2 (all or part of the string represented by q_2) or if there is a pointer q_3 such that q_1 depends on q_3 and q_3 depends on q_2. ○ A macro scheme is restricted to *no recursion* if dependent pointers are forbidden and *topological recursion* if no pointer may depend on itself; that is, there exists no circular sequence of pointer dependencies. Note that for external schemes, this definition applies only to the external dictionary.

Definition 5.1.6: Two pointers *overlap* if their targets overlap. A macro scheme is restricted to *no overlapping* if overlapping pointers are forbidden. ○

Definition 5.1.7: A compressed (original) pointer q *points to the left* if the leftmost character of its target is to the left of q (the leftmost character of the string represented by q). A *right pointer* is defined similarly. A macro scheme is restricted to *unidirectional pointers* if all pointers must point in the same direction. As a special case of this restriction, we can restrict a macro scheme to have only *left* or *right* pointers. Note that for external schemes, this definition applies only to the external dictionary. ○

The different combinations of the four basic macro schemes we have defined and the recursion, overlapping, and pointer direction restrictions provide us with a large number of data compression methods. The combinations are sufficiently general to cover a large number of the textual substitution schemes proposed in the literature.

5.2. INHERENT POWER OF THE MODEL

Simply examining how a data compression method compresses "easy" strings can say much about the basic power of the method, even though such strings may not be likely to occur in practice. Before proceeding to a theorem which addresses this issue, we first present a lemma which observes that a string that consists of a single character repeated must be as least as easy to compress as any other string of the same length.

Lemma 5.2.1: Let Σ be any alphabet, let a be any character in Σ, let s be any string over Σ, and let S be any macro scheme. Then:

$$|\Delta_S(s)| \geq |\Delta_S(a^{|s|})|$$

Proof: Construct the string α by replacing each character of Σ that appears in $\Delta_S(s)$ by a. Then $|\alpha| = |\Delta_S(s)|$ and α is a compressed form (using the scheme S) of $a^{|s|}$. Hence, since $|\Delta_S(a^{|s|})| \leq |\alpha|$, the lemma follows. $\bigcirc$

The following theorem addresses external schemes. A similar theorem can be proved for internal schemes (see the bibliographic notes).

Theorem 5.2.1: For all strings s, if only topological recursion is allowed, then (assuming s is compressible) both $|\Delta_{EPM}(s)|$ and $|\Delta_{OEPM}(s)|$ are:

(A) $\geq p^*\log_2(|s|/p) + 1.9p$.

(B) $\geq 3p^*\log_3(|s|/p) - .02p$ when overlapping is forbidden.

(C) $\geq 2(p|s|)^{\frac{1}{2}}$ when recursion is forbidden.

(D) $\geq 2(p|s|)^{\frac{1}{2}}$ when both recursion and overlapping are forbidden.

(E) (A) through (D) hold even if pointers are required to be unidirectional.

If non-topological recursion is allowed, then

(F) The bounds of (A) through (E) hold for the *EPM* scheme.

But:

(G) $|\Delta_{OEPM}(s)| \geq 2p+1$ independent of what overlapping and pointer direction restrictions are made.

Furthermore, all of the bounds in (A) through (G) are tight; that is, each is attained for infinitely many strings $s^{\dagger}$.

Proof of Part B: Since any compressed pointer may always be converted to an original pointer, $|\Delta_{OEPM}(s)| \leq |\Delta_{EPM}(s)|$. Hence, it is sufficient to show that the *OEPM* scheme satisfies this bound and the *EPM* scheme can

---

† Actually, the bound in (A) is just an approximation for the expression $\text{MIN}\{p\lceil\log_2|s|/i\rceil + i + p: p < i \leq 2p\}$ which is attained exactly infinitely often. Similarly, the bound in (B) is just an approximation for the expression $\textit{MIN}\{3p\lceil\log_3(|s|/i)\rceil + i: 2p < i \leq 4p\}$ which is attained exactly for infinitely many strings.

attain it infinitely often. By Lemma 5.2.1 we can assume that $s=a^{|s|}$. Since overlapping is forbidden, the pointers of $\Delta_{OEPM}(s)$ can be divided into a sequence of sets $S_1, \cdots, S_m$ such that the pointers in S_i, $1<i\leq m$, have targets whose compressed representation consists of pointers in some s_j, $j<i$; in fact, since we are concerned only with worst-case performance[†], we can assume that $j=i-1$. We can also assume that S_i, $1\leq i\leq m$, contains at most 3 pointers. This assumption is warranted because for any $k\geq4$, there are i and j such that $2i+3j\leq k\leq 2^i3^j$ and so we can replace a set S_i of 4 or more pointers by a sequence of sets having at most 3 pointers where the last set in the sequence will represent a string at least as long as that represented by the original sequence of 4 or more. Hence, for some $x\leq2$, we can assume that for all $i>x$, S_i contains exactly 3 pointers (because we can assume that the sets of 2 come first and a sequence of three 2-pointer sets can be replaced by two 3-pointer sets). Given this assumption, it can be assumed that for some $2p<k\leq4p$, $0\leq M\leq L\leq1$, and n, $\Delta_{OEPM}(s)$ is of the form:

$$a^k(q_0^2)^L(q_1^2)^M(\prod_{i=2}^{n}q_i^3)\#q_{n+1}^3$$

where q_0 points to a^k; q_1 points to q_0^2; q_2 points to a^K, q_0^2, or q_1^2 depending on the the values of L and M; and for $3\leq i\leq n+1$, q_i points to q_{i-1}^3. Thus we have:

$$|\Delta_{OEPM}(s)| \geq k+3np+2Lp+2Mp$$

$$\geq 3p\lceil\log_3(|s|/k2^L2^M)\rceil+k+2Lp+2Mp$$

$$\geq 3p\lceil\log_3(|s|/k)\rceil+k+3p(\frac{2}{3}-\log_32)(L+M)$$

$$\geq 3p\lceil\log_3(|s|/k)\rceil+k$$

$$\geq MIN\{3p\lceil\log_3(|s|/i)\rceil+i:\ 2p<i\leq4p\}$$

$$\geq 3p^*\log_3(|s|/p)+MIN\{p(h-3\log_3h):\ 2<h\leq4\}$$

$$> 3p^*\log_3(|s|/p)-.02p$$

For any $2p<i\leq4p$ and $n>1$, the bound of

[†] It is not necessary to consider a compressed form of length x for a string a^y if there is a compressed form of length $<x$ for a string a^z where $z\geq y$.

$$MIN\{3p\lceil\log_3(|s|/i)\rceil+i: 2p<i\leq 4p\}$$

is achieved using the *EPM* scheme with no overlapping on the string:

$$s=a^{i3^n} \bigcirc$$

Proof of Part D: By Lemma 5.2.1, we can assume that $s=a^{|s|}$. Consider a minimal length compressed form t for s. Without loss of generality we can assume that t has the form

$$t = (\prod_{j=1}^{k}x_j)\#(\prod_{j=1}^{k}q_j^{i_j})z$$

where

$$q_j^{i_j}$$

denotes i_j copies of a pointer to the string x_j. Given that $|t|<|s|$, we have:

$$|t| = |z|+\sum_{j=1}^{k}(|x_j|+pi_j)$$

$$= |z|+\sum_{j=1}^{k}(|x_j|+(pi_j|x_j|)/|x_j|)$$

$$\geq \lceil |z|+\sum_{j=1}^{k}2(pi_j|x_j|)^{\frac{1}{2}}\rceil$$

$$= \lceil |z|+2p^{\frac{1}{2}}\sum_{j=1}^{k}(i_j|x_j|)^{\frac{1}{2}}\rceil$$

$$\geq \lceil |z|+2p^{\frac{1}{2}}(|s|-|z|)^{\frac{1}{2}}\rceil$$

$$\geq \lceil 2(p|s|)^{\frac{1}{2}}\rceil$$

The first inequality appearing above follows from the fact that for any real

$h > 0$, the function (from positive reals to positive reals)

$$f(i) = i + (h/i)$$

achieves a minimum at $i = h^{\frac{1}{2}}$. The second inequality follows from the fact that for all integers $k \geq 0$ and all non-negative reals i_j, $1 \leq j \leq k$:

$$\sum_{j=1}^{k} i_j^{\frac{1}{2}} \geq (\sum_{j=1}^{k} i_j)^{\frac{1}{2}}$$

To see that the third inequality holds, let $i = |z|$ and $j = |s| - |z|$ and note that since $|t| < |s|$, it must be true that $p < j$. Hence, if the third inequality did not hold, we would have

$$i + 2(p\,j)^{\frac{1}{2}} < 2(p(i+j))^{\frac{1}{2}}$$

which implies

$$
\begin{aligned}
i + 4p \quad &< i + 4(p\,j)^{\frac{1}{2}} \quad \text{- since } p < j \\
&= (i^2 + 4(p\,j)^{\frac{1}{2}}i)/i \quad \text{- since } i > 0 \\
&= (i^2 + 4(p\,j)^{\frac{1}{2}}i + 4p\,j - 4p\,j)/i \\
&= ((i + 2(p\,j)^{\frac{1}{2}})^2 - 4p\,j)/i \\
&< ((2(p(i+j))^{\frac{1}{2}})^2 - 4p\,j)/i \quad \text{- by assumption} \\
&= (4p(i+j) - 4p\,j)/i \\
&= (4pi + (4p\,j - 4p\,j))/i \\
&= 4p
\end{aligned}
$$

which is a contradiction (since $i > 0$).

For any $i > 2$, the bound of (D) is achieved on the string

$$w_i = a^{p\,i^2}$$

by using the compressed form:

$$a^{pi} \# p^i$$

That is, this compressed form has length $2pi$, which is the same as:

$$2(pw_i)^{1/2} = 2(p(pi^2))^{1/2} = 2pi. \quad \bigcirc$$

The proofs of Parts (B) and (D) that were provided for the theorem above contain the key ideas; references to proofs for the other parts are contained at the end of this chapter. The theorem says that macro schemes are not as "wild" as methods considered in the next chapter but, if recursion is allowed, do have the ability to "count". That is, a string of n zeros can be represented with $O(log(n))$ bits. Bounds (C) and (D) show that recursion is in some sense a more serious restriction than overlapping. Bound (G) shows the limitations of a model that allows p to be independent of $|S|$; clearly, if p is constant, the set of all pointers cannot represent an infinite number of strings.

Another way to examine the power of the macro model is to consider worst-case performance ratios between schemes. For example, the next two theorems examine the relationships between compressed and original schemes and the relationships between internal and external schemes, respectively.

Theorem 5.2.2: For any string s,

$$|\Delta_{OPM}(s)| \leq |\Delta_{CPM}(s)|$$

independent of what restrictions are made (provided the same restrictions are used for both). Furthermore, for any real $h > 0$, using any alphabet of size ≥ 1, there are infinitely many strings s for which:

$$\frac{|\Delta_{OPM}(s)|}{|\Delta_{CPM}(s)|} < h$$

Proof: Since a compressed pointer may always be converted to an original pointer, it follows that for any string s, $|\Delta_{OPM}(s)| \leq |\Delta_{CPM}(s)|$, independent of what restrictions are made. Using a construction similar to that of the proof of Theorem 5.2.1, it can be shown that $|\Delta_{CPM}(a^n)|$ is $O(plog2(n))$. Hence, since $|\Delta_{OPM}(a^n)| = p+1^†$, the theorem follows. $\bigcirc$

---

† Recall that this string can be represented as $a(1,n-1)$ by employing the pointer $(1,n-1)$ which forms a degenerate cycle).

Theorem 5.2.3: For any string s,

(A) $\dfrac{2}{3} |\Delta_{CPM}(s)| < |\Delta_{EPM}(s)| \leq |\Delta_{CPM}(s)|+p$

(B) $\dfrac{1}{2} |\Delta_{OPM}(s)| < |\Delta_{OEPM}(s)| \leq |\Delta_{OPM}(s)|+p$

regardless of whether topological recursion is assumed. Furthermore, these bounds are tight[†].

Proof of Part A: The proof of the second inequality is trivial since $\Delta_{CPM}(s)$ may be used as the external dictionary. Let us now demonstrate the bound of 2/3. For this proof only, we use the notation: For strings uv and vw (v may be the null string), $uv-vw$ denotes w and $uv+vw$ denotes v. For a string s, consider $\Delta_{EPM}(s)=s_0\#s_1$. Write s_0 as

$$s_0 = \prod_{i=1}^{k} r_i$$

where r_1 is the first factor in s_0 and r_i, $2\leq i\leq k$, is $r_{i-1}-z$ where z is a substring of s_0 satisfying the following two conditions:

(1) z is a factor in s_0 that either overlaps with r_{i-1} or starts directly after r_{i-1}.

(2) There is no other factor in s_0 that satisfies condition 1 and extends further to the right in s_0 than z.

Since $\Delta_{EPM}(s)$ is (by definition) a minimal length compressed form, the partition of s_0 as described above is well defined. Furthermore, by construction, the following two facts hold:

(1) The set $\{R_i\colon r_i$ *is a compressed form for* $R_i\}$ is a set of non-overlapping substrings of s.

---

† For part (B) this tightness does not depend on the alphabet size; that is, for any real $h>0$, there are infinitely many strings over a 2-symbol alphabet for which the bound of $\dfrac{1}{2}+h$ can be achieved for (B). For Part (A) tightness does depend slightly on the alphabet size; more precisely, there are infinitely many strings over a k-symbol alphabet, $k\geq 2$, for which the bound of $\dfrac{2k-1}{3k-2}+h$ can be achieved for (A).

(2) Each factor in s_0 is, for some i, a substring of the string $r_i r_{i+1}$.

It is possible to construct a CPM compressed form t for s from s_1 as follows:

All characters (i.e., non-pointers) in s_1 are left intact. Find a pointer q in s_1 with r_1 as its target and replace q by r_1. For $2 \leq i \leq k$, find a pointer q in s_1 with a target z satisfying $r_i = r_{i-1} - z$ and replace q by $q' r_i$ where q' is a pointer to $r_{i-1} + z$. All other pointers q in s_1 point to a substring of $r_i r_{i+1}$ for some i and may be replaced by two pointers, one to r_i and one to r_{i+1}.

It is possible that for some strings, the substitutions described above cause some pointers to have targets of size p or smaller. In that case, we can reduce the size of t by deleting pointers of this kind and substituting their targets. Similarly, it may be possible to reduce the size of t by finding adjacent pairs of pointers that we created as described above and find a new target such that the pair of pointers can be replaced by a single pointer together with less than p characters. Since we are looking for a worst-case ratio (which we show to be tight shortly), we can assume that it is not possible to shorten t in the two ways described above. Having made this assumption, it follows that for a worst-case ratio, $|s_0| \geq pn$, where n denotes the number of pointers in s_1. Thus, if we let m denote the number of characters in s_1, we have:

$$\frac{|\Delta_{EPM}(s)|}{|\Delta_{CPM}(s)|} \geq \frac{|\Delta_{EPM}(s)|}{|t|}$$

$$\geq \frac{pn + m + |s_0|}{2pn + m + |s_0|}$$

$$\geq \frac{pn + |s_0|}{2pn + |s_0|}$$

$$\geq \frac{2}{3}$$

A more careful analysis shows that the inequality above must a strict ($>$, not $\geq$).

We now show the bound of 2/3 is tight. Let us first see how a bound of 3/4 may be achieved with a 2 symbol alphabet $\{a,b\}$. For n a multiple of p let:

$$s_n = \prod_{i=1}^{n/p} a^{ip} b^{n-(i-1)p}$$

Using the EPM scheme, s_n can be written as

$$a^n b^n \prod_{i=1}^{n/p}((n-i)p, n+p)$$

and so it follows that $|\Delta_{EPM}(s_n)| \leq 3n$. On the other hand, if we attempt to factor s_n using the CPM scheme, a shortest compressed form for s_n is

$$a^p b^n (\prod_{i=2}^{n/p-1} q_{1,i} q_{2,i}) a^n b^n$$

where $q_{1,i}$ denotes a pointer into a^n and $q_{2,i}$ denotes a pointer into b^n. Hence $|\Delta_{CPM}(s_n)| \geq 4n + O(p)$, and a bound of 3/4 follows.

For a k symbol alphabet, $k \geq 2$, we can generalize the above construction by defining

$$s_n = \prod_{i=1}^{K-1} (\prod_{j=1}^{n} a_i^{jp} a_{i+1}^{n-(j-1)p})$$

and the bound of $\dfrac{2k-1}{3k-2}$ follows. Hence, the bound of 2/3 follows for an unbounded alphabet size. $\bigcirc$

Proof of Part B: For a string s, we can consider $\Delta_{OEPM}(s) = s_0 \# s_1$ and proceed in a fashion analogous to the proof of part A, the only difference being that this proof is a bit simplier since we cannot make any claims about $|s_0|$. This is because with original pointers, pointers indicate the decompressed form of s_0, not s_0 itself; thus s_0 can be very small compared to the number of pointers in s_1. Hence, using the notation of part A:

$$\frac{|\Delta_{OEPM}(s)|}{|\Delta_{OPM}(s)|} > \frac{pn}{2pn} = \frac{1}{2}$$

This bound may be shown tight (even for two symbol alphabets) as follows:

For $n > 0$, let:

$$s_n = \prod_{i=1}^{n/p} a^{ip} b^{n-(i-1)p}$$

Using an external dictionary of $a^n b^n$, it follows that

$$|\Delta_{OEPM}(s_n)| \leq n + O(p \log_2(n))$$

regardless of whether topological recursion is used. Whereas it is easy to check that

$$|\Delta_{OPM}(s_n)| \geq 2n$$

regardless of whether topological recursion is used. Thus, the bound of 1/2 is approached arbitrarily closely as n gets large. $\bigcirc$

5.3. TWO NP-COMPLETE ENCODING PROBLEMS

A large number of results concerning the intractability of optimal encoding for the macro model are known. In this section, we present two sample theorems. These two theorems parallel two linear time algorithms (for restricted versions of these problems) to be presented in the next section. Section 5.5 then gives an informal characterization of what makes an encoding problem for the macro model intractable.

We assume that the reader is familiar with basic notions from the analysis of algorithms. However, before proceeding to the first theorem of this section, we briefly review the notion of *NP*-completeness. We shall use this notion to argue that certain problems are likely to be intractable. It simplifies the discussion to limit our attention to yes-no problems, or equivalently, language recognition problems; that is if the answer to some input is "yes", then that input is considered in the language accepted by the program, otherwise, the input is not in the language. Typically, computational problems can easily be formulated as language recognition problems. For example, the problem of finding a *Hamilton circuit* in a graph (a cycle that visits every vertex in the graph exactly once) can be formulated as the yes-no question (the classic *Hamilton circuit problem*):

"Given a graph G and an integer K, does G have a Hamilton circuit of length K?"

Clearly, if the Hamilton circuit problem is intractable, then so is the problem of actually finding the circuit.

The class P is the set of all languages that can be recognized in polynomial time[†]. The class NP is the set of all languages that can be recognized in polynomial time by a non-deterministic program[††]. Clearly, NP contains P. In addition, it would appear that this containment is proper. For example, no polynomial time algorithm has ever been found for the Hamilton circuit problem. Whereas, an NP algorithm can easily solve it by first guessing a sequence of edges, then checking if this sequence is one less than the number of nodes in the graph, then checking if this sequence forms a cycle, and then checking that the nodes are distinct. Unfortunately, to date, no one has been able to prove that NP properly contains P. However, hundreds of problems (which are not known to be in P), including the Hamilton circuit problem, have been shown to be NP-complete; such problems have the property that they are in NP and if any one of them could be shown to be in P, then $P=NP$. Thus, NP-complete problems are in some sense the "hardest" problems in NP. Hence, if one believes that NP properly contains P, then showing that a problem is NP-complete is tantamount to showing that the problem does not have a polynomial time solution (i.e., it is intractable for all practical purposes[†††]). A common way of proving that a problem X is NP-complete is to first show that X is in NP, and then show that if one had a (deterministic) polynomial time algorithm for X, you could use it to solve some known NP-complete problem in polynomial time.

The first theorem of this section shows that optimal encoding for the external models is likely to be, in general, intractable.

[†] That is, there exists a program (for a standard random access machine) which for every input of length n, always halts and correctly answers *yes* or *no* in at most $Q(n)$ steps, where $Q(n)$ is a polynomial (that depends on the language but not on the particular input).

[††] There are many equivalent ways of defining a *non-deterministic program*. One is to add a new statement of the form **choice**(*statement1,statement2*) which non-deterministically chooses to execute exactly one of the two statements. Note that *statement1* and *statement2* could be any legal statement, including a **begin .. end** block, a procedure call, or another **choice** statement. A non-deterministic program *accepts an input* if there is at least one way to execute **choice** statements to cause the program to answer *yes*; otherwise the program *rejects* the input.

[†††] We are not proposing that all problems in P are tractable in practice, only that problems not in P are not tractable.

Theorem 5.3.1: Given a string s and an integer K, it is NP-complete to determine whether $|\Delta_{EPM}(s)| \leq K$ or $|\Delta_{OEPM}(s)| \leq K$ when both recursion and overlapping are forbidden. Furthermore, this condition is true regardless if p is part of the problem input or is constrained to be a fixed integer ≥ 1.

Proof: We consider only the case $p > 1$; references for the case $p = 1$ are given in the bibliographic notes. Note that when both recursion and overlapping are forbidden, the EPM and OEPM schemes are equivalent.

We will show that if we could determine in polynomial time if $|\Delta_{EPM}(s)| \leq K$ (when recursion and overlapping are forbidden), then we could solve in polynomial time a well-known NP-complete problem, the *node cover problem*, which is: Given an undirected graph G and an integer K, is there a set of K or less nodes in G such that every edge of G is incident to at least one of these nodes.

Let

$$G = (V = \{v_1, ..., v_n\}, E = \{e_1, ..., e_m\}), K$$

be an instance of the node cover problem and let $p = p_0$. Let \$ be a special symbol and let @ denote a new, distinct symbol each time it occurs. For v_i in V, let $V_i = \$ v_i^{p-1} \$$ and for $e_i = (v_j, v_k)$ in E, let $E_i = \$ v_j^{p-1} \$ v_k^{p-1} \$$. Now let:

$$s = (\prod_{i=1}^{p} \prod_{j=1}^{n} V_j @)(\prod_{i=1}^{m} E_i @)$$

We claim that G has a node cover of size K if and only if $|\Delta(s)| \leq |s| + K - m$.

First suppose that G has a node cover X of size K. We shall construct a compressed form t for s (having length $|s| + K - m$) where t is of the form

$$s_0 \# (\prod_{i=1}^{p} \prod_{j=1}^{n} \overline{V}_j @)(\prod_{i=1}^{m} \overline{E}_i @)$$

where s_0 contains those V_i for which v_i is in X, and $\overline{V}_j$ is V_j if v_j is not in X and a pointer to v_j in s_0 if v_j is in X. If E_i is $\$ v_j^{p-1} \$ v_k^{p-1} \$$, then $\overline{E}_i$ is either $r v_k^{p-1} \$$ or $\$ v_j^{p-1} q$ where r is a pointer to v_j in s_0 and q is a pointer to v_k in s_0.

Since X is a node cover, this construction is always possible. We can now compute the length of t:

$$|s_0| = K(p+1)$$

$$\left|\prod_{i=1}^{p}\prod_{j=1}^{n}V_j@\right| = \left|\prod_{i=1}^{p}\prod_{j=1}^{n}V_j@\right| - pK$$

$$\left|\prod_{i=1}^{m}E_i@\right| = \left|\prod_{i=1}^{m}E_i@\right| - m.$$

Hence, $|\Delta(s)| \le |t| = |s| + K(p+1) - pK - m = |s| + K - m$, as was to be shown.

Conversely, suppose that $|\Delta(s)| \le |s| + K - m$. We shall show that G has a node cover of size at most K. First observe that since overlapping of pointer targets is forbidden, no pointer in $\Delta(s)$ can refer, for any strings x and y, to a string of the form $xv_i\$v_jy$, $x@y$, or $x@y$ since such a string can occur at most once in s and no gain can be achieved by factoring it out. Thus, $\Delta(s)$ is of the form

$$s_0\#\left(\prod_{i=1}^{p}\prod_{j=1}^{n}V_j@\right)\left(\prod_{i=1}^{m}E_i@\right)$$

where s_0 is a dictionary of macro bodies and the V_j's and E_i's are the shortest compressed forms of the V_j's and E_i's respectively using s_0. As mentioned earlier, without loss of generality we are assuming throughout this section that every pointer references a string of length at least $p+1$. Thus, since $|V_i| = p+1$, we can infer that each V_i is either V_i itself or a pointer to an occurrence of v_i in s_0. Similarly, since $|E_i| = 2p+1$, each E_i must either consist of E_i itself or else be a string of the form $rv_j^{p-1}\$$ or $\$v_j^{p-1}r$ where r is a pointer to some V_i in s_0. Now let L be the number of E_i's such that $E_i = E_i$; that is, the number of E_i's that have not had a factor removed. Then

$$\left|\prod_{i=1}^{m}E_i@\right| = \left|\prod_{i=1}^{m}E_i@\right| - (m-L)$$

since removing a factor from an E_i saves one character. Let J be the number of V_i's in s_0. Then $|s_0| = J(p+1)$ and

$$|\prod_{i=1}^{p}\prod_{j=1}^{n}V_j@| = |\prod_{i=1}^{p}\prod_{j=1}^{n}V_j@|-Jp$$

because each v_i that is replaced by a pointer saves one character. Thus $|\Delta(s)| = J(p+1)+|s|-Jp-(m-L) = |s|+J+L-m$, and so $J+L \leq K$. We now claim that G has a node cover of size $J+L$ formed by taking the J nodes represented in s_0 and one node from each of the L edges not factored in $\Delta(s)$. Therefore G has a node cover of size K, as was to be shown. $\bigcirc$

Theorem 5.3.2: Given a string s and an integer K, it is NP-complete to determine whether $|\Delta_{CPM}(s)|\leq K$ or $|\Delta_{OPM}(s)|\leq K$. Furthermore, this condition is true regardless if p is part of the problem input or is constrained to be a fixed integer ≥ 1. $\bigcirc$

References to a proof of the theorem above as well as related NP-completeness results (e.g., external schemes without restrictions or internal schemes with restrictions) are given in the bibliographic notes. Note that in the reduction used in the proof of the theorem above, the alphabet size is allowed to depend on the instance the NP-complete problem in question. However, all of the results above hold even when the alphabet is fixed.

5.4. TWO LINEAR-TIME ENCODING ALGORITHMS

In this section, we present linear time encoding algorithms for restricted versions of the problems shown NP-complete in the last section. We start with a restricted version of the *EPM* scheme where the dictionary is specified in advance.

Given a dictionary, a particular string may have many different compressed forms. For example, if the dictionary consists of the two strings ab and bab, the string $ababbab$ could be represented as $11b1$, $a22$, or $a2b1$, where 1 denotes a pointer to ab and 2 a pointer to bab. *Wagner's algorithm* is a simple dynamic programming algorithm to find a minimal length compressed form, when the dictionary is given in advance[†]. In fact, although his algorithm does not assume variable length pointers, the ability to point to a substring of a dictionary element, or pointers within dictionary elements, it

---

[†] Other methods for doing this are discussed in the bibliographic notes.

is so easily generalized to accommodate these features, that we do so to illustrate this fact. For D a given dictionary of strings, and $s = a_1 \cdots a_n$ a string to be compressed, let $q_{i,j}$ be defined as follows:

> DEFINITION OF $q_{i,j}$:
>
>> **if** $(i = j)$ **then** a_i
>>
>> **else if** (exists a pointer with expanded target $a_i \cdots a_j$)
>>> **then** the shortest one
>>
>> **else** a nil-pointer of infinite length

The representation and lengths of pointers are unimportant, but must be specified before $q_{i,j}$ can be defined. We extend the *MIN* function to apply to a set of strings X, where $MIN(X)$ denotes the shortest string in X[†].

$$SHORT(n+1) := \text{empty string}$$

> **for** $i = n$ **to** 1 **by** -1 **do**
>> $SHORT(i) := \text{MIN}\{q_{i,j}SHORT(j+1): i \le j \le n\}$

shortest compressed form of $s := SHORT[1]$

Algorithm 5.4.1
Wagner's Algorithm (slightly modified)

Algorithm 5.4.1 is a simple dynamic programming algorithm[††] that works from right to left in s. For each $1 \le i \le n$, it computes $SHORT(i)$, a shortest compressed form of the ith through n^{th} characters of s (using dictionary D). Algorithm 5.4.1 can clearly be implemented in polynomial time. As

---

† Ties are resolved using some lexicographic ordering.
†† Dynamic programming algorithms compute a solution to a large problem by first storing solutions to smaller problems (of the same type) in a table. See the bibliographic notes for references to introductory texts on dynamic programming.

presented above, however, it is not necessarily linear time. It is not necessarily true that the longest match possible is taken for the pointer to start $SHORT[i]$; it may be that it is better to choose a shorter match that is represented by a shorter pointer. Thus, in general, many different pointers $q_{i,j}$ may have to be checked at each iteration. However, with some reasonable assumptions about relative pointer sizes and by using appropriate data structures, this algorithm can be implemented in linear time.

A similar approach to that of Algorithm 5.4.1 (dynamic programming from right to left) works for the OPM/L scheme (OPM scheme restricted to left pointers). In contrast to our presentation of Wagner's algorithm, we will return to the basic assumption of this chapter that pointers have a single uniform size p (although our discussion can easily be generalized to variable length pointers). Let $s = a_1 \cdots a_n$ be a string to be compressed with the OPM/L scheme. The key to implementing this algorithm in linear time is to be able to quickly compute, for a position in the string, what is the longest substring that both starts at this position and occurs earlier in the string. The bibliographic notes contains references to a a number of data structures that can be constructed in linear time and used to compute this information in $O(1)$ time per querry. For the purposes of our presentation, we simply assume that along with a string s we are given an array of strings $MATCH$ where $MATCH[k]$, $1 \leq k \leq n$, is the longest substring $a_i \cdots a_j$ of s such that $i < k$ and $a_i \cdots a_j = a_k \cdots a_{k+j-i}$; we let q_k denote a pointer to $MATCH[k]$.

In a similar spirit to Algorithm 5.4.1, each string $SHORT[i]$ computed by Algorithm 5.4.2 is the shortest compressed form for the ith through n^{th} characters of s given that the string consisting of the first through $i-i^{th}$ characters of s is available as a "dictionary". To perform the main loop of Algorithm 5.4.2 in linear time, the array $SHORT$ can be represented by storing at $SHORT[i]$ its length together with a_i or q_i followed by a pointer to $SHORT[i+1]$ or $SHORT[i+|MATCH[i]|]$; this allows the body of the main loop to be executed in $O(1)$ time. The last step of the algorithm can output $SHORT[1]$ in linear time by following the sequence of pointers through the array $SHORT$.

Algorithm 5.4.1 was presented in general terms, and we did not worry about a linear time implementation (although under reasonable assumptions one is possible). By contrast, Algorithm 5.4.2 has been carefully presented to check only two possibilities in the body of the main loop. The key to verifying the correctness of Algorithm 5.4.2 is to note that, without loss of generality, we can assume that in any minimal length compressed form t for s, any substring that is represented by a pointer to an earlier occurrence is as long as

$SHORT[n+1] :=$ empty string

for $i:=n-1$ **downto** 1 **do**
        if $MATCH[i]$ is the empty string
                then $SHORT[i] := a_i SHORT[i+1]$
                else $SHORT[i] = \text{MIN}\{a_i SHORT[i+1],$
                                    $q_i SHORT[i+ |MATCH[i]\,|]\}$

$\Delta_{OPM/L}(s) = SHORT[1]$

Algorithm 5.4.2
Optimal OPM/L Algorithm

possible. That is, if the substring $a_i \cdots a_j$ of s is represented by a pointer q in t, then $a_i \cdots a_{j+1}$ is not a substring of $a_1 \cdots a_{i-1}$. Otherwise, we could obtain an equivalent compressed form of the same or shorter length than t by changing q to represent $a_i \cdots a_{j+1}$ and then either deleting a character (if q is followed by a character in t) or changing the pointer after q in t, call it r, as follows: Suppose that r represents the substring $a_{j+1} \cdots a_l$ of s. If the length of this string $(l-j)$ is greater than $p+1$, then replace r by a pointer that represents the string $a_{j+2} \cdots a_l$; otherwise, replace r by the string $a_{j+2} \cdots a_l$; note that if $l-j=p$, this substitution reduces the length of t by 1.

5.5. CHARACTERIZING TRACTABILITY

The difference between the compression methods considered in the last two sections is that with the schemes considered in Section 2.4, the set of legal pointers does not depend on the string being compressed, whereas this was not the case in Section 2.3. For example, suppose that positions 50 through 59 are identical to positions 100 through 109 of a string. Then with the OPM scheme, a pointer (100,10) may or may not be legal, depending on whether it causes a cycle of pointer dependences. However, this pointer is always legal for the OPM/L scheme. The following is an informal characterization of when encoding for the macro model is NP-complete:

> *If for a macro scheme the set of legal pointers does not depend on the string being compressed, then the scheme has a polynomial time encoding algorithm. Otherwise, encoding is NP-complete for this scheme.*

5.6. GREEDY VERSUS OPTIMAL ALGORITHMS

This section considers worst-case performance bounds between provably optimal off-line algorithms and on-line greedy heuristics of the type considered in Chapter 3. Our approach is to consider the static dictionary model in detail and present a theorem that can be easily modified to apply to a variety of other models (in particular, the OPM/L scheme).

$i := 1$

while $i \leq m$ **do begin**
      let j be such that $j-i-|q_{i,j}|$ is maximum
      replace $a_i, \ldots, a_j$ by $q_{i,j}$
      $i = j+1$
      end

Algorithm 5.6.1
Static Dictionary Greedy Encoding Algorithm

To simplify our presentation, we assume that dictionary elements do not contain pointers to other dictionary elements. Algorithm 5.6.1 is the greedy encoding algorithm of Chapter 3 for the static dictionary model expressed with the same notation that was used to present Wagner's algorithm. It simply proceeds through the string a character at a time, and at every opportunity, replaces a string by a pointer (choosing the best possible replacement). For a dictionary D and a string s, let $M(D,s)$ denote a compressed form obtained by Algorithm 5.4.1 (M for "minimum") and $G(D,s)$ denote the compressed form obtained by Algorithm 5.6.1 (G for "greedy").

Theorem 5.6.1: Let D be a dictionary and s a string. Given the following assumptions:

- No dictionary element contains a pointer.

- It is possible to point to any suffix of a dictionary element (it may be possible to point to other substrings as well).

- All pointers to substrings of the same dictionary element have the same length.

Then:

$$(1) \quad \frac{|M(D,s)|}{|G(D,s)|} \geq \frac{\rho}{p+\rho-1}$$

Furthermore, even if D is restricted to have only 2 elements and s is written over a 2 symbol alphabet, this bound may be obtained arbitrarily closely. That is, for any real $h > 0$, there are infinitely many strings such that:

$$(2) \quad \frac{|M(D,s)|}{|G(D,s)|} < \frac{\rho}{p+\rho-1} + h$$

Proof of Part (1): As discussed earlier, without loss of generality, we can assume that in any minimal length compressed form, any substring that is represented by a pointer to an earlier occurrence is as long as possible; that is, if the substring $a_i \cdots a_j$ of s is represented by a pointer, then $a_i \cdots a_{j+1}$ is not a suffix of a dictionary element. Otherwise, we could obtain an equivalent compressed form of the same or shorter length by changing the pointer to represent $a_i \cdots a_{j+1}$ and then either deleting a character (if the pointer was originally followed by a character) or changing the following pointer[†] (if the pointer was originally followed by another pointer).

To reduce notation, let $t = M(D,s)$ and $u = G(D,s)$. Form the finest partition of t and u into segments $t = t_1 \cdots t_m$ and $u = u_1 \cdots u_m$ such that for $1 \leq j \leq m$, t_j and u_j represent the same substring of s. In order to establish the bound claimed, it is sufficient to show that:

[†] Remember, it will always be possible to change the following pointer because any suffix of a dictionary element may be a pointer target.

$$\frac{\rho}{p+\rho-1} \le \frac{|t_j|}{|u_j|} \le 1 \text{ for } j>1$$

By definition of the greedy algorithm, it is impossible for some t_j to begin with a pointer while u_j begins with a character. Hence it must be that t_j begins with a character and u_j begins with a pointer; otherwise, both t_j and u_j must consist of a single character or pointer (the pointers must be of the same length, due to the greedy algorithm), and so $|t_j| = |u_j|$. Thus we can write

$$t_j = x_1 q_1 x_2 q_2 \cdots x_n q_n x_{n+1}$$

$$u_j = r_1 y_1 r_2 y_2 \cdots r_m y_m$$

where each of the q_i's and r_i's is a pointer, x_1 is a string of one or more characters, and each of the remaining x_i's and y_i's is a string of zero or more characters.

t_j: $\vdash x_1 \dashv \vdash q_1 \dashv \vdash x_2 \dashv \vdash q_2 \dashv \vdash x_3 \dashv$ ...
u_j: $\vdash r_1 \dashv \vdash y_1 \dashv \vdash r_2 \dashv \vdash y_2 \dashv \vdash r_3 \dashv$ ...

Figure 5.6.1

Any substring of s that is represented by characters (as opposed to pointers) in either t_j or u_j must be represented by a pointer in the other, since t_j and u_j have been defined in terms of a finest possible partition of t and u. Figure 5.6.1 suggests the structure of that portion of s represented by t_j and u_j. Notice that for each i, $1 \le i \le n$, q_i represents at least the last character represented by r_i, all of y_i, and at least the first character represented by r_{i+1}. Similarly, for $2 \le i \le m$, r_i represents at least the last character represented by q_{i-1}, all of x_i, and at least the first character represented by q_i. To verify the facts above, depicted in Figure 5.6.1, it is sufficient to observe that except at the end, if q_i starts within r_i, then q_i must go beyond the end of r_i since if q_i ended earlier then q_i wouldn't be as long as possible (as we assumed at the start of the proof) and if q_i ended at the same place we wouldn't have the finest possible partition. Similarly, if r_i starts within a q_i, then r_i

must go beyond the end of q_i since to end earlier would imply a violation of the greedy greedy rule and to end in the same place would violate the finest partition. Thus, it must be that either $m=n$ or $m=n+1$. In addition, for $1 \leq i < m$, $|y_i| \leq |q_i| - 1$, or else the greedy algorithm would have used a pointer instead of y_i (pointing to a suffix of the target of q_i).

Now, one of the following three cases must hold:

Case 1: $n=m$: Since $|x_1| \geq 1$, $|t_j| \geq 1 + \sum_{i=1}^{n} |q_i|$. Hence, since for $1 \leq i < n$, $|y_i| \leq |q_i| - 1$, $|y_n| \leq |q_n|$, and for $1 \leq i \leq n$, $|r_i| \leq p$, we have:

$$\frac{|t_j|}{|u_j|} \geq \frac{1 + \sum_{i=1}^{n} |q_i|}{np + \sum_{i=1}^{n} |y_i|}$$

$$\geq \frac{1 + \sum_{i=1}^{n} |q_i|}{1 + n(p-1) + \sum_{i=1}^{n} |q_i|}$$

$$\geq \frac{1 + np}{1 + n(p + \rho - 1)}$$

$$\geq \frac{\rho}{p + \rho - 1}$$

The inequalities above rest on the fact that if $0 < b \leq c$, then for any $a > 0$:

$$\frac{a+b}{a+c} \geq \frac{b}{c}$$

Case 2: $m=n+1$ and x_{n+1} is the empty string: Thus both t_j and u_j end in a pointer. It must be that y_{m-1} is also empty, or else the greedy algorithm would have replaced the string represented by $y_{m-1}r_m$ by a single pointer (to a suffix of the target of q_n). In addition, it must be that $|r_m| \leq |q_m|$, since the target of r_m is a suffix of the target of q_m. Hence

$$\frac{|t_j|}{|u_j|} \geq \frac{1+\sum_{i=1}^{n}|q_i|}{np+|r_m|+\sum_{i-1}^{n-1}y_i}$$

$$\geq \frac{1+\sum_{i=1}^{n}|q_i|}{1+n(p-1)+\sum_{i=1}^{n}|q_i|}$$

and we may now continue as in Case 1.

Case 3: $m=n+1$ and that x_{n+1} is not the empty string: By our definition of t and u in terms of a finest possible partition, it must be the case that y_{n+1} is the empty string. Also, the string represented by q_n extends at least $(|r_{n+1}|+1)-|x_{n+1}|$ characters past y_n. Hence, it must be that $(|y_n|+|r_{n+1}|+1-|x_{n+1}|) \leq |q_n|$; otherwise, the presence of q_n implies that the greedy algorithm must make y_n the empty string and place a pointer directly after r_n (to a suffix of the target of q_n). This inequality simplifies to $|y_n| \leq (|q_n|-|r_{n+1}|+|x_{n+1}|-1)$. Thus we have:

$$\frac{|t_j|}{|u_j|} \geq \frac{1+|x_{n+1}|+\sum_{i=1}^{n}|q_i|}{np+|r_{n+1}|+|y_n|+\sum_{i=1}^{n-1}y_i}$$

$$\geq \frac{1+|x_{n+1}|+\sum_{i=1}^{n}|q_i|}{n(p-1)+|x_{n+1}|+\sum_{i=1}^{n}|q_i|}$$

$$\geq \frac{1+|x_{n+1}|+n\rho}{|x_{n+1}|+n(p+\rho-1)}$$

$$\geq \frac{\rho}{p+\rho-1}$$

In all of the cases above we have $|t_j|/|u_j| \geq \rho/(p+\rho-1)$. ○

Proof of Part (2): We exhibit infinitely many strings that achieve the bound. Let

$$u = a(b^p), \quad v = (b^{p+\rho-1})a, \quad D = \{u,v\}$$

where any pointer to u has length p and any pointer to v has length ρ. Now, for any $i>0$, let:

$$s(i) = a(v^i)$$

For example, for $\rho=p=2$, $s(3) = abbbabbbabbba$. If q_1 denotes a pointer to u, q_2 a pointer to v, then $M(D,s(i)) = a(q_2^i)$ has length $1+i\rho$, whereas $G(D,s(i)) = (q_1 b^{\rho-1})^i a$ has length $1+i(p+\rho-1)$, from which the bound follows. ○

The theorem above says that the greedy algorithm and an optimal algorithm differ by at most a factor of $\rho/(p+\rho-1)$, which implies that for $p=1$, the greedy algorithm is optimal. Unfortunately, the second half of the theorem says that this bound can be obtained, even for large values of p (and small values of ρ). However, in practice, not only is p likely to be small (e.g., $p=2$) but this sort of worst-case performance is unlikely to occur. From a theoretical standpoint, we view the theorem above to mean that the greedy approach is a reasonable alternative to Wagner's algorithm (i.e., for small values of p, it differs from the optimal by at most a small constant factor).

The impact of Theorem 5.6.1 is somewhat lessened by the presence of the three conditions in its statement. Weaker forms of this theorem can be shown that do not rely on these conditions, but perhaps its greatest value is the techniques used in its proof, which yield insight into what the tradeoffs are between a greedy approach and and off-line approach. For example, with a proof that is very similar to the one above, the same theorem can be shown for bounds between the *OPM/L* scheme and the greedy sliding dictionary algorithm of Chapter 3.

5.7. COLLECTIONS OF STRINGS

We use the term *collection* like the term set, except that we allow an element to be present more than once[†]. We do not bother with a formal definition and formal notation for collections except to extend our notation $|S|$ for the number of elements in a set S to mean the total number of elements, when duplicates are counted, in a collection $|S|$. In practice, collections arise naturally when as list of items that contains duplicates is provided as input to an algorithm. Thus, we state our results for collections instead of sets to capture this generality. However, except when explicitly noted, the distinction between sets and collections is not technically important for the results presented in this section.

It is straightforward to generalize the macro model to compressing a collection of strings rather than just a single string. From a theoretical point of view, for a collection $\{s_1, \cdots ,_n\}$ of strings, we can simply consider the compression of the single string $s_1 \# s_2 \# \cdots \# s_n$. However, in practice, special purpose techniques may be much more appropriate.

A Large Number of Short Strings

A common application is when the collection consists of a large number of short strings. For example, consider the storage of the leaves of a Huffman trie that encodes strings of length $\leq k$ for some k as the basic "alphabet". One way to store such a collection of strings is to concatenate the strings together into one large "master string" and then replace leaves by a pair consisting of a pointer to the starting position of the corresponding string and its length. Given this representation, it is no less efficient to use any master string for the storage that contains all of the strings as substrings. This observation leads naturally to the following definition.

Definition 5.7.1: Given a collection $S = \{s_1 \cdots s_k\}$ of strings, the *superstring problem* for S is to find the shortest string t that contains all strings of S as substrings. ◯

If we let

$$n = \sum_{i=1}^{k} |s_i|$$

---

† In the literature, collections are often called *multi-sets*.

then it is possible to show that any superstring t must satisfy

$$|t| \geq \lfloor 2\sqrt{n} \rfloor - 1$$

and that there are infinitely many superstring problems that achieve this bound. Thus, there can be great savings achieved by computing minimal length superstrings. Unfortunately, the following two definitions and theorem show that the superstring problem is NP-complete even under restrictive conditions.

Definition 5.7.2: A string is *primitive* if no character appears more than once. ◯

Definition 5.7.3: The *directed Hamilton path (circuit) problem* is: Given a directed graph G, is there a path (cycle) that goes through each node of G exactly once. The *restricted directed Hamilton path problem* is the directed Hamilton path problem with the following restrictions:

(1) There is a designated start node s with no incoming edges and a designated end node t with no outgoing edges.

(2) Except for the end node t, all nodes have at least one outgoing edge. ◯

The directed Hamilton path problem is a well-known NP-complete problem from which the restricted version can easily be shown NP-complete. The following theorem uses this fact to show that the superstring problem is NP-complete.

Theorem 5.7.1: The superstring problem is NP-complete. Furthermore, this problem is NP-complete even if for any integer $H \geq 3$, the restriction is made that all strings in the collection must be primitive and of length H.

Proof: We first prove the theorem for non-primitive strings of length 3 and then show how to modify the construction to make all strings primitive and of length H, for $H \geq 3$. Let $G = (V, E)$ be an instance of the restricted directed Hamilton path problem where V is the set of integers from 1 to n (1 is the start node and n the end node) and $|E| = m$. We use the notation $IN(v)$ to denote the number of incoming edges to a vertex v and $OUT(v)$ to denote the number of outgoing edges from a vertex v. We construct strings for G over the alphabet $\Sigma = V \bigcup B \bigcup S$, where $B = \{\bar{v}: v \epsilon V - \{n\}\}$ is the set of barred symbols, and $S=\{@,\#,\$\}$ is the set of special symbols. In the reduction, the barred symbols may be thought of as local to a node while the unbarred symbols from V are thought of as global to the whole graph G.

For each node $v \epsilon V-\{n\}$ we create a set A_v of $2\,^*OUT(v)$ strings. Let

$$R_v = \{w_0, \cdots, w_{OUT(v)-1}\}$$

be the set of nodes adjacent to v. Then

$$A_v = \{\overline{v}w_i\overline{v}\colon\, w_i \epsilon R_v\}\bigcup\{w_i\overline{v}w_{iciplus1}\colon\, w_i \epsilon R_v\}$$

where *ciplus* denotes addition modulo $OUT(v)$.

For each node $v \epsilon V-\{1,n\}$ create a singleton set C_v containing a string of the form $v\#\overline{v}$ called a *connector*. Finally, create a set T that contains elements called *terminal strings:*

$$T = \{@\#\overline{1},n\#\$\}$$

Let S be the union of A_j, $1 \le j < n$, C_i, $1 \le i < n$, and T. We claim that G has a directed Hamilton path if and only if S has a superstring of length $2m+3n$.

Suppose G has a directed Hamilton path. Let (v,w_i) be an edge on the path. First, create a superstring of length $2(OUT(v))+2$ for A_v of the form

$$\overline{v}w_i\overline{v}w_{iciplus1}\overline{v} \cdots \overline{v}w_i$$

called the w_i-*standard superstring for* A_v. This superstring is formed by overlapping the strings of A_v in the order

$$\overline{v}w_i\overline{v}$$
$$w_i\overline{v}w_{iciplus1}$$
$$\overline{v}w_{iciplus1}\overline{v}$$
$$\cdot$$
$$\cdot$$
$$\cdot$$
$$\overline{v}w_{iciplusOUT(v)}\overline{v}$$
$$w_{iciplusOUT(v)}\overline{v}w_i$$

where adjacent pairs have an overlap of length two. Note that the set of w_i-standard superstrings for A_v is in one-to-one correspondence with the cyclic permutations of the integers 0 through $OUT(v)-1$. Also note that the standard superstrings for A_v are the only ones this short.

Let $(u_1, u_2, \cdots, u_n)$ denote the directed Hamilton path where $u_1=1$ and $u_n=n$, and denote the u_j-standard superstring for A_{u_i} as $STD(\overline{u}_i, u_j)$. We can form a superstring for S by overlapping the standard superstrings and the strings in S but not in any A_v in the order:

$$@\#\overline{1}$$
$$STD(\overline{1}, u_2)$$
$$u_2 \# \overline{u}_2$$
$$STD(\overline{u}_2$$
$$u_3)$$
$$u_3 \# \overline{u}_3$$
$$\cdot$$
$$\cdot$$
$$\cdot$$
$$u_{n-1} \# \overline{u}_{n-1}$$
$$STD(\overline{u}_{n-1}, n)$$
$$n \# \$$$

This superstring has length:

$$\sum_{i=1}^{n-1}(2*OUT(i)+2) + (n-2) + 4 = 2m+3n$$

The terms are for the standard superstrings, the $\#$'s from the connectors, and the additional symbols from the terminal strings, respectively.

To prove the converse, we show that $2m+3n$ is a lower bound for the size of a superstring for S and then show that this lower bound can only be achieved if the superstring encodes a directed Hamilton path.

There are a total of $2m+n$ strings, with a total length of $3(2m+n)$. The greatest amount of compression would result from an ordering in which each string except the first and last have an overlap of length 2 on both sides. This order would give a superstring of length $3(2m+n)-2(2m+n-1) = 2m+n+2$. However, the $n-2$ connectors can only have overlaps of length 1 on either side, since no string begins or ends with $\#$. In addition, the terminal strings can overlap at most one symbol on only one side. Observing these requirements, we get a lower bound of $(2m+n+2)+2(n-2)+2 = 2m+3n$ on the length of a superstring for S. Note that such a superstring must begin with $@\#\bar{1}$ and end with $n\#\$$.

Consider two consecutive occurrences of $\#$ in such a superstring. Let x be the string between the two $\#$'s. The first symbol of x must be barred, and the last unbarred, since they are substrings of connectors. Since there are no connectors in x, all substrings of x except the first and the last must have overlaps of length two on both sides. The first string must be $\bar{v}u_j\bar{v}$, the next $u_j\bar{v}u_{jciplus1}$, and so on. Furthermore, all strings in A_v except two must have overlaps of length 2 on both sides, so every string in A_v but one must be succeeded in order by the unique string that overlaps it by two. Thus all strings in A_v must occur contiguously in order and since x contains one string from A_v, it must contain them all. Thus, x is the w_j-standard superstring for A_v.

By applying the above analysis to all sequential pairs of $\#$'s, we obtain $n-1$ different standard strings. We can recover a directed Hamilton path by looking at the symbols next to each $\#$, since the barred and unbarred symbol of each connector correspond to the same node in G. Note that by the location of $@\#\bar{1}$ and $n\#\$$, the path is from node 1 to node n.

We now address the restriction that all strings be primitive and of exactly length H, for $H \geq 3$, by showing how to make the proper modifications on the strings in S. The alphabet Σ is augmented to include $\{\hat{a}: a\epsilon V\}$. For $H=3$, we need only change A_v. Replace strings of the form $\bar{v}a\bar{v}$ by the strings $\bar{v}a\hat{v}$, $a\hat{v}\hat{a}$, and $\hat{v}\hat{a}\bar{v}$. In addition, replace strings of the form $a\bar{v}b$ by $\hat{a}\bar{v}b$. For $H\geq 4$ let y and y' be primitive strings over an alphabet disjoint from Σ of length $H-4$ and $H-2$ respectively. Replace the $\#$ in all connectors and terminals by y'. For A_v, replace strings of the form $\bar{v}a\bar{v}$ by $\bar{v}ay\hat{a}\hat{v}$ and those of the form $a\bar{v}b$ by $\hat{a}\hat{v}y\bar{v}b$. The proofs with these changes differ only slightly from the one for the case of non-primitive strings of length three.

It is easy to check that the superstring problem is in NP and that the above reductions can be done in polynomial time. $\bigcirc$

One question, which naturally arises from the last theorem, is what happens if all strings are of a length shorter than 3. The next theorem and its corollary answer this question by showing a linear time algorithm to find a minimal length superstring for a set of strings of length less than or equal to 2 (we shall consider collections of strings in a later corollary). Before proceeding to this theorem we present a definition and a lemma that are used in the proof.

Definition 5.7.4: For a directed graph $G=(V,E)$, if $G_1=(V_1,E_1)$, $\cdots$, $G_k=(V_k,E_k)$ are the connected components of $G^\dagger$, then let

$$PATH(G) = \sum_{i=1}^{k} \max\{1, \sum_{v \in V_i} \frac{|IN(v)-OUT(v)|}{2}\}.$$

A *path-decomposition* of G is a partition of E into edge disjoint paths. $\bigcirc$

> **while** there is a node v in G with $IN(v) < OUT(v)$ **do**
>   Start at v, traverse edges randomly until a node with
>   no outgoing edges is found, delete the edges traversed
>   from G, and add this path to P.
> **while** G is not empty **do**
>   **if** there is a cycle c that intersects a path p in P
>   **then** delete c from G and "splice" it into p
>   **else** delete a cycle from G and add it to P

Algorithm 5.7.1
Minimal Path Decomposition Algorithm

Lemma 5.7.1: The number of paths in a minimal path-decomposition of a directed graph G is given by $PATH(G)$.

Proof: Algorithm 5.7.1 produces a minimal path decomposition P for a directed graph $G=(V,E)$. Each time a path p is deleted from G (and added to P) in the first **while** loop, the outdegree of the start node of p is reduced by 1, the indegree of the end node of p is reduced by 1, and all other nodes v of p have both $IN(v)$ and $OUT(v)$ reduced by 1 (i.e.,

---

† We consider the connected components of a directed graph to be the connected components of the undirected graph constructed by removing the direction from each edge.

$|IN(v)-OUT(v)|$ is unchanged). Hence, this loop produces

$$\sum_{v \in V} \frac{|IN(v)-OUT(v)|}{2}$$

paths. The second **while** loop adds a new path to P only when a connected component, consisting entirely of cycles (i.e., $IN(v)=OUT(v)$ for all nodes v in this component), is encountered for the first time. ◯

Theorem 5.7.2: For a set of strings $S=\{s_1 \cdots s_n\}$ and an integer K, if $|s_i| \leq 2$, $1 \leq i \leq n$, then there is a linear time and space algorithm to decide if S has a superstring of length K.

Proof: Let Σ denote the alphabet over which S is written. We can assume that all strings in S have length exactly 2 because strings of length 1 are either a substring of a string of length 2 or are a unique character not appearing anywhere else in S. We can also assume all strings in S to be primitive since for a non-primitive string $s_i=aa$ in S, if the character a does not appear anywhere else in S, then S has a superstring of length K if and only if $S-\{s_i\}$ has a superstring of length $K-2$; otherwise, S has a superstring of length K if and only if $S-\{s_i\}$ has a superstring of length $K-1$. We can associate a directed graph $G=(V,E)$ with S by letting $V=\Sigma$ and (a,b) be in E whenever ab is in S. The reader can now verify that S has a superstring of length K if and only if $PATH(G) \leq K-|S|$ and that $PATH(G)$ can be computed using linear time and space. ◯

The theorem above only addresses the decision problem of whether a superstring of length K exists. The following corollary and its proof provide a construction to produce such a superstring.

Corollary 5.7.2a: There is a linear time and space algorithm to find a minimal length superstring for a set of strings of length ≤ 2.

Proof: A single pass over S suffices to make a list of all the distinct characters in S and the number of times each character appears in strings of length 1 and strings of length 2. In a second pass over S, all strings of length 1 can be deleted from S and the strings of length 1 that are not a substring of any other string in S can be saved and concatenated on to the superstring produced for the remainder of S. Thus, in view of the proof of the above theorem it suffices to show a linear time and space algorithm to find a minimal size path-decomposition P for a directed graph G. Such an algorithm was presented in Lemma 5.7.1. Using linked lists, this algorithm may be implemented in linear time. ○

The corollary above addresses only sets of strings. In many practical applications, a string may appear more than once as part of the input. This has no effect on the size of the minimal length superstring or on the existence of a polynomial time algorithm, but does require slightly more work to identify identical strings.

Corollary 5.7.2b: For a collection of strings S over alphabet Σ such that each string in the collection has length less than or equal to 2, algorithms exist to find a minimal length superstring for S which use the following amounts of time and space:

  (1) Linear expected time and linear space.

  (2) $O(|S|\log_2|S|)$ time and linear space.

  (3) Linear time and $O(|S|+|\Sigma|^2)$ space.

Proof: An algorithm is easily constructed for (1) using hashing techniques and for (2) using dictionary techniques. For (3), strings of length 1 can be dealt with as in the above corollary and the number of times each string of length 2 occurs may be tabulated in linear time by using an $O(|\Sigma|)$ by $O(|\Sigma|)$ matrix. Note that this matrix may be effectively initialized to all zeros in $O(1)$ time by using a well-known technique that employs an $O(|S|)$ stack and a "hand shaking" protocol[†]. ○

The theorem above and its corollaries have many practical applications beyond data compression. One is for storing Huffman trees for encoding letter pairs. Another is for storing a directed graph G. The path decomposition of G can be computed and then the superstrings of the paths, separated by markers, can be stored. If d denotes the amount of space to store a node name, this scheme requires space $d(|E|+2PATH(G)-1)$. This size compares favorably with other methods such as storing a list of edges which takes space

---

† This technique for effectively initializing an array M (of any dimension) to 0 in $O(1)$ time will increase the running time and space used by a constant factor. The idea is to have a second (uninitialized) array P of pointers and an initially empty stack S of pointers. Each time an entry of M is accessed, a check is made as to whether the corresponding entry of P points into an active area of the stack, and if so, if that stack frame points back. If so, the entry of M must already contain a valid value; otherwise, this entry can be set to zero and P and S can be appropriately adjusted. See the bibliographic notes.

$2d|E|$ or storing an adjacency list which takes space $d(|E|+2|V|-1)$.

Although some special cases of the superstring problem, such as the one considered above, can be solved both efficiently and optimally, the NP-completeness of the problem in general implies that the use of approximation heuristics may be required to employ compression algorithms based on finding minimal length superstrings. The most common approach to approximation employs some sort of greedy algorithm. To discuss greedy superstring approximation algorithms for a collection $S = \{s_1 \cdots s_k\}$ of strings, we use the following notation:

OVERLAP(x,y): Denotes the string obtained by overlapping the right side of x with the left side of y as much as possible.

COMBINE(x,y): Denotes the smaller of the two strings $OVERLAP(x,y)$ and $OVERLAP(y,x)$. Note that the savings obtained by replacing the two strings x and y by $COMBINE(x,y)$ is given by $|x| + |y| - |COMBINE(x,y)|$; we denote this quantity by $SAVE(x,y)$.

SUBSTR(S,x,y): Denotes the set of all strings in S that are not equal to x or y but are a substring of $COMBINE(x,y)$.

Given this notation, Figure 5.7.1 presents successively more general notions of a greedy approximation algorithm to compute a superstring t for S; note that for simplicity of presentation, we assume that for no $i \neq j$ is s_i a substring of s_j.

It is not hard to see that G0, G1, and G2 have poor worst-case performance. Consider the set of strings:

$$s_1 = a_1 \cdots a_n$$
$$s_2 = a_n a_2$$
$$s_3 = a_2 \cdots a_{n+1}$$
$$s_4 = a_{n+1} a_3$$
$$.$$
$$.$$
$$.$$
$$s_{2n} = a_{2n-1} a_{n+1}$$
$$s_{2n+1} = a_{n+1} \cdots a_{2n}$$

G0: t := empty string
    for i:=1 to k **do** $t := OVERLAP(t,s_i)$

G1: t := empty string
    for i:=1 to k **do** $t := COMBINE(t,s_i)$

G2: t := empty string
    while $S \neq \{\}$ **do begin**
        s_i := an element of S that maximizes $SAVE(t,s_i)$
        $S := S-\{s_i\}$
        $t := COMBINE(t,s_i)$
    end

G3: **while** $|S|>1$ **do begin**
        s_i, s_j := elements of S that maximize $SAVE(s_i,s_j)$
        $S := (S-\{s_i,s_j\}) \bigcup \{COMBINE(s_i,s_j)\}$
    end
    t := the single string contained in S

G4: **while** $|S|>1$ **do begin**
        s_i, s_j := elements of S that maximize
            $SAVE(s_i,s_j)+||SUBSTR(S,s_i,s_j)||$
        $S := (S-\{s_i,s_j\}-SUBSTR(S,s_i,s_j)) \bigcup \{COMBINE(s_i,s_j)\}$
    end
    t := the single string contained in S

Figure 5.7.1
Superstring Greedy Algorithms

Then G0 and G1 simply overlap $s_1 \cdots s_{2n+1}$ to form a string of length $O(n^2)$, whereas the optimal superstring that overlaps $s_1 s_3 \cdots s_{2n+1}$ has length $O(n)$. By simply exchanging s_1 and s_2, the example above also works for $G2$[†].

The worst case performance of G3 and G4 is much better. One can argue that G3 and G4 always save a number of characters that is within a constant factor of the number of characters saved by an optimal algorithm[††]. as follows. Let $s_{i_1} \cdots s_{i_k}$ be the order in which an optimal algorithm overlaps the strings of $S = \{s_1 \cdots s_k\}$ and let O_{i_j}, $1 \leq j < k$, be the amount of overlap between s_{i_j} and $s_{i_{j+1}}$. Let $O_1 \cdots O_{k-1}$ be an ordering of the O_{i_j} from largest to smallest. Now consider the first iteration of G3. Suppose that it did $COMBINE(s_{i_x}, s_{i_y})$. This COMBINE operation must save at least O_1 characters. However, in the worst case we could forever loose the savings $O_{i_{x-1}}$, O_{i_x}, $O_{i_{y-1}}$, and O_{i_y}, which in the worst case could be O_1, O_2, O_3, O_4. It is not hard to see that when this reasoning is applied to successive iterations that it follows that G3 will always save at least $1/4$ the characters that an optimal algorithm would save. A more complicated argument shows that the savings obtained by G3 is within a factor of 2 of the savings obtained by an optimal algorithm[†††]. A similar argument applies to G4. Unfortunately, this bound is tight. For example, consider the following set of strings:

$$s_1 = ab^n$$
$$s_2 = b^{n-1}cb^{n-1}$$
$$s_3 = b^n a$$

Then both G3 and G4 save n characters by overlapping s_1 with s_3, whereas an optimal algorithm saves $2n-2$ characters by overlapping s_1 with s_2 with s_3.

In practice, even a factor of 2 in performance is very significant, and the discussion above of worst case performance can be viewed as a negative statement about G0 through G4. However, it is not likely that such worst case performance will occur for many practical applications.

---

† Note that the first iteration of $G2$ can select any string from S for s_i. Without loss of generality, we can assume that this string is s_1; otherwise, S can be permuted appropriately.

†† Note that this condition does not imply that the ratio between the size of a superstring obtained by G3 or G4 and an optimal one is bounded by a constant factor. See the bibliographic notes for further discussion of this point.

††† See the bibliographic notes.

Very Long, Highly Similar Strings

A rather specialized application is when the collection consists of very long strings that are highly similar. One example of such an application is the storage of information pertaining to long molecule chains (DNA, proteins, etc.). Similar to the above discussion, we can approach this problem by attempting to find a minimal length *supersequence* for the collection of strings; that is, a string that contains all of the strings in the collection as subsequences[†]. Given that the strings in the collection are highly similar, we should be able to point to a substring of this master string and "attach" to the pointer a list of changes that need to be made to the target to get the string in question. This idea is one example of the notion of generalizing the macro model to to allow the addition of *arguments* to pointers that can specify modifications to be made on a target before it is substituted. It is not clear whether such generality would have much practical value for standard sources such as English text, but this generality is clearly useful and necessary for special applications.

When Adjacent Strings are Highly Similar

Another specialized application is when there is an ordering of the strings such that adjacent strings in the ordering are highly similar in some fashion. A classic example of such application is compressing an English language dictionary. Here, adjacent entries often share large common prefixes (e.g., hip, hips, hipped, hippie, hippies, hippiedom, hippiehood, hippocratic, hippodrome, hippopotamus, hippopotamuses, hippy, etc.) Such a dictionary could be compressed with many of the techniques that we have discussed (e.g., sliding dictionary with a short window) but is most effectively compressed with a "finely tuned" algorithm that records one entry as its difference with the previous entry. This idea is an example of a general technique which is often referred to as *incremental coding*.

[†] Unfortunately, like the superstring problem, the supersequence problem is also NP-complete. Approximation heuristics would have to be employed for methods based on this problem.

5.8. MULTI-DIMENSIONAL DATA

Figure 5.8.1
A Hilbert Curve

For many applications of compressing multi-dimensional data (e.g., 2-dimensional digital images) lossy compression is most appropriate; either with a general purpose dynamic algorithm as considered in Chapter 3, or with special purpose techniques. However, if it is desired to perform lossless compression of a multi-dimensional input, there is an elegant construction due to Lempel and Ziv that shows how to reduce the problem of compressing an n-dimensional input optimally in the information-theoretic sense to that of compressing a (1-dimensional) string optimally in the information-theoretic sense.

The naive approach to such a reduction is to scan the matrix in row-major order (e.g., for the 2-dimensional case, scan the rows going from top to bottom) to produce a string; this order is often called a *raster* scan. The problem with the raster scan is that information about vertical correlations is lost. A solution to this problem is to scan the matrix with a finite approximation to a space filling curve such as the *Hilbert-curve* depicted in Figure 5.8.1 (for the two-dimensional case). The key property of this curve is that if one recursively divides space into quadrants, then it is always the case that a given quadrant is completely visited before the next one is entered. The proof of optimality given by Lempel and Ziv is an asymptotic result; it appears that in practice, the data must be quite large for the technique to be effective. However it is at the very least a useful theoretical tool.

One application of such a technique to lossy compression is to first apply lossy techniques to compress the multi-dimensional object as much as possible, then apply the above reduction to a one-dimensional problem, and finally, compress the resulting string with a lossless serial method. For example, with image compression, it can often be the case that a (lossless) on-line textual substitution method will achieve a significantly better compression ratio on an image that has already been compressed with standard lossy techniques than on the original uncompressed image. The lossy techniques have the ability to remove random or nearly random bits, thus making identification of patterns easier.

5.9. BIBLIOGRAPHIC NOTES

The macro model for data compression was introduced by Storer [1979] and Storer and Szymanski [1978,1982]. However, compression techniques that fall under the macro model have been considered by many authors, including: Storer [1985], Miller and Wegman [1984], Fraenkel and Mor [1983], Severance [1983], Choueka, Fraenkel, and Perl [1982], Gonzalez and Storer [1982], Pechura [1982], Tropper [1982], Rodeh, Pratt, and Even [1981], Langdon [1981], Gallant, Maier, and Storer [1980], Apostolico [1979], Maier and Storer [1978], Storer [1977,1977b], Sheifler [1977], Vasyukova [1977], Seery and Ziv [1977,1978], Lempel and Ziv [1976,1977,1978], Rubin [1976],

Visvalingham [1976], Dance and Pooch [1976], Mayne and James [1975], Hahn [1974], Morris and Thompson [1974], Wagner [1973], McCarthy [1973], Hagamen, Linden, Long, and Weber [1972], Ruth and Kreutzer [1972], Lesk [1970], Snyderman and Hunt [1970], White [1968], and Marron and DeMaine [1967]. Douchette, Harrison, and Schuegraf [1977] consider compressing French, German, and English with a static dictionary. Note also that most literature on on-line compression that was discussed in the bibliographic notes to Chapter 3 is relevant to off-line compression.

Pattern matching techniques have great importance for efficient implementation of off-line methods. Of particular interest for the *OPM/L* model (and the sliding dictionary method of Chapter 3) is to find the longest substring that occurs both starting at a specified point and at some point earlier in the string. Traditionally, a *position tree* or *suffix tree* data structure is used (e.g., Weiner [1973], McCreight [1976]). More recently, Blumer, Blumer, Ehrenfeuchtr, Haussler, and McConnel [1984,1984b] and Blumer and Blumer [1987], consider the *directed acyclic word graph* (DWAG) data structure that can be view as a position tree with isomorphic subtrees combined. Rodeh, Pratt, and Even [1976] give a linear time algorithm for computing match information (which they use to implement a greedy algorithm for a model similar to the OPM/L scheme) that is based on the work of McCreight [1976]. Bell [1986] considers a different approach that employs search trees. Landau, Schieber, and Vishkin [1987] and Apostolico, Iliopoulos, Landau, Schieber, and Vishkin [1987] consider parallel algorithms for suffix tree construction. Additional relevant references to position trees and pattern matching include: Apostolico [1985], Apostolico and Giancarlo [1986], Vishkin [1985], Chen and Seiferas [1984], Majster [1979], Seiferas [1977] Knuth, Morris, and Pratt [1977]. An important computation on a suffix tree is the lowest common ancestor operation; see Harel and Tarjan [1984] and Schieber and Vishkin [1987].

Pattern matching techniques have applications to lossy compression as well. Landau and Vishkin [1985,1986] consider string matching in the presence of errors. Ukkonen [1985] considers the problem of locating approximate patterns; that is, substrings that have a great similarity (small edit distance) to a given pattern. Lipton and Lopresti [1985] present a practical systolic array implementation for testing string similarity.

For an introduction to dynamic programming, see a text on algorithms such as Aho, Hopcroft, and Ullman [1974,1983]. Wagner's algorithm is presented in Wagner [1973]. Schuegraf and Heaps [1974] model the problem of optimally parsing a string with respect to a static dictionary as a shor-

test path problem in a directed acyclic graph that has one node for each prefix
of the input string (node 0 corresponds to the empty string, node 1
corresponds to the first character, node 2 to the first two characters, etc.) and
an edge between two nodes v and w if there is a string in the dictionary which
when concatenated to the prefix represented by v gives the prefix represented
by w. Katajainen and Raita [1987] uses this model to further study greedy
versus optimal parsings. The optimal dynamic programming algorithm for
the OPL/L scheme is due to Storer and Szymanski [1982]. Gonzalez and
Storer [1985] contains the proof of Section 6, which is a generalization of the
proof of greedy versus optimal for the OPM/L scheme that appears in Storer
and Szymanski [1982]. Hartman and Rodeh [1985] discuss an on-line algorithm for optimal parsing for certain compression problems.

Overlapping restrictions are considered in Storer [1977, 1979, 1982],
Gonzalez and Storer [1982], Choueka, Fraenkel, and Perl [1982] (prefix overlappings), and Fraenkel, Mor, and Perl [1983] (prefix and suffix overlappings).
For related results concerning pointer direction and overlapping, see Storer
and Szymanski [1982] and Storer [1979].

For a general introduction to NP-completeness (including classic
problems such as node cover and Hamilton path), see Garey and Johnson
[1979]. In addition, many texts on algorithms (e.g., Aho, Hopcroft, and Ullman [1974]) contain material on NP-completeness. Storer [1977,1979]
presents a number of NP-completeness results concerning encoding for the
macro model. Other NP-completeness results are contained in Gallant [1982],
Maier and Storer [1978], Maier [1977], and Gallant, Maier, and Storer [1980].
Proofs for these results include reductions from the various restricted forms of
the node cover problem (Maier and Storer [1978], Storer [1977,1979]), and the
superstring problem (Maier and Storer [1978], and Gallant, Maier, and Storer
[1980]). NP-completeness results for the case $p=1$ appear in Storer
[1977,1979]. See Storer [1977,1979] and Gallant [1982] for proofs NP-
completeness results pertaining to internal schemes.

In Gallant, Maier, and Storer [1980], the superstring problem is discussed and shown NP-complete under a variety of assumptions, including
binary alphabets. A simple NP-completeness proof for the restricted version
of the Hamilton path problem that was used in this chapter is presented as a
lemma in Gallant, Maier, and Storer [1980]; the directed Hamilton path problem is shown to be NP-complete in Karp [1972]. Maier and Storer [1978], as
well as Gallant, Maier, and Storer [1980], also contains a polynomial time algorithm for when all strings have length 2 or less. Turner [1986b] considers
approximation algorithms for the superstring problem; he propose that per-

formance be measured in terms of the ratio of savings achieved instead of the ratio of the sizes of the superstrings achieved and shows that G3 is within a factor of 2 under the savings measure. Kou [1977] shows NP-complete a variant of the superstring problem, which he calls the *consecutive set problem*, where the superstring is only required to contain as a substring a permutation of the characters of each of the input strings; he employs a reduction from the standard superstring problem. Turner [1986] also considers this problem, but calls it the *common matching string problem*. Maier [1978] proves that the supersequence problem is NP-complete under a variety of assumptions. Kruskal [1983] and Sankoff and Kruskal [1983] contains an overview of other related problems pertaining to strings.

Lathrop, Webster, and Smith [1987] discuss the analysis of protein sequences (and how it relates to various string problems) and contains references to related work on this sort of problem.

The hand-shaking protocol is a homework problem in Aho, Hopcroft, and Ullman [1974].

Gallant [1982] proposes *BPM schemes* as another generalization of the macro model along the lines of adding arguments; the idea is for internal schemes to allow extra data to be inserted into the compressed form that is not reproduced when decoding but can be used as part of pointer targets (i.e., a target of a pointer can overlap with part of one of these extra strings to form a target that would not otherwise be available).

Visvalingham [1976] and Laeser, McLaughlin, and Wolff [1986] consider incremental coding.

The material on multi-dimensional compression is from Lempel and Ziv [1985]. In an appendix on "pathological curves" Kasner and Newman [1940] provide an informal introduction to space filling curves, as does Gardner [1976]. Other references on the Hilbert curve and similar curves include Stevens, Lehar, and Preston [1983], Butz [1969,1971], Bially [1969], and Patrick, Anderson, and Bechtel [1968]. The Hilbert space filling curve is an example of a *fractal;* the book by Mandelbrot [1982] is a good reference on the subject. Fractals can be used to provide high-level descriptions of complex shapes; such descriptions can be the basis of lossy image compression algorithms where compressed forms describe features of the image; see Barnsley and Sloan [1988], Barnsley, Ervin, Hardin, and Lancaster [1986], and Barnsley and Demko [1985].

Another approach to "linearizing" a multi-dimensional problem is to perform compression on a structural representation. For example, for 2-dimensional data, compression can be performed on a *quadtree* representation (which gives rise to corresponding *quadcodes)*, which is based on recursively subdividing the matrix into quadrants. Samet [1984] is a survey paper on the subject. See also Li and Loew [1987,1987b], Abel and Smith [1983], Samet [1983,1985], Yau and Srihari [1983], and Gargantini [1982].

Even, Lichtenstein, and Shiloach [1979] consider the compression of sparse matrices.

Blumer [1985] considers what can be viewed as a generalization of run-length encoding that is similar to techniques considered here and in Chapter 3.

There has been considerable work on compression algorithms that take advantage of structure in the data. Young and Philip [1980] considers compression of fields in data files. Comer and Sethi [1977] and Ai-Sumaiyel and Horowitz [1984] considered the compression of trie data structures. Szymanski [1976], Robertson [1977], and Leverett and Szymanski [1979] consider the problem of minimizing the length of assembly language code where the length of an instruction depends on distance between the instruction and the location of its operands. Alsberg [1975] and Maier [1982] consider the compression of database relations. The compression of relational databases by taking explicit advantage of their structure (and possibly preserving some structure in the compressed form) appears to be an interesting area of future research. The texts by Ullman [1982] and Maier [1983] provide good references on the subject of relational databases. Severance [1983] is a survey on database compression. Cormack [1985] considers data compression of database files.

An important application of off-line data compression is the compaction of read-only data such as a laser disk (e.g., Urrows and Urrows [1984]) or data that is infrequently changed such as an electronic library (e.g., Weyer and Borning [1985]). In such applications, a large cost of computing time to compress the data can be justified.

6

PROGRAM SIZE COMPLEXITY

In this chapter we put aside practical concerns and focus on the theoretical issue of what sorts of compression can be achieved when unlimited computational resources are available. To do so, we employ the tools of abstract computational complexity theory.

Although we may have a "master program" that is used to decode compressed strings, each compressed string must contain all the information necessary to completely specify the original string except, possibly, for a fixed amount of information incorporated in the master program. Hence, in any data compression system, there is a correspondence between compressed forms of strings and computer programs. For example, a compressed form for a given macro scheme can be viewed as a program that can be "run", with the aid of a fixed decoding algorithm that is the same for all compressed forms (the "master program"), to produce the original string.

The observation above leads naturally to a very general model of data compression called *program size complexity*. In this model, a string is compressed by finding the shortest program that prints it. For such a program to be well defined, a particular programming language, as well as a cost function (typically the number of bits in the compressed form), must be agreed upon. In addition, this chapter generalizes this model by allowing the specification of a restricted domain of programs (such as those running in polynomial time) that may be candidates for the shortest programs.

Section 6.1 begins with an example that motivates why so much power is inherent in a model that is this general. In Section 6.2, the concept of a cost function is formally defined, and an abstract compression scheme is defined to be a set S of programs over a specified programming language (which has an associated complexity measure), subject to a specified cost function. The S-compression of a string is defined to be the program in S of least cost that produces this string. Section 6.3 discusses some basic properties of abstract compression schemes. Section 6.4 discusses complexity classes of schemes and considers the power of an important class of compression schemes called *good* compression schemes. Good compression schemes have basic properties that any useful compression scheme ought to have. Section 6.5 shows that many "useless" schemes also fall under the definition of good and motivates the need for additional criteria on which to judge the utility of a compression scheme.

Throughout this chapter, we use the following notation:

- N denotes the set of non-negative integers.

- We use the standard abbreviations of *i.o.* for *infinitely often* (i.e., for infinitely many values of N) and *a.e.* for *almost everywhere* (i.e., for all but finitely many values of N).

- For a function F from N to N,

  $$\liminf_{n \to \infty} F(i)$$

  denotes the "limiting value of the smallest values of F". That is, it denotes the largest real value h such that for any $\epsilon > 0$ there exists a k such that for all $n \geq k$, $F(n) \geq h - \epsilon$. Although a *liminf* expression may be undefined, we shall only use in in situations where it is always defined.

- For functions f and g from N to N, we use $f.g$ to denote the composition of f with g. That is, $f.g(i) = f(g(i))$. Note that if $g(i)$ is undefined or if $g(i)$ is defined but $f(g(i))$ is not, then $f.g(i)$ is undefined. Three or more function compositions are always evaluated from right to left; that is, $f.g.h(i) = f(g(h(i)))$.

- For functions f and g from N to N, $f \leq g$ if for all i, $f(i)$ and $g(i)$ are defined and $f(i) \leq g(i)$.

As we saw in Chapter 2 with the *INT* and *STR* functions, it is easy to define a correspondence between N and strings. Hence, without loss of generality, throughout this chapter our discussion will be in terms of N (however, when speaking informally, we may use "string" in place of "non-negative integer").

We assume that the reader is familiar with abstract computational complexity theory. In particular, the following are some informal definitions of terminology that will be used extensively.

- By a *program*, we mean a function that takes as input a non-negative integer (string) and is either undefined (the program runs forever) or produces as output a non-negative integer (string). To compute such a function, an unbounded amount of memory is available, but only a finite amount of memory is used for any particular successful computation. We often view programs as acceptors of sets; that is, for all inputs, the program either *accepts* by producing a 1 or *rejects* by either being undefined (the program runs forever) or producing a 0. We will also often view a program as defining a function from a number of inputs to a number of outputs; this notion can easily be realized by any encoding of a set of values into a single value[†].

- A *Gödel numbering* $\phi = (\phi_0, ...)$ is an infinite list of all programs over some programming language. We write $\phi_i = \phi_j$ if for all k, either both $\phi_i(k)$ and $\phi_j(k)$ are undefined or $\phi_i(k) = \phi_j(k)$. For most of what is to be presented, it suffices to simply think of a Gödel numbering as an infinite list of all Turing machines[††]. Some basic properties that are true of all Gödel numberings will be used throughout this chapter:

---

† Any of the techniques described in Chapter 2 for encoding commas can be used. For example, to encode n binary strings into a single binary string, we can first double the length of each string by replacing 0 by 00 and 1 by 01. The n strings can then be combined into a single string by adding 11 to the end of each string and then concatenating them together.

†† A Turing machine is a simple abstract model of computation. Although many equivalent definitions are used in the literature, a standard one is that a *Turing machine* consists of a finite-state control together with a single tape that has a left end but extends infinitely to the right. Initially, the input is written one character per tape cell at the left end of the tape; the remaining infinite portion of the tape going to the right is blank. The Turing machine starts its computation with its head on the leftmost tape cell (the first character of the input), and at each point in time, according to the finite-state control, may change the contents of the cell that the head is reading and then move its head left (but not off the left end of the tape) or right. Although the Turing machine's tape is infinite, any computation that halts will only use a finite portion of it. It is not hard to show that a Turing machine can simulate the usual notion of a random access machine and hence is equivalent in power to any practical computer (although the Turing machine may run much slower). Thus, for example, a Gödel numbering may also be thought of as as a list of all Pascal programs, provided that the notion of a Pascal program was appropriately generalized to allow an unbounded amount of memory. See the bibliographic notes for introductory texts on Turing machines and related subjects.

Universal program: There exists an i such that for all j and k, $\phi_i(j,k) = \phi_j(k)$. That is, ϕ_i is a program that is capable of simulating any other program on any input.

S-m-n function: For any $m,n \geq 1$, there exists a computable function S_n^m (which is computed by some ϕ_i) such that for all $x, y_1 \ \cdots \ y_m$, and $z_1 \ \cdots \ z_n$,

$$\phi_x(y_1 \ \cdots \ y_m, z_1 \ \cdots \ z_n) = \phi_{S_m^n(x, y_1 \ \cdots \ y_m)}(z_1 \ \cdots \ z_n)$$

That is, there is an effective way to translate between a program that takes $m+n$ variables to one that takes only n variables (while holding the other m variables fixed).

Padding property: For any i, there are infinitely many j (which are computable) such that $\phi_i = \phi_j$. That is, there are infinitely many copies of essentially the same program; in practice, such copies can be obtained by "padding" a given program with some number of useless instructions (that are never executed).

Isomorphism theorem: Any two Gödel numberings are recursively isomorphic. That is, for any two Gödel numberings ϕ and ψ, there exists a recursive permutation π (i.e., π is one-to-one and both π and π^{-1} are recursive) such that for all i $\phi_i = \psi_{\pi(i)}$.

Recursion theorem: In its most simple form, the recursion theorem states that for any recursive function f, there exists a "fixed point" i such that $\phi_i = \phi_{f(i)}$.

- A *total function* is function from N to N that is defined for all values. A *recursive function*, which we sometimes call a *computable function*, is a total function that can be computed by a program. A function with range $\{0,1\}$ is said to be *decidable* if it is computable. A *recursive set* is a subset X of N such that there exists a program which for any input i, always halts and prints 1 if i is in X and 0 otherwise.

- A *partial recursive function* is one that is not necessarily defined for all of N but is computed by a program on the values for which it is defined. A *recursively enumerable set*, usually called a *r.e. set*, is one that is accepted by a program[†].

- An *abstract computational complexity measure* is a Gödel numbering $\phi = (\phi_0, ...)$ together with a list of associated "step counting functions" $\Phi = (\Phi_0, ...)$. For most of what is to be presented, the reader may think of $\Phi_i(j)$ as the amount of time or memory that ϕ_i uses on input j. More formally, a legal step counting function is one that satisfies two axioms:

  (1) For all i and j, $\phi_i(j)$ is defined if and only if $\Phi_i(j)$ is.

  (2) For all i, j, and k, it is decidable if $\Phi_i(j)=k$.

As an example, consider how the amount of tape used by a Turing machine satisfies the two axioms above. Axiom (1) is satisfied so long as we adopt the convention that the amount of tape used is undefined if the Turing machine runs forever. For Axiom (2), if s denotes the number of states of the Turing machine and a the size of the tape alphabet, then observe that for each of the a^k different possible tape contents, the Turing machine can be in at most s different states with its head in at most k different positions. Hence, the Turing machine can run for at most $s*k*a^k$ steps before either visiting cell $k+1$, halting, or going into an infinite loop. Thus, we can decide if the Turing machine visits k tape cells on a particular input, by simply running it (simulating it using the universal program) until either it visits cell $k+1$, halts, or enters an infinite loop on the first k tape cells.

See the bibliographic notes for references to introductory material on abstract computational complexity theory.

[†] An equivalent definition of an r.e. set X is that X can be *enumerated* by a program. That is, there is an i such that: $\phi_i(j)\epsilon X$ for all j, and for every $x\epsilon X$, $\phi_i(j)=x$ for some j. In terms of a particular realization of a program such as a Turing machine, enumeration of X can be taken to mean that there is a program that lists the elements of X (and will run forever if X is infinite) in such a way that every element in X is listed after a finite number of steps.

6.1. AN EXAMPLE

As noted in the introduction to this chapter, the problem of finding the shortest representation for a string can be viewed as that of finding the shortest computer program that prints it. Before proceeding to the subsequent sections that formalize this notion, this section presents a small example that motivates not only the potential power of this general mechanism, but also why it embodies inherently intractable problems.

Example 6.1.1: Suppose that $F(i)$ is some very fast growing function (e.g., let $F(i) = ACKERMAN(i,i)$[†]). The following is clearly a well-defined and computable compression algorithm:

if $s=BIN(F(i))$ for some i

then $BIN(i)$

else $0s$

Although the method above is unlikely to have any practical value, it does compress infinitely many binary strings by an arbitrary amount (and does not increase the length of any string by more than one bit). ◯

6.2. DEFINITIONS

In order to have a general theory of data compression, we must allow for many different criteria on which to judge the cost of storing an integer. We call any such a criterion a *cost function*. Any reasonable cost function c should have the property that as i approaches infinity, so does $c(i)$; that is, we cannot have a fixed cost assigned to an infinite number of integers.

Definition 6.2.1: A recursive function $c:N{\rightarrow}N$ is a *cost function* if there exists an unbounded monotonic recursive function $\underline{c}:N{\rightarrow}N$ such that for all i, $\underline{c}(i){\leq}c(i)$. ◯

[†] Ackerman's function is a well-known function that grows faster than any primitive recursive function. See the bibliographic notes.

We could have defined a cost function as simply a recursive function c such that for any k, $c(i)=k$ for at most finitely many i, but then we are not guaranteed of having a recursive $\underline{c}$[†]. The way the definition stands, all cost functions have a recursive monotonic upper bound $\overline{c}$ (take $\overline{c}(i)$ to be 0 if $i=0$ and $MAX\{c(i), \overline{c}(i-1)\}$ otherwise), a recursive monotonic lower bound $\underline{c}$, and the cost function itself "wiggles" between these bounds in a recursive fashion. Some examples of cost functions are:

(1) $c(i)=\lceil \log_b(i)/a \rceil$. For $a=1$ this function might correspond to the number of digits needed to represent i in base b and for $a>1$ this function might correspond to the number of a-long disk blocks needed to store i when i is written in base b.

(2) $c(i)=i$.

(3) Any unbounded monotonic recursive function.

(4) For any $n,m>0$ consider:

$$c(i) = n(no.\ 0\text{'s in } BIN(i)) + m(no.\ 1\text{'s in } BIN(i))$$

That is, $c(i)$ is the amount of "ink" it takes to write i in binary. This function might model computer memories where the power required to store a 0 differs from that required to store a 1.

We let (ϕ,Φ) denote an abstract computational complexity measure where $\phi=\{\phi_0,\ \cdots\}$ is a Gödel numbering and $\Phi=\{\Phi_0,\ \cdots\}$ are the associated *step counting* functions. In order to completely specify a data compression scheme we must specify:

(1) A complexity measure (ϕ,Φ) that specifies a programming language and the cost of running programs.

(2) A recursive set S of programs in ϕ that may be used as compressed forms.

(3) A cost function c so that given two elements of S, we can judge which is "shorter".

---

† It can be shown that there exist recursive functions c for which no such $\underline{c}$ exists.

Our motivation for including (2) is that we may want to restrict the set of programs (we represent a program by its index in ϕ) we are allowed to use as encodings of strings so that we are assured that encodings of strings have some desirable property. For example, it might be desired to guarantee that decoding can be performed within a specific time or space bound[†]. As another example, we might want to restrict our attention only to programs which represent compressed forms for a particular macro scheme.

We define an *abstract compression scheme* as a triple consisting of a set of allowable programs over a given programming language subject to a cost function:

Definition 6.2.2: An *abstract compression scheme* is a triple $(S,(\phi,\Phi),c)$ where S is a recursive set, (ϕ,Φ) an abstract computational complexity measure, and c a cost function. $\bigcirc$

We refer to an abstract compression scheme as a compression scheme or simply a scheme and will not bother to include the word abstract in subsequent definitions. When (ϕ,Φ) and c are understood or may be arbitrary we refer to $(S,(\phi,\Phi),c)$ by simply writing S. We now define the concept of a compressed string.

Definition 6.2.3: The *S-contraction* of an integer i is the least integer $\Delta_S(i)$ in S such that:

(1) $\phi_{\Delta_S(i)}(0)=i$

(2) $(\forall j \epsilon S)[c(j) < c.\Delta_S(i) \rightarrow \phi_j(0) \neq i]$

The *proper S-contraction* of an integer i is defined by the function

---

[†] It is not, in general, decidable if a given program always halts within a given time bound $T(i)$, and hence the set of all i such that $\phi_i(j)$ always halts in $T(j)$ steps is not a recursive set. However, for each ϕ_i there is a ϕ_j which simulates ϕ_i and maintains a counter to shut off a computation on an input k after $T(k)$ steps. A list of these ϕ_j's is recursive.

$\delta_S:N\rightarrow N\bigcup\{no\}$ given by:

$$\delta_S(i) = \begin{cases} \Delta_S(i) \ if \ \Delta_S(i) \ is \ defined \ and \ c.\Delta_S(i)<c(i) \\ "no" \ otherwise \end{cases}$$

An integer i is *S-compressible* if $\delta_S(i)\neq$"no". ◯

The S-contraction of an integer i is the smallest (in the sense of the cost function) element in S which computes i, and i is S-compressible if the cost of the S-contraction of i is less than the cost of i. Note that Δ_S is not necessarily a total function whereas δ_S is.

For a given scheme S an obvious set to consider is the set of all integers which are S-compressible.

Definition 6.2.4: The *S-compression class* is given by:

$$A_S=\{i: i \ is \ S\text{-}compressible\} ◯$$

Another important set is the subset of A_S for which S gives the best compression possible (for the (ϕ,Φ) and c in question).

Definition 6.2.5: A compression scheme S is *optimal at* i if $i\epsilon A_S$ and $c.\Delta_S(i)=c.\Delta_N(i)$. The *S-compression optimal class* is given by $O_S=\{i: S \ is \ optimal \ at \ i\}$. A compression scheme S is *optimal i.o.* if O_S is infinite, *optimal a.e.* if A_N-O_S is finite, and *optimal* if $O_S=A_N$. ◯

At this point it is natural to ask why we insist that O_S be a subset of A_S. Why not simply define $O_S=\{i: c.\Delta_S(i)=c.\Delta_N(i)\}$? The reason is that we are not interested in the exact value of $\Delta_S(i)$ if $c.\Delta_S(i)\geq c(i)$; there may be hard results concerning situations where $c.\Delta_S(i)\geq c(i)$, but they are artificial in nature (as will be noted by the "Labeling Theorem" of the next section).

We now define the class of good schemes.

Definition 6.2.6: A compression scheme $(S,(\phi,\Phi),c)$ is *continuous* if $(\forall i\epsilon S)[\phi_i(0) \ is \ defined]$. A compression scheme S is *realizable* if Δ_S is recursive and *weakly realizable* if δ_S is recursive. A compression scheme S is *nontrivial* if A_S is infinite. A compression scheme is *good* if it is continuous, realizable, and non-trivial. ○

The English meaning of the terms just defined reflects their formal meaning. Clearly, if a scheme compresses only a finite number of strings it is not very interesting and so we have defined a scheme to be non-trivial only if it compresses an infinite number of strings (note that the condition non-trivial is weaker than that of optimal i.o.). It is also clear that, although a scheme S may be powerful, it may not be useful if we cannot compute Δ_S. This observation motivates our definition of realizability. Finally, it seems reasonable that the least we would require of a scheme S in order to call it good would be that S contain only useful programs (S is continuous), that there exists an effective procedure to find the S-contraction of a given integer i (S is realizable), and that S compresses many strings (S is non-trivial).

At this point we should prove that there actually exist good schemes (and hence there exist non-trivial and realizable schemes) but we will not bother since this fact will follow trivially from later results of this section. Note that we could have defined a scheme S to be realizable if δ_S is recursive (and there are schemes such that δ_S is recursive but Δ_S is not) but we shall see from the "Labeling Theorem" of the next section that there is little practical value in doing so.

6.3. BASIC PROPERTIES

Traditional program size complexity considers schemes of the form $(N,(\phi,\Phi),c)$ where N denotes the non-negative integers and c is often $\log_2$. One would think that so long as we use a reasonable programming language and cost function, the exact choice we make (i.e., ALGOL vs. PL/1 or $\log_2$ vs. $\log_{10}$) would not significantly change the difficulty of compressing strings. The following theorem notes that this intuition is correct; that is, any two schemes $(N,(\phi,\Phi),c)$ and $(N,(\phi,\Phi)',c)$ are recursively related, so that "modulo a recursive function", when choosing a scheme $(S,(\phi,\Phi),c)$, it is only the choice of S that really matters.

Theorem 6.3.1: For any two schemes $A=(N,(\phi,\Phi),c)$ and $B=(N,(\phi,\Phi)',c)$ there is a recursive f such that for all i both of the following hold:

$$c.\Delta_A(i) \leq f.c.\Delta_B(i)$$

$$c \cdot \Delta_B(i) \leq f \cdot c \cdot \Delta_A(i)$$

Proof: Since all Gödel numberings are recursively isomorphic (isomorphism theorem), there is a recursive bijection g such that:

$$(\forall i)[\phi_i = \phi'_{g(i)} \text{ and } \phi'_i = \phi_{g^{-1}(i)}]$$

Let:

$$f_1(i) = MAX\{c(i),\ c'(i)\}$$

$$f_2(i) = MAX\{g(i),\ g^{-1}(i)\}$$

$$f_3(i) = (least\ j)[\underline{c}(j) > i \text{ and } \underline{c}'(j) > i]$$

$$f = f_1 \cdot f_2 \cdot f_3$$

Since $(\forall i, j)[\underline{c}(j) > c(i) \rightarrow j > i]$, it follows that:

$$(\forall i)[f_3 \cdot c(i) > i \text{ and } f_3 \cdot c'(i) > i]$$

Hence we have:

$$c \cdot \Delta_A(i) \leq c \cdot g^{-1} \cdot \Delta_B(i)$$

$$\leq f_1 \cdot f_2 \cdot \Delta_B(i)$$

$$\leq f_1 \cdot f_2 \cdot f_3 \cdot c' \cdot \Delta_B(i)$$

$$= f \cdot c' \cdot \Delta_B(i)$$

Similarly we have $c \cdot \Delta_B(i) \leq f \cdot c \cdot \Delta_A(i)$. $\bigcirc$

Although we we shall show later in this section that we may be able to save great amounts of space with schemes, the next theorem shows that for any scheme S, there will always be an infinite number of strings that are not S-compressible. One might ask whether there are schemes S such that we have to use much more space to store some strings than if we did not use the scheme at all. There are indeed such schemes S, but following the next theorem the "Labeling Theorem" notes that we can always find an equivalent scheme S' such that the S'-contraction of any string is never significantly larger than the size of the string itself. This notion corresponds to what we might do on a real computer system; that is, we can attach a special bit to each file indicating whether or not the file is in compressed form. Thus using a compression scheme will cost us at most one extra bit per file.

Theorem 6.3.2: $N-A_S$ is infinite.

Proof: Define $CHAIN_i$ to be the set

$$CHAIN_i = \begin{cases} \{i\} \ if \ i \ is \ not \ S\text{-}compressible \\ \{i\} \ U \ CHAIN_{\Delta_S(i)} \ otherwise \end{cases}$$

and $TAIL_i$ to be the integer:

$$TAIL_i = \begin{cases} i \ if \ |CHAIN_i|=1 \\ TAIL_{\Delta_S(i)} \ otherwise \end{cases}$$

We say $CHAIN_i$ is *dead* if $\phi_i(0)$ is not defined. The reader can verify the following assertions:

(1) $CHAIN_i$ is always a well defined finite set and if $i \neq j$ then either $CHAIN_i$ is disjoint from $CHAIN_j$ or one of these sets is contained in the other.

(2) $TAIL_i$ is always well defined and not S-compressible.

(3) If $CHAIN_i$ is dead then $CHAIN_i$ cannot be a subset of any other chain.

(4) Since for any (ϕ,Φ), there are an infinite number of i for which $\phi_i(0)$ is not defined, there are an infinite number of i for which $CHAIN_i$ is dead.

From the above four facts it follows that $\{TAIL_i: CHAIN_i \ is \ dead\}$ is an infinite list of integers that are not S-compressible. ◯

Theorem 6.3.3 (Labeling Theorem): For any compression scheme $(S,(\phi,\Phi),c)$, there is a scheme $(S',(\phi,\Phi)',c)$ such that for all i:

$$c.\Delta'_S(i) \leq c(MIN\{2i,\ 2\Delta_S(i)+1\}).$$

Proof: We can let $\phi'=\{\phi'_0,\ \cdots\}$ where for all i, $\phi'_{2i}(0)=i$ and $\phi'_{2i+1}=\phi_i$, and let:

$$S'=\{i:\ i\ \text{even or}\ \frac{i-1}{2}\epsilon S\}\quad \bigcirc$$

Corollary 6.3.3: For any compression scheme $(S,(\phi,\Phi),\log_2)$, there is an equivalent scheme $(S',(\phi,\Phi)',\log_2)$ such that for all i:

$$\log_2.\Delta_S(i) \leq MIN\{\log_2(i)+1,\ \log_2.\Delta_S(i)+1\}\quad \bigcirc$$

Although the proof of the theorem above is trivial, the theorem has significance because it implies that schemes have potential practical value. That is, the corollary states that it costs us at most one bit per file to use a compression scheme and we shall see that the size of some files can be greatly reduced. It should also be noted that for all practical purposes, the concepts of realizability and weak realizability may be considered equivalent.

Choosing $S=N$, as in standard program size complexity, yields the most powerful schemes. In fact, it must be the case that when $S=N$ compression cannot even be recursively bounded; that is, for any recursive f there are infinitely many i such that:

$$f.c.\Delta_N(i) < c(i).$$

Unfortunately, along with this power comes undecidability. The following two theorems show that although A_S is always r.e., for any S that is optimal a.e. (in particular $S=N$) the complement of A_S is not r.e. (and so Δ_S cannot be recursive).

Theorem 6.3.4: For all schemes S, A_S is r.e.

Proof: For $S=\{S_0, \cdots\}$, to list A_S, compute $\phi_{S_0}, \cdots$ in parallel (with the standard "dovetailing" construction) and whenever $\phi_{S_i}=j$ is successfully computed, if $c(S_i)<c(j)$ and j is not already on the list then add j to the list. $\bigcirc$

Theorem 6.3.5: If S is a compression scheme that is optimal a.e. then $N-A_S$ is not r.e. In fact, no infinite subset of $N-A_S$ is r.e.

Proof: Assume the contrary; that is, assume that there exists a r.e. list L for an infinite subset of $N-A_S$. Let $g:N \rightarrow N$ be computed as follows:

To compute $g(i)=j$, we compute $\phi_i(0)$, $\phi_{i+1}(0)$, $\cdots$ in parallel until we find a $j \geq i$ such that $\phi_j(0)=i$.

By the "padding property" of a Gödel numbering it follows that g is recursive. Let x be such that:

$$(\forall i \geq x)[i \epsilon A_N \rightarrow i \epsilon O_S]$$

Then there exists the function f defined by:

$$f(i) = \begin{cases} g(\text{first } j \epsilon L \text{ such that } c(j)>c(x)) & \text{if } i = 0 \\ g(\text{first } j \epsilon L \text{ such that } c(j)>c.f(i-1)) & \text{if } i \mathrel{!=} 0 \end{cases}$$

By Theorem 6.3.2 and the definition of a cost function it follows that f is recursive. Since $i \epsilon L$ implies $\phi_j(0) \neq i$ for all j such that $c(j)<c(i)$, it must be that

$$\phi_0(0) \neq \phi_{f(0)}(0)$$

$$(\forall i>0)(\forall j \leq f(i-1))[\phi_j(0) \neq \phi_{f(i)}(0)]$$

and hence it follows that:

$$\phi_0 \neq \phi_{f(0)}$$

$$(\forall i>0)(\forall j \leq f(i-1))[\phi_j \neq \phi_{f(i)}]$$

In addition, a simple induction argument shows that $(\forall i>0)[i \leq f(i)]$. Thus, we have shown that

$$(\forall i)[\phi_i \neq \phi_{f(i)}]$$

which contradicts the recursion theorem of Kleene. $\bigcirc$

From the theorem above, many natural problems concerning schemes can easily be shown undecidable. For example, if S, S_1, and S_2 are arbitrary schemes, it can be shown that the following problems are undecidable:

(1) For S if $A_S=\{\}$, $O_S=\{\}$.

(2) For i,S if $i \epsilon A_S$ or $i \epsilon O_S$.

(3) For S_1,S_2 if $A_{S_1} \subseteq A_{S_2}$ or $O_{S_1} \subseteq O_{S_2}$.

(4) For S if S is continuous, realizable, non-trivial, or good.

(5) For S if S is optimal i.o., optimal a.e., or optimal.

Because of the inherent intractability of arbitrarily powerful schemes, this chapter proposes that schemes based on standard program size complexity ($S=N$) are too general, and that good schemes include all practical compression systems. We close this section with the following two theorems which show that although the amount of compression obtainable with a good scheme is recursively bounded, there is no limit on how large this recursive bound may be.

Theorem 6.3.6: If S is a good compression scheme, then the amount of compression obtained using S is recursively bounded; that is, there exists a recursive f such that $c(i) \leq f.c. \Delta_S(i)$ a.e.

Proof: Let:

$$f(i)=MAX(0,MAX\{c.\phi_j(0): j \epsilon S \text{ and } c(j)=i\})$$

Note that f is recursive, since to find all j in S such that $c(j)=i$, we check $j=0,1,\cdots$ until $c(j)>i$. $\bigcirc$

Theorem 6.3.7: For all (ϕ,Φ) and c, there is no recursive f such that for all good schemes S, $c(i) \leq f.c.\Delta_S(i)$ a.e.

Proof: Assume the contrary; that is, assume there exists such an f. By the S_n^m property of a Gödel numbering we know that there exists a recursive g such that:

$$(\forall i,j)[\phi_i(j) = \phi_{g(i,j)}(0)]$$

Due to the padding property of a Gödel numbering, we can also require that g be monotonic; that is:

$$(\forall i,j,k,l)[i \leq j \ \& \ k \leq l \rightarrow g(i,j) \leq g(k,l)])$$

Let $h(i) = (least \ j)[c(j) \geq i]$ and z be such that:

$$\phi_z(i) = h.\overline{f}.\overline{c}.g(i,i)$$

Clearly ϕ_z is recursive. In addition, for all $i > z$:

$$c.\phi_{g(z,i)}(0) = c.\phi_z(i)$$

$$= c.h.\overline{f}.\overline{c}.g(i,i)$$

$$\geq \overline{f}.\overline{c}.g(i,i)$$

$$\geq \overline{f}.\overline{c}.g(z,i)$$

$$\geq f.c.g(z,i)$$

Let $G = \{g(z,i): i > z\}$. Let $X = \{x_0, x_1, \cdots\}$ be a recursive list such that:

$$(\forall i)[\phi_{x_i}(0) = i]$$

Such an X can easily be constructed for any ϕ. Let S be the recursive set $S = X \bigcup G$. Clearly $i \epsilon S$ implies that $\phi_i(0)$ is defined. We can effectively compute $\Delta_S(i)$ as follows:

First find the $x \epsilon I$ such that $\phi_x(0) = i$; now calculate all $\phi_j(0)$ such that $j \epsilon S \ \& \ \underline{c}(j) \leq c(x)$ (thus we are guaranteed of looking at all j such that $c(j) \leq c(x)$) and pick the j of lowest cost such that $\phi_j(0) = i$.

Therefore S is realizable. Also, for infinitely many i in S, $c.\phi_i(0) > f.c(i)$. Thus it follows that there exist good schemes S such that $c(i) > f.c.\Delta_S(i)$ i.o. and we have a contradiction. $\bigcirc$

The proof above is constructive. A shorter (but less constructive) proof can be provided as follows. Let $g(i,0) = (least \ j)[c(j) > f.c(i)]$. The recursion theorem of Kleene[†] implies that there is an infinite set G satisfying $(\forall i \epsilon G)[\phi_i(0) = g(i,0)]$. Thus, for all i in G, $c(\phi_i(0)) > f.c(i)$, and we may now proceed as in the proof above (from the point "Let $G = ...$").

As promised at the beginning of this section, the following corollary notes that good schemes do exist.

Corollary 6.3.7: For all (ϕ,Φ) and c there exist good schemes. $\bigcirc$

6.4. GOOD VERSUS OPTIMAL I.O. SCHEMES

In this section, we start by defining complexity classes of schemes and then consider more carefully the class of good schemes. There are two natural ways to judge the complexity of a scheme; one way is by how difficult it is to compress or *encode* and the other is by how difficult it is to decompress or *decode*. Since functions exist that have no best algorithm[††], we cannot classify schemes by their "best" algorithms for encoding or decoding. Therefore we shall study encoding and decoding complexity classes.

Definition 6.4.1: A scheme S is *total* if Δ_S is total. For every recursive function f we define the *f-encoding complexity class* as

$$E_f = \{S: S \ total \ and \ (\exists \ j)[\phi_j = \Delta_S \ \& \ (\forall i)[\Phi_j(i) \leq f(i)]]\}$$

and the *f-decoding complexity class* as:

$$D_f = \{S: S \ total \ and \ (\forall i,j)[\Delta_S(i) = j \rightarrow \Phi_j(0) \leq f(i)]\}$$

If S is a compression scheme, then k is an *encoder* for S if $\phi_k = \Delta_S$ and k is a

---

† Note that here we are using the recursion theorem in the form: For a partial recursive function $f(x,y)$, there is an i such that $(\forall i)[f(i,j) = \phi_i(j)]$.
†† This fact follows from the "speed-up" theorem that applies to any Gödel numbering.

decoder for S if $(\forall i)[\,j=\Delta_S(i) \rightarrow \phi_k(\,j)=i]$. ○

The next two theorems give simple criteria for realizability and goodness of schemes.

Theorem 6.4.1: A compression scheme S is realizable if and only if
there exist some recursive f such that $S\epsilon D_f$.

Proof: Suppose there exists such an f. Then we can compute $\Delta_S(i)$
as follows:

> For $j=0,1,\cdots$ do {if $i\epsilon S$ then compute $\phi_j(0)$ for a max-
> imum of $f(i)$ steps} until we find a k such that $\phi_k(0)=i$.
> Then continue in this fashion for $j=k,k+1,\cdots$ until
> $\mathcal{L}(\,j)>c(k)$ and $\Delta_S(i)$ is the j of least cost such that $\phi_j(0)=i$.

Conversely, suppose that S is realizable. Then we see that if $\Delta_S(i)=j$ we can
compute $\phi_j(0)$ (i.e., decode) by computing $\Delta_S(0)$, $\Delta_S(1)$, ... until we find an i
such that $\Delta_S(i)=j$. Hence, if we let x be an index such that $\phi_x=\Delta_S$, then we
can let f be defined by:

$$f(i) = \sum_{k=0}^{i}\Phi_x(k) ○$$

Corollary 6.4.1a: If S is a compression scheme for which there exists an "efficient" encoder, then there exists a "reasonably efficient" encoder
for S; that is:

$$S\epsilon E_f \rightarrow S\epsilon D_g \quad where \quad g(i)=\sum_{j=0}^{i}f(\,j) ○$$

Corollary 6.4.1b: If S is a compression scheme for which there exists an "efficient" decoder, then there exists a "reasonably efficient" encoder
for S; that is, let f be any "sufficiently large" recursive function[†] and ϕ_k be a
recursive function such that $(\forall i)(\exists\,j)[\phi_j(0)=i,\ \Phi_j(0)\le f(0),\ \&\ c(\,j)\le\phi_k(i)]$
(such a k is easily found for any (ϕ,Φ) and c). Then:

[†] f must be large enough so that $(\forall i)(\exists\,j)[\phi_j(0)=i\ \&\ \Phi_j(0)\le f(0)]$.

$$S\epsilon D_f \;\rightarrow\; S\epsilon E_g \quad where \quad g=\Phi_k(i)+\sum_{j=0}^{\phi_k(i)} f(j) \quad \bigcirc$$

Continuity is a sufficient condition for weak realizability. A necessary condition for weak realizability is obtained by formalizing the concept of an abstract computational complexity measure for the set $N \bigcup \{\text{"no"}\}$ and proceeding as above. The next theorem states the criteria for goodness.

Theorem 6.4.2: A compression scheme is good if and only if it is continuous, total, and non-trivial.

Proof: The "only if" portion of the theorem follows directly from the definition of good. For the "if" portion, we can use the same construction as used in the first half of the proof of Theorem 6.4.1 except replace "compute $\phi_j(0)$ for a maximum of $f(i)$ steps" by "compute $\phi_j(0)$". $\bigcirc$

The next theorem shows that, even for good schemes, there is a rich hierarchy of encoding and decoding complexity classes; that is, there is no recursive bound on the encoding or decoding complexities of good schemes. Note that this theorem does not follow directly from Theorem 6.3.7 because these complexities are defined in terms of i, not $\Delta_S(i)$.

Theorem 6.4.3: For any recursive f, there exists a good scheme S such that S is not in E_f and S is not in D_f.

Proof: Let ϕ_k be a recursive function. By the S_n^m property of a Gödel numbering there exist a recursive g such that:

$$\phi_{g(i)}(0)=\phi_k(i).$$

Let $X=\{x_0, \cdots\}$ be a recursive list such that $(\forall i)[\phi_{x_i}(0)=i]$. Let $S=X\bigcup\{g(i): i\epsilon N\}$. Since we can pick k such that Φ_k is an arbitrarily "large" function, the theorem follows from Corollary 6.4.1a. $\bigcirc$

We now turn our attention from the complexity of good schemes to the performance of good schemes; in particular, to the relationship of the class of good schemes to the class of optimal i.o. schemes. We know that good schemes cannot be optimal a.e.[†]; hence for all (ϕ,Φ) and c, there exists an S that is optimal i.o. but not good. We now show that neither does good imply optimal i.o.

Theorem 6.4.4: For all (ϕ,Φ) and c there exists an S such that the scheme $(S,(\phi,\Phi),c)$ is good but not optimal i.o.

Proof: Let $X=\{x_0, \cdots\}$ be a recursive list such that $(\forall i)[c(x_i)>c(i)$ & $\phi_{x_i}(0)=i]$. Let $g:N\rightarrow N$ be computed as follows:

> To compute $g(i)=k$, compute $\phi_i(0)$, $\phi_{i+1}(0)$, ... in parallel until a j, k, and l are found satisfying $\phi_j(0)=\phi_k(0)=l$ and $c(j)<c(k)<c(l)$.

By the padding property of a Gödel numbering and the fact that there exist arbitrarily large recursive functions, it follows that g is recursive. Let f be the recursive function

$$f(i) = \begin{cases} g(0) \text{ if } i=0 \\ g.\phi_{f(i-1)}(0) \text{ otherwise} \end{cases}$$

and let $S=X\bigcup\{f(i): i\epsilon N\}$. By Theorem 6.4.2, S is good. However, by construction, S is nowhere optimal. $\bigcirc$

From the last theorem and the preceding remarks it follows that the class of good schemes and the class of optimal i.o. schemes are incomparable (i.e., neither one is contained in the other). Similar results hold for the other classes we have discussed. For the properties

(A) Continuous.

(B) Non-trivial.

(C) Realizable.

and for all (ϕ,Φ) and c, it can be shown that there exist schemes that are neither good nor optimal i.o. but do have:

(1) None of the properties A, B, and C.

---

† In fact, it can be shown that good schemes cannot even approximate optimal a.e. schemes by any recursive function.

(2) Exactly one of the properties A, B, and C.

(3) Exactly two of the properties A, B, and C.

At this point, our investigation of good versus optimal i.o. has reduced to the question of whether there are schemes that are both good and optimal i.o. The next definition and the following theorem provide a means for classifying good schemes that will allow us to address this question.

Definition 6.4.2: Given a recursive function f, an abstract computational complexity measure (ϕ, Φ), and a cost function c:

$$G_f = \{i: \Phi_i(0) < f(i)\} \quad \bigcirc$$

Theorem 6.4.5: For all (ϕ, Φ) and c

(A) There is a recursive function F such that for all $f \geq F$, G_f is good.

(B) For all good schemes G, there is a recursive function f such that $G = G_f$.

Proof: Let G be any good scheme (we know G exists by Corollary 6.3.7) and let F be the recursive function:

$$F(i) = \begin{cases} \Phi_i(0) + 1 & \text{if } i \text{ in } G \\ 0 & \text{otherwise} \end{cases}$$

Clearly, $G_F = G$. Now suppose f is a recursive function such that $f \geq F$. By definition, G_f is continuous. In addition, G being non-trivial implies that G_f is non-trivial. To see that Δ_{G_f} is realizable, for any i, $\Delta_{G_f}(i)$ can be calculated as follows.

Find a k in G such that $\phi_k(0) = i$ and then for all j such that $c(j) \leq c(i)$, compute $\phi_j(0)$ for at most $f(i)$ steps to check if $\phi_j(0) = i$. Then $\Delta_{G_f}(i)$ is the minimum of k and all such j for which the above computation is successful.

Thus, G_f is good for all $f \geq F$. ○

From the last theorem it follows that for a given (ϕ, Φ) and c, there exists an optimal i.o. scheme if and only if for some f, G_f is optimal i.o. Using this characterization, it is possible to construct schemes that are both good and optimal i.o.

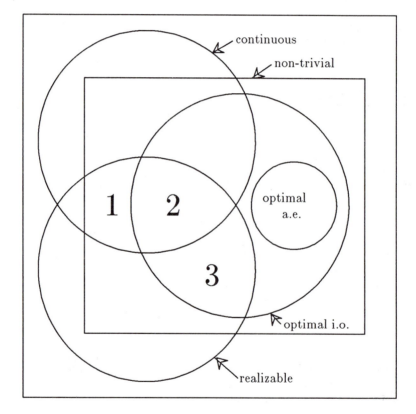

Figure 6.4.1

Figure 6.4.1 summarizes the relationship among the classes of schemes with which we have been concerned. Region 1 together with Region 2 represents the class of good schemes, Region 2 represents the class of good schemes that are optimal i.o., and Region 3 represents the class of realizable schemes that are not good but are optimal i.o. We have only seen rather artificial (ϕ,Φ) and c that have schemes in regions 2 and 3[†]. However, for all (ϕ,Φ) and c, using the theorems presented in this chapter, it is easy to show that all other regions of Figure 6.4.1 contain schemes. We note, however, that it is not decidable for which values a good scheme is optimal.

6.5. DENSITY

In this section we consider criteria for judging the utility of schemes. Given an abstract computational complexity measure and a cost function, we shall be interested in "how well" a scheme compresses strings that are on a given list of strings. The practical interpretation of such a list is that it consists of the strings that may be candidates for compression (e.g., the set of all strings that are valid English text). The following definition formalizes this notion of a data compression problem.

Definition 6.5.1: A *compression problem is a triple* $[T,(\phi,\Phi),c]$ where c is a cost function, (ϕ,Φ) is an abstract computational complexity measure, and $T = t_0, \cdots$ is an infinite recursive list satisfying[††]:

$$(\forall i)[i < j \rightarrow c(t_i) \leq c(t_j)] \qquad \bigcirc$$

When (ϕ,Φ) and c are understood or may be arbitrary, we refer to $[T,(\phi,\Phi),c]$ by simply writing T. Furthermore, if we discuss a scheme S in relation to a compression problem T, it will always be assumed that S and T refer to the same (ϕ,Φ) and c.

---

† As of the time of the writing of this book, it as an open problem whether for all (ϕ,Φ) and c there are schemes that are both good and optimal i.o. However, we conjecture that such schemes do in fact exist.
†† For any infinite recursive set T, a list $\{t_0, \cdots\}$ for T, satisfying the requirements of this theorem, can be effectively constructed. Without loss of generality we assume if $i < j$ and $c(t_i) = c(t_j)$ then $t_i < t_j$.

We now define two notions of density; first, what is meant by a scheme compressing many strings of a compression problem, and second, what is meant by a scheme providing a smaller representation for a compression problem. The theorems in this section exhibit schemes that help to motivate the need to study schemes with respect to a given compression problem T where T is "smaller" than N (such as the set of all strings that are valid English text).

Definition 6.5.2: If S is a scheme and T is a compression problem, then the *S-density function with respect to T* is given by

$$d_S^T(n) = \frac{|\{t_i:\ i \leq n\ and\ t_i\ is\ S\text{-}compressible\}|}{n+1}$$

and we refer to

$$d(S,T) = \liminf_{n \to \infty} d_S^T(n)$$

as the *density of S with respect to T*. We write d_S to mean d_S^N and $d(S)$ to mean $d(S,N)$. The *weighted S-density function with respect to T* is given by

$$D_S^T(n) = \begin{cases} 0\ if\ (\exists\ i \leq n)[\Delta_S(t_i)\ is\ not\ defined] \\[2mm] \dfrac{\displaystyle\sum_{i=0}^{n} c(t_i)}{\displaystyle\sum_{i=0}^{n} c \cdot \Delta_S(t_i)} \quad otherwise \end{cases}$$

and we refer to

$$D(S,T) = \liminf_{n \to \infty} D_S^T(n)$$

as the *weighted density of S with respect to T*. We write D_S to mean D_S^N and $D(S)$ to mean $D(S,N)$. ○

The following theorem supports the above definition by showing that $d(S)$ and $D(s)$ behave meaningfully.

Theorem 6.5.1: For all schemes S,

$$0 \leq d(S) \leq 1$$

$$0 \leq D(S) \leq 1$$

and there are good schemes that obtain these bounds.

Proof: Clearly 0 and 1 are lower and upper bounds for $d(S)$. For any (ϕ, Φ) and c, the construction to follow exhibits a scheme that obtains the lower bound of 0 and the proof of the last theorem of this section exhibits a scheme where the upper bound of 1 is obtained. We now consider $D(S)$. Clearly 0 is a lower bound for $D(S)$. Using techniques similar to those used in the proof of Theorem 6.3.7, it can be shown that for all (ϕ, Φ) and c, there exists a recursive set $X = \{x_0, \cdots\}$ satisfying $(\forall i)[c(x_i) < c. \phi_{x_i}(0) < c(x_{i+1})]$. Also, by the padding property of a Gödel numbering, it can be shown that for all (ϕ, Φ) and c, there exists a recursive set $Y = \{y_0, \cdots\}$ satisfying

$$(\forall i) \left[\phi_{y_i}(0) = i \quad \text{and} \quad c(y_i) > i \sum_{j=0}^{y_i} c(j) \right].$$

If we let $S = X \bigcup Y$, then the scheme $(S, (\phi, \Phi), c)$ is good, and we see:

$$D(S) \quad = \liminf_{n \to \infty} D_S(n)$$

$$= \liminf_{n \to \infty} \frac{\sum_{i=0}^{n} c(i)}{\sum_{i=0}^{n} c. \Delta_S(i)}$$

$$\leq \liminf_{n \to \infty} \frac{1}{n}$$

$$= 0$$

Hence the bound of 0 can be obtained. By the proof of Corollary 6.3.3, we see that for all (ϕ,Φ) and c, there are good schemes that obtain the bound of 1, since for the scheme S' of presented in the proof of Corollary 6.3.3,

$$D_S(n) \geq \frac{\sum\limits_{i=0}^{n} \log_2(i)}{\sum\limits_{i=0}^{n} (\log_2(i)+1)}$$

and so it follows that $D(S)=1$.

Thus, all that is left to prove is that 1 is, in fact, an upper bound for $D(S)$. For the case that c is monotonic, this proof follows from a simple "pigeon-hole" argument. We generalize this argument for non-monotonic c. Without loss of generality we can assume that Δ_S is total (otherwise, $D(S)=0$ and we are done). For $i,j>0$, define the sets

$$BIGCHAIN_{i,j} = \begin{cases} \{(j,\Delta_S(j))\} & \text{if } c.\Delta_S(j) \geq c(i) \\ \{(j,\Delta_S(j))\} \cup BIGCHAIN_{i,\Delta_S(j)} & \text{otherwise} \end{cases}$$

and let M_i and N_i be the integers:

$$M_i = \textit{sum of all first components in } BIGCHAIN_{i,i}$$

$$N_i = \textit{sum of all second components in } BIGCHAIN_{i,i}$$

Also, for $i \epsilon N$, let X_i be the set defined as

$$X_i = \begin{cases} BIGCHAIN_{0,0} & \text{if } i=0 \\ (X_{i-1} \cup BIGCHAIN_{f(i),f(i)}) - Y_i & \text{otherwise} \end{cases}$$

where $f(i)$ is the least j such that j is not the first component of any "bigchain" in X_{i-1} and Y_i is the set of all bigchains in X_{i-1} which are subsets of $BIGCHAIN_{f(i),f(i)}$. The reader can now verify, in order, the following assertions:

(1) $BIGCHAIN_{i,i}$ is always a well defined finite set and if $i \neq j$, either $BIGCHAIN_{i,i}$ is disjoint from $BIGCHAIN_{j,j}$ or one of these sets is a subset of the other.

(2) X_i is always a well defined finite set of disjoint sets ("bigchains").

(3) For $i \epsilon N$, $M_i \leq N_i$.

$$(4)\ D(S) = \liminf_{i \to \infty} \frac{\displaystyle\sum_{BIGCHAIN_{j,j} \epsilon X_i} M_j}{\displaystyle\sum_{BIGCHAIN_{j,j} \epsilon X_i} N_j}$$

(5) $D(S) \leq 1$ ○

We next note that there is no obvious relationship between d and D.

Theorem 6.5.2: For each of the following conditions, there exist good schemes that satisfy it:

(1) $d(S)=0$ and $D(S)=0$

(2) $d(S)=0$ and $D(S)=1$

(3) $d(S)=1$ and $D(S)=0$

(4) $d(S)=1$ and $D(S)=1$

Proof: A good scheme satisfying (1) is given the proof of Theorem 6.5.1, a good scheme satisfying (2) can be constructed using the techniques of Corollary 6.3.3, and a good scheme satisfying (4) is given in the proof of the next theorem. We can exhibit a good scheme satisfying (3) as follows. Let ϕ'

be arbitrary and let ϕ be defined as

$$\phi_i(k) = \begin{cases} IF \ (\forall j)[i \neq 2^j] \ THEN \ i{+}1 \\ ELSE \ IF \ (\exists j)[i{=}2^{2^j}] \ THEN \ j \\ ELSE \ \phi'_{f(i)}(k) \end{cases}$$

where $f(i)$ denotes that j such that ϕ'_j has yet to be used as the third condition in the definition of ϕ for any value less than i (i.e., $f(i)$ is approximately $\log_2(i) - \log_2\log_2(i)$). Intuitively, ϕ_i has been defined to be the constant function $i{+}1$ for all but an exponentially distributed number of "exceptional" values; among these exceptional values, exponentially few are used to fill in the "gaps" caused by exceptional values, and the remaining values are used to "sprinkle in" ϕ'.

Let Φ' be arbitrary, c the identity function, and:

$$S = \{i{:} (\forall j)[i \neq 2^j] \ or \ (\exists j)[i{=}2^{2^j}]\}$$

Then $(S,(\phi,\Phi),c)$ is a good scheme since it is non-trivial, realizable, and for infinitely many i, $c.\Delta_S(i) \leq c(i){-}1$. Also,

$$d_S(n) \geq \frac{n - \log_2(n)}{n{+}1}$$

$$D_S(n) \leq \frac{n^2{+}n}{n^2{+}2^n}$$

and so it follows that $d(S){=}1$ and $D(S){=}0$. $\bigcirc$

As indicated earlier, the goal of this section is to examine criteria for evaluating schemes. The following theorem uses density to exhibit a compression scheme that demonstrates a need for such criteria; it has desirable properties (e.g., good, optimal i.o., $d(s){=}1$) but is clearly not very useful.

Theorem 6.5.3: Let f be any (arbitrarily large) recursive function and g be any (arbitrarily small) strictly monotonic non-linear recursive function; that is, $(\forall i)[g(i{+}1) > g(i)]$ and $(\forall k)(\exists i)[g(i) \geq ki]$. Then there exists a scheme S which has all of the following properties:

(1) S is good.

(2) S is optimal i.o.

(3) $d(S)=D(S)=1$.

(4) c is monotonic.

(5) $f.c. \Delta_S(i) < c(i)$ i.o.

(6) $c. \Delta_S(i) \le g(i)$ a.e.

Proof: Let H be any strictly monotonic non-linear recursive function such that:

$$H(i+\log_2(i)) \le MIN\{g(i), i^2\} \text{ a.e.}$$

By the definition of g, there exists such an H and H^{-1} (the inverse of H) is recursive. Let $L(i)$ denote the function:

$$L(i) = \begin{cases} 0 & \text{if } i=0 \\ \lceil \log_2(i) \rceil & \text{otherwise} \end{cases}$$

For c the identity function and ϕ' arbitrary, let ϕ be defined as

$$\phi_i(k) = \begin{cases} IF \ i=0 \ THEN \ 0 \\ ELSE \ IF \ (\forall j)[i \ne H(j)] \ THEN \ i+1 \\ ELSE \ IF \ (\forall j)[i \ne H(2^j)] \ THEN \ H(H^{-1}(i)-L.H^{-1}(i))+1 \\ ELSE \ IF \ (\exists j)[i=H(2^j) \text{ and } j \ even] \ THEN \ \phi'_{j/2}(k) \\ ELSE \ f(i) \end{cases}$$

Intuitively, ϕ_i has been defined to be the constant function $i+1$ for all but a number of "exceptional" values that are distributed by the function H; among these exceptional values, some are used to fill in the "gaps" caused by exceptional values (the third condition), some are used to "sprinkle in" ϕ' (the fourth condition), and some are used to get high compression (the fifth condition).

For all values of i, ϕ_i is either a constant function or ϕ_j' for some j. Furthermore, for all i, there exists a j such that $\phi_i = \phi'_j$. Hence, ϕ is a well defined Gödel numbering. Now let:

$$S = \{i: (\forall j)[j \ odd \ or \ i \neq H(2^j)]\}$$

We claim that for any Φ_i the scheme $(S,(\phi,\Phi),c)$ satisfies our requirements. Since S consists entirely of (effectively defined) constant functions, S is continuous and realizable. S is also non-trivial since for infinitely many i, $c.\Delta_S(i) \leq c(i)-1$. Hence S is good. From the definition of S it can be seen that:

$$d_S(n) \geq \frac{n - H^{-1}(n)}{n+1}$$

$$D_S(n) \geq \frac{n^2}{n^2 + 2H^{-1}(n)H^{-1}(n+L(n))}$$

Hence, by the definition of h, it follows that $d(S)=D(S)=1$. From a simple "pigeon hole" argument it follows that S is optimal i.o. Condition (6) is satisfied since $c.\Delta_S(i) \leq c.H(i+L(i)) \leq c.g(i)$. ◯

The last theorem exhibited a rather "pathological" scheme; that is, the properties listed in the statement of the theorem "sound nice" but the proof of the theorem constructs a scheme that achieves insignificant compression on "most" values. Although the definition of an abstract compression scheme captures a great deal of generality, included in this definition are schemes which we would like to rule out. At the very least, we would like to have more stringent criteria with which to judge the utility of schemes. Density and optimality with respect to a compression problem can be the basis of such criteria. For example, if S is a scheme, T a compression problem, and f and g recursive functions, consider the following criteria:

(1) S is *(f,g)-dense with respect to* T if $d_S^T = f$ and $D_S^T = g$.

(2) S is *optimal i.o. with respect to* T if the intersection of O_S with T is infinite. The concepts of optimal a.e. and optimal can be extended in a similar fashion.

(3) S is *(f,g)-tractable with respect to* T if the complexities of decoding and encoding over T are bounded by f and g.

Given a scheme S and a problem T, the above criteria can be used to make a quantitative evaluation of how useful S is for compressing strings of T.

6.6. BIBLIOGRAPHIC NOTES

For an easy to read introduction to the notion of program size complexity, see Chaitin [1975b]. The notion of an abstract compression scheme as presented in this chapter is due to Storer [1979,1983]. Many authors in the past have considered program size complexity (also known as *Kolmogorov* complexity); including, Chaitin [1987, 1976, 1975, 1969, 1969b, 1966], Katseff and Sipser [1977], Daley [1976, 1974, 1973], Daley [1974], Kamae [1973], Kolmogorov [1969, 1965], Loveland [1969, 1969b], Blum [1967], Martin-Lof [1966]) Goldberg and Sipser [1985] consider a notion similar to program size complexity when programs are restricted to lie within a particular complexity class.

For an introduction to Turing machines, recursive functions, decidability, and related issues see a text on the theory of computation such as Hopcroft and Ullman [1979]; other texts include Lewis and Papadimitriou [1981], Brainerd and Landweber [1974], Toulakis [1984], Hermes [1969], Hennie [1977], Davis and Weyuker [1983], Boolos and Jeffrey [1980], and Machtey and Young [1978]. Trakhtenbrot [1963] is a dated but delightful little paperback (translated from Russian) that includes a discussion of Turing machines. For an introduction to Ackerman's function, see Henie [1977]. For an introduction to the dovetailing construction, see Lewis and Papadimitriou [1981]. For a formal introduction to recursive function theory see Soare [1987], Cutland [1980], or Rogers [1967].

The notion of an abstract computational complexity measure is due to Blum [1967b]. An excellent discussion of this subject is contained in Hartmanis and Hopcroft [1971].

The isomorphism theorem is due to Rogers [1958]. The recursion theorem of Kleene appears in Kleene [1952]. For a presentation of the speed-up theorem, see Blum [1967, 1971], Hartmanis and Hopcroft [1971].

Chaitin [1969b] considers the weaker notion of a cost function that was discussed earlier (a recursive function c such that for any k, $c(i)=k$ for at most finitely many i). Our definition of a cost function can easily be shown equivalent to the "measure of size of machines" defined in Blum [1967b].

An interesting direction for future research would be to investigate useful restrictions that may be placed on (ϕ,Φ) and c for a scheme $(S,(\phi,\Phi),c)$. In this chapter, when defining good schemes, etc., we have been primarily concerned with restricting the set S. We might, for example, want to restrict ϕ to be an optimal Gödel numbering (Schnorr [1974]) or to have other characteristics such as those discussed in Hartmanis [1974], Hartmanis and Baker [1975], and Machtey and Young [1976].

Letting the set S in an abstract compression scheme be a proper subset of N can be viewed as "bounding the resources" that are available for performing compression. Resource-bounded versions of standard program size complexity have a number of applications to complexity theory. Hartmanis [1983] defines *generalized Kolmogorov complexity* as the smallest program operates within specified time and space bounds to produce a given string. Applications of resource-bounded versions of Kolmogorov complexity such as this can be found in Allender [1987], Huyn [1986], Luc Longpre [1986], Rubinstein [1986], Watanabe [1986], Li [1985], Hartmanis [1983], Sipser [1980], and Peterson [1980].

APPENDIX

A.1. ENGLISH STATISTICS

This appendix contains statistics obtained from the following English text files, which collectively total 1,042,927 characters.

ea	9084	author 2	undergraduate music paper
eb	13340	author 1	CS article on trees
ec	19294	author 3	undergraduate English paper
ed	19763	author 3	undergraduate English paper
ee	23794	author 4	undergraduate English paper
ef	25331	author 4	undergraduate English paper
eg	35394	author 5	CS article on garbage collection
eh	39922	author 4	undergraduate linguistics paper
ei	41238	author 1	CS article on data compression
ej	43180	author 1	CS article on NP-complete string problems
ek	49248	author 6	CS article on data compression
el	68002	author 1	CS article on planar embeddings
em	76605	author 1	CS article on data compression
en	80951	author 7	manual for the "Caesar" VLSI layout editor
eo	102235	author 8	chapter of an undergraduate data structures text
ep	105152	author 8	chapter of an undergraduate data structures text
eq	136729	author 1	CS grant proposal
er	153665	author 9	undergraduate English paper

These files were obtained by rummaging through the file system on the authors local UNIX system[†]. The following sections of this appendix are approximate[††] lists of the most common n-grams (character strings of length n) for $1 \leq n \leq 8$ and a list of the most common strings of length ≤ 8. Entries in these tables are accompanied by their frequency of occurrence. To make the gram files printable, the following substitutions have been made:

newline	→	@
tab	→	~
!,@, ~, non-printing character	→	!

[†] In all cases, carriage return / line feed was stored as a single newline character. Some files were stored in directly printable form whereas others contained UNIX *troff* typesetting commands. To make the data more uniform, all of the troff files had the formatting commands removed (all lines that either started with a period or contained a back-slash). Even with this modification, the troff files were not totally "pure" text; there were still some lines of formatting information that remained. However, such formatting information amounted to an insignificant portion of the text (less than one percent).

[††] See the discussion in Chapter 1 about possible inaccuracies in these statistics.

A.1.1. ONE-GRAMS (All)

167429	' '	2872	' " '	904	'] '
93318	'e'	2747	'S'	852	'W'
67459	't'	2623	') '	755	'4'
57065	'a'	2619	'A'	717	'<'
56947	'o'	2442	'x'	714	' | '
55598	'i'	2269	'I'	707	'8'
53738	'n'	2189	'C'	634	'5'
52353	's'	1923	'P'	583	'>'
48305	'r'	1767	'2'	537	'6'
34858	'h'	1682	'E'	516	'U'
31324	'@'	1658	'_'	504	' ; '
29503	'l'	1458	'F'	478	'J'
26787	'c'	1434	' : '	453	'+'
25508	'd'	1366	'M'	425	' * '
21098	'u'	1344	'L'	411	'V'
19188	'm'	1257	'9'	404	'{'
18252	'p'	1243	'R'	385	'}'
17015	'f'	1231	'G'	375	'K'
14383	'g'	1213	'N'	231	' / '
12011	'b'	1193	'\'	194	'Y'
11283	' . '	1151	'B'	175	'Q'
10737	'y'	1138	'q'	152	' ! '
9572	'w'	1101	' ' '	117	' ? '
9088	' , '	1080	'D'	111	' ' '
7114	'v'	1054	'7'	102	'Z'
6059	'%'	1045	'='	102	'X'
5443	' ! '	1037	'3'	77	'$'
3666	'k'	1035	'O'	61	' ! '
3652	'T'	1019	'j'	55	' ! '
3094	' ~ '	955	'H'	32	' ! '
3070	' - '	929	'0'	29	' ^ '
3037	' ('	913	' ['	26	'&'
2931	'1'	910	'z'	26	'#'

A.1.2. TWO-GRAMS (100 MOST COMMON)

27249	'e '	6368	'al'	3985	'ct'
21536	' '	6367	'of'	3978	'as'
20247	' t'	6336	'nt'	3902	'll'
19244	'th'	5975	'y '	3803	'. '
17412	's '	5937	'st'	3760	'om'
17133	'he'	5801	'to'	3721	' m'
14645	' a'	5611	'.@'	3701	',@'
14467	'in'	5492	' p'	3637	'ic'
11878	're'	5474	'o '	3617	'ou'
11319	'er'	5410	'le'	3555	' d'
11200	't '	5371	'io'	3508	'pr'
11188	'n '	5280	' b'	3489	'h '
10768	'on'	5241	'ha'	3487	'be'
10340	'd '	5142	'se'	3457	' r'
10248	' o'	5012	'co'	3408	' e'
10064	' i'	4884	' w'	3405	'su'
10014	'an'	4769	'ra'	3331	'ac'
9818	' s'	4762	'de'	3258	' n'
8958	'es'	4727	', '	3246	'ta'
8238	'or'	4701	'ro'	3225	'ec'
8138	'ti'	4647	' f'	3150	'ea'
8075	'at'	4639	've'	3132	'ur'
8002	'en'	4423	'l '	3109	'ca'
7689	'is'	4229	'hi'	3077	' h'
7476	'r '	4147	'me'	3046	'ns'
7241	' c'	4131	'ch'	2975	'fo'
7216	'te'	4106	'a '	2961	'ma'
6957	'ar'	4069	'@@'	2948	' l'
6696	'nd'	4067	'ce'	2943	'la'
6388	'ng'	4035	'si'	2877	'tr'
6388	'ed'	4015	'g '	2845	'mp'
6383	'it'	4010	'ri'	2812	'ss'
6382	'f '	3988	'ne'	2798	'di'
				2748	'el'

A.1.3. THREE-GRAMS (100 MOST COMMON)

14364	' '	2512	'at '	1696	'his'
13953	' th'	2500	's t'	1688	'ly '
12847	'the'	2492	'for'	1686	'e i'
10890	'he '	2485	' be'	1681	'The'
5783	' of'	2456	'ati'	1679	'ch '
5555	'of '	2355	'@@ '	1678	' no'
5132	'ing'	2332	'hat'	1655	'@ '
4980	'ion'	2294	'tha'	1654	't t'
4945	'is '	2292	'e s'	1639	'ith'
4558	'and'	2271	'e a'	1637	'omp'
4262	'tio'	2230	'n t'	1635	'ons'
4206	' an'	2189	'al '	1607	'int'
4191	'nd '	2138	'her'	1565	'nte'
4176	' in'	2126	'f t'	1546	'll '
4030	'ed '	2124	'res'	1531	' ar'
3887	' to'	2093	'pro'	1513	'ere'
3879	'to '	2089	'e c'	1511	' de'
3873	'ng '	1991	' fo'	1504	'cti'
3651	' co'	1962	' pr'	1494	'be '
3568	'er '	1931	's o'	1478	'ver'
3441	'on '	1890	' st'	1477	'nt '
3275	'es '	1869	'e o'	1476	'st '
3238	' a '	1831	'as '	1451	'd t'
3188	're '	1819	'sub'	1442	'ers'
3092	' is'	1793	'. '	1434	' wi'
3040	'ent'	1791	'all'	1434	' wh'
2844	'in '	1776	'en '	1432	'str'
2821	's a'	1770	'com'	1398	'e p'
2772	'e t'	1766	'an '	1385	'nce'
2746	'or '	1734	' on'	1379	'ts '
2699	'ter'	1731	'con'	1338	' ma'
2676	' re'	1719	'are'	1328	'ate'
2567	' su'	1712	'ess'	1323	'@th'
				1317	'thi'

A.1.4. FOUR-GRAMS (100 MOST COMMON)

Count	Four-gram	Count	Four-gram	Count	Four-gram
11823	' '	1276	'he s'	818	' str'
10531	' the'	1263	'comp'	809	'hich'
9177	'the '	1226	'The '	806	'ting'
5139	' of '	1216	'are '	800	'to t'
4237	'tion'	1197	' are'	798	'oint'
3649	'ing '	1135	'he c'	798	' not'
3614	'and '	1121	't th'	787	'd th'
3308	' to '	1082	'with'	779	'he p'
3000	' and'	1052	'ent '	777	'the@'
2729	' is '	1037	'e of'	775	'ere '
2397	'ion '	1007	'ions'	756	'ding'
2075	' in '	991	' thi'	754	'ring'
2062	'that'	987	'e co'	754	' by '
2023	'f th'	981	'ment'	750	's a '
2003	' tha'	977	'.@Th'	744	' it '
1969	'atio'	968	'in t'	738	'____'
1952	'hat '	957	'ted '	730	'ich '
1940	'of t'	946	'inte'	727	' whi'
1833	'n th'	941	'@the'	722	's to'
1765	' sub'	940	'nter'	722	's in'
1647	'@ '	937	'this'	722	'not '
1568	's th'	905	'@The'	718	'e in'
1560	' for'	897	' wit'	716	'cess'
1548	'e th'	881	'ng t'	712	'form'
1507	'his '	870	'ter '	707	's an'
1459	' pro'	850	'here'	705	'r th'
1443	'ther'	846	' as '	704	'is a'
1415	' com'	843	'mple'	703	'gram'
1394	'for '	842	'o th'	700	'ed t'
1381	' be '	840	'her '	699	'ture'
1353	' con'	838	'ith '	699	'one '
1316	'sub '	834	'pres'	697	't of'
1291	's of'	827	'@and'	692	' poi'
				689	't is'

A.1.5. FIVE-GRAMS (100 MOST COMMON)

9638	' '	782	'point'	561	' can '
8416	' the '	754	' the@'	557	'from '
2760	' and '	747	'inter'	549	'other'
1984	'tion '	728	'to th'	548	'ointe'
1955	'ation'	727	'hich '	546	' cont'
1861	'of th'	723	'_____'	540	'progr'
1814	' of t'	692	'the p'	539	' of a'
1809	' that'	689	'ther '	533	's are'
1807	'f the'	687	'truct'	533	' one '
1739	'that '	677	'o the'	520	'at th'
1561	'@ '	675	' .@The'	517	'ed in'
1487	'n the'	669	'@The '	517	'ding '
1316	' sub '	653	' to t'	516	'he co'
1153	'ction'	652	'struc'	512	'e is '
1140	's of '	637	'@the '	509	'r the'
1138	' for '	636	'here '	506	'g the'
1109	'the s'	635	's to '	503	'proce'
1053	' comp'	635	'ion o'	501	'ocess'
994	's the'	634	'ions '	498	'd to '
991	' are '	624	't of '	496	', and'
973	'the c'	621	'@and '	494	'ould '
938	'e the'	616	'@@ '	492	' is a'
928	'e of '	614	'ting '	491	'cture'
920	'tions'	608	' not '	490	's and'
894	' with'	607	'ng th'	489	'the f'
886	'in th'	600	'ogram'	488	', the'
880	't the'	600	'ition'	477	'ing a'
842	'ing t'	598	'n of '	474	'nd th'
835	' this'	594	't is '	474	' have'
833	'this '	593	'd the'	471	's tha'
802	'which'	586	'on of'	471	'and t'
794	'with '	580	'ement'	461	'have '
786	' in t'	566	' from'	460	'will '
				457	' The '

A.1.6. SIX-GRAMS (100 MOST COMMON)

8083	' '	531	'on of '	386	'ed by '
1743	' of th'	528	'ointer'	383	'ed to '
1665	'of the'	513	' .@The '	382	' struc'
1501	' that '	507	' from '	380	'presen'
1500	'f the '	505	'ng the'	380	' the a'
1277	'n the '	501	'rocess'	376	'ed in '
1028	' the s'	483	'ations'	375	'resent'
976	'@ '	481	'tation'	375	'e that'
942	'ation '	476	's are '	375	' the r'
883	' the c'	464	'at the'	372	'other '
816	's the '	462	'ction '	372	' the n'
778	'in the'	460	', and '	364	' sub i'
736	' this '	453	's that'	362	'hat th'
727	'e the '	453	' the f'	355	'racter'
724	' in th'	450	's and '	351	'gorith'
720	'which '	449	'ructur'	350	'orithm'
708	'_____'	447	' proce'	348	'that t'
691	' point'	430	'the co'	346	'can be'
682	't the '	428	'ucture'	344	'the st'
666	' with '	428	'r the '	344	'ection'
651	'struct'	426	' have '	344	' The '
650	'to the'	421	' ~ '	340	'or the'
650	' which'	421	'g the '	340	' other'
632	' the p'	412	'd the '	338	'nguage'
596	'rogram'	412	'@~ '	338	'mpress'
594	'o the '	411	'e of t'	336	's of t'
594	' to th'	409	' will '	325	' the o'
580	'@@ '	402	' the t'	323	'there '
578	'ion of'	398	'nd the'	322	' the e'
575	'tions '	395	'string'	321	'for th'
572	'ing th'	395	' the l'	321	'an be '
548	'tion o'	394	'and th'	315	'on the'
541	'pointe'	388	'lement'	312	'Figure'
				309	' of a '

A.1.7. SEVEN-GRAMS (100 MOST COMMON)

7071	' '	335	'that th'	238	' the re'
1563	' of the'	335	'ompress'	235	'ntation'
1393	'of the '	325	' the st'	233	'nstruct'
839	'@ '	324	'hat the'	231	'. The '
691	'_____'	321	'can be '	227	'mplemen'
686	'in the '	320	's of th'	227	' sub i%'
644	' in the'	307	' that t'	226	'plement'
580	' which '	303	'e that '	225	' other '
576	'to the '	300	' string'	224	'formati'
528	' to the'	299	'ations '	222	'tional '
524	'program'	298	'Figure '	222	'tation '
523	'ion of '	290	'rogram '	222	'rmation'
521	'pointer'	289	'or the '	221	' comput'
507	'tion of'	282	'for the'	220	' recurs'
488	' pointe'	281	' for th'	219	'n of th'
471	'ing the'	277	' scheme'	218	'es the '
449	'tructur'	274	' can be'	214	'rom the'
428	'ructure'	273	'on the '	212	' there '
420	'ng the '	270	'ointers'	211	'with th'
419	'@@ '	270	' the pr'	210	't of th'
407	'@@~ '	267	'ocessor'	208	'from th'
404	'@~ '	267	'nd the '	207	' would '
398	's that '	266	' follow'	207	' repres'
397	'e of th'	265	'@Figure'	206	'on of t'
380	' the co'	262	' on the'	204	'-------'
377	'process'	256	'ation o'	204	' first '
373	'present'	256	' number'	203	'example'
357	'at the '	252	' to be '	202	'@@@@@@@'
355	'aracter'	250	' and th'	202	' subpro'
351	'lgorith'	245	'unction'	201	'mpressi'
350	'gorithm'	242	' compre'	200	'.@This '
338	'anguage'	239	'recursi'	199	' from t'
337	'and the'	238	'the pro'	198	'cessor '
				196	'ould be'

A.1.8. EIGHT-GRAMS (100 MOST COMMON)

Count	Gram	Count	Gram	Count	Gram
6199	' '	242	'for the '	194	' subprog'
1296	' of the '	237	'ation of'	193	'rom the '
710	'@ '	236	'function'	191	' from th'
677	'_____'	235	' compres'	190	'from the'
568	' in the '	234	'epresent'	188	't of the'
472	' pointer'	234	'@Figure '	187	'with the'
458	'tion of '	232	' on the '	187	'pression'
457	' to the '	231	'hat the '	187	'of the s'
428	'tstructure'	229	' algorit'	186	' impleme'
413	'structur'	228	'represen'	182	'@@@@@@@@'
400	'@@ '	227	'entation'	180	' with th'
388	'ing the '	226	'mplement'	179	'position'
381	' structu'	224	'and the '	175	'variable'
355	'haracter'	222	'ormation'	174	'ould be '
352	'e of the'	222	'formatio'	174	' number '
350	'lgorithm'	219	' the pro'	172	'mpressio'
345	'characte'	219	' recursi'	166	'pointer '
328	' process'	218	' functio'	166	'nstructi'
303	'that the'	215	' and the'	164	'ictionar'
299	' charact'	210	'ubprogra'	163	'omponent'
298	' that th'	210	'bprogram'	162	' is the '
293	'@@ '	206	' represe'	160	'dictiona'
290	' program'	205	'subprogr'	160	'ctionary'
284	'compress'	203	'ion of t'	158	'putation'
279	's of the'	202	'implemen'	158	'consider'
267	'rocessor'	200	'ompressi'	158	'componen'
266	'language'	199	'n of the'	157	'processo'
265	'pointers'	197	'on of th'	157	'ointers '
258	'algorith'	197	'nformati'	157	'ed in th'
255	'program '	197	'--------'	156	'ith the '
253	' languag'	196	'ocessor '	155	'omputati'
251	' can be '	196	' example'	155	'mputatio'
244	' for the'	195	'ructures'	154	'umber of'
				154	'truction'

A.1.9. 500 MOST COMMON SUBSTRINGS

167429	' '	10737	'y'	5474	'o '
93318	'e'	10531	' the'	5443	'!'
67459	't'	10340	'd '	5410	'le'
57065	'a'	10248	' o'	5371	'io'
56947	'o'	10064	' i'	5280	' b'
55598	'i'	10014	'an'	5241	'ha'
53738	'n'	9818	' s'	5142	'se'
52353	's'	9638	' '	5139	' of '
48305	'r'	9572	'w'	5132	'ing'
34858	'h'	9177	'the '	5012	'co'
31324	'@'	9088	','	4980	'ion'
29503	'l'	8958	'es'	4945	'is '
27249	'e '	8416	' the '	4884	' w'
26787	'c'	8238	'or'	4769	'ra'
25508	'd'	8002	'en'	4762	'de'
21536	' '	7689	'is'	4727	', '
21098	'u'	7476	'r '	4701	'ro'
20247	' t'	7241	' c'	4647	' f'
19244	'th'	7216	'te'	4639	've'
19188	'm'	7114	'v'	4558	'and'
18252	'p'	7071	' '	4423	'l '
17412	's '	6957	'ar'	4262	'tio'
17133	'he'	6696	'nd'	4237	'tion'
17015	'f'	6388	'ng'	4229	'hi'
14645	' a'	6388	'ed'	4206	' an'
14467	'in'	6383	'it'	4191	'nd '
14383	'g'	6382	'f '	4176	' in'
14364	' '	6368	'al'	4147	'me'
13953	' th'	6367	'of'	4067	'ce'
12847	'the'	6336	'nt'	4035	'si'
12011	'b'	6199	' '	4030	'ed '
11878	're'	6059	'%'	4015	'g '
11823	' '	5975	'y '	4010	'ri'
11319	'er'	5937	'st'	3988	'ne'
11283	'.'	5801	'to'	3985	'ct'
11200	't '	5783	' of'	3978	'as'
11188	'n '	5611	'.@'	3902	'll'
10890	'he '	5555	'of '	3887	' to'
10768	'on'	5492	' p'	3879	'to '

3873	'ng '	2948	' l'	2308	'nc'
3803	'. '	2943	'la'	2299	'li'
3760	'om'	2931	'l'	2294	'tha'
3721	' m'	2877	'tr'	2292	'e s'
3701	',@'	2872	'""'	2271	'e a'
3666	'k'	2845	'mp'	2269	'I'
3652	'T'	2844	'in '	2245	'ot'
3651	' co'	2821	's a'	2230	'n t'
3649	'ing '	2812	'ss'	2225	'ge'
3637	'ic'	2798	'di'	2222	'lo'
3617	'ou'	2772	'e t'	2215	'Th'
3614	'and '	2760	' and '	2155	'm '
3568	'er '	2748	'el'	2138	'her'
3555	' d'	2747	'S'	2126	'f t'
3508	'pr'	2746	'or '	2124	'res'
3489	'h '	2729	' is '	2110	'am'
3487	'be'	2728	'em'	2093	'pro'
3457	' r'	2699	'ter'	2089	'e c'
3441	'on '	2686	'rs'	2075	' in '
3408	' e'	2676	' re'	2062	'that'
3405	'su'	2665	'no'	2023	'f th'
3331	'ac'	2623	')'	2013	'wi'
3308	' to '	2619	'A'	2003	' tha'
3275	'es '	2615	'ut'	1991	' fo'
3258	' n'	2567	' su'	1984	'tion '
3246	'ta'	2518	'@~'	1980	'im'
3238	' a '	2512	'at '	1975	'pl'
3225	'ec'	2502	'po'	1970	'ee'
3188	're '	2500	'us'	1969	'atio'
3150	'ea'	2500	's t'	1962	' pr'
3132	'ur'	2492	'for'	1958	'ts'
3109	'ca'	2485	' be'	1955	'ation'
3094	'~'	2456	'ati'	1952	'hat '
3092	' is'	2447	'ly'	1940	'of t'
3077	' h'	2442	'x'	1933	'ul'
3070	'-'	2397	'ion '	1931	's o'
3046	'ns'	2387	'e@'	1929	'ub'
3040	'ent'	2386	'et'	1923	'P'
3037	'('	2355	'@@~'	1896	'so'
3000	' and'	2332	'hat'	1890	'ow'
2975	'fo'	2328	'pe'	1890	' st'
2961	'ma'	2317	'il'	1880	'@a'

1869	'e o'	1648	'od'	1443	'ther'
1861	'of th'	1647	'@ '	1442	'ig'
1851	'@t'	1643	'ol'	1442	'ers'
1846	'ho'	1639	'ith'	1441	'b '
1833	'n th'	1637	'omp'	1434	':'
1831	'as '	1635	'ons'	1434	' wi'
1819	'sub'	1620	'os'	1434	' wh'
1814	' of t'	1607	'int'	1432	'str'
1809	' that'	1583	'@%'	1430	' S'
1807	'f the'	1581	' u'	1427	'iv'
1806	'wh'	1569	' g'	1415	' com'
1801	'ie'	1568	's th'	1403	'uc'
1793	'. '	1565	'nte'	1401	'ab'
1791	'all'	1563	' of the'	1398	'e p'
1777	'rt'	1561	'@ '	1394	'for '
1776	'un'	1560	' for'	1393	'of the '
1776	'en '	1548	'e th'	1385	'nce'
1770	'com'	1546	'll '	1381	' be '
1767	'2'	1542	'gr'	1379	'ts '
1766	'an '	1541	'ay'	1368	'ap'
1765	' sub'	1535	'ad'	1366	'M'
1756	'mo'	1531	' ar'	1359	'id'
1739	'that '	1519	'tu'	1358	's,'
1734	' on'	1513	'ere'	1353	' con'
1731	'con'	1511	' de'	1348	'@i'
1729	'ex'	1507	'his '	1344	'L'
1719	'are'	1504	'cti'	1338	'sh'
1716	'@ '	1501	' that '	1338	' ma'
1713	'fi'	1500	'f the '	1335	'bl'
1712	'ess'	1494	'be '	1328	'ate'
1696	'his'	1491	'we'	1323	'ai'
1688	'ly '	1489	'ir'	1323	'@th'
1686	'e i'	1487	'n the'	1317	'thi'
1682	'E'	1478	'ver'	1316	'ub '
1681	'The'	1477	'nt '	1316	'sub '
1679	'ch '	1476	'st '	1316	' sub '
1678	' no'	1472	'oc'	1311	' T'
1665	'of the'	1471	'@T'	1310	' ha'
1658	'_'	1459	' pro'	1309	'ef'
1655	'@ '	1458	'F'	1305	's i'
1654	't t'	1453	's.'	1296	'le '
1652	'ni'	1451	'd t'	1296	' po'

1296	' of the '	1147	'wo'	1046	'tur'
1293	'n a'	1140	's of '	1045	'='
1278	'it '	1140	'ld'	1043	' di'
1277	'n the '	1140	' ('	1042	' mo'
1276	'he s'	1138	'q'	1041	'n@'
1274	'ure'	1138	'd@'	1037	'e of'
1271	've '	1138	' for '	1037	'3'
1269	' ca'	1136	'ry'	1036	'ns '
1265	't i'	1135	'wit'	1035	'O'
1263	'comp'	1135	'he c'	1034	'ove'
1259	'se '	1132	'ci'	1028	' the s'
1258	'e,'	1128	'e.'	1026	'ces'
1257	'@Th'	1121	'vi'	1019	'j'
1257	'9'	1117	' %'	1018	'eve'
1255	'ted'	1116	'e f'	1018	'ble'
1255	' it'	1109	'the s'	1017	'ce '
1254	' as'	1105	'pre'	1013	't o'
1251	'ect'	1101	''''	1013	'sp'
1243	'R'	1099	'r t'	1010	'ut '
1238	' al'	1099	'%@'	1009	' ex'
1237	'ov'	1092	'me '	1008	'ia'
1231	'ev'	1088	' se'	1007	'ions'
1231	'G'	1082	'with'	1000	'ram'
1229	'rm'	1081	'.@T'	1000	' A'
1228	'mi'	1080	'D'		
1226	'The '	1079	'wa'		
1216	'are '	1078	'by'		
1213	'N'	1073	'ive'		
1212	' C'	1070	'ty'		
1211	'ep'	1064	'tin'		
1203	'bo'	1064	'sc'		
1197	' are'	1064	'mpl'		
1193	'\'	1063	'gra'		
1191	'rd'	1062	'ne '		
1191	'if'	1055	'n o'		
1178	'one'	1054	'7'		
1178	'act'	1053	'cal'		
1174	'not'	1053	' comp'		
1171	'op'	1052	'ru'		
1171	'cu'	1052	'ent '		
1153	'ction'	1049	'ag'		
1151	'B'	1048	' v'		

A.2. SAMPLE FILES USED FOR EXPERIMENTS

The labeling of authors for these files is consistent with that used for files *ea* through *er* used for the English statistics. The English text files were obtained in the same manner as *ea* through *er* but are different files with the exception of *e*1 and *eg*, which are different versions of the same paper. The Pascal and Lisp files are all undergraduate student programs found on the author's UNIX system. Pascal and Lisp provide two nice alternative languages to English. It seemed appropriate to leave the comments in the Pascal programs, since Pascal is more English-like to begin with, and then for contrast, to remove all comments from the Lisp programs to produce a more "pure" programming language source.

English Files:

e1	31799	author 5	CS journal article on garbage collection
e2	39046	author 10	undergraduate art paper
e3	58295	author 1	CS journal article on VLSI routing
e4	62463	author 11	interlisp manual
e5	69130	author 8	chapter of an undergraduate data structures text
e6	82300	author 12	manual for the UNIX bb screen editor
e7	343033	misc	files e1 through e6
e8	505291	author 1	concatenation of 7 CS journal articles
e9	724133	author 8	undergraduate data structures book
e10	1042927	misc	files *ea* through *er*

Pascal files (including comments):

p1	21727	author 13	command processing module
p2	40234	author 14	PDP8 assembler simulator
p3	83696	author 15	polynomial manipulation package
p4	132142	author 1	concatenation of 10 misc. programs
p5	236295	misc	6 (about equal size) programs by different authors
p6	514094	misc	files p1 through p5

Lisp files (comments have been removed):

l1	25302	author 16	Chinese checkers
l2	55240	author 4	Alpha-Beta game playing program
l3	93672	author 17	battle game program
l4	134940	misc	5 (about equal size) programs by different authors
l5	254044	misc	6 (about equal size) programs by different authors
l6	563198	misc	files l1 through l5

The above files are referred to as the *sample files*. All of our statisitics pertaining to these files will be reported as the compression ratio expressed as a percentage:

$$\frac{(number\ of\ bytes\ in\ compressed\ file)}{(number\ of\ bytes\ in\ original\ file)} * 100$$

A.3. HUFFMAN CODING

Some entries have been omitted due to limits on computational resources.

file name	number of bits per input code			
	8	16	24	32
e1	59	57	67	82
e2	56	53	63	80
e3	58	54	61	75
e4	65	60	70	84
e5	57	52	56	68
e6	64	55	56	63
e7	61	55	55	55
e8	63	57	56	
e9	59	53	50	
e10	60			
p1	57	50	52	57
p2	59	49	49	53
p3	61	51	50	53
p4	59	49	48	51
p5	64	54	51	53
p6	63	53	49	
l1	53	49	54	60
l2	60	53	55	61
l3	43	37	35	36
l4	56	49	49	54
l5	55	47	45	
l6	54	47	45	

A.4. STATIC DICTIONARY METHOD

Due to limits on computational resources, only statistics on English sample files with less than 100,000 characters have been reported. However, it should be noted that the static dictionary method has no startup overhead to build a dictionary. Hence, for a given source, its performance on small files will be identical to that on big files.

file name	pointer size				
	10	11	12	13	14
e1	53	50	47	45	41
e2	51	49	48	47	45
e3	53	49	46	43	41
e4	65	65	64	63	59
e5	50	47	47	43	41
e6	65	63	62	58	55

A.5. SLIDING DICTIONARY METHOD

All of these statistics were gathered using uniform length pointers; that is, the same number of bits was used for a pointer even during the start-up phase when the dictionary was not yet full. For small files with big dictionaries (e.g. file p1 with 16-bit pointers), the compression ratios would be better if variable-length pointers were used; however, for most of the statistics reported, the difference is less that 1 percent. The advantage of using uniform length pointers is that most other authors do so as well (because it is not worth the bother to to include the extra code when it only pertains to the initial portion of the input stream) and hence these statistics are more consistent with other literature.

The software used to gather the following statistics was coded by at least two different programmers (and then it was checked that the two different versions were interchangeable). In addition, for each compression ratio reported, the corresponding decompression program was run to check that the decompressed file was the same as the original. However, we caution the reader that these statistics give only an indication of the relative performance of the heuristics in question, and do not represent any sort of definitive reference. The sample files chosen may not be truly representative of technical English, Pascal, and Lisp; it may be that the reader will obtain significantly different results with a different body of test files.

A.5.1. SLIDING DICTIONARY METHOD

all files on selected parameter values						
file name	bits for displacement,length					
	10,6	11,5	12,4	13,3	14,2	15,1
e1	66	55	48	46	53	73
e2	65	56	49	46	52	71
e3	62	52	45	43	50	70
e4	69	59	52	49	54	72
e5	60	50	44	41	49	70
e6	47	41	37	38	48	70
e7	60	51	44	42	49	69
e8	62	52	46	43	50	70
e9	61	52	45	42	48	69
e10	63	53	46	43	49	69
p1	40	32	30	35	48	71
p2	40	33	31	34	46	70
p3	40	34	31	34	46	70
p4	39	34	32	34	47	69
p5	36	30	29	33	45	69
p6	38	32	30	33	46	69
l1	35	30	30	35	47	70
l2	39	34	32	34	47	70
l3	27	22	22	29	44	68
l4	36	31	30	33	45	69
l5	39	33	30	33	45	68
l6	36	31	29	32	45	68

A.5.2. SLIDING DICTIONARY METHOD

Some entries have been omitted due to limits on computational resources.

file e2 on many parameter values						
distance bits	length bits					
	1	2	3	4	5	6
10	59	56	54	57	61	65
11	59	52	50	52	56	
12	61	51	48	49	52	
13	64	51	46	47	49	
14	67	52	45	45		
15	71	54	46			
16	75	57				

file p2 on many parameter values						
distance bits	length bits					
	1	2	3	4	5	6
10	56	46	40	37	38	40
11	58	45	37	34	34	
12	60	45	35	31	30	
13	63	45	34	29	27	
14	66	46	34	28		
15	70	49	35			
16	75	51				

file l2 on many parameter values						
distance bits	length bits					
	1	2	3	4	5	6
10	55	44	38	36	37	39
11	57	45	37	34	35	
12	60	45	36	32	32	
13	62	45	34	29	27	
14	66	47	35	29		
15	70	49	35			
16	74	51				

A.6. IMPROVED SLIDING DICTIONARY METHOD

The same comments pertaining to the use of fix-length pointers and the accuracy of the reported statistics that were made in Appendix A.5 apply here as well.

Entries for $e8$, $e9$, and $e10$ have been omitted due to limits on computational resources.

all files on selected parameter values					
file	bits for displacement,length				
name	10,6	11,5	12,4	13,3	14,2	15,1
e1	65	54	48	45	52	73
e2	64	55	49	45	50	71
e3	61	51	45	42	48	70
e4	68	59	52	48	52	72
e5	59	50	43	40	47	69
e6	46	39	36	36	46	69
e7	59	50	44	41	46	68
p1	39	31	29	33	48	71
p2	39	32	28	31	46	70
p3	39	32	29	31	45	68
p4	37	31	28	31	44	69
p5	35	29	26	30	43	68
p6	37	30	27	30	43	68
l1	33	30	29	34	47	71
l2	38	34	31	32	46	70
l3	26	21	20	26	42	68
l4	36	31	28	31	44	68
l5	38	33	30	31	43	68
l6	35	30	28	30	43	67

A.7. DYNAMIC DICTIONARY METHOD

The same comments pertaining to the use of fix-length pointers and the accuracy of the reported statistics that were made in Appendix A.5 apply here as well.

A.7.1. FC-FREEZE HEURISTIC

file	pointer size			
name	10	12	14	16
e1	59	50	53	60
e2	55	49	51	58
e3	58	49	47	54
e4	58	52	51	59
e5	56	49	43	50
e6	72	62	40	45
e7	64	57	53	47
e8	67	61	53	44
e9	62	51	44	39
e10	65	58	53	46
p1	48	36	41	46
p2	47	36	37	42
p3	52	40	33	38
p4	81	46	33	35
p5	82	65	46	36
p6	65	59	46	34
l1	48	39	41	47
l2	71	47	40	46
l3	48	26	24	27
l4	57	53	39	39
l5	66	54	39	36
l6	55	53	43	35

A.7.2. FC-LRU HEURISTIC

file	pointer size			
name	10	12	14	16
e1	55	48	53	60
e2	53	47	51	58
e3	54	46	47	54
e4	67	56	52	59
e5	51	43	43	50
e6	49	40	40	45
e7	53	45	42	43
e8	55	47	43	43
e9	52	44	39	37
e10	53	45	42	41
p1	39	35	41	46
p2	39	33	37	42
p3	40	32	33	38
p4	37	31	31	35
p5	40	33	33	36
p6	39	32	31	33
l1	38	36	41	47
l2	43	38	40	46
l3	27	23	24	27
l4	38	33	34	39
l5	38	33	33	36
l6	37	31	31	33

A.7.3. AP-LRU HEURISTIC

file name	pointer size			
	10	12	14	16
e1	57	49	46	50
e2	56	49	46	49
e3	56	47	43	44
e4	60	53	49	49
e5	54	45	40	40
e6	53	39	34	33
e7	56	46	40	38
e8	57	48	42	39
e9	54	46	40	35
e10	56	47	41	38
p1	43	31	28	32
p2	40	32	27	29
p3	41	31	26	26
p4	37	30	25	24
p5	40	29	25	24
p6	39	30	25	24
l1	39	31	31	34
l2	44	35	30	32
l3	31	22	19	18
l4	39	31	28	28
l5	40	33	30	29
l6	39	31	27	27

A.7.4. ID-LRU HEURISTIC

The first page of this appendix presents statistics for the standard ID-LRU heuristic. The second and third pages show how much worse these statistics become when the standard ID-LRU heuristic is restricted so that every non-leaf node of the trie that represents the local dictionary must always satisfy

$$height(leftsubtree) \leq r*(height(rightsubtree))+d$$
$$height(rightsubtree) \leq r*(height(leftsubtree))+d$$

where r is the "ratio" parameter and d is the "difference parameter". The fourth page of this appendix shows how much the standard ID-LRU heuristic is improved when various numbers of characters of lookahead are allowed; note that the size of the lookahead buffer is how far ahead the algorithm can compute a match that *starts* at that location.

A.7.4.1. ID-LRU, STANDARD ALGORITHM

file name	pointer size			
	10	12	14	16
e1	49	44	49	57
e2	49	45	49	56
e3	47	41	44	50
e4	53	46	49	56
e5	45	38	40	46
e6	36	31	33	38
e7	45	38	37	40
e8	48	39	37	38
e9	46	37	32	32
e10	47	39	36	37
p1	27	27	31	36
p2	28	25	29	33
p3	27	24	26	29
p4	27	22	24	27
p5	25	22	23	26
p6	26	22	22	25
l1	29	30	35	40
l2	32	28	31	36
l3	18	16	18	21
l4	29	26	29	33
l5	31	27	29	33
l6	28	25	26	28

A.7.4.2. ID-LRU, WITH BALANCING

file name	all files on selected parameter values dictionary size = 12 bits					
	difference,ratio					
	0,1	1,1.5	2,2	3,2.5	4,3	5,4
e1	57	48	46	45	45	44
e2	56	46	45	45	45	45
e3	53	44	42	41	41	41
e4	58	50	47	47	47	47
e5	51	42	40	39	39	38
e6	48	38	34	32	32	31
e7	50	42	39	38	38	38
e8	51	43	41	40	40	40
e9	48	40	38	38	37	37
e10	49	42	40	39	39	39
p1	49	36	31	29	28	28
p2	44	33	29	27	27	26
p3	42	32	28	26	25	24
p4	38	30	26	25	24	23
p5	46	32	26	24	23	22
p6	40	30	26	24	23	23
l1	52	38	35	33	32	31
l2	47	37	31	30	29	28
l3	32	25	21	19	18	18
l4	46	34	30	29	28	27
l5	41	33	30	29	28	28
l6	39	32	28	27	26	25

A.7.4.3. ID-LRU, WITH BALANCING

file e2 on different parameters dictionary size = 12 bits					
diff	ratio				
	1	1.5	2	2.5	3	4
0	56	56	47	47	45	45
1	48	48	47	47	45	45
2	46	46	45	45	45	45
3	45	45	45	45	45	45
4	45	45	45	45	45	45
5	45	45	45	45	45	45

file p2 on different parameters dictionary size = 12 bits					
diff	ratio				
	1	1.5	2	2.5	3	4
0	44	44	31	31	27	27
1	34	33	31	31	27	27
2	30	30	29	28	27	27
3	28	28	28	27	27	27
4	27	27	27	27	27	26
5	27	27	27	26	26	26

file l2 on different parameters dictionary size = 12 bits					
diff	ratio				
	1	1.5	2	2.5	3	4
0	47	47	36	34	30	29
1	38	37	35	34	30	29
2	33	32	31	30	30	29
3	31	30	30	30	29	29
4	30	29	29	29	29	29
5	29	29	29	29	29	28

A.7.4.4. ID-LRU, WITH LOOKAHEAD

| file | \multicolumn{6}{c}{pointer size = 12 bits} |
| name | \multicolumn{6}{c}{buffer length} |
	1	2	4	8	16	64
e1	44	44	43	43	42	42
e2	45	44	44	43	43	43
e3	41	40	39	38	38	38
e4	46	45	45	44	44	44
e5	38	38	37	36	36	36
e6	31	30	30	30	29	29
e7	38	37	36	36	36	36
e8	39	38	38	37	37	37
e9	37	36	35	35	35	35
e10	39	38	37	37	37	37
p1	27	27	26	26	26	26
p2	25	25	24	24	24	24
p3	24	23	23	23	22	22
p4	22	22	21	21	21	21
p5	22	21	21	20	20	20
p6	22	21	21	21	20	20
l1	30	30	29	29	28	28
l2	28	27	27	27	26	26
l3	16	16	16	15	15	15
l4	26	26	25	25	25	25
l5	27	27	26	26	26	26
l6	25	24	24	23	23	23

A.7.5. SAMPLE IMPLIED DICTIONARIES

All of the all implied dictionaries to be presented were obtained by compressing the first half of file e2, which we henceforth refer to as *e2.first*, using 10-bit pointers. The motivation for using e2.first rather than e2 is that the state of the dictionary is more "typical" in the middle of the file. A small pointer size was chosen to reduce the size of the implied dictionary. To make the implied dictionaries readable, all instances of the newline character (the only non-printing character in e2) have been replaced by @ (which does not occurr in e2). For the FC and AP update heuristics, only the root-to-leaf paths of length greater than one are listed; this omission looses no information because all 1 character strings are always in the dictionary, and if a string is in the dictionary, then so are all of its prefixes. For the ID update heuristic, each entry of 2 or more characters is listed along with its index in the trie and the indices of the two nodes from which it was formed.

To help interpret these implied dictionaries, the following is a listing of e2.first. Note that this text is a bit rough because not only is it a first draft of a student paper, but it has been stripped of lines containing text formatting information. Note also that for all implied dictionaries except for the one for FC-FREEZE, it is the text at the end of the listing that was being processed just before the dictionary was dumped. With the FC-FREEZE heuristic, the dictionary was frozen after reading only 1,546 characters.

> Art can be seen as the mirror of society. It is a picture of man's
> greatest aspirations and triumphs as well as his defeats. Art can be said
> to reflect a culture in its ability to show us the cultural concerns and
> self-image of an age and a civilization. The cultures of East and West
> may on the surface appear entirely different but in examining the art of
> these cultures, I would like to show that there are also similarities, and
> that the concerns of men everywhere, as reflected in their art, are not
> altogether different.
> A topic dealing with the principles of art in the East and the West is
> extremely broad. For the purpose of a more concentrated study. I have
> chosen to deal with two seminal periods in the history of both cultures.
> In the East I will be dealing with the Sung period. In the West, I will
> deal with the period of rebirth or the Renaissance, as the age aptly named
> itself. Within these periods I have chosen to deal with art in terms of
> genres or types. These subdivisions will allow a comparison of
> different works within the same general subject. These types of painting
> will be: the human figure, landscape, animals, and still-life. Before comparing the
> paintings, however, I will give a cultural background of each period and
> examine the guiding principles of their respective art.
> I will also offer a brief explanation of the different materials used by
> the Eastern and Western artist in order to more accurately compare their
> art.
> In examining the art of the East and West it is instructive to examine
> certain cultural differences in these two societies. Both the Renaissance
> and the Sung period represented extremely important and flourishing eras

in their respective cultures. These periods are also similar in that in
the Quattrocentto in Florence there was a decline in commercial enterprise
but there was also great artistic productivity, while in the Sung, there
was a decline in social and political conditions but at the same time a
rise in the production of important Chinese Art.

In the writings of the fourteenth to the sixteenth century in Europe we
find an interest in the revival of man's relationship to both Antiquity
and nature. Durer says: "For art standeth firmly fixed in nature, and
The Writings of Albrecht Durer.
London, 1958.

Alberti stated his view on the artists relationship to the ancients:
We should not simply take over into our work the formulas of the Ancients
and there by remain chained by ancient rules; rather, we should let
ourselves be stimulated by Antiquity to discover our true selves and to
make the effort not just equal the ancient masters but, where it is still

Renaissance art was also influenced by the dynastic ruling houses that
came to power, such as the Medicis, who patronized and guided the
development of important artists. Another important development in the
Renaissance was a loosening of the social stronghold of the class system.
The "Renaissance man" was recognized not solely for his class or importance
in society but for this intellectual and artistic capabilities as well.

Artists in the Renaissance took on new social importance, and it became
acceptable for an artist to be of noble rank. Art also became linked with
the sciences; mathematicians and artists were often brought together in
the Medici circle, to make new discoveries such as linear perspective.

The most noteworthy change however was the attitude that the art object
was no longer of highest value, but the "idea" within the object was of
greatest importance. This idea can be compared with the Chinese "spirit
resonance" of an object which will later be discussed. The Renaissance,
with its emphasis on learning, science, and religion formed the bedrock of
artistic accomplishment of the time.

The Sung dynasty, like the Renaissance, was a period of great patronage.
The emperors of the Sung Dynasty maintained their state by bribing
barbarians rather than by keeping up military power. This gave the Sung
A History of Far Eastern Art,
N.Y. 1973, p. 338

Because of the lack of invaders and consequent cultural isolation, the
Sung culture did not have a foreign influence on their art and thus
turned to past artistic periods for guidance. In the late Northern Sung,
Archaism flourished and went on to influence Southern Sung art as well.
Ancient bronzes were collected and often copied to look like "antiques".
The Art of Southern Sung China,
New York, 1962, p.8

This revival of the past can be compared to the Renaissance's classical
concerns, and the importance of the past in forming the art of that period.
Like the Renaissance period, the Sung was a time of educational endeavor.
Treatises were published on various subjects and book printing reached a
The Northern Sung also produced a type of artist comparable to the
Renaissance man, known as the "gentleman-painter". These men were often
scholars, officials and philosophers as well as artists and
The Chinese on the Art of Painting,
N.Y., 1963, p. 52

The gentleman painter embodied a type of "man for all seasons" - a man
who, like the Renaissance man, was learned as well as artistic and
embodied the tenants of his age.

Important academies were also formed during the Sung such as the academy
of painter-emperor Hui-Tsung. These academies like the "academies" of the
Medici's offered the artist training in the important principles of their
art.

Though both the Renaissance and the Sung periods were similar in their
general environment for the artist of great learning, philosophy,
admiration of ancient art and flourishing patronage, many differences

existed in the intellectual climate and formation of artistic ideals.
In Western Europe, the importance of the individual person and his
handling of technical problems was paramount. In China, the way on looked
at life and then interpreted it was the most important aspect of art.
The
Chinese did not create art based solely on religion, philosophy or
science, but an art reflective of certain ideas which were embodied in
these fields. The European artists was more bound to religion in his
choice of subject matter and his scientific thought led him to search
for greater and greater accuracy in his portrayal of reality, rather than
the "idea" of reality. For the Chinese the natural world, rather than
religion, was where the artist received his greatest inspiration, and his
portrayal of the natural world contained many conventions that the
Western eye could not comprehend. For example, a mountain to the Chinese
has a certain character and that character should be evident in the
painting while to the Western artist a mountain represents a solid mass
which must be portrayed as realistically and as monumentally as possible.
In the West, Christianity, and the Hellenic tradition were largely
responsible for molding European art, while Taoism and Confusionism
created the climate for Chinese art. While Christianity sought a kind of
perpetuation of religion through its representation, Taoism and
Confusionism were philosophies that encouraged not just representation of
stories but of a certain way of thinking.
Christianity established for the Western mind a series of extremes such as
Good and Evil, God and Man, Spirit and Matter. Though Taoism allowed for
extremens, it generally avoided them. In the Eastern philosophy, the Tao
is impersonal and therefore the Western duality between divine and human
did not arise.
The Contrast, for example, between spirit and matter in the West (the
spirit belonging to religion, the matter belonging to science) did not
exist in the East. To the Chinese, the realm of spirit and matter are
one. In the West, the duality of spirit and matter lead to very extreme
representations of either religious or natural subjects. To the Eastern artist
art is a combination of beliefs and feelings, as well as naturalistic
understanding.
The combination of spirit and naturalism are embodied in the Chinese "six Fa"
or six principles. These principles, as set forth by Hsieh Ho, are the
guiding principles of Chinese art. The six Fa are: Spirit Resonance and Life Movement, Bone manner (brush
use), conformity to objects, coloration, plan and design (composition), and
These principles have no direct counterpart in Western artistic history,
yet there are in the Renaissance some similar values set forth by Angiolo
Galli in 1442. These were Arte, Mesura, Aera, Desegna, Manera, and
The Art of the Italian Renaissance
p. 15
Before comparing these principles, a short explanation of each will help
to simplify the comparison.
Spirit Resonance and Life Movement are perhaps the most difficult
principles for the Western mind to understand. What the Westerner views as
reality is most often a conformity to an outer reality. To the Chinese,
this is reversed: The inner reality can be said to be the most important
thing - that is the spirit which must resonate in order to be felt.
Life-Movement is likewise the life given to an inanimate object by the
artist. The artist gives his painting movement and the breath of life in
order to animate it. This principle can be compared to the Renaissance
term
Arte
which means the artist's way of giving life to his art.
Arte
is more general, however, than spirit resonance and does not really
include the philosophy that lies behind the Chinese first principle.
Arte
defines the artist's cause but not really the effect of that cause.
The second principle Bone Manner or brushwork is very important to the

Chinese painter in a completely different way than the brush was important
to his Western counterpart. To the Chinese, the brush could designate
emotions and feeling. The Chinese could portray a mood or the personality
of a person with a few characteristic brushstrokes whereas the Western
artist sought the make his brushstrokes indistinguishable.
The Western artist believed that the smoother the surface the more real
the illusion. The other major difference in brushwork is that the
Chinese worked primarily in ink while the Western artist sometimes
sketched in ink but painted in oil or other heavy paint with a rich
consistency that was not conducive to the kind of brushwork that the
Chinese were able to achieve. The importance of this principle in the
Sung dynasty is summed up by Kuojo-hsu in "Merits and Faults in the use of
the Brush":
...The brush must be nimble, move swiftly in a continuous and connecting
manner, so that the flow (arteries) of life is not interrupted as the
thoughts precede the brush. But the brush is also in the thoughts, and
when the picture is finished, all the thoughts are there, and the image
p. 79
The third principle, Conformity to Objects, is the artists' depiction of
forms as they are, or as they appear in nature. This principle can be
compared to
Naturale
or
truth to nature
in the Renaissance terminology. The primary differences, however,
betweens these two terms is that the Eastern artist saw objects as having
a certain life that Western artists did not see. For example, a rock to
the Chinese is an animate object while to his Western counterpart it is an
inanimate object.
The Chinese also created a pictorial language of
reality that to the Western eye may seem quite foreign. One can think of
a child's drawing in which the young "artist" has taken up certain
conventions in drawing the human figure; perhaps he has drawn a round
circle for a head with stick-like lines denoting arms and legs. This
drawing is recognizable as a human figure although it might not conform
exactly to the reality of human anatomy. The Renaissance artist thought
in terms of great reality and studied the human figure in depth as to
render his anatomy and musculature with great faithfulness, while the
Chinese artist rarely if ever drew from a nude, except in their erotic art. The Eastern artist strove
to capture spirit, not imitation.
This idea is expressed by the Sung connoisseur Tung Yu who writes:
Likeness is much appreciated in painting, but is that merely a matter of
outer form? The important point is not to look for this quality in that
The fourth principle of Hsieh Ho, Coloration, is quite different from the
Western concept of the coloring of an object. The Renaissance artist rarely
worked in black and white except for drawings and ink sketches. To the
Western artist, color was what gave life and reality to his work. Color
was used first to give likeness and then to create harmony whereas to the
Eastern artist, the colors must blend harmoniously first and foremost.
The Eastern artist also worked often in black and white for ink works of
favorite subjects such as bamboo. This was unthinkable to the Western
artist who believed that a finished work must be colored. Also, the
Renaissance artist's choice of color differed greately from the Easterner's
choice of palette. The Renaissance artist used bold clear colors applied
in glazes for a bright surface while Chines artists usually used subtle washes of
color. The subject of color is also dependent upon the different mediums used by the
the Western and Eastern artist and this will be discussed later.
Symbolism in color was also an important difference in Eastern and Western
cultures. For example, the color white to the Chinese is the color of
simplicity to the point of barreness and is also the color of mourning
while to the Westerner white is the color of purity. Red for the Chinese
is a festive color while for the Westerner it is a color of anger and
passion.

Another important difference is that whereas the Europeans depended upon
color to give mass to the objects, the Chinese painter used a combination
of color and line as a means of constructing his painting.
The principle of Plan and Design (Composition) correlates to the
Renaissance
Mesurea
(measure and proportion),
Designo, (design) and
Prospectiva
(linear perspective).
These principles in both cultures served to remind the artist of the
importance of placement and harmony of objects in his work. The emphasis,
however, is different in both cultures. The Western artist used
mathamatics to formulate strict rules of proportion that ruled much of
his composition, be it of the human figure or of a landscape. The Chinese
would have found these theories abhorrant in that rationalization in
connection with creation was contrary to Chinese Taoist freedom.
In terms of the composition of a landscape, the Westerners adhered to a
linear perspective system while the Chinese used a moving focus, which allowed
the eye to wander freely throughout the scene. Spatial depth or
Ch'i-fu
in Eastern art remained at the level of the early Renaissance three-depth
system (foreground, middle ground, background - each parallel to the
picture plane) up until the Ming Dynasty.
The Eastern artist did adhere to certain rules in terms of composition as
explained by the Sung landscape painter Ching Hao:
The faults in painting are of two kinds: those dependent on shapes and
those independent of shapes. Flowers and trees which do not conform in
season, figures which are larger than the buildings, trees which are
higher than the mountains, bridges which do not rest on their banks, are
These rules are rules of proportion but they are guided by the painter's
eye rather than a mathematical formula or a series of ideal proportions.
The final principle of Chinese painting is the drawing from past models.
This was important to both the Renaissance as well as the Sung painter.
Classicism was one of the guiding forces of the Renaissance and artist's
studied and drew from classical models at length. Likewise, in Chinese
culture, the copying of ancient models was an integral part of the
The Chinese Theory of Art,
N.Y., 1967, p. 14
Copying was included in the six principles but is not really a principle
of art; rather it was a widely accepted and practised part of an artist's
training.
The two Renaissance terms not yet discussed are
Aere
or aerial perspective and
Manera
or the manner and facility of execution. Aerial perspective in the
Renaissance was most often associated with Leonardo's technique of
"sfumato" or atmospheric treatment giving the painting a mist-like
quality. This technique was also used by the Sung landscape painter in
his treatment of the mist and atmosphere. In the treatise
Lin Ch'iian Kao Chih
(The Great Message of Forests and Streams) we see an explanation of the
importance and variation of
aere
in Chinese painting:
Clouds and vapours of real landscapes are not the same at the four
seasons. In Spring they are light and diffused. In summer rich and dense.
In Autumn scattered and thin. In Winter, dark and solitary. When not
simply disrupted shapes but such general effects are to be seen in the
Maniera
of facility of execution was seen by the Renaissance artist as a gift from
God. It was seen as an outer force that graced the gifted artist. In the

classifications of painters the "divine painters" in the Sung period were
described as those who did not make an effort but whose forms were arrived
This is perhaps closest to the Western conceptions of artists who achieve
maniera.
Yet for all Chinese artists, the manner of working came from within; that
is, from inner contemplation rather than a God-given gift. This is
explained also in the Lin Ch'iian Kao Chih:
He (the artist) let the thoughts settle in his soul, and then he
worked... He planned and penetrated it thoroughly,', he added to it, made
For the Chinese artist
maniera
was the result of inner tranquility while for the Western artist it was seen as the
result of the gift of an outer force that was beyond his control.
The main difference between East and West in terms of these principles
seems to be a different way of viewing the world. Many of the principles
correspond to one another such as the principle of likeness to objects and
the principle of naturale; however, the manifestations of these principles
are quite different. An example of this is best seen in E.H. Gombrich's
Art and Illusion.
In his section on "The Limits of Likeness", Gombrich includes a
juxtaposition of two landscapes of the same site, one done by an Eastern
artist, the other by a Westerner (see figs 1 and 2). This striking
comparison illustrates the marked difference in the Eastern and Western
interpretation of the same scene. Gombrich calls this "a selective
screen" which allows for only certain features of the landscape to exist.
The Western interpretation seems very bucolic and naturalistic, while the
Eastern interpretation seems much more mysterious and full of character as
evidenced by the mist around the mountains and the gnarled and
individualistic trees. Even the cows in Chiang Lee's work have a
uniqueness, each with its own personality that is not present in the cows
of the English work.   Gombrich calls this difference in interpretation
the difference in the "language of art" and this language cannot be
divorced from the cultures which create it. To the Western and Eastern
artist it is not a matter of translation but a matter of interpretation of
the world around him.
Before continuing a comparison between Chinese and Western paintings, a
short explanation of the different types of formats and materials used by
each culture is in order. The formats of Eastern painting include the
hanging scroll, the hand scroll, and the album leaf. The hanging scroll
may be seen as comparable to the Western canvas but the Chinese hanging scrolls

A.7.5.1. FC-FREEZE

`" "`	`"-l"`	`"Be"`	`"ena"`
`" In"`	`". B"`	`"bir"`	`"enr"`
`" a b"`	`". F"`	`"bo"`	`"ent"`
`" a cu"`	`". Th"`	`"bri"`	`"ent."`
`" A"`	`". W"`	`"bu"`	`"er,"`
`" ag"`	`".@In"`	`"by"`	`"era"`
`" and We"`	`": "`	`"c"`	`"ere"`
`" ap"`	`"@A"`	`"can"`	`"eria"`
`" ar"`	`"@a"`	`"cap"`	`"erio"`
`" be:"`	`"@ce"`	`"ce "`	`"erm"`
`" comp"`	`"@di"`	`"ce,"`	`"ern a"`
`" cult"`	`"@e"`	`"ch "`	`"ery"`
`" de"`	`"@ge"`	`"cipl"`	`"es "`
`" e"`	`"@I"`	`"civ"`	`"es,"`
`" g"`	`"@i"`	`"com"`	`"ese"`
`" ha"`	`"@n"`	`"ct "`	`"est "`
`" ho"`	`"@p"`	`"cte"`	`"et"`
`" I "`	`"@s"`	`"ctiv"`	`"eve"`
`" in"`	`"@the"`	`"cul"`	`"exam"`
`" it"`	`"@w"`	`"cur"`	`"exp"`
`" ma"`	`"A "`	`"d an"`	`"ext"`
`" mo"`	`"a c"`	`"d b"`	`"f a"`
`" n"`	`"acc"`	`"d i"`	`"f b"`
`" of p"`	`"ack"`	`"d l"`	`"f E"`
`" of t"`	`"ad"`	`"d st"`	`"f e"`
`" of@"`	`"ag"`	`"d. "`	`"f t"`
`" off"`	`"ain"`	`"d@"`	`"f-"`
`" or"`	`"ais"`	`"deal "`	`"f."`
`" per"`	`"al b"`	`"der"`	`"f@"`
`" pri"`	`"al p"`	`"diff"`	`"fa"`
`" re"`	`"al s"`	`"div"`	`"fe."`
`" sam"`	`"all"`	`"ds"`	`"fer "`
`" se"`	`"als "`	`"dy"`	`"feren"`
`" sh"`	`"alt"`	`"e al"`	`"ffe"`
`" so"`	`"ame"`	`"e ar"`	`"fi"`
`" T"`	`"ami"`	`"e ch"`	`"fl"`
`" the a"`	`"an f"`	`"e co"`	`"Fo"`
`" the E"`	`"an'"`	`"e d"`	`"g t"`
`" the h"`	`"ana"`	`"e E"`	`"g wi"`
`" the pe"`	`"anc"`	`"e m"`	`"ge a"`
`" the W"`	`"ands"`	`"e of"`	`"gen"`
`" thei"`	`"ap"`	`"e p"`	`"get"`
`" ther"`	`"are"`	`"e s"`	`"gi"`
`" top"`	`"aris"`	`"e th"`	`"gro"`
`" tr"`	`"art o"`	`"e W"`	`"gui"`
`" tw"`	`"Art"`	`"@"`	`"h a"`
`" ty"`	`"art."`	`"eac"`	`"h c"`
`" us"`	`"arti"`	`"eal "`	`"h o"`
`" W"`	`"as "`	`"ear"`	`"ha"`
`" wil"`	`"asp"`	`"East "`	`"he E"`
`" with"`	`"ast"`	`"Easte"`	`"he g"`
`" wo"`	`"at "`	`"eb"`	`"he s"`
`" 's"`	`"ate"`	`"ect"`	`"her"`
`" , and"`	`"ation"`	`"ed@"`	`"hese "`
`" , ar"`	`"ats"`	`"ee"`	`"his"`
`" , as "`	`"ave"`	`"efo"`	`"hose"`
`" , I "`	`"ba"`	`"ely "`	`"how"`
`" , l"`	`"bd"`	`"en"`	`"hs"`
`" -i"`	`"be "`	`"en t"`	`"hu"`

``I h''
``I wil''
``ic''
``idi''
``ief''
``ies''
``iff''
``ig''
``ila''
``ili''
``ill''
``imi''
``in th''
``In''
``inc''
``ine''
``ing t''
``ing@''
``int''
``iods''
``ion''
``ir r''
``ire''
``is ''
``is@''
``ist''
``It''
``ith t''
``ithin''
``iti''
``its''
``ity''
``iu''
``ive''
``iz''
``je''
``ke''
``kg''
``ks''
``l a''
``l c''
``l@''
``la''
``lec''
``les ''
``lf''
``lif''
``lik''
``ling''
``ll a''
``ll g''
``ll-''
``lo''
``ls,''
``ltur''
``ly''
``mag''
``mal''
``may''
``me ''
``mel''
``mina''
``mine''

``mini''
``mo''
``mpar''
``ms''
``n a''
``n b''
``n ex''
``n i''
``n of''
``n te''
``n the ''
``na''
``nc''
``nd o''
``nd@e''
``ne''
``ng ''
``ngs''
``nim''
``no''
``ns o''
``ns w''
``nst''
``nt''
``nti''
``ntr''
``o m''
``o si''
``oc''
``od ''
``of a ''
``of e''
``of m''
``of t''
``of@''
``on ''
``on.''
``oncen''
``or t''
``ord''
``ore a''
``ork''
``ory''
``os''
``oth''
``oun''
``ow ''
``owe''
``pai''
``par''
``pe,''
``pec''
``peri''
``pes ''
``ph''
``pic''
``pir''
``pla''
``po''
``pp''
``pt''
``pu''
``r d''

``r e''
``r to''
``r@''
``rate''
``re a''
``re n''
``re t''
``Re''
``re,''
``rea''
``refl''
``rem''
``ren''
``res ''
``resp''
``ring''
``riod''
``rn''
``roa''
``rr''
``rt ''
``rt,''
``rt.''
``rth''
``s ab''
``s an''
``s as''
``s I''
``s in''
``s of''
``s r''
``s t''
``s wi''
``s, ''
``s.''
``s@''
``s@''
``sa''
``sc''
``se o''
``sed''
``self''
``sen''
``sh''
``si''
``so ''
``son''
``ss''
``st i''
``sto''
``stu''
``Su''
``subj''
``t an''
``t b''
``t c''
``t I''
``t in o''
``t is''
``t t''
``t,''
``t.''
``t@a''

``ted''
``th ''
``that''
``the a''
``the d''
``the E''
``the h''
``the R''
``the S''
``The''
``th@''
``their''
``ther''
``til''
``tin''
``tl''
``to de''
``to e''
``tog''
``tru''
``ts''
``tura''
``ture''
``typ''
``uc''
``ud''
``uld''
``ultu''
``ura''
``un''
``ura''
``ure,''
``urf''
``urp''
``us''
``ut''
``ve t''
``ve@''
``vis''
``w t''
``we''
``Weste''
``wh''
``Wi''
``will ''
``wo ''
``xam''
``y b''
``y d''
``y of''
``y. ''
``y@''
``yp''
``yw''
``za''

A.7.5.2. FC-LRU

```
" a "          "@c"           "col"          "exi"
"ʒ@u"          "@d"           "comp"         "exp"
"and th"       "@E"           "cows"         "f ar"
"bu"           "@ea"          "cro"          "f th"
"by"           "@h"           "cte"          "f tw"
"ca"           "@i"           "cti"          "f."
"Ch"           "@n"           "cu"           "fea"
"co"           "@s"           "d and"        "fer"
"cu"           "@the"         "d ar"         "for "
"do"           "a ma"         "d f"          "fore"
"e"            "ʒ@"           "d h"          "forma"
"fi"           "ach"          "d m"          "fr"
"G"            "af"           "d W"          "fu"
"hang"         "ainti"        "d@"           "g "
"in t"         "alb"          "de "          "ge"
"inte"         "alit"         "den"          "gi"
"is "          "all"          "der"          "gl"
"it"           "als"          "differen"     "Cambri"
"la"           "ame "         "divo"         "gs,"
"Le"           "an E"         "ds"           "gu"
"m"            "and E"        "e a"          "h c"
"no"           "and s"        "e ca"         "h m"
"of c"         "and t"        "e co"         "h wo"
"of the "      "and W"        "e E"          "han"
"of tr"        "ands"         "e f"          "hav"
"on"           "ang"          "e is"         "he a"
"pa"           "ann"          "e my"         "he C"
"scr"          "ape"          "e of"         "he di"
"see"          "ara"          "e ot"         "he E"
"the c"        "aris"         "e sa"         "he s"
"the m"        "aro"          "e se"         "he We"
"the@"         "as "          "e w"          "hil"
"to "          "as@"          "e,"           "him"
"tre"          "at "          "ea"           "hin"
"W"            "ate"          "Eastern"      "hor"
"whic"         "ation of"     "ed by"        "ia"
"wo"           "ation@"       "ed d"         "ic "
" " a "        "ats"          "ee"           "ic,"
" "a "         "att"          "een"          "ich c"
" "] "         "atur"         "ees"          "iff"
"'s "          "Be"           "ef"           "ig"
"(s"           "b@"           "el"           "iki"
")."           "bet"          "ems"          "ill"
", a"          "bl"           "en "          "in f"
", e"          "bum"          "En"           "in o"
", o"          "but"          "en""          "in the"
", the "       "by "          "enc"          "inc"
", w"          "c"            "ene"          "ind"
". "           "cal"          "er a"         "ing i"
". E"          "can"          "eri"          "ing sc"
". G"          "ce in"        "ern "         "ing@"
". The "       "ced"          "er@i"         "inter"
". Thi"        "cen"          "erpr"         "ion "
". To"         "cer"          "es "          "iq"
".@B"          "ch al"        "ess,"         "is ""
"@Th"          "cha"          "est"          "is l"
"1 "           "Chia"         "eta"          "is st"
"2)"           "Chin"         "Ev"           "iso"
"@art"         "clud"         "ev"           "ist."
```

''isti''
''it ''
''it.''
''iv''
''k ''
''l ''
''lana''
''land''
''langu''
''lat''
''le to''
''lea''
''lec''
''led''
''lic''
''lish''
''ll, ''
''l@ ''
''llo''
''lls''
''ls''
''lu''
''ly ''
''m l''
''m.''
''mar''
''mate''
''mats''
''may''
''mis''
''mou''
''mpa''
''ms v''
''mu''
''n as''
''n b''
''n i''
''n pa''
''n t''
''nar''
''nat''
''nce ''
''nd 2''
''nd f''
''nd t''
''ne.''
''ner (''
''nese ''
''ng ''
''ngin''
''nl''
''not''
''ns ''
''nsl''
''nt i''
''nta''
''nu''
''nv''
''o th''
''of i''
''of the''
''of@ ''
''oll''

''amp''
''on i''
''ona''
''one b''
''ont''
''orc''
''ord''
''ore''
''ork.''
''ot a''
''oun''
''ous''
''ow''
''par''
''pe ''
''per''
''pes''
''pl''
''pres''
''preta''
''que''
''r.''
''rab''
''ran''
''rea''
''ree''
''renc''
''rent''
''res w''
''reta''
''rich''
''rio''
''rke''
''rl''
''rn ''
''rn@ ''
''rol''
''rou''
''rp''
''rs''
''rt e''
''rt"''
''rta''
''rtis''
''s l''
''s and''
''s c''
''s d''
''s f''
''s i''
''s m''
''s n''
''s of E''
''s of f''
''s ow''
''s the ''
''s this''
''s u''
''s.''
''s@ ''
''sa''
''scap''
''scrol''

''see ''
''seem''
''sen''
''sh''
''site''
''son''
''st a''
''st i''
''st,''
''ster''
''sti''
''t a''
''t b''
''t th''
''tati''
''ter o''
''tern c''
''terpr''
''tes''
''th ''
''tha''
''the "''
''the c''
''the gn''
''the m''
''the W''
''th@ ''
''ther ''
''thi''
''ting''
''tion b''
''tion s''
''tis''
''trat''
''tri''
''ts''
''tt''
''tur''
''tw''
''typ''
''uage''
''uch''
''ui''
''ull''
''ultu''
''und''
''uni''
''ura''
''ure''
''use''
''ust''
''ut''
''va''
''ve ''
''ve@s''
''ven''
''very''
''vidu''
''wee''
''Western ''
''whi''
''wit''
''wn''

''wo ''
''world''
''ws ''
''y a ''
''y be''
''y t ''
''y@ ''
''ys''

A.7.5.3. AP-LRU

`` a mat''
`` be ''
`` inc''
`` is in ''
`` is not ''
`` matter of ''
`` of tr''
`` of@the ''
`` pa''
`` se''
`` the Chin''
`` the cul''
`` the Western ''
`` th@' '
`` to the ''
`` whi''
``'' and ''
``''lan''
``, the ''
``. The ''
``,@'
``@art''
``@B''
``@eac''
``@ha''
``@ra''
``@s''
``@the wor''
``a co''
``a m''
``a@' '
``ab''
``ainting''
``als ''
``and Eastern''
``and the a''
``and Western ''
``ans''
``aris''
``artist ''
``as but''
``ate ''
``ation ''
``ats and ''
``ats of ''
``atter''
``Be''
``be@' '
``ble''
``bum ''
``but the ''
``by''
``canv''
``ced f''
``ch c''
``Chinese ''
``cl''
``compar''
``cont''

``cre''
``crolls''
``cult''
``d aro''
``d b''
``d hi''
``d scr''
``de the''
``der''
``difference in the ''
``different ''
``divor''
``e al''
``e and ''
``e ca''
``e form''
``e hang''
``e it''
``e of ''
``e@div''
``each ''
``eaf''
``Eastern p''
``Eastern@' '
``een ''
``ef''
``en ''
``er. T''
``eri''
``es w''
``ese hanging s''
``et''
``ex''
``f for''
``f. Th''
``fore ''
``formats ''
``fro''
``g a ''
``ge ''
``gua''
``h c''
``hand ''
``hanging scroll''
``he ''
``hich ''
``him''
``hor''
``ial''
``in interpre''
``in or''
``ing scro''
``ings, ''
``interpretation of''
``inting in''
``inu''
``ion bu''
``ion of the ''
``is lang''

``ison''
``ist it''
``it is ''
``it. ''
``l, and th''
``lanat''
``languag''
``lat''
``lbu''
``ld a''
``le t''
``lea''
``ll@' '
``lu''
``m l''
``m the c''
``m.''
``mater''
``may''
``mp''
``n a''
``n Chi''
``nes''
``nging ''
``nnot''
``not a''
``ntin''
``o the Western ''
``of ar''
``of Eastern''
``of the differen''
``oll, ''
``on b''
``orced ''
``ord''
``ore co''
``ort ''
``paint''
``para''
``pes o''
``plan''
``ran''
``reat''
``ram''
``roun''
``s and mat''
``s cam''
``s of ''
``s this di''
``s u''
``s, a''
``scrol''
``sed ''
``see''
``sh''
``sla''
``t a''
``t e''
``t ty''

``t" ''
``tation@' '
``ter of interpretation''
``ter of t''
``the "''
``the difference in ''
``the han''
``this ''
``tion ''
``To''
``tur''
``tw''
``type''
``uage ''
``ude''
``uin''
``ulture''
``und ''
``ure is ''
``ures''
``use''
``vas ''
``wee''
``Western and ''
``Western can''
``Western pa''
``worl''
``xp''
``y be''
``y@' '

A.7.5.4. ID-LRU

```
 389 =   32 +   97 '' a''
 715 =  389 +   10 '' a@''
 806 =  620 +   32 '' and ''
 625 =  806 +  102 '' and f''
1023 =  806 +  696 '' and nat''
 652 =  806 +  274 '' and th''
 421 =  806 +  685 '' and Western ''
 620 =  389 +  332 '' and''
 591 =  389 +  272 '' as ''
 368 =  389 +  314 '' as@''
 263 =   32 +   98 '' b''
 646 =  263 +  584 '' bet''
 587 =  263 +  117 '' bu''
 259 =   32 +   99 '' c''
 307 =  259 +  261 '' can''
 895 =  259 +  415 '' cer''
 461 =   32 +  914 '' Chi''
 736 =  461 +  880 '' Chine''
 473 =  259 +  111 '' co''
 869 =  259 +  542 '' creat''
 699 =   32 +  100 '' d''
 889 =   32 +   69 '' E''
 859 =   32 +  102 '' f''
 324 =  859 +  111 '' fo''
 468 =   32 +  103 '' g''
 796 =   32 +  669 '' Gombrich ''
 665 =   32 +  104 '' h''
 705 =  665 +   97 '' ha''
 770 =  665 +  424 '' him''
1020 =   32 +  105 '' i''
 983 = 1020 +  339 '' ill''
 711 = 1020 +  262 '' in ''
 312 =  711 +  496 '' in interpre''
 822 =  711 +  405 '' in the ''
 544 =  822 +  402 '' in the cow''
 469 =  822 +  731 '' in the Easter''
 887 = 1020 +  110 '' in''
 505 = 1020 +  567 '' it is ''
 534 =   32 +   76 '' L''
 794 =   32 +  812 '' landscap''
 310 =   32 +  109 '' m''
 788 =  310 +  281 '' mor''
 283 =   32 +  111 '' o''
 920 =  504 +   32 '' of ''
1004 =  920 +  502 '' of art''
 524 =  920 +  923 '' of ch''
 354 =  920 +  383 '' of interpretation''
 342 =  599 +  313 '' of the same ''
 599 =  920 +  573 '' of the''
 791 =  920 +  631 '' of tra''
 504 =  283 +  102 '' of''
 956 =  504 +  611 '' of@the ''
 391 =  283 +  110 '' on''
 301 =   32 +  112 '' p''
 732 =  301 +  290 '' prin''
 941 =  732 +  764 '' princip''
 266 =   32 +  115 '' s''
 313 =  266 +  640 '' same ''
 984 =  313 +  982 '' same sc''

 608 =  266 +   99 '' sc''
 804 =  266 +  101 '' se''
 768 =  804 +  756 '' seems''
 273 =   32 +  116 '' t''
 529 =  273 +  104 '' th''
 423 =  529 +  319 '' that''
 500 =  273 +  275 '' the ''
 767 =  500 +  716 '' the differen''
1008 =  500 +  355 '' the mo''
 509 =  529 +  773 '' the@''
 264 =  273 +  978 '' tree''
 260 =   32 +  659 '' ve''
 514 =   32 +  119 '' w''
 976 =  953 +  266 '' was s''
 953 =  514 +  271 '' was''
 463 =  514 +  104 '' wh''
 921 =  463 +  105 '' whi''
 387 =  921 +  303 '' which a''
 945 =  514 +  281 '' wor''
 269 =   34 +  806 '' '' and ''
 430 =   34 +  921 '' '' whi''
 712 =   34 +  300 '' ''a ''
 622 =   34 +  412 '' ''la''
 861 =   39 +  105 '' ''i''
 947 =   39 +  272 '' ''s ''
 401 =   39 +  314 '' ''s@''
 865 =   44 +   32 '' , ''
 876 =  865 +  453 '' , and ''
 929 =  865 +  405 '' , the ''
 655 =  929 +  606 '' , the ha''
 854 =  865 +  754 '' , whi''
 775 =  358 +   32 '' . ''
 358 =  293 +   32 '' . ''
 831 =  358 +   69 '' . E''
 346 =  358 +  853 '' . Gombric''
 877 =  358 +   73 '' . I''
 443 =  358 +   84 '' . T''
 687 =  443 +  275 '' . The ''
 297 =  687 +  714 '' . The hang''
 677 =  443 +  558 '' . This ''
 311 =  443 +  371 '' . To ''
 293 =   46 +   32 '' . ''
 593 =   46 +   10 '' .@''
 398 =  593 +   66 '' .@B''
 901 =  593 +   84 '' .@T''
 308 =  901 +  275 '' .@The ''
 458 =  308 +  685 '' .@The Western ''
 668 =   58 +   10 '' .@''
 960 =   10 +  904 '' @comp''
 647 =   10 +  826 '' @eac''
 944 =   10 +  425 '' @ma''
 884 =  944 +  479 '' @may ''
 450 =   10 +  982 '' @sc''
 611 =   10 +  405 '' @the ''
 517 =  611 +  704 '' @the wor''
 588 =   10 +  117 '' @u''
 300 =   97 +   32 '' a ''
 837 =  300 +  962 '' a compar''
 618 =  300 +  425 '' a ma''
```

```
 959 =  618 + 390  ''a matter''
 536 =  300 + 267  ''a se''
 667 =   97 +  10  ''a@''
 760 =  667 + 428  ''a@h''
 446 =   97 +  98  ''ab''
 913 =   97 +  99  ''ac''
 942 =  913 + 540  ''ach ''
 289 =  913 + 780  ''acter''
 538 =   97 + 102  ''af''
 323 =   97 + 287  ''age''
 366 =   97 + 105  ''ai''
 971 =  366 + 262  ''ain ''
 488 =  366 + 110  ''ain''
 740 =  366 + 115  ''ais''
 933 =  535 + 301  ''al p''
 535 =   97 + 108  ''al''
 379 =  535 + 776  ''albu''
 897 =  535 + 811  ''alisti''
 749 =  535 + 700  ''alit''
1016 =  535 + 108  ''all''
 360 =  535 + 272  ''als ''
 337 =  535 + 557  ''also''
 621 =   97 + 109  ''am''
 640 =  621 + 265  ''ame ''
1015 =  261 +  32  ''an ''
 268 = 1015 + 917  ''an ou''
 261 =   97 + 110  ''an''
 453 =  433 +  32  ''and ''
 660 =  453 + 405  ''and the ''
 832 =  453 + 802  ''and Wester''
 433 =  261 + 100  ''and''
 870 =  261 + 103  ''ang''
 759 =  261 + 985  ''annot ''
 722 =  261 + 118  ''anv''
 809 =   97 + 111  ''ao''
 808 =   97 + 112  ''ap''
 972 =   97 + 114  ''ar''
 343 =  972 +  97  ''ara''
 444 =  972 + 913  ''arac''
 671 =  972 + 684  ''aris''
 815 =  972 + 375  ''arle''
 928 =  972 + 917  ''arou''
 502 =   97 + 257  ''art''
 411 =  502 +  34  ''art"''
 562 =  502 + 684  ''artis''
 302 =  707 +  32  ''artist ''
 707 =  562 + 116  ''artist''
 734 =  271 + 263  ''as b''
 543 =  271 + 259  ''as c''
 271 =   97 + 115  ''as''
 319 =   97 + 116  ''at''
 327 =  319 + 105  ''ati''
 692 =  441 + 599  ''ation of the''
 441 =  327 + 329  ''ation''
 939 =  441 + 460  ''ations of ''
 333 =  319 + 306  ''atur''
 682 =  333 + 404  ''atures of the''
 907 =   97 + 659  ''ave''
 842 =   98 + 265  ''be ''
 406 =   66 + 101  ''Be''
 654 =   98 + 773  ''be@''
 843 =   98 + 106  ''bj''
 882 =   98 +1012  ''ble ''

 442 =   98 + 426  ''bric''
 776 =   98 + 117  ''bu''
 883 =  776 + 813  ''buco''
 511 =  776 + 394  ''bun ''
 462 =  776 + 258  ''but ''
 998 =   98 + 479  ''by ''
 641 =  998 + 405  ''by the ''
 386 =   98 + 121  ''by''
 836 =   99 + 806  ''c and ''
 256 =   99 + 273  ''c t''
 967 =   99 + 865  ''c, ''
 814 =   99 + 535  ''cal''
 341 =  814 + 634  ''calls t''
 916 =   99 + 261  ''can''
 679 =  414 + 822  ''ce in the ''
 414 =   99 + 101  ''ce''
 863 =  414 + 518  ''ced ''
 661 =  863 + 839  ''ced from ''
 828 =  414 + 112  ''cep''
 303 =  923 + 389  ''ch a''
 365 =  303 + 339  ''ch all''
 476 =  923 + 259  ''ch c''
 388 =  923 + 310  ''ch m''
 628 =   67 + 104  ''Ch''
 923 =   99 + 104  ''ch''
 856 =  923 + 972  ''char''
 914 =   67 + 683  ''Chi''
 918 =  914 + 261  ''Chian''
 786 =  914 + 110  ''Chin''
1018 =  786 + 765  ''Chinese ''
 653 = 1018 + 357  ''Chinese hanging sc''
 288 =   99 + 105  ''ci''
 764 =  288 + 112  ''cip''
 581 =   99 + 108  ''cl''
 813 =   99 + 111  ''co''
 954 =  813 + 393  ''coli''
 904 =  813 + 338  ''comp''
 962 =  904 + 972  ''compar''
 467 =  962 + 506  ''comparison''
 858 =  813 + 110  ''con''
 909 =  858 + 633  ''contin''
 402 =  813 + 119  ''cow''
 777 =  402 + 314  ''cows@''
 582 =   99 + 478  ''croll''
 304 =   99 + 116  ''ct''
 739 =  304 + 105  ''cti''
 925 =   99 + 381  ''cul''
 518 =  100 +  32  ''d ''
 482 =  518 +  97  ''d a''
 891 =  482 +1001  ''d and@''
 395 =  482 + 821  ''d aro''
 449 =  518 +  98  ''d b''
 936 =  518 + 998  ''d by ''
 785 =  518 + 716  ''d differen''
 720 =  100 +  46  ''d.''
 878 =  352 + 529  ''de th''
 352 =  100 + 101  ''de''
 803 =  352 + 110  ''den''
 615 =  352 + 114  ''der''
 481 =  100 + 105  ''di''
 508 =  481 + 968  ''differ''
 716 =  508 + 474  ''differen''
 318 =  410 + 711  ''difference in ''
```

829 =	318 + 405	''difference in the ''
410 =	716 + 414	''difference''
380 =	716 + 258	''different ''
673 =	481 + 118	''div''
521 =	481 + 664	''divi''
603 =	100 + 117	''du''
265 =	101 + 32	''e ''
513 =	265 + 858	''e con''
527 =	265 + 908	''e is ''
637 =	265 + 700	''e it''
408 =	265 + 109	''e m''
369 =	265 + 550	''e see''
799 =	265 + 439	''e to ''
525 =	101 + 39	''e'''
298 =	101 + 358	''e. ''
773 =	101 + 10	''d@ ''
747 =	773 + 481	''d@di''
681 =	773 + 606	''d@ha''
826 =	101 + 913	''eac''
656 =	826 + 545	''each c''
774 =	69 + 271	''Eas''
731 =	774 + 780	''Easter''
657 =	731 + 262	''Eastern ''
331 =	657 + 496	''Eastern interpre''
602 =	657 + 686	''Eastern painting''
551 =	731 + 810	''Eastern@artist''
546 =	101 + 333	''eatur''
376 =	101 + 304	''ect''
977 =	376 + 299	''ects a''
570 =	101 + 518	''ed ''
1021 =	570 + 453	''ed and ''
833 =	101 + 101	''ee''
824 =	730 + 461	''een Chi''
730 =	101 + 474	''een''
898 =	101 + 899	''efor''
797 =	756 + 32	''ems ''
597 =	797 + 109	''ems m''
756 =	101 + 727	''ems''
474 =	101 + 110	''en''
728 =	474 + 101	''ene''
934 =	728 + 115	''enes''
465 =	69 + 498	''Eng''
415 =	101 + 114	''er''
572 =	415 + 105	''eri''
552 =	415 + 328	''erio''
910 =	415 + 116	''ert''
678 =	321 + 32	''es ''
800 =	404 + 32	''es of the ''
404 =	678 + 413	''es of the''
448 =	678 + 754	''es whi''
321 =	101 + 115	''es''
765 =	321 + 265	''ese ''
456 =	321 + 116	''est''
584 =	101 + 116	''et''
583 =	584 + 119	''etw''
676 =	69 + 659	''Eve''
893 =	101 + 659	''eve''
563 =	101 + 664	''evi''
748 =	101 + 120	''ex''
817 =	748 + 684	''exis''
629 =	748 + 112	''exp''
938 =	629 + 412	''expla''
980 =	101 + 121	''ey''
963 =	102 + 500	''f the ''
789 =	102 + 687	''f. The ''
374 =	102 + 97	''fa''
783 =	102 + 101	''fe''
841 =	102 + 102	''ff''
968 =	841 + 415	''ffer''
578 =	899 + 283	''for o''
874 =	70 + 281	''For''
899 =	102 + 281	''for''
1000 =	899 + 265	''fore ''
873 =	899 + 986	''format''
879 =	873 + 460	''formats of ''
1022 =	102 + 821	''fro''
839 =	1022 + 394	''from ''
452 =	839 + 405	''from the ''
437 =	102 + 258	''ft ''
703 =	102 + 381	''ful''
848 =	103 + 32	''g ''
793 =	287 + 259	''ge c''
900 =	287 + 920	''ge of ''
287 =	103 + 101	''ge''
758 =	103 + 104	''gh''
522 =	103 + 105	''gi''
872 =	522 + 102	''gif''
586 =	103 + 110	''gn''
695 =	71 + 111	''Go''
807 =	695 + 109	''Gom''
853 =	807 + 442	''Gombric''
669 =	853 + 540	''Gombrich ''
769 =	669 + 814	''Gombrich cal''
540 =	104 + 32	''h ''
545 =	540 + 99	''h c''
486 =	545 + 999	''h cult''
604 =	540 + 700	''h it''
737 =	540 + 119	''h w''
606 =	104 + 97	''ha''
743 =	606 + 332	''hand''
714 =	606 + 498	''hang''
357 =	714 + 485	''hanging sc''
864 =	357 + 478	''hanging scroll''
275 =	104 + 265	''he ''
706 =	72 + 265	''He ''
350 =	275 + 873	''he format''
735 =	104 + 101	''he''
683 =	104 + 105	''hi''
558 =	683 + 272	''his ''
708 =	558 + 34	''his "''
549 =	558 + 410	''his difference''
651 =	558 + 908	''his is ''
762 =	105 + 535	''ial''
906 =	105 + 1015	''ian ''
846 =	105 + 99	''ic''
424 =	105 + 109	''im''
949 =	424 + 593	''im@ ''
438 =	424 + 639	''impo''
294 =	438 + 257	''import''
326 =	73 + 262	''In ''
385 =	105 + 262	''in ''
911 =	385 + 914	''in Chi''
492 =	385 + 281	''in or''
497 =	105 + 110	''in''
519 =	497 + 481	''indi''
729 =	627 + 32	''ing ''

490 = 729 + 300 ''ing a ''		339 = 108 + 108 ''ll''
485 = 729 + 982 ''ing sc''		336 = 339 + 929 ''ll, the ''
935 = 485 + 478 ''ing scroll''		403 = 339 + 693 ''llow''
627 = 497 + 103 ''ing''		868 = 339 + 658 ''llus''
396 = 627 + 10 ''ing@''		470 = 108 + 111 ''lo''
419 = 497 +1005 ''inner''		634 = 108 + 636 ''ls t''
741 = 497 + 320 ''inte''		577 = 634 + 558 ''ls this ''
675 = 741 + 114 ''inter''		605 = 108 + 258 ''lt ''
496 = 675 + 595 ''interpre''		489 = 108 + 117 ''lu''
849 = 383 + 504 ''interpretation of''		975 = 784 + 259 ''ly c''
717 = 496 + 987 ''interpretation se''		784 = 108 + 121 ''ly''
383 = 496 + 526 ''interpretation''		394 = 109 + 32 ''m ''
328 = 105 + 111 ''io''		292 = 394 + 375 ''m le''
619 = 340 + 283 ''ion o''		425 = 109 + 97 ''ma''
991 = 619 + 102 ''ion of''		612 = 77 + 261 ''Man''
340 = 328 + 110 ''ion''		825 = 425 + 114 ''mar''
422 = 328 + 658 ''ious''		986 = 425 + 116 ''mat''
908 = 684 + 32 ''is ''		691 = 986 + 415 ''mater''
560 = 908 + 385 ''is in ''		316 = 986 + 663 ''mats and ''
322 = 908 +1006 ''is lang''		755 = 109 + 101 ''me''
844 = 908 + 985 ''is not ''		277 = 109 + 105 ''mi''
684 = 105 + 115 ''is''		278 = 277 + 990 ''mist ''
672 = 506 + 263 ''ison b''		355 = 109 + 111 ''mo''
506 = 684 + 329 ''ison''		507 = 355 + 117 ''mou''
819 = 684 + 116 ''ist''		338 = 109 + 112 ''mp''
811 = 819 + 105 ''isti''		650 = 338 + 972 ''mpar''
855 = 811 + 99 ''istic''		727 = 109 + 115 ''ms''
700 = 105 + 116 ''it''		992 = 109 + 117 ''mu''
778 = 700 + 443 ''it. T''		950 = 109 + 121 ''my''
501 = 700 + 540 ''ith ''		262 = 110 + 32 ''n ''
510 = 700 + 272 ''its ''		435 = 262 + 453 ''n and ''
964 = 700 + 479 ''ity ''		989 = 435 + 731 ''n and Easter''
745 = 105 + 659 ''ive''		418 = 262 + 271 ''n as''
830 = 107 + 358 ''k. ''		823 = 262 + 99 ''n c''
270 = 75 + 809 ''Kao''		649 = 262 + 102 ''n f''
643 = 107 + 101 ''ke''		547 = 262 + 981 ''n pe''
779 = 643 + 518 ''ked ''		397 = 262 + 405 ''n the ''
674 = 643 + 880 ''kene''		750 = 110 + 34 ''n"''
885 = 108 + 920 ''l of ''		367 = 110 + 10 ''n@''
412 = 108 + 97 ''la''		940 = 810 +1020 ''n@artist i''
378 = 412 + 696 ''lanat''		810 = 367 + 707 ''n@artist''
503 = 412 + 332 ''land''		434 = 367 + 741 ''n@inte''
812 = 503 + 726 ''landscap''		589 = 110 + 535 ''nal''
862 = 812 + 265 ''landscape ''		709 = 110 + 972 ''nar''
1006 = 412 + 498 ''lang''		696 = 110 + 319 ''nat''
866 = 1006 + 345 ''langua''		1014 = 696 + 619 ''nation o''
670 = 412 + 601 ''lation ''		459 = 696 + 579 ''natural''
835 = 108 + 482 ''ld a''		285 = 110 + 99 ''nc''
1012 = 375 + 32 ''le ''		701 = 110 + 414 ''nce''
400 = 1012 + 432 ''le the@''		662 = 332 + 665 ''nd h''
915 = 1012 + 439 ''le to ''		624 = 332 + 266 ''nd s''
375 = 108 + 101 ''le''		946 = 332 + 500 ''nd the ''
924 = 76 + 101 ''Le''		332 = 110 + 100 ''nd''
330 = 375 + 97 ''lea''		1001 = 332 + 10 ''nd@''
417 = 375 + 304 ''lect''		892 = 1001 + 497 ''nd@in''
541 = 375 + 482 ''led a''		880 = 110 + 101 ''ne''
377 = 375 + 314 ''les@''		1005 = 110 + 415 ''ner''
393 = 108 + 105 ''li''		763 = 880 + 267 ''nese''
487 = 76 + 105 ''Li''		644 = 498 + 32 ''ng ''
295 = 393 + 99 ''lic''		498 = 110 + 103 ''ng''
609 = 487 + 262 ''Lin ''		961 = 498 + 729 ''nging ''
974 = 393 + 428 ''lish''		973 = 498 + 393 ''ngli''
427 = 393 + 291 ''lity''		1002 = 498 + 117 ''ngu''

553 =	110 + 105	''ni''
680 =	553 + 415	''nier''
471 =	553 + 614	''niqu''
718 =	110 + 784	''nly''
875 =	110 + 111	''no''
985 =	875 + 258	''not ''
569 =	985 + 300	''not a ''
919 =	985 + 98	''not b''
751 =	985 + 595	''not pre''
881 =	110 + 663	''ns and ''
466 =	110 + 115	''ns''
531 =	475 + 822	''nt in the ''
475 =	110 + 116	''nt''
532 =	475 + 366	''ntai''
371 =	111 + 32	''o ''
792 =	371 + 440	''o the Wester''
309 =	284 + 32	''of ''
952 =	309 + 116	''of t''
1003 =	413 + 32	''of the ''
413 =	952 + 735	''of the''
284 =	111 + 102	''of''
554 =	111 + 338	''omp''
571 =	329 + 1020	''on i''
329 =	111 + 110	''on''
753 =	329 + 518	''ond ''
958 =	329 + 265	''one ''
528 =	281 + 32	''or ''
281 =	111 + 114	''or''
344 =	281 + 863	''orced ''
970 =	281 + 352	''orde''
282 =	281 + 265	''ore ''
416 =	281 + 107	''ork''
771 =	281 + 258	''ort''
607 =	111 + 690	''osi''
457 =	111 + 573	''othe''
917 =	111 + 117	''ou''
857 =	917 + 758	''ough''
816 =	917 + 332	''ound''
693 =	111 + 119	''ow''
548 =	693 + 262	''own ''
454 =	693 + 272	''ows ''
623 =	112 + 97	''pa''
455 =	623 + 497	''pain''
431 =	455 + 780	''painter''
353 =	686 + 1020	''painting i''
686 =	455 + 666	''painting''
349 =	686 + 495	''paintings, ''
981 =	112 + 101	''pe''
598 =	981 + 114	''per''
886 =	981 + 460	''pes of ''
464 =	112 + 412	''pla''
639 =	112 + 111	''po''
595 =	112 + 317	''pre''
592 =	595 + 267	''prese''
746 =	595 + 526	''pretation''
772 =	112 + 290	''prin''
757 =	772 + 764	''princip''
931 =	757 + 375	''principle''
614 =	113 + 117	''qu''
932 =	614 + 728	''quene''
890 =	614 + 105	''qui''
943 =	114 + 32	''r ''
356 =	943 + 564	''r tha''

840 =	114 + 443	''r. T''
409 =	114 + 97	''ra''
616 =	409 + 573	''rathe''
600 =	114 + 414	''rce''
317 =	114 + 101	''re''
542 =	317 + 319	''reat''
795 =	542 + 265	''reate ''
978 =	317 + 101	''ree''
838 =	978 + 110	''reen''
499 =	978 + 115	''rees''
738 =	82 + 474	''Ren''
361 =	738 + 740	''Renais''
1013 =	361 + 363	''Renaissance''
491 =	317 + 979	''resu''
724 =	317 + 116	''ret''
335 =	114 + 105	''ri''
426 =	335 + 99	''ric''
290 =	335 + 110	''rin''
613 =	114 + 643	''rke''
821 =	114 + 111	''ro''
478 =	821 + 339	''roll''
845 =	478 + 865	''roll, ''
568 =	478 + 944	''roll@ma''
922 =	478 + 314	''rolls@''
512 =	821 + 117	''rou''
827 =	114 + 112	''rp''
556 =	114 + 557	''rso''
257 =	114 + 116	''rt''
617 =	114 + 479	''ry ''
272 =	115 + 32	''s ''
299 =	272 + 97	''s a''
663 =	493 + 32	''s and ''
993 =	663 + 986	''s and mat''
790 =	663 + 405	''s and the ''
493 =	299 + 332	''s and''
480 =	272 + 899	''s for''
515 =	272 + 385	''s in ''
460 =	272 + 309	''s of ''
713 =	460 + 657	''s of Eastern ''
445 =	460 + 899	''s of for''
555 =	272 + 693	''s ow''
636 =	272 + 116	''s t''
373 =	636 + 275	''s the ''
610 =	373 + 425	''s the ma''
781 =	636 + 558	''s this ''
533 =	272 + 912	''s use''
484 =	272 + 721	''s work''
951 =	115 + 34	''s"''
495 =	115 + 865	''s, ''
969 =	495 + 667	''s, @''
280 =	495 + 101	''s, e''
988 =	115 + 358	''s. ''
314 =	115 + 10	''s@''
447 =	314 + 101	''s@e''
965 =	314 + 413	''s@f the''
742 =	115 + 261	''san''
363 =	742 + 414	''sance''
982 =	115 + 99	''sc''
726 =	982 + 808	''scap''
702 =	982 + 474	''scen''
559 =	982 + 978	''scree''
888 =	982 + 821	''scro''
348 =	267 + 806	''se and ''

```
 267 =  115 +  101 ''se''              539 =  432 +  657 ''the@Eastern ''
 550 =  267 +  101 ''see''             820 =  573 +  267 ''these''
 575 =  550 +  262 ''seen ''           994 =  274 +  908 ''this ''
 733 =  267 +  375 ''sele''            566 =  116 +  105 ''ti''
 279 =  267 +  475 ''sent''            633 =  566 +  110 ''tin''
 436 =  428 +  514 ''sh w''            666 =  633 +  103 ''ting''
 428 =  115 +  104 ''sh''              626 =  633 +  117 ''tinu''
 359 =  428 +  281 ''shor''            601 =  392 +   32 ''tion ''
 690 =  115 +  105 ''si''              957 =  601 +  776 ''tion bu''
 689 =  115 +  412 ''sla''             392 =  566 +  329 ''tion''
 557 =  115 +  111 ''so''              439 =  370 +   32 ''to ''
 818 =  557 +  110 ''son''             805 =  439 +  748 ''to ex''
 451 =  115 +  112 ''sp''              580 =  439 +  440 ''to the Wester''
 725 =  451 +  376 ''spect''           370 =  116 +  111 ''to''
 399 =  115 +  495 ''ss, ''            631 =  116 +  409 ''tra''
 990 =  276 +   32 ''st ''            1011 =  631 +  110 ''tran''
 697 =  990 +  972 ''st ar''           905 =  631 +  320 ''trate''
 276 =  115 +  116 ''st''              801 =  116 +  272 ''ts ''
 719 =  276 +  415 ''ster''            867 =  390 +  920 ''tter of ''
 979 =  115 +  117 ''su''              390 =  116 +  780 ''tter''
 258 =  116 +   32 ''t ''              561 =  116 +  306 ''tur''
 635 =  258 +  618 ''t a ma''          291 =  116 +  121 ''ty''
 860 =  258 +  453 ''t and ''          710 =  291 +  981 ''type''
 574 =  258 +  629 ''t exp''           345 =  117 +   97 ''ua''
1019 =  258 +  102 ''t f''             896 =  345 +  287 ''uage''
 567 =  258 +  908 ''t is ''           852 =  117 +  535 ''ual''
 594 =  567 +  985 ''t is not ''       798 =  117 +  923 ''uch''
 420 =  258 +  405 ''t the ''          834 =  117 +  352 ''ude''
 384 =  420 + 1018 ''t the Chinese ''  902 =  117 +  729 ''uing ''
 847 =  258 +  291 ''t ty''            381 =  117 +  108 ''ul''
 688 =  258 +  119 ''t w''             315 =  381 +  108 ''ull''
 752 =  116 +  308 ''t.@The ''         999 =  381 +  116 ''ult''
 787 =  116 +  366 ''tai''             483 =  999 +  306 ''ultur''
 987 =  526 +  804 ''tation se''       530 =  117 +  332 ''und''
 347 =  987 +  797 ''tation seems ''   871 =  117 +  553 ''uni''
 526 =  116 +  441 ''tation''         1010 =  117 +  475 ''unt''
 851 =  526 +   10 ''tation@ ''        306 =  117 +  114 ''ur''
 320 =  116 +  101 ''te''              579 =  306 +  535 ''ural''
 694 =  320 +  518 ''ted ''            948 =  579 +  819 ''uralist''
 372 =  780 +  389 ''ter a''           927 =  306 +  265 ''ure ''
 766 =  780 +  324 ''ter fo''          850 =  306 +  678 ''ures ''
 286 =  780 +  920 ''ter of ''         632 =  658 +  806 ''us and ''
 780 =  320 +  114 ''ter''             658 =  117 +  115 ''us''
 477 =  320 +  373 ''tes the ''        912 =  117 +  267 ''use''
 274 =  116 +  104 ''th''              429 =  912 +  518 ''used ''
 564 =  274 +   97 ''tha''             520 =  658 +  631 ''ustra''
 955 =  564 +  258 ''that ''           966 =  117 +  420 ''ut the ''
 405 =  274 +  265 ''the ''            585 =  118 +  271 ''vas''
 630 =  405 +   34 ''the "''           930 =  659 +  389 ''ve a''
 997 =  405 +  535 ''the al''          659 =  118 +  101 ''ve''
 296 =  405 +   99 ''the c''           523 =  659 +   10 ''ve@ ''
 903 =  405 +  813 ''the co''          642 =  659 +  262 ''ven ''
 996 =  405 +  318 ''the difference in '' 638 = 659 + 114 ''ver''
 590 =  405 +  103 ''the g''           664 =  118 +  105 ''vi''
 472 =  405 +  425 ''the ma''          894 =  664 +  100 ''vid''
 364 =  405 +  277 ''the mi''         1007 =  664 +  352 ''vide''
 698 =  405 +  931 ''the principle''   926 =  118 +  281 ''vor''
 440 =  405 +  802 ''the Wester''      596 =  576 +   32 ''was ''
 744 =  440 +  262 ''the Western ''    576 =  119 +  271 ''was''
 407 =  440 +  435 ''the Western and '' 648 = 119 + 730 ''ween''
 362 =   84 +  735 ''The''             782 =   87 +  456 ''West''
 573 =  274 +  101 ''the''             802 =  782 +  415 ''Wester''
 432 =  573 +   10 ''the@ ''           685 =  802 +  262 ''Western ''
```

```
 723 =  685 +  675 ''Western inter''
 761 =  685 +  686 ''Western painting''
 351 =  802 +  367 ''Western@''
 382 =  119 +  104 ''wh''
 754 =  119 +  683 ''whi''
 334 =  754 +  923 ''which''
 305 =  754 + 1012 ''while ''
1017 =  119 +  700 ''wit''
 704 =  119 +  281 ''wor''
1009 =  721 +  665 ''work h''
 721 =  704 +  107 ''work''
 565 =  704 +  108 ''worl''
 325 =  119 +  272 ''ws ''
 479 =  121 +   32 ''y ''
 537 =  479 +   98 ''y b''
 937 =  479 +  776 ''y bu''
 645 =  479 +  309 ''y of ''
 516 =  479 +  564 ''y tha''
 995 =  121 +   10 ''y@''
 494 =  121 +  276 ''yst''
```

A.7.5.5. ID-LRU WITH BALANCING (difference=2, ratio=2)

633 =	32 +	34	`` " ''
595 =	32 +	40	`` (''
504 =	32 +	50	`` 2 ''
464 =	389 +	449	`` a co ''
389 =	32 +	97	`` a ''
402 =	389 +	10	`` a@ '
390 =	1004 +	828	`` and f ''
369 =	1004 +	525	`` and th ''
1004 =	389 +	332	`` and ''
575 =	389 +	114	`` ar ''
937 =	575 +	880	`` arou ''
986 =	575 +	458	`` arti ''
859 =	389 +	272	`` as ''
841 =	389 +	314	`` as@ '
263 =	32 +	98	`` b ''
286 =	263 +	754	`` bet ''
661 =	263 +	117	`` bu ''
259 =	32 +	99	`` c ''
667 =	259 +	531	`` cal ''
910 =	32 +	736	`` Chi ''
449 =	259 +	111	`` co ''
1020 =	449 +	338	`` comp ''
858 =	32 +	100	`` d ''
574 =	32 +	101	`` e ''
840 =	32 +	677	`` Eas ''
681 =	840 +	1023	`` Eastern ''
879 =	574 +	120	`` ex ''
828 =	32 +	102	`` f ''
420 =	828 +	318	`` fea ''
648 =	828 +	394	`` fig ''
373 =	828 +	281	`` for ''
421 =	373 +	680	`` format ''
802 =	828 +	381	`` ful ''
716 =	32 +	103	`` g ''
847 =	32 +	997	`` ha ''
973 =	32 +	105	`` i ''
771 =	973 +	379	`` illus ''
839 =	537 +	32	`` in ''
694 =	839 +	954	`` in interpre ''
885 =	678 +	840	`` in the Eas ''
678 =	537 +	447	`` in the ''
537 =	973 +	110	`` in ''
407 =	537 +	1005	`` incl ''
728 =	407 +	890	`` include ''
558 =	973 +	272	`` is ''
480 =	558 +	385	`` is in ''
730 =	973 +	258	`` it ''
942 =	730 +	797	`` it is ''
378 =	973 +	428	`` its ''
725 =	32 +	76	`` L ''
823 =	725 +	101	`` Le ''
700 =	32 +	680	`` mat ''
588 =	32 +	512	`` mo ''
483 =	32 +	912	`` nat ''
283 =	32 +	111	`` o ''
883 =	500 +	32	`` of ''
533 =	883 +	886	`` of ch ''

990 =	883 +	954	`` of interpre ''
665 =	883 +	274	`` of th ''
422 =	883 +	900	`` of tra ''
614 =	883 +	679	`` of tw ''
500 =	283 +	102	`` of ''
957 =	500 +	10	`` of@ '
598 =	283 +	110	`` on ''
301 =	32 +	112	`` p ''
934 =	301 +	696	`` pain ''
936 =	301 +	335	`` pri ''
266 =	32 +	115	`` s ''
682 =	266 +	491	`` same ''
287 =	266 +	99	`` sc ''
651 =	266 +	414	`` sce ''
440 =	266 +	101	`` se ''
793 =	440 +	411	`` seems ''
273 =	32 +	116	`` t ''
525 =	273 +	104	`` th ''
687 =	525 +	319	`` that ''
496 =	273 +	275	`` the ''
447 =	525 +	101	`` the ''
392 =	525 +	797	`` this ''
746 =	273 +	371	`` to ''
707 =	273 +	625	`` tree ''
351 =	273 +	121	`` ty ''
486 =	32 +	499	`` use ''
510 =	32 +	119	`` w ''
983 =	510 +	97	`` wa ''
479 =	983 +	272	`` was ''
515 =	510 +	668	`` whi ''
327 =	515 +	929	`` which a ''
877 =	510 +	281	`` wor ''
1017 =	34 +	300	`` "a ''
322 =	34 +	562	`` "lan ''
359 =	39 +	105	`` 'i ''
388 =	39 +	272	`` 's ''
339 =	39 +	314	`` 's@ '
596 =	40 +	570	`` (see ''
834 =	44 +	32	`` , ''
721 =	834 +	450	`` , and ''
346 =	834 +	311	`` , one ''
733 =	834 +	405	`` , the ''
958 =	733 +	312	`` , the other ''
361 =	834 +	295	`` , whi ''
984 =	358 +	32	`` . ''
358 =	293 +	32	`` . ''
925 =	358 +	636	`` . Gambri ''
895 =	358 +	73	`` . I ''
903 =	895 +	262	`` . In ''
441 =	358 +	84	`` . T ''
605 =	441 +	275	`` . The ''
948 =	605 +	519	`` . The hang ''
532 =	441 +	893	`` . This ''
467 =	441 +	371	`` . To ''
293 =	46 +	32	`` . ''
587 =	46 +	10	`` .@ '
497 =	587 +	66	`` .@B ''

635 =	587 +	84	''.@T''
637 =	635 +	275	''.@The ''
798 =	637 +	702	''.@The Western ''
848 =	50 +	41	''2)''
607 =	10 +	997	''@ha''
835 =	10 +	106	''@j ''
664 =	10 +	424	''@ma''
931 =	10 +	521	''@man''
374 =	10 +	691	''@sc''
719 =	10 +	398	''@sh''
511 =	10 +	117	''@u''
300 =	97 +	32	''a ''
368 =	300 +	424	''a ma''
683 =	368 +	789	''a matter''
333 =	300 +	267	''a se''
926 =	300 +	904	''a West''
527 =	97 +	10	''a@''
530 =	97 +	98	''ab''
876 =	97 +	99	''ac''
397 =	876 +	759	''acil''
938 =	876 +	755	''acter''
881 =	97 +	102	''af''
816 =	97 +	103	''ag''
366 =	97 +	105	''ai''
919 =	696 +	828	''ain f''
696 =	366 +	110	''ain''
269 =	696 +	927	''ains and''
767 =	696 +	755	''ainter''
296 =	696 +	632	''ainting''
720 =	366 +	115	''ais''
531 =	97 +	108	''al''
892 =	531 +	326	''albu''
711 =	531 +	105	''ali''
772 =	711 +	978	''alist''
826 =	711 +	291	''ality''
647 =	531 +	108	''all''
503 =	531 +	272	''als ''
544 =	531 +	285	''also''
992 =	97 +	109	''am''
491 =	992 +	265	''ame ''
484 =	491 +	584	''ame si''
548 =	261 +	32	''an ''
693 =	548 +	677	''an Eas''
586 =	548 +	880	''an ou''
261 =	97 +	110	''an''
450 =	431 +	32	''and ''
418 =	450 +	758	''and Easter''
638 =	450 +	405	''and the ''
280 =	450 +	702	''and Western ''
431 =	261 +	100	''and''
979 =	261 +	103	''ang''
794 =	261 +	813	''annot ''
1011 =	97 +	111	''ao''
731 =	97 +	112	''ap''
930 =	731 +	662	''aposi''
868 =	97 +	114	''ar''
438 =	868 +	876	''arac''
805 =	868 +	669	''aris''
613 =	805 +	329	''arison''
396 =	868 +	375	''arle''
498 =	97 +	257	''art''
894 =	498 +	34	''art"''
608 =	749 +	730	''artist it ''

749 =	498 +	775	''artist''
777 =	749 +	733	''artist, the ''
941 =	271 +	32	''as ''
436 =	941 +	555	''as but ''
871 =	941 +	612	''as compar''
271 =	97 +	115	''as''
412 =	319 +	973	''at i''
319 =	97 +	116	''at''
659 =	783 +	665	''ation of th''
433 =	783 +	500	''ation of''
516 =	783 +	440	''ation se''
675 =	516 +	411	''ation seems ''
783 =	319 +	465	''ation''
790 =	66 +	101	''Be''
932 =	98 +	766	''be@''
706 =	98 +	375	''ble''
843 =	98 +	335	''bri''
380 =	843 +	886	''brich''
326 =	98 +	117	''bu''
481 =	326 +	788	''buco''
1016 =	326 +	901	''bum ''
555 =	326 +	258	''but ''
583 =	555 +	405	''but the ''
946 =	98 +	475	''by ''
556 =	946 +	300	''by a ''
849 =	946 +	548	''by an ''
861 =	946 +	405	''by the ''
1018 =	861 +	444	''by the mist''
478 =	98 +	121	''by''
367 =	99 +	261	''can''
944 =	367 +	118	''canv''
578 =	414 +	525	''ce th''
414 =	99 +	101	''ce''
874 =	414 +	514	''ced ''
620 =	414 +	110	''cen''
652 =	414 +	112	''cep''
727 =	414 +	257	''cert''
699 =	886 +	32	''ch ''
929 =	886 +	389	''ch a''
911 =	929 +	345	''ch all''
666 =	886 +	259	''ch c''
443 =	666 +	647	''ch call''
960 =	666 +	323	''ch creat''
981 =	886 +	537	''ch in''
967 =	699 +	726	''ch wit''
601 =	67 +	104	''Ch''
886 =	99 +	104	''ch''
933 =	886 +	868	''char''
736 =	67 +	668	''Chi''
442 =	736 +	261	''Chian''
786 =	736 +	110	''Chin''
536 =	786 +	321	''Chines''
288 =	99 +	105	''ci''
864 =	288 +	270	''ciple''
1005 =	99 +	108	''cl''
695 =	1005 +	117	''clu''
788 =	99 +	111	''co''
743 =	788 +	393	''coli''
528 =	788 +	338	''comp''
612 =	528 +	868	''compar''
489 =	788 +	110	''con''
1022 =	489 +	760	''contin''
591 =	788 +	622	''cows ''

```
1012 =   99 +  348 "cro"              836 =  415 +   32 "er "
 452 = 1012 +  345 "croll"           415 =  101 +  114 "er"
 304 =   99 +  116 "ct"              993 =  415 +  766 "er@ "
 307 =  304 +  952 "ctive"          355 =  415 +  105 "eri"
 704 =   99 +  117 "cu"             741 =  415 +  328 "erio"
 572 =  704 +  108 "cul"            336 =  415 +  262 "ern "
 435 =  572 +  810 "culture"        427 =  415 +  563 "erner"
 514 =  100 +   32 "d "             321 =  101 +  115 "es"
 842 =  514 +   97 "d a"            276 =  321 +  705 "ess, "
 806 =  842 + 1019 "d and@ "        453 =  321 +  116 "est"
 278 =  842 +  348 "d aro"          698 =  101 +  258 "et "
 745 =  514 +   98 "d b"            754 =  101 +  116 "et"
 945 =  514 +  569 "d fro"         1014 =  754 +  377 "etwe"
 921 =  100 +   46 "d."             485 =  101 +  118 "ev"
 888 =  100 +   10 "d@"             913 =   69 +  645 "Eve"
 352 =  100 +  101 "de"             488 =  101 +  120 "ex"
 455 =  352 +  114 "der"            987 =  488 +  101 "exe"
 386 =  352 +  299 "des a"          487 =  488 +  775 "exist"
 477 =  100 +  105 "di"             492 =  488 +  112 "exp"
 589 =  477 +  102 "dif"            857 =  101 +  121 "ey"
 642 =  589 +  102 "diff"           688 =  102 +  101 "fe"
 340 =  642 +  415 "differ"         829 =  792 +  283 "for o"
 577 =  360 +  678 "difference in the"  290 =   70 +  281 "For"
 360 =  340 +  646 "difference"     792 =  102 +  281 "for"
 590 =  340 +  482 "different"      462 =  792 +  265 "fore "
 776 =  477 +  118 "div"            419 =  792 +  680 "format"
 752 =  477 +  884 "divid"          569 =  102 +  348 "fro"
 265 =  101 +   32 "e "             856 =  569 +  901 "from "
1009 =  265 +  450 "e and "         735 =  103 +  725 "g L"
 316 =  265 +  498 "e art"          674 =  103 +  265 "ge "
 640 =  265 +  489 "e con"          850 =  674 +   99 "ge c"
 922 =  265 +  809 "e it"           573 =  103 +  104 "gh"
 526 =  265 +  309 "e of "          663 =  103 +  105 "gi"
 618 =  265 +  824 "e sa"           429 =  663 +  102 "gif"
 568 =  265 +  267 "e se"           907 =  663 +  118 "giv"
 324 =  568 +  977 "e seen "        955 =  103 +  110 "gn"
 657 =  101 +   39 "e'"             953 =   71 +  111 "Go"
1010 =  101 +  358 "e. "            774 =  953 +  109 "Gom"
 766 =  101 +   10 "@"              636 =  774 +  843 "Gombri"
 985 =  766 +  477 "@di"            961 =  636 +  666 "Gombrich c"
 318 =  101 +   97 "ea"             517 =  103 +  117 "gu"
 980 =  318 +  699 "each "          709 =  104 +  973 "h i"
 451 =  980 +  572 "each cul"       997 =  104 +   97 "ha"
 677 =   69 +  271 "Eas"            545 =  997 +  770 "hand "
 758 =  677 +  755 "Easter"         519 =  997 +  494 "hang"
 724 =  318 +  810 "eature"         552 =  519 +  395 "hanging s"
 376 =  101 +  304 "ect"            963 =  552 +  452 "hanging scroll"
 564 =  101 +  514 "ed "            439 =  997 +  645 "have"
 970 =  101 +  101 "ee"             275 =  104 +  265 "he "
 616 =  101 +  792 "efor"           313 =   72 +  265 "He "
 411 =  101 +  753 "ems "           576 =  275 +  792 "he for"
 869 =  411 +  645 "ems ve"         628 =  275 +  424 "he ma"
 977 =  470 +   32 "en "            417 =  104 +  101 "he"
 969 =  977 +  941 "en as "         668 =  104 +  105 "hi"
 356 =  977 +  536 "en Chines"      303 =  668 +  109 "him"
 470 =  101 +  110 "en"             893 =  668 +  272 "his "
 634 =  646 +  678 "ence in the"    399 =  104 +  111 "ho"
 646 =  470 +  414 "ence"           594 =  105 +  531 "ial"
1021 =  646 +  514 "enced "         445 =  105 +  548 "ian "
 538 =  470 +  321 "enes"           801 =  460 +  273 "ic t"
 490 =   69 +  494 "Eng"            460 =  105 +   99 "ic"
 630 =  482 +  273 "ent t"          550 =  460 +  834 "ic, "
 482 =  470 +  116 "ent"            599 =  105 +  100 "id"
```

```
454 = 599 + 646  ''idence''          345 = 108 + 108  ''ll''
289 = 105 + 101  ''ie''              673 = 345 +  10  ''ll@''
872 = 289 + 409  ''iera''            631 = 345 + 111  ''llo''
394 = 105 + 103  ''ig''              379 = 345 + 689  ''llus''
401 = 394 + 272  ''igs ''            406 = 379 + 900  ''llustra''
759 = 105 + 108  ''il''              768 = 108 + 617  ''ls t''
423 = 105 + 109  ''im''              795 = 865 +  32  ''ly ''
968 = 423 + 112  ''imp''             713 = 795 + 414  ''ly ce''
385 = 105 + 262  ''in ''             865 = 108 + 121  ''ly''
701 =  73 + 262  ''In ''             901 = 109 +  32  ''m ''
833 = 385 + 736  ''in Chi''          520 = 901 + 375  ''m le''
535 = 385 + 281  ''in or''           951 = 901 + 405  ''m the ''
915 = 385 + 732  ''in the co''       508 = 109 + 587  ''m@''
493 = 105 + 110  ''in''              424 = 109 +  97  ''ma''
264 = 493 + 477  ''indi''            521 = 424 + 110  ''man''
554 = 493 + 564  ''ined ''           650 = 424 + 114  ''mar''
714 = 943 + 389  ''ing a''           680 = 424 + 116  ''mat''
395 = 943 + 266  ''ing s''           294 = 680 + 415  ''mater''
540 = 395 +1012  ''ing scro''        762 = 680 + 927  ''mats and''
943 = 493 + 103  ''ing''             426 = 680 + 509  ''mats of''
971 = 493 + 563  ''inner''           906 = 424 + 475  ''may ''
404 = 493 + 755  ''inter''           660 = 734 + 266  ''me s''
954 = 404 + 737  ''interpre''        734 = 109 + 101  ''me''
328 = 105 + 111  ''io''              277 = 109 + 105  ''mi''
465 = 328 + 110  ''ion''             791 = 444 + 575  ''mist ar''
982 = 328 + 689  ''ious''            444 = 277 + 978  ''mist''
797 = 669 +  32  ''is ''             512 = 109 + 111  ''mo''
896 = 797 + 891  ''is lang''         260 = 512 + 611  ''more ''
1013 = 797 + 813 ''is not ''         656 = 512 + 117  ''mou''
669 = 105 + 115  ''is''              338 = 109 + 112  ''mp''
624 = 669 + 329  ''ison''            838 = 338 + 805  ''mparis''
775 = 669 + 116  ''ist''             753 = 109 + 272  ''ms ''
472 = 775 + 637  ''ist.@The ''       815 = 109 + 117  ''mu''
787 = 775 + 460  ''istic''          1007 = 109 + 121  ''my''
809 = 105 + 116  ''it''              262 = 110 +  32  ''n ''
781 = 809 + 441  ''it.  T''         1002 = 262 + 101  ''n e''
742 = 712 + 883  ''ity of ''         827 = 262 + 949  ''n pe''
712 = 105 + 291  ''ity''             814 = 262 + 405  ''n the ''
952 = 105 + 645  ''ive''             715 = 110 +  34  ''n"''
887 = 952 +  10  ''iv@''             740 = 110 +  10  ''n@''
918 = 106 + 117  ''ju''              522 = 740 + 493  ''n@n''
764 = 107 + 358  ''k.  ''            819 = 110 + 711  ''nali''
723 =  75 +1011  ''Kao''             773 = 110 + 868  ''nar''
757 = 107 + 101  ''ke''              912 = 110 + 319  ''nat''
600 = 757 + 514  ''ked ''            765 = 912 + 998  ''natural''
785 = 107 + 943  ''king''            863 = 110 + 288  ''nci''
610 = 108 +  97  ''la''              653 = 863 + 270  ''nciple''
562 = 108 + 261  ''lan''             770 = 332 +  32  ''nd ''
615 = 562 + 100  ''land''            539 = 770 + 668  ''nd hi''
344 = 615 + 551  ''landsca''         383 = 770 + 691  ''nd sc''
891 = 562 + 103  ''lang''           1003 = 770 + 405  ''nd the ''
974 = 891 + 996  ''langua''          332 = 110 + 100  ''nd''
391 = 610 + 349  ''lation''         1019 = 332 +  10  ''nd@''
956 = 375 + 447  ''le the''          606 =1019 + 493  ''nd@n''
867 = 375 + 746  ''le to ''          592 = 110 + 101  ''ne''
375 = 108 + 101  ''le''              506 = 563 +  32  ''ner ''
684 = 375 +  97  ''lea''             563 = 110 + 415  ''ner''
898 = 375 + 304  ''lect''            690 = 110 + 321  ''nes''
729 = 375 + 842  ''led a''           854 = 494 +  32  ''ng ''
393 = 108 + 105  ''li''              494 = 110 + 103  ''ng''
565 =  76 + 105  ''Li''              331 = 494 + 943  ''nging''
457 = 393 +  99  ''lic''             292 = 494 + 393  ''ngli''
603 = 393 + 398  ''lish''            297 = 110 + 105  ''ni''
```

448 = 297 + 909 ''niqu''
341 = 110 + 795 ''nly ''
800 = 110 + 563 ''nner''
763 = 110 + 111 ''no''
813 = 763 + 258 ''not ''
947 = 813 + 300 ''not a ''
846 = 813 + 737 ''not pre''
916 = 110 + 115 ''ns''
579 = 471 + 32 ''nt ''
860 = 579 + 385 ''nt in ''
471 = 110 + 116 ''nt''
965 = 471 + 696 ''ntain''
371 = 111 + 32 ''o ''
897 = 371 + 488 ''o ex''
310 = 371 + 615 ''o land''
747 = 371 + 405 ''o the ''
571 = 111 + 100 ''od''
309 = 284 + 32 ''of ''
708 = 309 + 498 ''of art''
641 = 309 + 405 ''of the ''
284 = 111 + 102 ''of''
644 = 329 + 263 ''on b''
817 = 329 + 973 ''on i''
329 = 111 + 110 ''on''
330 = 329 + 514 ''ond ''
311 = 329 + 265 ''one ''
469 = 311 + 946 ''one by ''
281 = 111 + 114 ''or''
364 = 281 + 414 ''orce''
821 = 281 + 352 ''orde''
866 = 281 + 107 ''ork''
543 = 279 + 574 ''ort e''
279 = 281 + 116 ''ort''
561 = 279 + 261 ''ortan''
643 = 111 + 267 ''ose''
662 = 111 + 584 ''osi''
362 = 662 + 349 ''osition''
513 = 111 + 274 ''oth''
312 = 513 + 836 ''other ''
437 = 312 + 946 ''other by ''
880 = 111 + 117 ''ou''
988 = 880 + 770 ''ound ''
649 = 111 + 119 ''ow''
751 = 649 + 262 ''own ''
365 = 112 + 97 ''pa''
315 = 365 + 493 ''pain''
808 = 315 + 632 ''painting''
703 = 949 + 273 ''pe t''
949 = 112 + 101 ''pe''
686 = 112 + 470 ''pen''
853 = 949 + 114 ''per''
882 = 949 + 509 ''pes of''
382 = 112 + 562 ''plan''
270 = 112 + 375 ''ple''
825 = 112 + 111 ''po''
737 = 112 + 317 ''pre''
459 = 737 + 267 ''prese''
413 = 737 + 116 ''pret''
430 = 112 + 353 ''prin''
909 = 113 + 117 ''qu''
474 = 909 + 470 ''quen''
831 = 114 + 32 ''r ''
282 = 114 + 834 ''r, ''

409 = 114 + 97 ''ra''
611 = 317 + 32 ''re ''
609 = 611 + 109 ''re m''
317 = 114 + 101 ''re''
323 = 317 + 319 ''reat''
962 = 323 + 265 ''reate ''
625 = 317 + 101 ''ree''
748 = 625 + 110 ''reen''
832 = 625 + 298 ''rees. ''
718 = 82 + 470 ''Ren''
1006 = 718 + 720 ''Renais''
935 = 317 + 432 ''resu''
639 = 317 + 116 ''ret''
335 = 114 + 105 ''ri''
908 = 335 + 785 ''riking''
353 = 335 + 110 ''rin''
547 = 114 + 757 ''rke''
348 = 114 + 111 ''ro''
446 = 348 + 345 ''roll''
991 = 446 + 834 ''roll, ''
372 = 348 + 117 ''rou''
855 = 114 + 285 ''rso''
257 = 114 + 116 ''rt''
582 = 257 + 696 ''rtain''
529 = 114 + 117 ''ru''
672 = 114 + 475 ''ry ''
272 = 115 + 32 ''s ''
744 = 272 + 49 ''s 1''
299 = 272 + 97 ''s a''
425 = 299 + 10 ''s @''
553 = 927 + 496 ''s and the ''
927 = 299 + 332 ''s and''
739 = 272 + 792 ''s for''
717 = 272 + 813 ''s not ''
976 = 509 + 681 ''s of Eastern''
502 = 509 + 373 ''s of for''
466 = 509 + 301 ''s of p''
796 = 509 + 447 ''s of the''
509 = 272 + 284 ''s of''
617 = 272 + 116 ''s t''
384 = 617 + 275 ''s the ''
738 = 617 + 893 ''s this ''
779 = 738 + 360 ''s this difference''
784 = 272 + 499 ''s use''
619 = 272 + 295 ''s whi''
468 = 272 + 780 ''s work''
627 = 115 + 34 ''s"''
705 = 541 + 32 ''s, ''
1001 = 705 + 97 ''s, a''
851 = 705 + 318 ''s, ea''
541 = 115 + 44 ''s,''
298 = 357 + 32 ''s. ''
357 = 115 + 293 ''s. ''
314 = 115 + 10 ''s@''
534 = 314 + 101 ''s@e''
710 = 314 + 309 ''s@of ''
824 = 115 + 97 ''sa''
995 = 824 + 734 ''same''
722 = 115 + 261 ''san''
1008 = 722 + 414 ''sance''
691 = 115 + 99 ''sc''
551 = 691 + 97 ''sca''
473 = 551 + 949 ''scape''

629 =	691 +	625	"scree"
408 =	691 +	446	"scroll"
585 =	267 +	936	"se pri"
267 =	115 +	101	"se"
597 =	570 +	828	"see f"
570 =	267 +	101	"see"
685 =	267 +	470	"seen"
940 =	267 +	375	"sele"
476 =	267 +	579	"sent"
875 =	398 +	510	"sh w"
398 =	115 +	104	"sh"
889 =	398 +	279	"short"
584 =	115 +	105	"si"
676 =	584 +	320	"site"
964 =	115 +	610	"sla"
285 =	115 +	111	"so"
818 =	285 +	110	"son"
769 =	115 +	112	"sp"
347 =	769 +	376	"spect"
870 =	978 +	32	"st "
978 =	115 +	116	"st"
803 =	978 +	415	"ster"
692 =	978 +	460	"stic"
623 =	978 +	335	"stri"
432 =	115 +	117	"su"
837 =	83 +	117	"Su"
334 =	432 +	886	"such"
258 =	116 +	32	"t "
862 =	258 +	368	"t a ma"
989 =	258 +	450	"t and "
844 =	258 +	309	"t of "
845 =	116 +	731	"tap"
320 =	116 +	101	"te"
523 =	320 +	834	"te, "
505 =	320 +	514	"ted "
914 =	320 +	842	"ted a"
873 =	755 +	389	"ter a"
403 =	755 +	373	"ter for"
812 =	755 +	883	"ter of "
755 =	320 +	114	"ter"
1000 =	755 +	109	"term"
621 =	1023 +	1004	"tern and"
1023 =	755 +	110	"tern"
761 =	755 +	112	"terp"
626 =	320 +	617	"tes t"
274 =	116 +	104	"th"
405 =	274 +	265	"the "
799 =	84 +	275	"The "
560 =	405 +	531	"the al"
461 =	405 +	536	"the Chines"
732 =	405 +	788	"the co"
902 =	405 +	704	"the cu"
302 =	405 +	429	"the gif"
778 =	405 +	424	"the ma"
905 =	405 +	512	"the mo"
920 =	405 +	430	"the prin"
581 =	405 +	702	"the Western "
655 =	405 +	658	"the worl"
567 =	274 +	101	"the"
959 =	567 +	10	"the@"
400 =	274 +	111	"tho"
458 =	116 +	105	"ti"
760 =	458 +	110	"tin"

268 =	632 +	407	"ting incl"
632 =	760 +	103	"ting"
507 =	632 +	705	"tings, "
750 =	760 +	117	"tinu"
593 =	349 +	263	"tion b"
923 =	349 +	883	"tion of "
349 =	458 +	329	"tion"
878 =	370 +	32	"to "
604 =	878 +	98	"to b"
370 =	116 +	111	"to"
900 =	116 +	409	"tra"
999 =	900 +	110	"tran"
602 =	900 +	320	"trate"
428 =	116 +	272	"ts "
559 =	428 +	649	"ts ow"
463 =	789 +	883	"tter of "
789 =	116 +	755	"tter"
305 =	116 +	117	"tu"
416 =	810 +	558	"ture is "
810 =	305 +	317	"ture"
899 =	810 +	272	"tures "
363 =	810 +	796	"tures of the"
679 =	116 +	119	"tw"
924 =	679 +	371	"two "
350 =	291 +	525	"ty th"
291 =	116 +	121	"ty"
996 =	117 +	97	"ua"
256 =	996 +	674	"uage "
807 =	117 +	711	"uali"
410 =	117 +	886	"uch"
820 =	890 +	447	"ude the"
890 =	117 +	352	"ude"
1015 =	117 +	943	"uing"
381 =	117 +	108	"ul"
928 =	381 +	108	"ull"
542 =	117 +	770	"und "
387 =	117 +	297	"uni"
939 =	117 +	471	"unt"
306 =	117 +	114	"ur"
998 =	306 +	531	"ural"
566 =	998 +	775	"uralist"
495 =	689 +	1004	"us and"
689 =	117 +	115	"us"
499 =	117 +	267	"use"
580 =	499 +	514	"used "
342 =	117 +	258	"ut "
557 =	117 +	120	"ux"
549 =	118 +	941	"vas "
822 =	645 +	389	"ve a"
645 =	118 +	101	"ve"
804 =	645 +	262	"ven "
756 =	645 +	114	"ver"
884 =	118 +	599	"vid"
782 =	884 +	117	"vidu"
917 =	118 +	281	"vor"
994 =	119 +	941	"was "
434 =	994 +	685	"was seen"
377 =	119 +	101	"we"
518 =	377 +	977	"ween "
904 =	87 +	453	"West"
456 =	904 +	415	"Wester"
702 =	904 +	336	"Western "
972 =	702 +	450	"Western and "

```
654 = 702 + 404 ''Western inter''
325 = 702 + 315 ''Western pain''
295 = 119 + 668 ''whi''
852 = 295 + 666 ''which c''
501 = 295 + 375 ''while''
670 = 119 + 399 ''who''
524 = 119 + 943 ''wing''
726 = 119 + 809 ''wit''
337 = 726 + 104 ''with''
697 = 119 + 281 ''wor''
780 = 697 + 107 ''work''
658 = 697 + 108 ''worl''
343 = 658 + 842 ''world a''
622 = 119 + 272 ''ws ''
830 = 622 + 385 ''ws in ''
671 = 119 + 314 ''ws@''
950 = 120 + 116 ''xt''
475 = 121 +  32 ''y ''
308 = 475 +  98 ''y b''
546 = 475 + 326 ''y bu''
975 = 475 + 309 ''y of ''
811 = 121 +  10 ''y@''
354 = 121 + 949 ''ype''
966 = 121 + 978 ''yst''
```

A.7.5.6. ID-LRU WITH LOOKAHEAD (buffer=16)

469 =	32 +	97	'' a''
393 =	469 +	10	'' a@''
377 =	469 +	262	'' an ''
936 =	322 +	32	'' and ''
279 =	936 +	50	'' and 2''
838 =	936 +	437	'' and nat''
903 =	936 +	369	'' and this ''
322 =	469 +	332	'' and''
750 =	322 +	10	'' and@''
634 =	750 +	498	'' and@in''
1003 =	469 +	438	'' aro''
585 =	1003 +	751	'' around''
894 =	632 +	32	'' as ''
632 =	469 +	115	'' as''
428 =	632 +	10	'' as@''
263 =	32 +	98	'' b''
259 =	32 +	99	'' c''
398 =	259 +	261	'' can''
390 =	32 +	885	'' Chi''
619 =	32 +	615	'' comp''
786 =	32 +	102	'' f''
860 =	786 +	961	'' fig''
690 =	770 +	32	'' for ''
795 =	690 +	329	'' for on''
770 =	786 +	281	'' for''
973 =	32 +	323	'' Gombrich ''
735 =	32 +	104	'' h''
581 =	735 +	97	'' ha''
889 =	735 +	423	'' him''
520 =	32 +	105	'' i''
563 =	444 +	32	'' in ''
682 =	563 +	885	'' in Chi''
760 =	563 +	662	'' in interpreta''
591 =	563 +	404	'' in the ''
974 =	591 +	289	'' in the cows''
396 =	591 +	458	'' in the Eastern ''
444 =	32 +	498	'' in''
957 =	444 +	704	'' inclu''
966 =	444 +	779	'' inter''
363 =	539 +	32	'' is ''
984 =	363 +	385	'' is in ''
947 =	363 +	970	'' is not ''
849 =	947 +	300	'' is not a ''
539 =	32 +	686	'' is''
310 =	32 +	109	'' m''
576 =	310 +	121	'' my''
283 =	32 +	111	'' o''
916 =	505 +	32	'' of ''
436 =	916 +	503	'' of art''
1013 =	916 +	919	'' of ch''
861 =	916 +	378	'' of interpretation''
1004 =	916 +	933	'' of tr''
505 =	283 +	102	'' of''
708 =	505 +	784	'' of@he ''
301 =	32 +	112	'' p''
399 =	32 +	852	'' paint''
802 =	301 +	944	'' par''
292 =	301 +	335	'' pri''
671 =	292 +	723	'' princi''
357 =	671 +	510	'' principle''
725 =	357 +	807	'' principles@''
473 =	32 +	875	'' seen''
273 =	32 +	116	'' t''
531 =	273 +	104	'' th''
967 =	531 +	442	'' that ''
501 =	273 +	275	'' the ''
915 =	501 +	912	'' the differen''
993 =	501 +	741	'' the mo''
313 =	531 +	402	'' the@''
1021 =	313 +	458	'' the@Eastern ''
870 =	313 +	1023	'' the@ha''
395 =	273 +	371	'' to ''
790 =	395 +	98	'' to b''
534 =	395 +	643	'' to the Western ''
653 =	273 +	317	'' tre''
797 =	32 +	661	'' ve''
515 =	32 +	119	'' w''
454 =	515 +	685	'' whi''
589 =	454 +	427	'' which ''
345 =	454 +	911	'' which a''
939 =	345 +	722	'' which all''
514 =	450 +	313	'' while the@''
450 =	454 +	375	'' while''
658 =	34 +	936	''" and ''
550 =	34 +	345	''" which a''
364 =	34 +	300	''"a ''
831 =	34 +	639	''"la''
609 =	39 +	105	''' i''
688 =	39 +	272	''' s ''
1012 =	39 +	807	''' s@ ''
836 =	41 +	440	''). This ''
806 =	44 +	32	'', ''
823 =	806 +	453	'', and ''
621 =	806 +	404	'', the ''
979 =	621 +	104	'', the h''
839 =	44 +	450	'', while''
583 =	358 +	32	''. ''
358 =	293 +	32	''. ''
601 =	358 +	69	''. E''
805 =	358 +	732	''. Gombric''
549 =	358 +	73	''. I''
443 =	358 +	84	''. T''
848 =	443 +	275	''. The ''
981 =	848 +	992	''. The hang''
440 =	443 +	497	''. This ''
392 =	440 +	1015	''. This st''
536 =	443 +	371	''. To ''
293 =	46 +	32	''. ''
595 =	46 +	10	''.@''
513 =	595 +	66	''.@B''
834 =	595 +	84	''.@T''
924 =	834 +	275	''.@The ''
379 =	924 +	1011	''.@The Western''
910 =	49 +	936	''1 and ''
604 =	50 +	41	''2)''
648 =	58 +	10	'' ;@''
579 =	10 +	772	''@com''
799 =	10 +	482	''@li''

906 =	10 +	101	''@e''	837 =	982 +	116 ''artist''
826 =	906 +	97	''@ea''	820 =	271 +	32 ''as ''
707 =	10 +	664	''@inte''	290 =	820 +	928 ''as but ''
652 =	10 +	424	''@ma''	271 =	97 +	115 ''as''
990 =	10 +	696	''@man''	442 =	319 +	32 ''at ''
471 =	10 +	734	''@of the ''	485 =	319 +	363 ''at is ''
987 =	10 +	883	''@sc''	319 =	97 +	116 ''at''
784 =	10 +	404	''@the ''	327 =	319 +	105 ''ati''
312 =	784 +	835	''@the wor''	441 =	327 +	329 ''ation''
651 =	10 +	117	''@u''	777 =	441 +	627 ''ations of ''
300 =	97 +	32	''a ''	613 =	319 +	306 ''atur''
307 =	300 +	615	''a comp''	477 =	613 +	308 ''atures of ''
599 =	300 +	424	''a ma''	446 =	97 +	661 ''ave''
850 =	599 +	665	''a matter''	726 =	264 +	32 ''be ''
868 =	300 +	267	''a se''	264 =	98 +	101 ''be''
448 =	97 +	10	''a@'	467 =	264 +	10 ''be@'
681 =	448 +	115	''a@s''	719 =	66 +	663 ''Bef''
978 =	97 +	98	''ab''	935 =	264 +	486 ''betw''
909 =	97 +	99	''ac''	814 =	98 +	106 ''bj''
752 =	97 +	977	''ach c''	736 =	98 +	375 ''ble''
584 =	909 +	779	''acter''	940 =	98 +	487 ''bric''
743 =	97 +	102	''af''	522 =	98 +	117 ''bu''
554 =	97 +	1002	''age''	830 =	522 +	811 ''buco''
366 =	97 +	105	''ai''	931 =	522 +	1006 ''bum ''
937 =	366 +	262	''ain ''	928 =	522 +	258 ''but ''
468 =	366 +	110	''ain''	986 =	928 +	404 ''but the ''
740 =	366 +	115	''ais''	412 =	98 +	480 ''by ''
758 =	537 +	32	''al ''	637 =	412 +	404 ''by the ''
537 =	97 +	108	''al''	325 =	637 +	557 ''by the mist''
706 =	537 +	522	''albu''	611 =	98 +	121 ''by''
342 =	537 +	541	''alistic''	266 =	99 +	936 ''c and ''
934 =	537 +	387	''alit''	932 =	99 +	97 ''ca''
302 =	537 +	108	''all''	330 =	932 +	722 ''call''
787 =	537 +	272	''als ''	898 =	330 +	451 ''calls t''
854 =	537 +	524	''also''	533 =	932 +	110 ''can''
429 =	261 +	32	''an ''	470 =	413 +	591 ''ce in the ''
261 =	97 +	110	''an''	413 =	99 +	101 ''ce''
453 =	433 +	32	''and ''	474 =	413 +	257 ''cert''
333 =	453 +	720	''and Easter''	427 =	919 +	32 ''ch ''
336 =	453 +	1010	''and scro''	911 =	919 +	469 ''ch a''
768 =	453 +	404	''and the ''	977 =	427 +	99 ''ch c''
656 =	453 +	700	''and Wes''	901 =	977 +	569 ''ch culture''
472 =	713 +	32	''and Western ''	560 =	427 +	741 ''ch mo''
713 =	656 +	887	''and Western''	703 =	427 +	824 ''ch wit''
433 =	261 +	100	''and''	294 =	67 +	104 ''Ch''
843 =	97 +	647	''ang ''	919 =	99 +	104 ''ch''
506 =	261 +	970	''annot ''	484 =	919 +	944 ''char''
625 =	261 +	115	''ans''	885 =	67 +	685 ''Chi''
504 =	97 +	111	''ao''	959 =	885 +	97 ''Chia''
956 =	97 +	112	''ap''	401 =	885 +	110 ''Chin''
256 =	65 +	114	''Ar''	829 =	401 +	321 ''Chines''
944 =	97 +	114	''ar''	818 =	401 +	764 ''Chinese ''
592 =	944 +	97	''ara''	512 =	818 +	713 ''Chinese and Western''
324 =	944 +	909	''arac''	746 =	818 +	837 ''Chinese artist''
761 =	944 +	265	''are ''	567 =	818 +	766 ''Chinese hanging sc''
489 =	944 +	686	''aris''	288 =	99 +	105 ''ci''
532 =	489 +	655	''arison ''	930 =	99 +	108 ''cl''
851 =	944 +	375	''arle''	704 =	930 +	117 ''clu''
503 =	97 +	257	''art''	629 =	704 +	352 ''clude''
1019 =	503 +	34	''art"''	811 =	99 +	111 ''co''
982 =	503 +	686	''artis''	729 =	811 +	521 ''coli''
578 =	837 +	32	''artist ''	772 =	811 +	109 ''com''
328 =	578 +	387	''artist it''	615 =	772 +	112 ''comp''

983 =	615 +	944	''compar''
1017 =	615 +	489	''comparis''
411 =	99 +	329	''con''
949 =	411 +	545	''conti''
289 =	99 +	388	''cows''
507 =	289 +	10	''cows@ ''
938 =	99 +	354	''creat''
304 =	99 +	116	''ct''
519 =	100 +	32	''d ''
374 =	100 +	750	''d and@ ''
874 =	100 +	1003	''d aro''
460 =	519 +	98	''d b''
815 =	519 +	637	''d by the ''
819 =	519 +	912	''d differen''
406 =	519 +	756	''d from ''
353 =	352 +	313	''de the@ ''
352 =	100 +	101	''de''
410 =	100 +	490	''dence''
871 =	352 +	114	''der''
482 =	100 +	105	''di''
270 =	482 +	102	''dif''
879 =	270 +	564	''diffe''
921 =	879 +	114	''differ''
912 =	921 +	475	''differen''
465 =	287 +	563	''difference in ''
447 =	465 +	404	''difference in the ''
287 =	912 +	413	''difference''
721 =	912 +	258	''different ''
529 =	482 +	118	''div''
775 =	482 +	577	''divid''
265 =	101 +	32	''e ''
886 =	265 +	411	''e con''
788 =	265 +	387	''e it''
607 =	265 +	900	''e to ''
922 =	101 +	358	''e. ''
402 =	101 +	10	''@ ''
318 =	101 +	97	''ea''
701 =	318 +	427	''each ''
998 =	69 +	271	''Eas''
720 =	998 +	779	''Easter''
458 =	998 +	702	''Eastern ''
897 =	458 +	656	''Eastern and Wes''
546 =	458 +	972	''Eastern inter''
908 =	458 +	791	''Eastern painting''
880 =	720 +	896	''Eastern@ ''
376 =	101 +	304	''ect''
466 =	376 +	105	''ecti''
389 =	466 +	661	''ective''
479 =	389 +	10	''ective@ ''
571 =	101 +	519	''ed ''
553 =	571 +	453	''ed and ''
988 =	101 +	101	''ee''
278 =	988 +	39	''ee''
712 =	988 +	262	''een ''
663 =	101 +	102	''ef''
617 =	663 +	281	''efor''
475 =	101 +	110	''en''
1005 =	475 +	34	''en"''
490 =	475 +	413	''ence''
1001 =	490 +	519	''enced ''
765 =	475 +	101	''ene''
616 =	765 +	115	''enes''
347 =	69 +	499	''Eng''
343 =	414 +	32	''er ''
646 =	343 +	1000	''er than ''
414 =	101 +	114	''er''
920 =	414 +	448	''era@ ''
544 =	414 +	105	''eri''
714 =	544 +	537	''erial''
269 =	414 +	628	''ersp''
884 =	321 +	32	''es ''
308 =	884 +	309	''es of ''
461 =	308 +	404	''es of the ''
556 =	884 +	404	''es the ''
321 =	101 +	115	''es''
660 =	321 +	358	''es. ''
764 =	321 +	265	''ese ''
298 =	101 +	661	''eve''
570 =	69 +	661	''Eve''
623 =	101 +	508	''evi''
657 =	101 +	120	''ex''
555 =	657 +	686	''exis''
945 =	657 +	112	''exp''
893 =	945 +	639	''expla''
757 =	102 +	501	''f the ''
372 =	102 +	848	''f. The ''
813 =	102 +	97	''fa''
564 =	102 +	101	''fe''
349 =	564 +	613	''featur''
491 =	70 +	281	''For''
882 =	102 +	281	''for''
351 =	882 +	260	''format''
952 =	351 +	627	''formats of ''
626 =	102 +	438	''fro''
756 =	626 +	1006	''from ''
976 =	756 +	496	''from the c''
368 =	102 +	753	''ful''
789 =	1002 +	259	''ge c''
864 =	1002 +	916	''ge of ''
1002 =	103 +	101	''ge''
727 =	103 +	104	''gh''
303 =	103 +	105	''gi''
380 =	303 +	102	''gif''
610 =	103 +	110	''gn''
803 =	71 +	111	''Go''
314 =	803 +	109	''Gom''
732 =	314 +	940	''Gombric''
323 =	732 +	435	''Gombrich ''
941 =	323 +	330	''Gombrich call''
435 =	104 +	32	''h ''
1022 =	435 +	932	''h ca''
783 =	435 +	387	''h it''
717 =	435 +	710	''h work''
1023 =	104 +	97	''ha''
809 =	104 +	453	''hand ''
992 =	1023 +	499	''hang''
766 =	992 +	856	''hanging sc''
666 =	766 +	679	''hanging scroll''
275 =	104 +	265	''he ''
407 =	72 +	265	''He ''
525 =	275 +	351	''he format''
526 =	104 +	101	''he''
685 =	104 +	105	''hi''
497 =	685 +	272	''his ''
694 =	497 +	34	''his "''
315 =	497 +	287	''his difference''

716 = 104 + 281 ''hor''
667 = 105 + 429 ''ian ''
950 = 105 + 99 ''ic''
895 = 950 + 44 ''ic,''
917 = 105 + 920 ''iera@'
483 = 105 + 102 ''if''
961 = 105 + 103 ''ig''
297 = 961 + 272 ''igs ''
737 = 105 + 722 ''ill''
423 = 105 + 109 ''im''
631 = 423 + 595 ''im.@'
636 = 423 + 386 ''import''
385 = 105 + 262 ''in ''
929 = 73 + 262 ''In ''
650 = 385 + 281 ''in or''
498 = 105 + 110 ''in''
509 = 498 + 482 ''indi''
350 = 846 + 32 ''ing ''
383 = 350 + 300 ''ing a ''
856 = 350 + 883 ''ing sc''
597 = 856 + 679 ''ing scroll''
846 = 498 + 103 ''ing''
859 = 846 + 10 ''ing@'
356 = 846 + 794 ''ings, ''
669 = 498 + 943 ''inner''
664 = 498 + 320 ''inte''
972 = 664 + 114 ''inter''
662 = 972 + 608 ''interpreta''
863 = 378 + 505 ''interpretation of''
378 = 662 + 923 ''interpretation''
709 = 853 + 283 ''ion o''
793 = 709 + 102 ''ion of''
853 = 105 + 329 ''ion''
926 = 105 + 913 ''iou''
817 = 105 + 463 ''iqu''
692 = 686 + 363 ''is is ''
686 = 105 + 115 ''is''
285 = 686 + 329 ''ison''
434 = 686 + 116 ''ist''
535 = 541 + 273 ''istic t''
541 = 434 + 950 ''istic''
699 = 387 + 32 ''it ''
759 = 387 + 947 ''it is not ''
387 = 105 + 116 ''it''
767 = 387 + 443 ''it. T''
547 = 387 + 272 ''its ''
778 = 387 + 480 ''ity ''
676 = 75 + 504 ''Kao''
812 = 107 + 101 ''ke''
449 = 812 + 519 ''ked ''
670 = 812 + 280 ''kene''
326 = 107 + 846 ''king''
828 = 108 + 916 ''l of ''
639 = 108 + 97 ''la''
624 = 639 + 437 ''lanat''
776 = 639 + 543 ''landscap''
340 = 776 + 265 ''landscape ''
925 = 639 + 499 ''lang''
711 = 925 + 459 ''langua''
649 = 639 + 382 ''lation ''
869 = 108 + 100 ''ld''
445 = 375 + 395 ''le to ''
375 = 108 + 101 ''le''

980 = 375 + 97 ''lea''
337 = 108 + 389 ''lective''
502 = 375 + 100 ''led''
311 = 76 + 988 ''Lee''
521 = 108 + 105 ''li''
948 = 76 + 105 ''Li''
841 = 521 + 99 ''lic''
963 = 948 + 262 ''Lin ''
684 = 521 + 115 ''lis''
558 = 521 + 116 ''lit''
722 = 108 + 108 ''ll''
808 = 722 + 806 ''ll, ''
296 = 722 + 621 ''ll, the ''
995 = 722 + 677 ''llow''
339 = 722 + 272 ''lls ''
672 = 722 + 598 ''llus''
744 = 108 + 111 ''lo''
733 = 108 + 804 ''lt of ''
876 = 108 + 480 ''ly ''
881 = 876 + 413 ''ly ce''
1006 = 109 + 32 ''m ''
409 = 1006 + 375 ''m le''
424 = 109 + 97 ''ma''
365 = 77 + 261 'Man''
696 = 424 + 110 ''man''
452 = 424 + 114 ''mar''
260 = 424 + 116 ''mat''
548 = 260 + 544 ''materi''
359 = 260 + 381 ''mats and ''
511 = 424 + 480 ''may ''
495 = 109 + 265 ''me ''
1014 = 495 + 883 ''me sc''
277 = 109 + 105 ''mi''
748 = 557 + 469 ''mist a''
557 = 277 + 1015 ''mist ''
741 = 109 + 111 ''mo''
360 = 741 + 317 ''more''
754 = 741 + 117 ''mou''
538 = 109 + 112 ''mp''
419 = 763 + 32 ''ms ''
299 = 419 + 109 ''ms m''
763 = 109 + 115 ''ms''
965 = 109 + 117 ''mu''
262 = 110 + 32 ''n ''
989 = 262 + 818 ''n Chinese ''
439 = 262 + 564 ''n fe''
888 = 262 + 600 ''n pe''
478 = 262 + 404 ''n the ''
896 = 110 + 10 ''n@'
291 = 896 + 578 ''n@artist ''
968 = 110 + 537 ''nal''
462 = 110 + 944 ''nar''
437 = 110 + 319 ''nat''
562 = 437 + 709 ''nation o''
517 = 437 + 551 ''natural''
723 = 110 + 288 ''nci''
816 = 332 + 501 ''nd the ''
332 = 110 + 100 ''nd''
516 = 332 + 883 ''ndsc''
543 = 516 + 956 ''ndscap''
280 = 110 + 101 ''ne''
943 = 110 + 414 ''ner''
647 = 499 + 32 ''ng ''

840 = 647 + 76 ''ng L''	996 = 463 + 765 ''quene''
499 = 110 + 103 ''ng''	425 = 463 + 105 ''qui''
877 = 499 + 350 ''nging ''	951 = 114 + 32 ''r ''
780 = 499 + 521 ''ngli''	985 = 114 + 443 ''r. T''
892 = 499 + 117 ''ngu''	481 = 114 + 97 ''ra''
367 = 110 + 105 ''ni''	527 = 481 + 274 ''rath''
858 = 110 + 111 ''no''	927 = 317 + 310 ''re m''
970 = 858 + 258 ''not ''	317 = 114 + 101 ''re''
492 = 970 + 264 ''not be''	354 = 317 + 319 ''reat''
400 = 970 + 832 ''not pre''	873 = 354 + 265 ''reate ''
561 = 110 + 381 ''ns and ''	969 = 317 + 475 ''reen''
630 = 476 + 591 ''nt in the ''	559 = 317 + 321 ''rees''
476 = 110 + 116 ''nt''	738 = 82 + 475 ''Ren''
582 = 476 + 366 ''ntai''	341 = 738 + 740 ''Renais''
792 = 110 + 117 ''nu''	999 = 341 + 348 ''Renaissance''
904 = 110 + 118 ''nv''	488 = 317 + 590 ''resu''
371 = 111 + 32 ''o ''	612 = 317 + 845 ''reta''
687 = 371 + 643 ''o the Western ''	335 = 114 + 105 ''ri''
309 = 284 + 32 ''of ''	487 = 335 + 99 ''ric''
734 = 309 + 404 ''of the ''	962 = 335 + 107 ''rik''
644 = 734 + 69 ''of the E''	958 = 114 + 812 ''rke''
284 = 111 + 102 ''of''	438 = 114 + 111 ''ro''
655 = 329 + 32 ''on ''	679 = 438 + 722 ''roll''
891 = 655 + 264 ''on be''	605 = 679 + 10 ''rol@ ''
329 = 111 + 110 ''on''	865 = 679 + 807 ''rolls@ ''
857 = 329 + 519 ''ond ''	391 = 438 + 117 ''rou''
620 = 329 + 265 ''one ''	674 = 114 + 112 ''rp''
416 = 329 + 876 ''only ''	762 = 114 + 524 ''rso''
426 = 281 + 32 ''or ''	257 = 114 + 116 ''rt''
281 = 111 + 114 ''or''	946 = 257 + 366 ''rtai''
718 = 281 + 413 ''orce''	855 = 114 + 480 ''ry ''
769 = 718 + 519 ''orced ''	272 = 115 + 32 ''s ''
593 = 281 + 352 ''orde''	295 = 272 + 49 ''s 1''
518 = 281 + 265 ''ore ''	689 = 272 + 97 ''s a''
346 = 281 + 258 ''ort ''	381 = 272 + 453 ''s and ''
821 = 111 + 267 ''ose''	842 = 381 + 102 ''s and f''
847 = 111 + 574 ''othe''	899 = 381 + 260 ''s and mat''
913 = 111 + 117 ''ou''	418 = 381 + 404 ''s and the ''
867 = 913 + 727 ''ough''	430 = 115 + 690 ''s for ''
603 = 913 + 381 ''ous and ''	627 = 272 + 309 ''s of ''
677 = 111 + 119 ''ow''	588 = 627 + 458 ''s of Eastern ''
902 = 677 + 262 ''own ''	918 = 627 + 882 ''s of for''
724 = 388 + 563 ''ows in ''	415 = 272 + 677 ''s ow''
388 = 677 + 115 ''ows''	451 = 272 + 116 ''s t''
594 = 112 + 366 ''pai''	954 = 451 + 497 ''s this ''
852 = 594 + 476 ''paint''	373 = 272 + 801 ''s use''
586 = 852 + 414 ''painter''	580 = 115 + 454 ''s whi''
822 = 791 + 444 ''painting in''	1008 = 272 + 710 ''s work''
791 = 852 + 846 ''painting''	540 = 115 + 34 ''s"''
905 = 112 + 944 ''par''	794 = 115 + 806 ''s, ''
600 = 112 + 101 ''pe''	844 = 794 + 448 ''s, a@ ''
731 = 600 + 114 ''per''	1009 = 794 + 318 ''s, ea''
276 = 600 + 627 ''pes of ''	807 = 115 + 10 ''s@ ''
568 = 112 + 639 ''pla''	728 = 115 + 97 ''sa''
510 = 112 + 375 ''ple''	742 = 115 + 261 ''san''
641 = 112 + 111 ''po''	348 = 742 + 413 ''sance''
386 = 641 + 257 ''port''	883 = 115 + 99 ''sc''
421 = 641 + 774 ''posi''	403 = 883 + 475 ''scen''
832 = 112 + 317 ''pre''	417 = 883 + 317 ''scre''
773 = 832 + 267 ''prese''	1010 = 883 + 438 ''scro''
608 = 832 + 845 ''preta''	997 = 1010 + 722 ''scroll''
691 = 608 + 747 ''pretation see''	267 = 115 + 101 ''se''
463 = 113 + 117 ''qu''	422 = 464 + 786 ''see f''

```
 464 =  267 +  101 ''see''              878 =  643 +  453 ''the Western and ''
 500 =  464 +  763 ''seems''            455 =  643 +  932 ''the Western ca''
 862 =  875 +  632 ''seen as''          574 =  274 +  101 ''the''
 875 =  267 +  475 ''seen''             523 =  574 +   10 ''the@ ''
 397 =  267 +  108 ''sel''              730 =  574 +  267 ''these''
 872 =  267 +  476 ''sent''             369 =  116 +  497 ''this ''
 457 =  115 +  435 ''sh ''              642 =  369 +  925 ''this lang''
 338 =  115 +  104 ''sh''               545 =  116 +  105 ''ti''
 774 =  115 +  105 ''si''               614 =  545 +  110 ''tin''
 678 =  115 +  639 ''sla''              382 =  923 +   32 ''tion ''
 524 =  115 +  111 ''so''               833 =  382 +  522 ''tion bu''
 749 =  524 +  110 ''son''              739 =  382 +  309 ''tion of ''
 628 =  115 +  112 ''sp''               334 =  739 +  994 ''tion of the sa''
 953 =  115 +  794 ''ss, ''             747 =  382 +  464 ''tion see''
 975 = 1015 +   32 ''st ''              781 =  747 +  419 ''tion seems ''
1015 =  115 +  116 ''st''               923 =  545 +  329 ''tion''
 991 = 1015 +  414 ''ster''             698 =  923 +   10 ''tion@ ''
1016 = 1015 +  335 ''stri''             900 =  370 +   32 ''to ''
 590 =  115 +  117 ''su''               668 =  900 +  657 ''to ex''
 800 =   83 +  117 ''Su''               370 =  116 +  111 ''to''
 258 =  116 +   32 ''t ''               933 =  116 +  114 ''tr''
 705 =  258 +  599 ''t a ma''           645 =  933 +  261 ''tran''
 596 =  258 +  453 ''t and ''           618 =  933 +  319 ''trat''
 420 =  258 +  945 ''t exp''            659 =  618 +  884 ''trates ''
 573 =  258 +  102 ''t f''              528 =  116 +  272 ''ts ''
 804 =  258 +  309 ''t of ''            431 =  665 +  916 ''tter of ''
 361 =  258 +  116 ''t t''              665 =  116 +  779 ''tter''
 697 =  116 +  924 ''t.@The ''          305 =  116 +  117 ''tu''
 845 =  116 +   97 ''ta''               715 =  305 +  317 ''ture''
 693 =  845 +  382 ''tation ''          680 =  715 +  115 ''tures''
 572 =  845 +  739 ''tation of ''       486 =  116 +  119 ''tw''
 320 =  116 +  101 ''te''               362 =  486 +  988 ''twee''
 640 =  779 +  632 ''ter as''           796 =  116 +  121 ''ty''
 960 =  779 +  786 ''ter f''            459 =  117 +   97 ''ua''
1007 =  779 +  916 ''ter of ''          355 =  459 + 1002 ''uage''
 779 =  320 +  114 ''ter''              633 =  117 +  537 ''ual''
 827 =  779 +  109 ''term''             344 =  117 +  427 ''uch ''
 702 =  779 +  262 ''tern ''            384 =  117 +  350 ''uing ''
 887 =  779 +  110 ''tern''             753 =  117 +  108 ''ul''
 408 =  887 +   10 ''tern@ ''           695 =  753 +  108 ''ull''
 268 =  779 +  832 ''terpre''           942 =  569 +  363 ''ulture is ''
 274 =  116 +  104 ''th''               569 =  753 +  715 ''ulture''
 606 =   84 +  104 ''Th''               683 =  117 +  110 ''un''
1000 =  274 +  429 ''than ''            542 =  751 +  735 ''und h''
 964 =  274 +  319 ''that''             751 =  117 +  332 ''und''
 404 =  274 +  265 ''the ''             494 =  117 +  476 ''unt''
 782 =   84 +  275 ''The ''             306 =  117 +  114 ''ur''
 755 =  404 +   34 ''the "''            551 =  306 +  537 ''ural''
 635 =  404 +  537 ''the al''           432 =  551 +  434 ''uralist''
 496 =  404 +   99 ''the c''            598 =  117 +  115 ''us''
 566 =  404 +  818 ''the Chinese ''     801 =  117 +  267 ''use''
 622 =  496 +  753 ''the cul''          771 =  801 +  519 ''used ''
 785 =  404 +  465 ''the difference in '' 286 =  598 +  618 ''ustrat''
 602 =  404 +  103 ''the g''            331 =  118 +  820 ''vas ''
1018 =  404 +  380 ''the gif''          914 =  661 +  469 ''ve a''
 456 =  404 +  776 ''the landscap''     661 =  118 +  101 ''ve''
 530 =  404 +  424 ''the ma''           673 =  661 +  262 ''ven''
 575 =  404 +  696 ''the man''          405 =  661 +  114 ''ver''
 654 =  574 +  357 ''the principle''    508 =  118 +  105 ''vi''
 994 =  404 +  728 ''the sa''           577 =  508 +  100 ''vid''
 810 =  994 +  495 ''the same ''        394 =  577 +  117 ''vidu''
 638 =  404 +  700 ''the Wes''          552 =  118 +  718 ''vorce''
 643 =  638 +  702 ''the Western ''     493 =  119 +  820 ''was ''
```

```
 955 =  493 +  875 ''was seen''
 700 =   87 +  321 ''Wes''
 890 = 1011 +  444 ''Western in''
1011 =  700 +  887 ''Western''
 587 =  119 +  104 ''wh''
 824 =  119 +  387 ''wit''
 565 =  824 +  435 ''with ''
 835 =  119 +  281 ''wor''
 825 =  710 +  735 ''work h''
 710 =  835 +  107 ''work''
 745 =  710 +  358 ''work.  ''
 866 =  835 +  108 ''worl''
 480 =  121 +   32 ''y ''
1020 =  480 +  264 ''y be''
 907 =  480 +  522 ''y bu''
 282 =  480 +  309 ''y of ''
 316 =  480 +  274 ''y th''
 798 =  121 +  906 ''y@e''
 971 =  121 +  600 ''ype''
 675 =  121 + 1015 ''yst''
```

A.8. PASCAL FOR DYNAMIC METHODS

DELETION HEURISTIC: Default is LRU (Least Recently Used).
All prefixes of a string are considered used when the string is used;
in this case, it is moved to the front of the LRU queue, after its ancestors.
A flag can be set to use the FREEZE heuristic instead of LRU.

UPDATE HEURISTIC: Default is AP (All Prefixes).
That is, after a match has been found, update the dictionary
by adding the last match concatenated with each of the prefixes of
the current match. This heuristic may be modified via the program
parameters to add only a portion of these prefixes; e.g., the FC
(First Character) heuristic allows only length 1 prefixes to be used.

ORGANIZATION OF THE CODE:
        squeeze.p - encoder
        unsqueeze.p - decoder
The following files are included by both squeeze.p and unsqueeze.p:
        declare.i - program parameters, declarations, etc.
        map.i - maps between external and internal pointer values
        dictionary_.i - trie implementation of the dictionary
        queue.i - doubly linked list implementation of LRU queue
        io_byte.i - routines to read and write bytes
        io_ptr.i - routines to read and write pointers
        dump.i - code to dump the dictionary
        start.i - initialization of variables and structures
        update.i - update code

PROGRAM PARAMETERS: May be set by changing constants and re-compiling.
For a listing of parameters and their defaults, see the file "declare.i".

HOW TO COMPILE THE CODE:
On a Berkeley Unix operating system do "pc -O squeeze.p" to compile the
encoder and "pc -O unsqueeze.p" to compile the decoder.
For other systems, note that code is standard PASCAL except for #include
directives and some i/o statements in io_byte.i and dump.i.

{ squeeze.p }

```
program MAIN(input,output);
#include "declare.i"
#include "map.i"
#include "dictionary.i"
#include "queue.i"
#include "io_byte.i"
#include "io_ptr.i"
#include "dump.i"
begin
#include "start.i"

inputbyte:=READBYTE;
while (not ENDINPUT) do begin

        {save queue head, initialize trieptr, and initialize parameters}
        place:=qin;
        trieptr:=CHILD(INT(nilptr),inputbyte);
        prevptr:=curptr;
        prevlen:=curlen;
        curlen:=0;

        {calculate current match by moving down trie as far as possible}
        while (EXT(trieptr)<>nilptr) do begin
                if (EXT(trieptr)>=StaticSize) then if (trieptr=place)
                        then place:=OLDER(trieptr)
                        else begin DEQUEUE(trieptr); ENQUEUE(trieptr,place) end;
                curptr:=trieptr;
                curlen:=curlen+1;
                match[curlen]:=inputbyte;
                if (ENDINPUT)
                        then trieptr:=INT(nilptr)
                        else begin
                                inputbyte:=READBYTE;
                                trieptr:=CHILD(curptr,inputbyte)
                                end
            end;

        {calculate match start and output the current pointer}
        mstart:=1;
        WRITEPTR(curptr);

#include "update.i"
        end;

{output last pointer and flush any leftover bits}
WRITEPTR(INT(inputbyte));
FLUSHBITS;
end.
```

{ unsqueeze.p }

```
program MAIN(input,output);
#include "declare.i"
#include "map.i"
#include "dictionary.i"
#include "queue.i"
#include "io_byte.i"
#include "io_ptr.i"
#include "dump.i"
begin
#include "start.i"

while (not ENDINPUT) do begin

        {set trieptr to next pointer and initialize parameters}
        trieptr:=READPTR;
        prevptr:=curptr;
        prevlen:=curlen;
        curptr:=trieptr;
        curlen:=0;

        {calculate current match by moving up trie as far as possible}
        while (EXT(trieptr)<>nilptr) do begin
                if (EXT(trieptr)>=StaticSize) and (trieptr<>qin) then begin
                        DEQUEUE(trieptr);
                        ENQUEUE(trieptr,qin)
                        end;
                match[MaxMatch-curlen]:=CTR(trieptr);
                curlen:=curlen+1;
                trieptr:=PARENT(trieptr);
                end;

        {calculate match start and output the current match}
        mstart:=MaxMatch-curlen+1;
        for mindex:=mstart to MaxMatch do WRITEBYTE(match[mindex]);

#include "update.i"
        end;

end.
```

{ declare.i }

```
const    {program parameters}
         FreezeFlag=0; {0 for LRU queue, 1 to FREEZE dictionary when full}
         MaxChildren=256; {max number of children allowed per non-root node}
         MaxDict=4096; {max dict size; e.g. 4096, 8192, 16384, 32768, 65536}
         MaxIncrement=100; {maximum increase in length to make a new entry}
         MaxMatch=100; {maximum allowable length for a trie string}
         PtrType=0; {0 for fixed length pointers, 1 for variable length}
         StaticSize=256; {input alphabet is 0...(StaticSize-1); StaticSize<=256}

type     TypePointer = integer; {arrays will be used to store linked structures}

var      {special pointer values}
         maxptr: integer; {max "real" pointer value; always equal to MaxDict-2}
         nilptr: integer; {nil pointer; always equal to MaxDict-1}

         {trie data structure for the dictionary}
         ctrfield: array [0..MaxDict] of integer; {character}
         parfield: array [0..MaxDict] of TypePointer; {parent}
         lcfield: array [0..MaxDict] of TypePointer; {left child}
         countfield: array [0..MaxDict] of integer; {number of children}
         rsibfield: array [StaticSize..MaxDict] of TypePointer; {right sibling}
         lsibfield: array [StaticSize..MaxDict] of TypePointer; {left sibling}
         dictsize: integer; {current size of the dictionary}
         trieptr: TypePointer; {used to walk up and down trie}

         {LRU queue data structure}
         olderfield: array [StaticSize..MaxDict] of TypePointer; {left pointer}
         newerfield: array [StaticSize..MaxDict] of TypePointer; {right pointer}
         qin: TypePointer; {right end of LRU queue, where things enter}
         qout: TypePointer; {left end of LRU queue, where things leave}
         place: TypePointer; {used to point into LRU queue}

         {previous match data structure}
         prevptr: TypePointer; {used to hold pointer to previous match}
         prevlen: TypePointer; {length of previous match}

         {current match data structure}
         curptr: TypePointer; {used to hold pointer to current match}
         curlen: integer; {length of current match}
         match: array [1..MaxMatch] of integer; {holds current match}
         mstart: integer; {positions mstart thru mstart+curlength-1 hold match}
         mindex: integer; {used to walk thru match array}
         mval: integer; {used by update code to hold current element of match}

         {variables used for input and output}
         leftover: integer; {holds leftover <8 bits for pointer io routines}
         losize: integer; {1,2...256 indicates 0 to 8 leftover bits}
         inputbyte: integer; {holds current input byte}
```

{ map.i }

{NOTE: for this implementation, internal and external pointer
representations are identical. Hence, all calls to INT and EXT
could be removed from the code to reduce overhead}

function INT(extpointer:integer):TypePointer; begin INT:=extpointer end;

function EXT(intpointer:TypePointer):integer; begin EXT:=intpointer end;

{ dictionary.i }

function CTR(ptr:TypePointer):integer; begin CTR:=ctrfield[ptr] end;

function PARENT(ptr:TypePointer):TypePointer; begin PARENT:=parfield[ptr] end;

function COUNT(ptr:TypePointer):integer; begin COUNT:=countfield[ptr] end;

```
function CHILD(ptr:TypePointer; c:integer):TypePointer;
begin
if (ptr=nilptr) then CHILD:=c
else begin
    ptr:=lcfield[ptr];
    while (ptr<>nilptr) and (c<>ctrfield[ptr]) do ptr:=rsibfield[ptr];
    CHILD:=ptr
    end;
end {CHILD};
```

```
procedure ADDLEAF(parptr,ptr:TypePointer; c:integer);
begin
ctrfield[ptr]:=c;
countfield[ptr]:=0;
parfield[ptr]:=parptr;
lcfield[ptr]:=nilptr;
lsibfield[ptr]:=nilptr;
if (parptr=nilptr) then rsibfield[ptr]:=nilptr
else begin
    rsibfield[ptr]:=lcfield[parptr];
    if (lcfield[parptr]<>nilptr) then lsibfield[lcfield[parptr]]:=ptr;
    lcfield[parptr]:=ptr;
    countfield[parptr]:=countfield[parptr]+1
    end;
end {ADDLEAF};
```

```
procedure DELETELEAF(ptr:TypePointer);
begin
countfield[parfield[ptr]]:=countfield[parfield[ptr]]-1;
if (lsibfield[ptr]<>nilptr)
        then rsibfield[lsibfield[ptr]]:=rsibfield[ptr]
        else lcfield[parfield[ptr]]:=rsibfield[ptr];
if (rsibfield[ptr]<>nilptr) then
        lsibfield[rsibfield[ptr]]:=lsibfield[ptr]
end {DELETELEAF};
```

{ queue.i }

function OLDER(place:integer):integer; begin OLDER:=olderfield[place] end;

{remove arg1 from LRU queue; assumes queue size >1 and place not right end}
procedure DEQUEUE(trieptr: integer);
begin
if (trieptr=qout) then begin {delete from left}
       qout:=newerfield[trieptr];
       olderfield[qout]:=nilptr
       end
else begin {delete from middle}
       newerfield[olderfield[trieptr]]:=newerfield[trieptr];
       olderfield[newerfield[trieptr]]:=olderfield[trieptr]
       end
end {DEQUEUE};

{put arg1 after arg2 in LRU queue; if arg2=nilptr, insert at left end}
procedure ENQUEUE(trieptr,place:integer);
begin
if (qin=nilptr) then begin {empty queue}
       olderfield[trieptr]:=nilptr;
       newerfield[trieptr]:=nilptr;
       qin:=trieptr;
       qout:=trieptr
       end
else if (place=nilptr) then begin {insert at left}
       olderfield[trieptr]:=nilptr;
       newerfield[trieptr]:=qout;
       olderfield[qout]:=trieptr;
       qout:=trieptr
       end
else if (place=qin) then begin {append to right}
       olderfield[trieptr]:=qin;
       newerfield[trieptr]:=nilptr;
       newerfield[qin]:=trieptr;
       qin:=trieptr
       end
else begin {append somewhere in middle}
       olderfield[trieptr]:=place;
       newerfield[trieptr]:=newerfield[place];
       olderfield[newerfield[place]]:=trieptr;
       newerfield[place]:=trieptr;
       end
end {ENQUEUE};

```
{ io_byte.i }

function ENDINPUT:boolean;
begin
if (eof) then ENDINPUT:=true else ENDINPUT:=false
end {ENDINPUT};

function READBYTE:integer;
var c:char; b:integer;
begin
if (eof) then b:=0
else if (eoln) then begin
        read(c); {read blank that PASCAL replaced for line end}
        b:=10 {10 is ascii code for carriage-return}
        end
else begin
        read(c);
        b:=ord(c);

        {check for two's complement form of a non-ascii character}
        if (b<0) then b:= b+256

        end;
READBYTE:=b
end {READBYTE};

procedure WRITEBYTE(b:integer);
begin
write(chr(b))
end {WRITEBYTE};
```

{ io_ptr.i }

```
function READPTR:TypePointer;
var ptr,length,maxlength,maxvalue:integer;
begin
if (PtrType=0) then maxvalue:=MaxDict else maxvalue:=dictsize;
ptr:=0;
length:=1;
maxlength:=2; while (maxlength<maxvalue) do maxlength:=maxlength*2;
while (length<maxlength) do begin
        if (losize=1) then begin
                leftover:=READBYTE;
                losize:=256
                end;
        losize:=(losize div 2);
        ptr:=(ptr*2)+(leftover div losize);
        leftover:=(leftover mod losize);
        length:=length*2
        end;
READPTR:=ptr
end {READPTR};

procedure WRITEPTR(ptr:TypePointer);
var length,maxlength,maxvalue:integer;
begin
if (PtrType=0) then maxvalue:=MaxDict else maxvalue:=dictsize;
maxlength:=2; while (maxlength<maxvalue) do maxlength:=maxlength*2;
length:=maxlength;
while (length>1) do begin
        length:=(length div 2);
        leftover:=(leftover*2)+(ptr div length);
        losize:=losize*2;
        ptr:=(ptr mod length);
        if (losize=256) then begin
                WRITEBYTE(leftover);
                losize:=1;
                leftover:=0
                end
        end
end {WRITEPTR};

procedure FLUSHBITS;
begin
if (losize>1) then begin
        while (losize<256) do begin leftover:=leftover*2;losize:=losize*2 end;
        WRITEBYTE(leftover)
        end
end {FLUSHBITS};
```

{This procedure is not normally called.
However, at any place in squeeze.p or unsqueeze.p the call
          DUMPDICT(INT(nilptr),0);
may be inserted to dump the current dictionary to the file "dumpdict".
The code is a recursive pre-order traversal of a subtree of the trie.
Argument 1 = root of sub-tree (INT(nilptr) specifies the root).
Argument 2 = depth of Argument 1 (0 for the root).
One root-to-leaf path is written per line.
Unreadable ASCII characters are printed as @.}

```
procedure DUMPDICT(ptr:TypePointer; pathlen:integer);
var i:integer; f:text;
begin
rewrite(f,'dumpdict'); {associate the file variable f with file name}
if (pathlen>0) then match[pathlen]:=CTR(ptr);
if ((EXT(ptr)<>nilptr) and (COUNT(ptr)=0))
    then begin
        write(f,'"');
        for i:=1 to pathlen do if ((match[i]<32) or (match[i]>126))
            then write(f,'@') {character is unprintable}
            else write(f,chr(match[i]));
        write(f,'"');
        writeln(f)
        end
    else for i:=0 to StaticSize-1 do if (EXT(CHILD(ptr,i))<>nilptr) then
        DUMPDICT(CHILD(ptr,i),pathlen+1)
end {DUMPDICT};
```

{ start.i }

{check for illegal values of program parameters}
if ((FreezeFlag<0) or (FreezeFlag>1)) then FreezeFlag:=0;
if (MaxChildren<0) then MaxChildren:=0;
if (MaxIncrement<0) then MaxIncrement:=0;
if (MaxMatch<1) then MaxMatch:=1;
if ((PtrType<0) or (PtrType>1)) then PtrType:=0;
if (StaticSize<1) then StaticSize:=1;
if (MaxDict<StaticSize) then MaxDict:=StaticSize;

{initialize maxptr and nilptr}
nilptr:=MaxDict-1;
maxptr:=MaxDict-2;

{initialize static portion of the dictionary trie}
dictsize:=0;
while (dictsize<StaticSize) do begin
        ADDLEAF(nilptr,INT(dictsize),dictsize);
        dictsize:=dictsize+1;
        end;

{initialize LRU queue}
qin:=INT(nilptr);
qout:=INT(nilptr);

{initialize parameters for current match}
curptr:=INT(nilptr);
curlen:=0;

{initialize i/o variables}
leftover:=0;
losize:=1;

{ update.i }

```
if (EXT(prevptr)<>nilptr) then begin
        mindex:=0;
        while (mindex<curlen)
                and (mindex<MaxIncrement)
                and ((prevlen+mindex)<MaxMatch)
                and (COUNT(prevptr)<MaxChildren)
                and ((FreezeFlag=0) or (dictsize<=maxptr))
                and ((prevptr<>qout) or (dictsize<=maxptr)) do begin

                {if can't match, add a new node to the tie}
                mval:=match[mstart+mindex];
                trieptr:=CHILD(prevptr,mval);
                if (EXT(trieptr)=nilptr) then begin

                        {get a free pointer}
                        if (dictsize<=maxptr)
                                then begin
                                        trieptr:=INT(dictsize);
                                        dictsize:=dictsize+1
                                        end
                                else begin
                                        trieptr:=qout;
                                        DEQUEUE(trieptr);
                                        DELETELEAF(trieptr)
                                        end;

                        {add new pointer to trie}
                        ADDLEAF(prevptr,trieptr,mval);

                        {add new pointer to left of current in LRU queue}
                        if (EXT(prevptr)<StaticSize)
                                then place:=qin
                                else place:=OLDER(prevptr);
                        ENQUEUE(trieptr,place)

                        end;

                {move down one level in trie}
                prevptr:=trieptr;
                mindex:=mindex+1;

                end

        end;
```

A.9. PASCAL FOR LOSSY COMPRESSION

This code is intended to be used only for experimentation.
It uses linear search for dictionary look-up and runs very slowly.

ORGANIZATION OF THE CODE:
     vsqueeze.p - encoder
     vunsqueeze.p - decoder
The following files are included by both vsqueeze.p and vunsqueeze.p:
     declare.i - declarations (including program parameters)
     utility.i.i - utility routines to read in parameters, etc.
     dictionary.i - dictionary data structure
     queue.i - LRU queue
     dump.i - routines to dump statistics, etc.
     heur_init.i - initialization heuristics
     heur_delete.i - deletion heuristics
     heur_delete.i - update heuristics
     io.i - input-output routines
     start.i - initialization of variables and structures
     finish.i - finish up code (dictionary dump, etc.)

THE PROGRAM PARAMETERS:
Defaults to lossles compression ID-LRU compression on 8-bit data.
Lossy compression is controlled by parameters listed in "declare.i".
See the end of the file "utility.i" for samples of parameter settings.

HOW TO COMPILE THE CODE:
On a Berkeley Unix operating system do "pc -O squeeze.p" to compile the
encoder and "pc -O unsqueeze.p" to compile the decoder.
For other systems, note that code is standard PASCAL except for #include
directives and some i/o statements in io_byte.i, utility.i, and dump.i.

HOW TO USE THE CODE:
On a Berkeley Unix operating system,
vsqueeze and vunsqueeze must be given identical command-line parameters
of the form paremeter=value or parameter=value_argument.
Case is ignore with command line parameters and parameters may be
abbreviated as described in the file "declare.i".
For example, the following is a slow way to print a file on Berkely Unix:
     cat file | vsqueeze hi=log_1 e=4 | vunsqueeze hi=log_1 e=4

```
{ vsqueeze.p }

program MAIN(input,output);
#include "declare.i"
#include "utility.i"
#include "dictionary.i"
#include "queue.i"
#include "dump.i"
#include "heur_init.i"
#include "heur_delete.i"
#include "heur_update.i"
#include "io.i"
begin
#include "start.i"

while ((not ENDINPUT) or (buffer[0]>0)) do begin

    {fill input buffer and compute current match}
    while ((not ENDINPUT) and (buffer[0]<MaxMatch)) do begin
        buffer[0]:=buffer[0]+1;
        buffer[buffer[0]]:=READCTR;
        end;
    prevptr:=curptr;
    curptr:=FIND;

    {output escape-raw sequence or a pointer}
    if (curptr=nilptr) then begin
        WRITEPTR(dictsize);
        if (tflag) then DUMPTRACE('esc',dictsize);
        curptr:=DELETE;
        ADDPTR(curptr,1,nilptr,nilptr,buffer[1]);
        WRITERAW(buffer[1]);
        if (tflag) then DUMPTRACE('raw',buffer[1]);
        mcount[0]:=mcount[0]+1;
        end
    else begin
        WRITEPTR(curptr);
        if (tflag) then DUMPTRACE('ptr',curptr);
        mcount[SIZE(curptr)]:=mcount[SIZE(curptr)]+1;
        end;

    {move current pointer to front of LRU queue}
    PROMOTE(curptr);

    {shift current match out of the buffer}
    buffer[0]:=buffer[0]-SIZE(curptr);
    for bindex:=1 to buffer[0] do buffer[bindex]:=buffer[bindex+SIZE(curptr)];

    {update the dictionary}
    UPDATE;
    end;

#include "finish.i"
end.
```

{ vunsqueeze.p }

```
program MAIN(input,output);
#include "declare.i"
#include "utility.i"
#include "dictionary.i"
#include "queue.i"
#include "dump.i"
#include "heur_init.i"
#include "heur_delete.i"
#include "heur_update.i"
#include "io.i"
begin
#include "start.i"

while (not ENDINPUT) do begin

    {compute current pointer}
    prevptr:=curptr;
    curptr:=READPTR;

    {place next match in expand buffer}
    if (curptr=dictsize)
        then begin
            if (tflag) then DUMPTRACE('esc',dictsize);
            curptr:=DELETE;
            buffer[0]:=1; buffer[1]:=READRAW;
            ADDPTR(curptr,1,nilptr,nilptr,buffer[1]);
            if (tflag) then DUMPTRACE('raw',buffer[1]);
            mcount[0]:=mcount[0]+1;
            end
        else begin
            EXPAND(curptr);
            if (tflag) then DUMPTRACE('ptr',curptr);
            mcount[buffer[0]]:=mcount[buffer[0]]+1;
            end;

    {move current pointer to front of LRU queue}
    PROMOTE(curptr);

    {output current match}
    for bindex:=1 to buffer[0] do WRITECTR(buffer[bindex]);

    {update the dictionary}
    UPDATE;
    end;

{execute finish-up code}
#include "finish.i"
end.
```

```
{ declare.i }

const    {array limits}
         DictLimit=65535;
         MatchLimit=1024;
         StringLimit=80;

type     {types}
         TypeDictArray = array [0..DictLimit] of integer;
         TypeBuffer = array [0..MatchLimit] of integer; {entry 0 holds length}
         TypeString = packed array [1..StringLimit] of char;

var      {primary program parameters}
         {NOTE: enter parameters as parameter=value or parameter=value_argument}
         {NOTE: can specify parameters with upper-case only; eg CB for CharBytes}
         {NOTE: for string values, only the first character is significant}
         CharBytes:TypeString; {one=1-byte, hl=high-low, lh=low-high}
         CharDiv:integer; {divide all chars into encoder by this amount}
         CharMult:integer; {multiply all chars out of decoder by this amount}
         CharForm:TypeString; {tc = twos-comp integer, nn = non-neg integer}
         CharInit:integer; {max positive value of a char that can be added by
                              an init heuristic (max negative value is minus this
                              minus 1); -1 to set to max possible value}
         CharQuant:TypeString; {yes to quantize all chars input to the encoder
                              to the closest vector of length 1 in the static
                              portion of the dictionary}
         Epsilon:integer; {acceptable closeness for two characters}
         HeurD:TypeString; {deletion heuristic - FREEZE, LRU}
         HeurI:TypeString; {init heur - EMPTY, ALL, COVER, FILE, LOG, UNIFORM}
         HeurU:TypeString; {update heuristic - EMPTY, AP, FC, ID}
         Ignore:integer; {how many leading characters to ignore}
         MaxMatch:integer; {maximum allowable length for a match}
         PtrSize:integer; {maximum number of bits per pointer}
         PtrType:TypeString; {fixed (max length) or variable length pointers}
         VecMetric:TypeString; {vector dist metric - 1L, 2L, MAX, SMAX}

         {secondary program parameters}
         {NOTE: enter parameters as parameter=value}
         {NOTE: can specify parameters with upper-case only; eg DD for DumpDict}
         {NOTE: all characters of a string value may be significant}
         DumpDict:TypeString; {dump dictionary to file ('off' to disable)}
         DumpStats:TypeString; {dump statistics to file ('off' to disable)}
         DumpTrace:TypeString; {dump execution trace to file ('off' to disable)}
         DumpUpdate:TypeString; {yes to include updates in trace file}
         HeurIParam:integer; {stores an integer argument to HeurI heuristic}
         HeurIString:TypeString; {stores a string argument to HeurI heuristic}
         LineLength:integer; {maximum length of an output line}
         Readable:TypeString; {yes if data is readable}
         ReadChar:char; {character used to write unreadable characters}
         ReadLow:integer; {lowest value that is readable}
         ReadHigh:integer; {highest value that is readable}

         {variables used for only dump options}
         dictfile:text; {dictionary dump file}
         statsfile:text; {stats dump file}
         tracefile:text; {trace dump file}
```

dflag:boolean; {true if dict dump option in effect}
sflag:boolean; {true if stats dump option in effect}
tflag:boolean; {true if trace dump option in effect}
uflag:boolean; {true if trace dump option with updates in effect}
rflag:boolean; {true if readable option in effect}
bytesin:integer; {total number of bytes in}
bytesout:integer; {total number of bytes out}
minval:integer; {minimum character value encountered}
maxval:integer; {maximum character value encountered}
mcount:TypeBuffer; {contains number of matches of each length}

{special characters}
nilctr:integer; {one bigger than largest possible character}
maxctr:integer; {maximum possible character value}
initctr:integer; {computed from CharInit and maxctr}

{special pointers}
nilptr:integer; {nil pointer = largest legal pointer value}
maxptr:integer; {largest possible dictionary pointer = nilptr-1}
prevptr:integer; {dictionary pointer to previous match}
curptr:integer; {dictionary pointer to current match}

{dictionary data structure}
sizefield:TypeDictArray; {number of characters in this entry}
leftfield:TypeDictArray; {left parent}
rightfield:TypeDictArray; {right parent}
ctrfield:TypeDictArray; {raw character}
refsfield:TypeDictArray; {current number of pointers to this entry}
staticsize:integer; {size of static portion of the dictionary}
dictsize:integer; {current size of the dictionary}
dindex:integer; {used to sequence through dictionary}

{LRU queue data structure}
olderfield:TypeDictArray; {left pointer}
newerfield:TypeDictArray; {right pointer}
qin:integer; {right end of LRU queue, where things enter}
qout:integer; {left end of LRU queue, where things leave}

{variables used for input and output}
rleftover:integer; {holds leftover <8 bits for bit-read routine}
wleftover:integer; {holds leftover <8 bits for bit-write routine}
rlosize:integer; {1...256 = 0 to 8 leftover bits for bit-read routine}
wlosize:integer; {1...256 = 0 to 8 leftover bits for bit-write routine}
nilptrflag:boolean; {true if nilptr will never need to be sent}
buffer:TypeBuffer; {io buffer}
bindex:integer; {used to sequence through io buffer}

{ utility.i }

```
function MINIMUM(i,j:integer):integer;
begin
if (i<j)
    then MINIMUM:=i
    else MINIMUM:=j;
end {MINIMUM};

function MAXIMUM(i,j:integer):integer;
begin
if (i>j)
    then MAXIMUM:=i
    else MAXIMUM:=j;
end {MINIMUM};

{test whether a (positive) integer is a power of 2}
function POWEROF2(n:integer):boolean;
var i:integer;
begin
POWEROF2:=false;
i:=1;
while (i<=(maxint div 2)) do begin
        if (n=i) then POWEROF2:=true;
        i:=i*2;
        end;
end {POWEROF2};

{return the number of digits needed to write argument in given base}
function DIGITS(num,base:integer):integer;
var i:integer;
begin
num:=abs(num);
base:=abs(base);
i:=1;
while (num>(base-1)) do begin
    i:=i+1;
    num:=(num div base);
    end;
DIGITS:=i;
end {DIGITS};

{return the length of the alph-numeric prefix of a string}
function LENGTH(s:TypeString):integer;
var i,j:integer;
begin
i:=0;
j:=0;
while (i<StringLimit) do begin
    i:=i+1;
    if ((ord(s[i])>=ord('a')) and (ord(s[i])<=ord('z')))
```

```
    or  (ord(s[i])>=ord('A')) and (ord(s[i])<=ord('Z'))
    or  (ord(s[i])>=ord('0')) and (ord(s[i])<=ord('9')))
        then j:=j+1
        else i:=StringLimit;
    end;
LENGTH:=j;
end {LENGTH};

{make a character string blank}
procedure BLANK(var s:TypeString);
var i:integer;
begin
for i:=1 to StringLimit do s[i]:=' ';
end {BLANK};

{make a character string lower case}
procedure LOWER(var s:TypeString);
var i:integer;
begin
for i:=1 to StringLimit do
    if ((s[i]>='A') and (s[i]<='Z'))
        then s[i]:=chr(ord('a')+ord(s[i])-ord('A'));
end {LOWER};

{make a character string upper case}
procedure UPPER(var s:TypeString);
var i:integer;
begin
for i:=1 to StringLimit do
    if ((s[i]>='a') and (s[i]<='z'))
        then s[i]:=chr(ord('A')+ord(s[i])-ord('a'));
end {UPPER};

{assign the first string the value of the second}
procedure ASSIGN(var first:TypeString;second:TypeString);
var i:integer;
begin
for i:=1 to StringLimit do first[i]:=second[i];
end {ASSIGN};

{assign the first string the value of the second in lower case}
procedure ASSIGNLOW(var first:TypeString;second:TypeString);
begin
LOWER(second);
ASSIGN(first,second);
end {ASSIGNLOW};

{assign the first string the value of the second in upper case}
procedure ASSIGNUP(var first:TypeString;second:TypeString);
begin
UPPER(second);
```

```
ASSIGN(first,second);
end {ASSIGNUP};

{assign the first string 'yes' or 'no' according to the value of the second}
procedure ASSIGNBOOL(var first:TypeString;second:TypeString);
var i:integer;
begin
if (second[1] in [' ','y','Y'])
        then begin
                    first[1]:='y';
                    first[2]:='e';
                    first[3]:='s';
                    for i:=4 to StringLimit do first[i]:=' ';
                    end
        else begin
                    first[1]:='n';
                    first[2]:='o';
                    for i:=3 to StringLimit do first[i]:=' ';
                    end;
end {ASSIGNBOOL};

{convert an integer to a readable character}
function MAKECHAR(i:integer):char;
begin
if ((i>=ReadLow) and (i<=ReadHigh))
    then MAKECHAR:=chr(i)
    else MAKECHAR:=ReadChar;
end {MAKECHAR};

{convert a character string (padded with spaces) to an integer}
function MAKEINT(s:TypeString):integer;
var sign,val,i:integer;
begin
if (s[1]<>'-')
    then sign:=1
    else begin
        sign:=-1;
        s[1]:='0';
        end;
val:=0;
i:=0;
while (i<StringLimit) do begin
    i:=i+1;
    if ((ord(s[i])>=ord('0')) and (ord(s[i])<=ord('9')))
        then val:=(val*10)+ord(s[i])-ord('0')
        else i:=StringLimit+1;
    end;
MAKEINT:=sign*val;
end {MAKEINT};

{read program arguments of the form identifier=value_parameter}
```

```
procedure READARGS;
var  arg,ident,value,param: TypeString;
     argnum,i,j,k: integer;
begin
for argnum:=1 to (argc-1) do begin

    {place next argument in string variable}
    argv(argnum,arg);

    {get identifier portion of argument}
    BLANK(ident);
    i:=1;
    while ((i<StringLimit) and (arg[i]<>'=') and (arg[i]<>' ')) do begin
        ident[i]:=arg[i];
        i:=i+1;
        end;

    {get value portion of argument}
    BLANK(value);
    j:=i+1;
    while ((j<StringLimit) and (arg[j]<>'_') and (arg[j]<>' ')) do begin
        value[j-i]:=arg[j];
        j:=j+1;
        end;

    {get paramater portion of argument}
    BLANK(param);
    k:=j+1;
    while ((k<StringLimit)  and (arg[k]<>' ')) do begin
        param[k-j]:=arg[k];
        k:=k+1;
        end;

    {map ident argument to lower case and ignore a leading -}
    LOWER(ident);
    if (ident[1]='-') then for i:=1 to (StringLimit-1) do
        ident[i]:=ident[i+1];

    {process argument}
    if ((ident='charbytes') or (ident='cb'))
        then ASSIGNLOW(CharBytes,value);
    if ((ident='chardiv') or (ident='cd'))
        then CharDiv:=MAXIMUM(1,MAKEINT(value));
    if ((ident='charmult') or (ident='cm'))
        then CharMult:=MAXIMUM(1,MAKEINT(value));
    if ((ident='charform') or (ident='cf'))
        then ASSIGNLOW(CharForm,value);
    if ((ident='charinit') or (ident='ci'))
        then CharInit:=MAXIMUM(-1,MAKEINT(value));
    if ((ident='charquant') or (ident='cq'))
        then ASSIGNBOOL(CharQuant,value);
```

```
if ((ident='dumpdict') or (ident='dd'))
    then ASSIGN(DumpDict,value);
if ((ident='dumpstats') or (ident='ds'))
    then ASSIGN(DumpStats,value);
if ((ident='dumptrace') or (ident='dt'))
    then ASSIGN(DumpTrace,value);
if ((ident='dumpupdate') or (ident='du'))
    then ASSIGNBOOL(DumpUpdate,value);
if ((ident='epsilon') or (ident='e '))
    then Epsilon:=MAXIMUM(0,MAKEINT(value));
if ((ident='heurd') or (ident='hd'))
    then ASSIGNUP(HeurD,value);
if ((ident='heuri') or (ident='hi')) then begin
    ASSIGNUP(HeurI,value);
    if (LENGTH(param)>0) then begin
        HeurIParam:=MAKEINT(param);
        ASSIGN(HeurIString,param);
        end;
    end;
if ((ident='heuriparam') or (ident='hip'))
    then HeurIParam:=MAKEINT(value);
if ((ident='heuristring') or (ident='his'))
    then ASSIGN(HeurIString,value);
if ((ident='heuru') or (ident='hu'))
    then ASSIGNUP(HeurU,value);
if ((ident='ignore') or (ident='i '))
    then Ignore:=MAXIMUM(0,MAKEINT(value));
if ((ident='maxmatch') or (ident='mm'))
    then MaxMatch:=MAXIMUM(1,MINIMUM(MatchLimit,MAKEINT(value)));
if ((ident='ptrsize') or (ident='ps'))
    then PtrSize:=MAXIMUM(1,MINIMUM(DIGITS(DictLimit,2),MAKEINT(value)));
if ((ident='ptrtype') or (ident='pt'))
    then ASSIGNLOW(PtrType,value);
if ((ident='readable') or (ident='r '))
    then ASSIGNBOOL(Readable,value);
if ((ident='readchar') or (ident='rc'))
    then ReadChar:=value[1];
if ((ident='readlow') or (ident='rl'))
    then ReadLow:=MAXIMUM(0,MINIMUM(255,MAKEINT(value)));
if ((ident='readhigh') or (ident='rh'))
    then ReadHigh:=MAXIMUM(0,MINIMUM(255,MAKEINT(value)));
if ((ident='vecmetric') or (ident='vm')) then begin
    ASSIGNUP(VecMetric,value);
    if (VecMetric='L1') then VecMetric:='1L';
    if (VecMetric='L2') then VecMetric:='2L';
    end;

{SHORT WAYS TO SPECIFY DUMP OPTIONS}
if (ident='dict') then DumpDict:='dumpdict';
if (ident='stats') then DumpStats:='dumpstats';
if (ident='trace') then DumpTrace:='dumptrace';
```

```
if (ident='traceu') then begin
    DumpTrace:='dumptrace';
    DumpUpdate:='yes';
    end;
if (ident='dump') then begin
    DumpDict:='dumpdict';
    DumpStats:='dumpstats';
    DumpTrace:='dumptrace';
    DumpUpdate:='yes';
    end;

{LOSSY COMPRESSION OF DIGITIZED SPEECH}
if (ident='speech') then begin
    CharBytes:='lh'; {2 bytes per char, low followed by high byte}
    CharDiv:=16; {divide input chars by 16 to get 12-bit speech}
    CharMult:=16; {multiply output chars by 16 to rescale to 16 bits}
    CharForm:='tc'; {input and output chars in two's-complement form}
    CharInit:=-1; {no assumption is made on size of char values}
    CharQuant:='no'; {disable character quantization facility}
    Epsilon:=64; {allow errors of at most 64}
    HeurI:='EMPTY'; {initialize dictionary to be empty}
    HeurU:='FC'; {use FC update heuristic}
    HeurD:='LRU'; {use LRU deletion heuristic}
    Ignore:=512; {pass thru unchanged the first 512 bytes}
    MaxMatch:=500; {max length of a dictionary entry = 500}
    PtrSize:=12; {12-bit pointers}
    PtrType:='variable'; {pointers grow to a maximum of PtrSize bits}
    VecMetric:='MAX'; {use MAX metric ("L infinity metric")}
    end;

{2:1 LOG SCALAR QUANTIZATION OF A B&W DIGITAL IMAGE}
if (ident='image') then begin
    CharBytes:='one'; {one byte per character}
    CharDiv:=1; {disable input character scale-down facility}
    CharMult:=1; {disable output character scale-up facility}
    CharForm:='nn'; {characters represented as non-negative integers}
    CharInit:=-1; {no assumption is made on size of char values}
    CharQuant:='yes'; {map each input char to closest dictionary entry}
    Epsilon:=0; {allow no errors; i.e., lossless compression}
    HeurI:='LOG'; {use LOG initialization of dictionary}
    HeurIParam:=1; {LOG routine should save 1 additional bit}
    {HeurU value is not relevant because MaxMatch=1}
    {HeurD value is not relevant because MaxMatch=1}
    Ignore:=0; {disable option to ignore a file header}
    MaxMatch:=1; {force scalar quantization}
    PtrSize:=4; {use 4-bit pointers since LOG_1 produces 16 values}
    PtrType:='fixed'; {fixed size pointers}
    {VecMetric value not relevant because Epsilon=0}
    end;

{LOSSLESS COMPRESSION OF ASCII TEXT}
```

```
if (ident='ascii') then begin
    CharBytes:='one'; {one byte per character}
    CharDiv:=1; {disable input character scale-down facility}
    CharMult:=1; {disable output character scale-up facility}
    CharForm:='nn'; {characters represented as non-negative integers}
    CharInit:=127; {largest possible character value is 127}
    CharQuant:='no'; {disable character quantization facility}
    Epsilon:=0; {allow no errors; i.e., lossless compression}
    HeurI:='ALL'; {initialize dictionary with all vaules 0 - 127}
    HeurU:='ID'; {use ID update heuristic}
    HeurD:='LRU'; {use LRU deletion heuristic}
    Ignore:=0; {disable option to ignore a file header}
    MaxMatch:=100; {max length of a dictionary entry = 100}
    PtrSize:=12; {12-bit pointers}
    PtrType:='variable'; {pointers grow to a maximum of PtrSize bits}
    {VecMetric value not relevant because Epsilon=0}
    Readable:='yes'; {a dictionary dump may print in readable format}
    end;

{DUPLICATE DEFAULT SETTINGS OF LOSSLESS SQUEEZE PASCAL CODE}
if (ident='squeeze') then begin
    CharBytes:='one'; {one byte per character}
    CharDiv:=1; {disable input character scale-down facility}
    CharMult:=1; {disable output character scale-up facility}
    CharForm:='nn'; {characters represented as non-negative integers}
    CharInit:=255; {largest possible character value is 255}
    CharQuant:='no'; {disable character quantization facility}
    Epsilon:=0; {allow no errors; i.e., lossless compression}
    HeurI:='ALL'; {initialize dictionary with all vaules 0 - 255}
    HeurU:='AP'; {use AP update heuristic}
    HeurD:='LRU'; {use LRU deletion heuristic}
    Ignore:=0; {disable option to ignore a file header}
    MaxMatch:=100; {max length of a dictionary entry = 100}
    PtrSize:=12; {12-bit pointers}
    PtrType:='fixed'; {fixed size pointers of PtrSize bits}
    {VecMetric value not relevant because Epsilon=0}
    end;

    end;
end {READARGS};
```

{In addition to a size field (that contains the size of the entry) and
a reference field (that contains the number of other entries that refer
to the entry), a dictionary entry consists of a left pointer, right pointer,
and character; the only legal combinations are:

```
        left=nilptr         right=nilptr         character present
        left<>nilptr        right=nilptr         character present
        left<>nilptr        right<>nilptr        character not present
```

The target of a pointer is computed by concatenating the target of the left,
the target of the right, and the character.}

```
{return the size of a pointer's target}
function SIZE(ptr:integer):integer;begin SIZE:=sizefield[ptr] end;

{return the character stored at pointer}
function CTR(ptr:integer):integer;begin CTR:=ctrfield[ptr] end;

{add a pointer to the dictionary}
procedure ADDPTR(ptr,size,left,right,ele:integer);
begin
sizefield[ptr]:=size;
leftfield[ptr]:=left;
rightfield[ptr]:=right;
ctrfield[ptr]:=ele;
refsfield[ptr]:=0;
if (left<>nilptr) then refsfield[left]:=refsfield[left]+1;
if (right<>nilptr) then refsfield[right]:=refsfield[right]+1;
end {ADDPTR};

{delete a pointer from the dictionary}
procedure REMPTR(ptr:integer);
begin
if (leftfield[ptr]<>nilptr)
        then refsfield[leftfield[ptr]]:=refsfield[leftfield[ptr]]-1;
if (rightfield[ptr]<>nilptr)
        then refsfield[rightfield[ptr]]:=refsfield[rightfield[ptr]]-1;
end {REMPTR};

{return the index of the smallest single-character entry}
function MINENTRY:integer;
var i,m:integer;
begin
MINENTRY:=-1;
m:=maxint;
for i:=0 to (dictsize-1) do if ((SIZE(i)=1) and (CTR(i)<m)) then begin
        MINENTRY:=i;
        m:=CTR(i);
        end;
end {MINENTRY};

{return the index of the largest single-character entry}
function MAXENTRY:integer;
```

```
var i,m:integer;
begin
MAXENTRY:=-1;
m:=minint;
for i:=0 to (dictsize-1) do if ((SIZE(i)=1) and (CTR(i)>m)) then begin
        MAXENTRY:=i;
        m:=CTR(i);
        end;
end {MAXENTRY};

{return the element in the ith position of ptr}
{no check is made for illegal arguments}
function POS(ptr,i:integer):integer;
begin
while ((rightfield[ptr]<>nilptr) or (i<sizefield[ptr])) do
        if (i<=sizefield[leftfield[ptr]])
                then ptr:=leftfield[ptr]
                else begin
                        ptr:=rightfield[ptr];
                        i:=i-sizefield[leftfield[ptr]];
                        end;
POS:=ctrfield[ptr];
end {POS};

{expand ptr into io buffer}
{for speed, this is done non-recursively using a stack}
procedure EXPAND(ptr:integer);
var stack:TypeBuffer; top,stop,left,right,pos:integer;
begin
buffer[0]:=sizefield[ptr];
pos:=sizefield[ptr];
stack[1]:=ptr;
top:=1;
while (top>0) do begin
    stop:=stack[top];
    left:=leftfield[stop];
    right:=rightfield[stop];
    top:=top-1;
    if (left<>nilptr) then begin top:=top+1; stack[top]:=left end;
    if (right<>nilptr)
        then begin top:=top+1; stack[top]:=right end
        else begin buffer[pos]:=ctrfield[stop]; pos:=pos-1 end;
    end;
end {EXPAND};

{find the longest acceptable match to a prefix of the io buffer}
function FIND:integer;
var tbuffer:TypeBuffer; bptr,bsize,bval,tptr,tsize,tval:integer;
    stack:TypeBuffer; top,stop,left,right,pos:integer; {expand variables}
    i,d:integer; {variables used in distance computations}
begin
```

```
bptr:=nilptr;
bsize:=0;
bval:=maxint;
for tptr:=0 to (dictsize-1) do begin
    tsize:=sizefield[tptr];
    if ((tsize>=bsize) and (tsize<=buffer[0])) then begin

        {expand pointer into test buffer}
        {for speed, this is in-line rather than a (recursive) sub-routine}
        tbuffer[0]:=tsize;
        pos:=tsize;
        stack[1]:=tptr;
        top:=1;
        while (top>0) do begin
            stop:=stack[top];
            left:=leftfield[stop];
            right:=rightfield[stop];
            top:=top-1;
            if (left<>nilptr) then begin top:=top+1; stack[top]:=left end;
            if (right<>nilptr)
                then begin top:=top+1; stack[top]:=right end
                else begin tbuffer[pos]:=ctrfield[stop]; pos:=pos-1 end;
            end;

        {compute distance between test buffer and (prefix of) input buffer}
        {for speed, this code is in-line rather than a sub-routine}
        case VecMetric[1] of

            '1': begin {L1 metric}
                tval:=0;
                for i:=1 to tsize do tval:=tval+abs(tbuffer[i]-buffer[i]);
                if ((Epsilon=0) and (d>0))
                    then tval:=maxint
                    else tval:=(tval div tsize);
                end;

            '2': begin {L2 metric}
                tval:=0;
                for i:=1 to tsize do tval:=tval+sqr(tbuffer[i]-buffer[i]);
                if ((Epsilon=0) and (d>0))
                    then tval:=maxint
                    else tval:=trunc(sqrt(tval/tsize));
                end;

            'M': begin {maximum metric - "L infinity metric"}
                tval:=0;
                for i:=1 to tsize do begin
                    d:=abs(tbuffer[i]-buffer[i]);
                    if (tval<d) then tval:=d;
                    end;
                end;
```

```
            'S': begin {signed-maximum metric}
                tval:=0;
                for i:=1 to tsize do begin
                    d:=abs(tbuffer[i]-buffer[i]);
                    if (tval<d) then tval:=d;
                    if ((tbuffer[i]<0) and (buffer[i]>0))
                    or ((tbuffer[i]>0) and (buffer[i]<0))
                        then tval:=maxint;
                    end;
                end;

            end;

        {replace best ptr if ptr is acceptable and better or bigger}
        if ((tval<=Epsilon) and ((tval<bval) or (tsize>bsize))) then begin
            bptr:=tptr;
            bsize:=tsize;
            bval:=tval;
            end;

        end;
    end;
FIND:=bptr;
end {FIND};

{quantize a char to closest char in the static portion of the dictionary}
procedure QUANTIZE(var c:integer);
var ptr,savee,saveds,saveb0,saveb1: integer;
begin
savee:=Epsilon; Epsilon:=maxint;
saveds:=dictsize; dictsize:=staticsize;
saveb0:=buffer[0]; buffer[0]:=1;
saveb1:=buffer[1]; buffer[1]:=c;
ptr:=FIND;
if (ptr<>nilptr) then c:=ctrfield[ptr];
Epsilon:=savee;
dictsize:=saveds;
buffer[0]:=saveb0;
buffer[1]:=saveb1;
end {QUANTIZE};
```

{ queue.i }

{return next newer element after a given element in LRU queue}
function NEWER(place:integer):integer;begin NEWER:=newerfield[place] end;

{remove pointer from LRU queue}
procedure DEQUEUE(ptr:integer);
begin
if (qin=qout) then begin {delete only element}
        qin:=nilptr;
        qout:=nilptr;
        end
else if (ptr=qin) then begin {delete newest}
        qin:=olderfield[ptr];
        newerfield[qin]:=nilptr;
        end
else if (ptr=qout) then begin {delete oldest}
        qout:=newerfield[ptr];
        olderfield[qout]:=nilptr
        end
else begin {delete from middle}
        newerfield[olderfield[ptr]]:=newerfield[ptr];
        olderfield[newerfield[ptr]]:=olderfield[ptr]
        end
end {DEQUEUE};

{put pointer after place in LRU queue; if place is nilptr, insert as oldest}
procedure ENQUEUE(ptr,place:integer);
begin
if (qin=nilptr) then begin {empty queue}
        olderfield[ptr]:=nilptr;
        newerfield[ptr]:=nilptr;
        qin:=ptr;
        qout:=ptr
        end
else if (place=nilptr) then begin {prepend as oldest}
        olderfield[ptr]:=nilptr;
        newerfield[ptr]:=qout;
        olderfield[qout]:=ptr;
        qout:=ptr
        end
else if (place=qin) then begin {append as newest}
        olderfield[ptr]:=qin;
        newerfield[ptr]:=nilptr;
        newerfield[qin]:=ptr;
        qin:=ptr
        end
else begin {insert somewhere in middle}
        olderfield[ptr]:=place;
        newerfield[ptr]:=newerfield[place];
        olderfield[newerfield[place]]:=ptr;

```
        newerfield[place]:=ptr;
        end;
end {ENQUEUE};

{promote a legal non-static pointer to the front of the LRU queue}
procedure PROMOTE(ptr:integer);
begin
if ((ptr>=staticsize) and (ptr<dictsize)) then DEQUEUE(ptr);
if ((ptr>=staticsize) and (ptr<=dictsize)) then ENQUEUE(ptr,qin);
end;
```

{ dump.i }

{dump values that remain constant after initialization}
procedure DUMPCONST;
begin
```
writeln(statsfile,'DictLimit = ',DictLimit:0);
writeln(statsfile,'MatchLimit = ',MatchLimit:0);
writeln(statsfile,'StringLimit = ',StringLimit:0);
writeln(statsfile,'CharBytes = ',CharBytes:LENGTH(CharBytes));
writeln(statsfile,'CharDiv = ',CharDiv:0);
writeln(statsfile,'CharMult = ',CharMult:0);
writeln(statsfile,'CharForm = ',CharForm:LENGTH(CharForm));
writeln(statsfile,'CharInit = ',CharInit:0);
writeln(statsfile,'CharQuant = ',CharQuant:LENGTH(CharQuant));
writeln(statsfile,'DumpDict = ',DumpDict:LENGTH(DumpDict));
writeln(statsfile,'DumpStats = ',DumpStats:LENGTH(DumpStats));
writeln(statsfile,'DumpTrace = ',DumpTrace:LENGTH(DumpTrace));
writeln(statsfile,'DumpUpdate = ',DumpUpdate:LENGTH(DumpUpdate));
writeln(statsfile,'Epsilon = ',Epsilon:0);
writeln(statsfile,'HeurD = ',HeurD:LENGTH(HeurD));
writeln(statsfile,'HeurI = ',HeurI:LENGTH(HeurI));
writeln(statsfile,'HeurIParam = ',HeurIParam:0);
writeln(statsfile,'HeurIString = ',HeurIString:LENGTH(HeurIString));
writeln(statsfile,'HeurU = ',HeurU:LENGTH(HeurU));
writeln(statsfile,'Ignore = ',Ignore:0);
writeln(statsfile,'LineLength = ',LineLength:0);
writeln(statsfile,'MaxMatch = ',MaxMatch:0);
writeln(statsfile,'PtrSize = ',PtrSize:0);
writeln(statsfile,'PtrType = ',PtrType:LENGTH(PtrType));
writeln(statsfile,'Readable = ',Readable:LENGTH(Readable));
writeln(statsfile,'ReadChar = ',ReadChar);
writeln(statsfile,'ReadLow = ',ReadLow:0);
writeln(statsfile,'ReadHigh = ',ReadHigh:0);
writeln(statsfile,'VecMetric = ',VecMetric:LENGTH(VecMetric));
writeln(statsfile,'nilptr = ',nilptr:0);
writeln(statsfile,'maxptr = ',maxptr:0);
writeln(statsfile,'nilctr = ',nilctr:0);
writeln(statsfile,'maxctr = ',maxctr:0);
writeln(statsfile,'initctr = ',initctr:0);
writeln(statsfile,'staticsize = ',staticsize:0);
end {DUMPCONST};
```

{dump program variables that may change after initialization}
procedure DUMPVAR;
begin
```
writeln(statsfile,'dictsize = ',dictsize:0);
writeln(statsfile,'prevptr = ',prevptr:0);
writeln(statsfile,'curptr = ',curptr:0);
writeln(statsfile,'qin = ',qin:0);
writeln(statsfile,'qout = ',qout:0);
end {DUMPVAR};
```

```
{dump statistics gathering variables}
procedure DUMPDATA;
var ncr:real;
begin
writeln(statsfile,'minimum data value encountered = ',minval:0);
writeln(statsfile,'maximum data value encountered = ',maxval:0);
writeln(statsfile,'bytes in = ',bytesin:0);
writeln(statsfile,'bytes out = ',bytesout:0);
writeln(statsfile,'compression ratio = ',(bytesout/bytesin):0:3);
if (bytesin>Ignore) then begin
    ncr:=(bytesout-Ignore)/(bytesin-Ignore);
    if (CharDiv>1) then begin
        if (CharBytes[1]='o')
            then ncr:=ncr/(1-(DIGITS(CharDiv-1,2)/8))
            else ncr:=ncr/(1-(DIGITS(CharDiv-1,2)/16));
        end;
    writeln(statsfile,'normalized (by Ignore and CharDiv) ratio = ',ncr:0:3);
    end;
end {DUMPDATA};

{dump distribution of non-empty matches}
procedure DUMPMATCH;
var i,j,k,m,n:integer;
begin
writeln(statsfile,'# of raw data elements transmitted = ',mcount[0]:0);
i:=0;
j:=1;
m:=MaxMatch;
while ((mcount[m]=0) and (m>0)) do m:=m-1;
while(j<m) do begin
    k:=0; for n:=i+1 to j do k:=k+mcount[n];
    if (i=(j-1))
        then writeln(statsfile,'matches of length ',j:0,' = ',k:0)
        else writeln(statsfile,'matches of length >',
                            i:0,' and <=',j:0,' = ',k:0);
    i:=j;
    if (i<8)
        then j:=i+1
        else j:=((i*4) div 3);
    end;
if (m>0) then writeln(statsfile,'matches of length ',m:0,' = ',mcount[m]:0);
writeln(statsfile,'length of longest match = ',m:0);
end {DUMPMATCH};

{dump a trace line}
procedure DUMPTRACE(s:TypeString;val:integer);
var i:integer;
begin
if (s='esc') then writeln(tracefile,'esc=',val:0);
if (s='raw') then begin
        write(tracefile,'raw=',val:0,' (ptr=',curptr:0,')');
```

```
                if (rflag) then write(tracefile,' (',MAKECHAR(val),')');
                writeln(tracefile);
                end;
if (s='ptr') then begin
                write(tracefile,'ptr=',val:0,' (size=',SIZE(val):0,')');
                if (rflag) then begin
                        write(tracefile,' (');
                        for i:=1 to SIZE(val) do write(tracefile,MAKECHAR(buffer[i]));
                        write(tracefile,')');
                        end;
                writeln(tracefile);
                end;
if (s='upd') then
                writeln(tracefile,'upd=',val:0,' (size=',sizefield[val]:0,')');
end {DUMPTRACE};

{dump the contents of the dictionary}
procedure DUMPDICT;
var pwidth,ewidth,enum,ptr,i:integer;
begin
pwidth:=DIGITS((dictsize-1),10);
ewidth:=DIGITS(maxctr,10);
if (CharForm='tc') then ewidth:=ewidth+1;
enum:=(LineLength-pwidth-2) div ewidth;
for ptr:=0 to dictsize-1 do begin
    EXPAND(ptr);
    write(dictfile,ptr:pwidth,' =');
    if (rflag)
        then begin
            write(dictfile,'"');
            for i:=1 to buffer[0] do write(dictfile,MAKECHAR(buffer[i]));
            write(dictfile,'"');
            end
        else for i:=1 to buffer[0] do begin
            if ((i>1) and (((i-1) mod enum)=0)) then begin
                writeln(dictfile);
                write(dictfile,' ':(pwidth+2));
                end;
            write(dictfile,buffer[i]:(ewidth+1));
            end;
    writeln(dictfile);
    end;
end {DUMPDICT};
```

{ heur_init.i }

{initialize dictionary with enough elements (symetrical about 0 for tc data)
so that any value is within the specified distance of some dictionary element;
if second argument is true, 0 is forced to be one of the elements;
a third "seed" argument specifies the smallest positive value
(the largest negative value is -seed); an argument of 0 sets seed to
distance if zflag is true and (2*distance)+1 otherwise}

```
procedure COVERTEST(distance:integer; zflag:boolean; seed:integer);
var i,minusi:integer;
begin
if (distance<0) then distance:=0;
if (zflag)
    then begin
        ADDPTR(0,1,nilptr,nilptr,0);
        dictsize:=1;
        if ((seed<=0) or (seed>((2*distance)+1))) then seed:=(2*distance)+1;
        end
    else begin
        dictsize:=0;
        if ((seed<=0) or (seed>distance)) then seed:=distance;
        end;
i:=seed;
while (i<=(initctr+1)) do begin
    if ((i<=initctr) and (dictsize<=maxptr)) then begin
        ADDPTR(dictsize,1,nilptr,nilptr,i);
        dictsize:=dictsize+1;
        end;
    if ((CharForm[1]='t') and (dictsize<=maxptr)) then begin
        if (zflag) then minusi:=(-i) else minusi:=(-i-1);
        if (minusi>=(-initctr-1))
            then ADDPTR(dictsize,1,nilptr,nilptr,minusi);
        dictsize:=dictsize+1;
        end;
    i:=i+(2*distance)+1;
    end;
if ((CTR(MAXENTRY)<(initctr-distance)) and (dictsize<=maxptr)) then begin
    ADDPTR(dictsize,1,nilptr,nilptr,initctr);
    dictsize:=dictsize+1;
    end;
if ((CharForm[1]='t')
and (CTR(MINENTRY)>(distance-initctr-1))
and (dictsize<=maxptr)) then begin
    ADDPTR(dictsize,1,nilptr,nilptr,(-initctr-1));
    dictsize:=dictsize+1;
    end;
end {COVERTEST};
```

{dynamic version of COVERTEST that adjusts the distance
down as far possible (and still yield the same.dictionary size)

and then moves seed down as far as possible}
procedure COVER(distance:integer);
var d,s,saveds,i:integer; z:boolean;
begin

{comput initial cover}
COVERTEST(distance,false,0);
saveds:=dictsize;
z:=false;

{check if as good or better to include 0}
COVERTEST(distance,true,0);
if (dictsize<=saveds) then begin
        saveds:=dictsize;
        z:=true;
        end;

{minimize distance}
d:=distance;
if (d>0) then begin
        repeat
                    d:=d-1;
                    COVERTEST(d,z,0);
                    until (dictsize>saveds);
        d:=d+1;
        end;

{minimize seed}
if (z) then s:=(2*d)+1 else s:=d;
if (s>0) then begin
        repeat
                    s:=s-1;
                    COVERTEST(d,z,s);
                    until ((dictsize>saveds) or (s=0));
        s:=s+1;
        end;

{compute final cover}
COVERTEST(d,z,s);
if ((initctr-CTR(MAXENTRY))<d) then for i:=0 to (dictsize-1) do
        if (CTR(i)>0) then ADDPTR(i,1,nilptr,nilptr,CTR(i)-1);
end {COVER};

{initialize dictionary with integers from a text file; one integer per line}
procedure FILE(name:TypeString);
var initfile:text; x:integer;
begin
reset(initfile,name);
dictsize:=0;
while ((not eof(initfile)) and (dictsize<=maxptr)) do begin

```
        readln(initfile,x);
        ADDPTR(dictsize,1,nilptr,nilptr,x);
        dictsize:=dictsize+1;
        end;
end {FILE};
```

{Initialize dictionary by sliding a window that is a 1 followed by all
combinations of extrabits over each possible bit position of a data element.
For example, LOG(0) creates 0, all powers of 2 less than initctr, and initctr.
If CharForm=tc, then negatives of all values are created as well.
Let b denote the number of bits per character and i the paramater to LOG, and:
        nn(b,i) = number of entries generated when CharForm is 'nn'
        tc(b,i) = number of entries generated when CharForm is 'tc'
Then:

$$nn(b,i) = (b\text{-}i\text{+}1)*2^{**}i + 1, \quad \text{if } 0<=i<=(b\text{-}2)$$
$$2^{**}b, \quad \text{if } (b\text{-}1)<=i$$

$$tc(b,i) = (b\text{-}i)*2^{**}(i\text{+}1) + 1 = nn(b,i\text{+}1), \quad \text{if } 0<=i<=(b\text{-}3)$$
$$2^{**}b, \quad \text{if } (b\text{-}2)<=i$$

The values of nn(b,i) look as follows:

	b=8	b=16
0	10	18
1	17	33
2	29	61
3	49	113
4	81	209
5	129	385
6	193	705
7	256	1281
8	256	2305
9	256	4097
10	256	7169
11	256	12289
12	256	20481
13	256	32769
14	256	49153
15	256	65536

It is possible for both nn(b,i) and tc(b,i) to be just 1 more than
a power of 2; in the case that scalar quantization is being performed
(i.e., CharQuant=yes and MaxMatch=1), the largest possible
positive value is not added so that this will not happen;
in addition, for the case i=0 nn(b,i) is 2 greater than b (which is typically
a power of two - 8 or 16); in this case 0 is not added either.}

```
procedure LOG(extrabits:integer);
var i,j,n:integer;
begin
```

```
dictsize:=0;
if ((CharQuant[1]='n') or (MaxMatch>1) or (CharForm[1]='t') or (extrabits>0))
then begin
            ADDPTR(0,1,nilptr,nilptr,0);
            dictsize:=dictsize+1;
            end;
n:=1;
for i:=1 to extrabits do n:=n*2;
for i:=1 to n-1 do if (i<=initctr) then begin
    if (dictsize<=maxptr) then begin
        ADDPTR(dictsize,1,nilptr,nilptr,i);
        dictsize:=dictsize+1;
        end;
    if ((CharForm[1]='t') and (dictsize<=maxptr)) then begin
        ADDPTR(dictsize,1,nilptr,nilptr,-i);
        dictsize:=dictsize+1;
        end;
    end;
i:=1;
while ((i*n)<=initctr) do begin
    for j:=n to ((2*n)-1) do if ((i*j)<=initctr) then begin
        if (dictsize<=maxptr) then begin
            ADDPTR(dictsize,1,nilptr,nilptr,i*j);
            dictsize:=dictsize+1;
            end;
        if ((CharForm[1]='t') and (dictsize<=maxptr)) then begin
            ADDPTR(dictsize,1,nilptr,nilptr,-i*j);
            dictsize:=dictsize+1;
            end;
        end;
    i:=i*2;
    end;
if (((CharQuant[1]='n')
    or (MaxMatch>1)
    or ((CharForm[1]='n') and (not POWEROF2(dictsize)))
    or ((CharForm[1]='y') and (not POWEROF2(dictsize+1))))
and (abs(CTR(dictsize-1))<initctr)
and (dictsize<=maxptr)) then begin
    ADDPTR(dictsize,1,nilptr,nilptr,initctr);
    dictsize:=dictsize+1;
    end;
if ((CharForm[1]='t')
and (abs(CTR(dictsize-1))<=initctr)
and (dictsize<=maxptr)) then begin
    ADDPTR(dictsize,1,nilptr,nilptr,(-initctr-1));
    dictsize:=dictsize+1;
    end;
end {LOG};
```

{create uniformly spaced elements going up (and down if appropriate) from 0

also, insure that largest possible positive and negative values are present}
procedure UNIFORM(spacing:integer);
var i:integer;
begin
if (spacing<1) then spacing:=1;
dictsize:=0;
i:=0;
while (i<=(initctr+1)) do begin
       if ((i<=initctr) and (dictsize<=maxptr)) then begin
           ADDPTR(dictsize,1,nilptr,nilptr,i);
           dictsize:=dictsize+1;
           end;
       if ((CharForm[1]='t') and (i>0) and (dictsize<=maxptr)) then begin
           ADDPTR(dictsize,1,nilptr,nilptr,-i);
           dictsize:=dictsize+1;
           end;
       i:=i+spacing;
       end;
if ((CTR(MAXENTRY)<initctr) and (dictsize<=maxptr)) then begin
       ADDPTR(dictsize,1,nilptr,nilptr,initctr);
       dictsize:=dictsize+1;
       end;
if ((CharForm[1]='t')
and (CTR(MINENTRY)>(-initctr-1))
and (dictsize<=maxptr)) then begin
       ADDPTR(dictsize,1,nilptr,nilptr,-initctr-1);
       dictsize:=dictsize+1;
       end;
end {UNIFORM};

{ heur_delete.i }

```
function DELETE:integer;
var ptr:integer;
begin
DELETE:=nilptr;
if (dictsize<=maxptr) then begin
        ENQUEUE(dictsize,nilptr);
        DELETE:=dictsize;
        dictsize:=dictsize+1;
        end
else if ((HeurD[1]='L') and (qout<>nilptr)) then begin
        ptr:=qout;
        while ((refsfield[ptr]>0) and (ptr<>nilptr)) do ptr:=NEWER(ptr);
        if (ptr<>nilptr) then begin
                REMPTR(ptr);
                DELETE:=ptr;
                end;
        end;
end {DELETE};
```

•

```
{ heur_update.i }

{AP heuristic}
{for speed, no check is made for string already present}
procedure AP;
var ptr,saveptr,i:integer;
begin
ptr:=prevptr;
i:=0;
while ((i<SIZE(curptr)) and ((SIZE(prevptr)+i)<MaxMatch)) do begin
        i:=i+1;
        saveptr:=ptr;
        ptr:=DELETE;
        if (ptr<>nilptr) then begin
                ADDPTR(ptr,(SIZE(prevptr)+i),saveptr,nilptr,POS(curptr,i));
                PROMOTE(ptr);
                if (uflag) then DUMPTRACE('upd',ptr);
                end;
        end;
end {AP};

{FC heuristic}
{for speed, no check is made for string already present}
procedure FC;
var ptr:integer;
begin
ptr:=DELETE;
if (ptr<>nilptr) then begin
        ADDPTR(ptr,(SIZE(prevptr)+1),prevptr,nilptr,POS(curptr,1));
        PROMOTE(ptr);
        if (uflag) then DUMPTRACE('upd',ptr);
        end;
end {FC};

{ID heuristic}
{for speed, no check is made for string already present}
procedure ID;
var prefix,ptr,s:integer;
begin
s:=MaxMatch-SIZE(prevptr);
prefix:=curptr;
while (SIZE(prefix)>s) do prefix:=leftfield[prefix];
if (prefix<>nilptr) then begin
   ptr:=DELETE;
   if (ptr<>nilptr) then begin
      ADDPTR(ptr,(SIZE(prevptr)+SIZE(prefix)),prevptr,prefix,nilctr);
      PROMOTE(ptr);
      if (uflag) then DUMPTRACE('upd',ptr);
      end;
   end;
end {ID};
```

```
procedure UPDATE;
begin
if ((prevptr< >nilptr)
and (SIZE(prevptr)<MaxMatch)
and (curptr< >nilptr)) then case (HeurU[1]) of
        'A': AP;
        'F': FC;
        'I': ID;
        end;
end {UPDATE};
```

{ io.i }

{check for end of input stream}
function ENDINPUT:boolean;
begin
ENDINPUT:=eof;
end {ENDINPUT};

{read a byte from the input stream}
function READBYTE:integer;
var c:char; b:integer;
begin
if (eof) then b:=0
else if (eoln) then begin
        read(c); {read blank that PASCAL replaced for line end}
        b:=10 {10 is ascii code for carriage-return}
        end
else begin
        read(c);
        b:=ord(c);

        {check for two's complement form of a non-ascii character}
        if (b<0) then b:= b+256

        end;
if (bytesin<maxint) then bytesin:=bytesin+1;
READBYTE:=b
end {READBYTE};

{write a byte to the output stream}
procedure WRITEBYTE(b:integer);
begin
write(chr(b));
if (bytesout<maxint) then bytesout:=bytesout+1;
end {WRITEBYTE};

{pass through a number of bytes given by argument}
procedure PASSTHRU(num:integer);
var i:integer;
begin
i:=0;
while ((i<num) and (not eof)) do begin
        i:=i+1;
        WRITEBYTE(READBYTE);
        end;
end {PASSTHRU};

{read a character from input stream to the encoder}
function READCTR:integer;
var c:integer;
begin

```
case (CharBytes[1]) of
        'o': c:=READBYTE;
        'h': begin
                c:=READBYTE*256;
                c:=c+READBYTE;
                end;
        'l': begin
                c:=READBYTE;
                c:=(READBYTE*256)+c;
                end;
        end;
if (CharForm[1]='t') then begin {convert two's comp form to negative value}
        if ((CharBytes[1]='o') and (c>=128)) then c:=c-256
        else if (c>=32768) then c:=c-65536;
        end;
minval:=MINIMUM(minval,c);
maxval:=MAXIMUM(maxval,c);
if (CharDiv<>1) then c:=(c div CharDiv);
if (CharQuant[1]='y') then QUANTIZE(c);
READCTR:=c;
end {READCTR};

{write a character to output stream from decoder}
procedure WRITECTR(c:integer);
begin
if (CharMult<>1) then c:=(c*CharMult);
if (c>maxctr) then c:=maxctr;
if (c<(-maxctr-1)) then c:=-maxctr-1;
if ((CharForm[1]='n') and (c<0)) then c:=0;
minval:=MINIMUM(minval,c);
maxval:=MAXIMUM(maxval,c);
if (c<0) then begin {convert negative value to two's comp form}
        if (CharBytes[1]='o')
                then c:=c+256
                else c:=c+65536;
        end;
case (CharBytes[1]) of
        'o': WRITEBYTE(c);
        'h': begin
                WRITEBYTE(c div 256);
                WRITEBYTE(c mod 256);
                end;
        'l': begin
                WRITEBYTE(c mod 256);
                WRITEBYTE(c div 256);
                end;
        end;
end {WRITECTR};

{read smallest number of bits capable of holding the argument}
{used to read data into decoder}
```

```
function READBITS(maxvalue:integer):integer;
var ptr,length,maxlength:integer;
begin
ptr:=0;
length:=1;
maxlength:=2; while (maxlength<=maxvalue) do maxlength:=maxlength*2;
while (length<maxlength) do begin
        if (rlosize=1) then begin
                    rleftover:=READBYTE;
                    rlosize:=256;
                    end;
        rlosize:=(rlosize div 2);
        ptr:=(ptr*2)+(rleftover div rlosize);
        rleftover:=(rleftover mod rlosize);
        length:=length*2
        end;
READBITS:=ptr
end {READBITS};


{write arg1 using the smallest number of bits capable of holding arg2}
{used to write data out from encoder}
procedure WRITEBITS(ptr:integer;maxvalue:integer);
var length,maxlength:integer;
begin
maxlength:=2; while (maxlength<=maxvalue) do maxlength:=maxlength*2;
length:=maxlength;
while (length>1) do begin
        length:=(length div 2);
        wleftover:=(wleftover*2)+(ptr div length);
        wlosize:=wlosize*2;
        ptr:=(ptr mod length);
        if (wlosize=256) then begin
                    WRITEBYTE(wleftover);
                    wlosize:=1;
                    wleftover:=0;
                    end;
        end;
end {WRITEBITS};


{flush to output any left over fraction of a byte}
{used by encoder to finish up its output}
procedure FLUSHBITS;
begin
if (wlosize>1) then begin
        while (wlosize<256) do begin
                    wleftover:=wleftover*2;
                    wlosize:=wlosize*2;
                    end;
        WRITEBYTE(wleftover);
        end;
end {FLUSHBITS};
```

```
{read a raw character that has been sent by the encoder}
function READRAW:integer;
var c:integer;
begin
case (CharBytes[1]) of
        'o': c:=READBITS(255);
        'h': c:=READBITS(65535);
        'l': begin
                c:=READBITS(65535);
                c:=((c mod 256)*256)+(c div 256);
                end;
        end;
if (CharForm[1]='t') then begin {convert two's comp form to negative value}
        if ((CharBytes[1]='o') and (c>=128)) then c:=c-256
        else if (c>=32768) then c:=c-65536;
        end;
READRAW:=c;
end {READRAW};

{write a raw character to be sent to the decoder}
procedure WRITERAW(c:integer);
begin
if (c<0) then begin {convert negative value to two's comp form}
        if (CharBytes[1]='o')
                then c:=c+256
                else c:=c+65536;
        end;
case (CharBytes[1]) of
        'o': WRITEBITS(c,255);
        'h': WRITEBITS(c,65535);
        'l': WRITEBITS((((c mod 256)*256)+(c div 256)),65535);
        end;
end {WRITERAW};

{read a dictionary pointer that has been sent by the encoder}
function READPTR:integer;
begin
if (PtrType[1]='f') then READPTR:=READBITS(nilptr)
else if (nilptrflag) then READPTR:=READBITS(dictsize-1)
else READPTR:=READBITS(dictsize);
end {READPTR};

{write a dictionary pointer to be sent to the decoder}
procedure WRITEPTR(ptr:integer);
begin
if (PtrType[1]='f') then WRITEBITS(ptr,nilptr)
else if (nilptrflag) then WRITEBITS(ptr,(dictsize-1))
else WRITEBITS(ptr,dictsize);
end {WRITEPTR};
```

{ start.i }

{parameter defaults for general-purpose lossless compression}
CharBytes:='one';
CharDiv:=1;
CharMult:=1;
CharForm:='nn';
CharInit:=-1;
CharQuant:='no';
DumpDict:='off';
DumpStats:='off';
DumpTrace:='off';
DumpUpdate:='no';
Epsilon:=0;
HeurD:='LRU';
HeurI:='ALL';
HeurIParam:=0;
HeurIString:='initfile';
HeurU:='ID';
Ignore:=0;
LineLength:=72;
MaxMatch:=100;
PtrSize:=12;
PtrType:='variable';
Readable:='no';
ReadChar:='@';
ReadLow:=32;
ReadHigh:=126;
VecMetric:='MAX';

{read in optional arguments to program}
READARGS;

{initialize trace variables}
if (DumpDict='off')
        then dflag:=false
        else begin rewrite(dictfile,DumpDict); dflag:=true end;
if (DumpStats='off')
        then sflag:=false
        else begin rewrite(statsfile,DumpStats); sflag:=true end;
if (DumpTrace='off')
        then tflag:=false
        else begin rewrite(tracefile,DumpTrace); tflag:=true end;
if ((tflag) and (DumpUpdate[1]='y'))
        then uflag:=true
        else uflag:=false;
if (Readable[1]='y')
        then rflag:=true
        else rflag:=false;
bytesin:=0;
bytesout:=0;

```
minval:=maxint;
maxval:=minint;
for bindex:=0 to MaxMatch do mcount[bindex]:=0;

{initialize special elements}
nilctr:=256;
if (CharBytes[1]< >'o') then nilctr:=nilctr*256;
if (CharForm[1]='t') then nilctr:=(nilctr div 2);
maxctr:=nilctr-1;
CharDiv:=MINIMUM(maxctr,CharDiv);
CharMult:=MINIMUM(maxctr,CharMult);
if (CharInit>maxctr) then CharInit:=maxctr;
if (CharInit<0)
        then initctr:=maxctr
        else initctr:=CharInit;
initctr:=MINIMUM((maxctr div CharDiv),initctr);

{initialize special pointers}
nilptr:=1; for curptr:=1 to PtrSize do nilptr:=nilptr*2; nilptr:=nilptr-1;
maxptr:=nilptr-1;
prevptr:=nilptr;
curptr:=nilptr;

{initialize fields of nilptr to make checking of degenerate conditions easier}
sizefield[nilptr]:=0;
leftfield[nilptr]:=nilptr;
rightfield[nilptr]:=nilptr;
ctrfield[nilptr]:=nilctr;
refsfield[nilptr]:=0;
olderfield[nilptr]:=nilptr;
newerfield[nilptr]:=nilptr;

{initialize the static portion of the dictionary}
case (HeurI[1]) of {these routines must set dictsize}
        'A': UNIFORM(1);
        'C': COVER(HeurIParam);
        'E': {do nothing};
        'F': FILE(HeurIString);
        'L': LOG(HeurIParam);
        'U': UNIFORM(HeurIParam);
        end;
staticsize:=dictsize;

{initialize LRU queue}
qin:=nilptr;
qout:=nilptr;

{initialize i/o variables}
rleftover:=0;
wleftover:=0;
rlosize:=1;
```

```
wlosize:=1;
buffer[0]:=0;
nilptrflag:=false;
if (CharQuant[1]='y') then
          for dindex:=0 to (staticsize-1) do
                    if (SIZE(dindex)=1) then nilptrflag:=true;

{process ignore option}
PASSTHRU(Ignore);

{dump to stats file if appropriate}
if (sflag) then begin;
    write(statsfile,'*********INITIALIZAZTION COMPLETED');
    if (bytesin>0) then write(statsfile,' (',bytesin:0,' bytes ignored)');
    writeln(statsfile,':');
    DUMPCONST;
    DUMPVAR;
    end;
```

{ finish.i }

{flush any leftover bits to output stream}
FLUSHBITS;

{dump final values of variables to stats file if appropriate}
if (sflag) then begin
        writeln(statsfile,'**********EXECUTION COMPLETED:');
        DUMPMATCH;
        DUMPVAR;
        DUMPDATA;
        end;

{dump dictionary to dict file if appropriate}
if (dflag) then DUMPDICT;

BIBLIOGRAPHY

D. J. Abel and J. L. Smith [1983]. "A Data Structure and Algorithm Based on a Linear Key for a Rectangle Retrieval Problem", *Computer Graphics Image Processing* 24:1, 1-13.

N. Abramson [1963]. *Information Theory and Coding*, McGraw-Hill, New York, NY.

A. V. Aho, J. E. Hopcroft, and J. D. Ullman [1974]. *The Design and Analysis of Computer Algorithms*, Addison-Wesley, Reading, MA.

A. V. Aho, J. E. Hopcroft, and J. D. Ullman [1983]. *Data Structures and Algorithms*, Addison-Wesley, Reading, MA.

M Ai-Suwaiyel and E. Horowitz [1984]. "Algorithms for Trie Compaction", *ACM Transactions on Database Systems* 9:2, 243-263.

E. W. Allender [1987]. "Some Consequences of the Existence of Pseudorandom Generators", *Proceedings Nineteenth Annual ACM Symposium on the Theory of Computing*, New York City, NY, 151-159.

P. A. Alsberg [1975]. "Space and Time Savings Through Large Data Base Compression and Dynamic Restructuring", *Proceedings of the IEEE* 63:8, 1114-1122.

D. Angluin [1986]. "Learning Regular Sets from Querries and Counter-Examples", *Technical Report TR-464*, Computer Science Dept., Yale University, New Haven, CT.

A. Apostolico [1979]. "Linear Pattern Matching and Problems of Data Compression", *Proceedings IEEE International Symposium on Information Theory*.

A. Apostolico [1985]. "The Myriad Virtues of Subword Trees", *Combinatorial Algorithms on Words*, Springer-Verlag (A. Apostolico and

Z. Galil, editors), 85-95.

A. Apostolico and A. S. Fraenkel [1985]. "Robust Transmission of Unbounded Strings Using Fibonacci Representations", TR-CS545, Purdue University.

A. Apostolico and R. Giancarlo [1986]. "The Boyer-Moore-Galil String Searching Strategies Revisited", *SIAM Journal on Computing* 15:1.

A. Apostolico and E. Guerrieri [1983]. "Linear Time Universal Compression Techniques Based on Pattern Matching", *Proceedings Twenty-First Allerton Conference on Communication, Control, and Computing*, Monticello, Ill., 70-79.

A. Apostolico, C. Iliopoulos, G. M. Landau, B. Schieber, and U. Vishkin [1987]. "Parallel Construction of a Suffix Tree with Applications", *Technical Report*, Department of Computer Science, Purdue University, West Lafayette, IN.

R. Aravind and A. Gersho [1987]. "Image Compression based on Vector Quantization with Finite Memory", *Optical Engineering* 26:7, 570-580.

Ash [1965]. *Information Theory*, John Wiley and Sons, New York, NY.

R. F. Ayres [1983]. *VLSI: Silicon Compilation and the Art of Automatic Microchip Design*, Prentice-Hall, Englewood Cliffs, NJ.

F. L. Bacon and D. J. Houde [1986]. "Data Compression Apparatus and Method", U.S. Patent No. 4,612,532.

J. L. Balcazar and R. V. Book [1987]. "Sets with Small Generalized Kolmogorov Complexity", to appear, *Acta Informatica*.

F. Banchilon, P. Richard, M. Scholl [1982]. "On Line Processing of Compacted Relations", *Proceedings of the Eighth International Conference on Very Large Data Bases*, September 1982, 263-269.

M. F. Barnsley and A. D. Sloan [1988]. "A Better Way to Compress Images", *Byte Magazine* (January), 215-223.

M. F. Barnsley, V. Ervin, D. Hardin, and J. Lancaster [1986]. "Solution of an Inverse Problem for Fractals and Other Sets", Proceedings of the National Academy of Science 83, 1975-1977.

M. F. Barnsley and S. Demko [1985]. "Iterated Function Systems and the Global Construction of Fractals", Proceedings of the Royal Society of London A399, 243-275.

R. H. T. Bates and M. J. McDonnell [1986]. *Image Restoration and Reconstruction*, Oxford University Press, New York, NY.

T. C. Bell [1985]. "Better OPM/L Text Compression", *IEEE Transactions on Communications* 34:12, 1176-1182.

F. Benford [1938]. *Proc. American Philopsophical Society 78*, 551.

W. R. Bennett [1976]. *Scientific and Engineering Problem-Solving with the Computer* (Chapter 4), Prentice-Hall, Englewood Cliffs, NJ.

J. L. Bentley, D. D. Sleator, R. E. Tarjan, and V. K. Wei [1985]. "A Locally Adaptive Data Compression Scheme", *Communications of the ACM* 29:4, 320-330.

J. L. Bentley and A. C. Yao [1976]. "An Almost Optimal Algorithm for Unbounded Searching", *Information Processing Letters* 5, 1976.

T. Berger [1971]. *Rate Distortion Theory: A Mathematical Basis for Data Compression*, Prentice-Hall, Englewood Cliffs, NJ.

J. Berstel and D. Perrin [1985]. *Theory of Codes*, Academic Press, New York, NY.

P. Bertolazzi and F. Luccio [1985]. *VLSI Algorithms and Architectures*, North-Holland, New York, NY.

S. N. Bhatt and C. E. Leiserson [1982]. "How to Assemble Tree Machines", *Proceedings Fourteenth Annual ACM Symposium on the Theory of Computing*, 77-83.

T. Bially [1969]. "Space-Filling Curves: Their Generation and Their Application to Bandwidth Reduction", *IEEE Transactions on Computers* 15:6, 658-664.

G. Bilardi, M. Pracchi, and F. P. Preparata [1981]. "A Critique and Appraisal of VLSI Models of Computation", *Conference on VLSI Systems and Computations*, Carnegie-Mellon University, 81-88.

R. E. Blahut [1983]. *Theory and Practice of Error Control Codes*, Addison-Wesley, Reading, MA.

R. E. Blahut [1983]. *Fast Algorithms for Digital Signal Processing*, Addison-Wesley, Reading, MA.

M. Blum [1967]. "On the Size of Machines", *Information and Control* 11, 257-265.

M. Blum [1967b]. "A Machine Independent Theory of Recursive Functions", *Journal of the ACM* 14:2, 322-336.

M. Blum [1971]. "On effective Procedures for Speeding Up Algorithms", *Journal of the ACM* 18:2, 290-305.

A. Blumer [1985]. "A Generalization of Run-Length Encoding", *Proceedings IEEE Symposium on Information Theory.*

A. Blumer [1987]. "Min-Max Universal Noiseless Coding with Unifilar and Markov Sources", *IEEE Transactions on Information Theory.*

A. Blumer [1988]. "Arithmetic Coding with Non-Markov Sources", *Technical Report,* Tufts University, Medford, MA.

A. Blumer and J. Blumer [1987]. "On-Line Construction of a Complete Inverted File", *Technical Report,* Dept. of Mathematics and Computer Science, University of Denver, Denver, CO.

A. Blumer, A. Ehrenfeuchtr, D. Haussler, and M. Warmuth [1986]. "Classifying Learnable Geometric Concepts with the Vapnik-Chervonekis Dimension", *Proceedings Eighteenth Annual ACM Symposium on the Theory of Computing*, Berkeley, CA, 273-282.

A. Blumer, J. Blumer, A. Ehrenfeuchtr, D. Haussler, and R. McConnell [1984]. "Building the Minimal DFA for the Set of all Sub-words of a Word in Linear Time", *Lecture Notes in Computer Science* 172, Springer-Verlag, New York, NY, 109-118.

A. Blumer, J. Blumer, A. Ehrenfeuchtr, D. Haussler, and R. McConnell [1984b]. "Building a Complete Inverted File for a Set of Text Files in Linear Time", *Proceedings Sixteenth Annual ACM Symposium on the Theory of Computing*, Washington, DC, 349-358.

A. Blumer and R. J. McEliece [1988]. "The Renyi Redundancy of Generalized Huffman Codes", submitted to *IEEE Transactions on Information Theory*.

J. Blumer and A. Blumer [1986]. "OnLine Construction of a Complete Inverted File", *Technical Report*, Department of Mathematics and Computer Science, University of Denver, Denver, CO.

G. S. Boolos and R. C. Jeffrey [1980]. *Computability and Logic* (second edition), Cambridge University Press, New York, NY.

R. S. Boyer [1977]. "A Fast String Searching Algorithm", *Communications of the ACM* 20:10, 762-772.

W. S. Brainerd and L. H. Landweber [1974]. *Theory of Computation*, John Wiley and Sons, New York, NY.

R. P. Brent and H. T. Kung [1980]. "On the Area of Binary Tree Layouts", *Information Processing Letters* 11:1, 46-48.

D. J. Brown and P. Elias [1976]. "Complexity of Acceptors for Prefix Codes", *IEEE Transactions on Information Theory* 22:3, 357-359.

A. W. Burks [1970]. *Essays on Cellular Automata*, University of Illonois Press, Urbana, Illonois.

P. J. Burville and J. F. C. Kingman [1973]. "On a Model for Storage and Search", *Journal of Applied Probability* 10, 697-701.

A. R. Butz [1969]. "Convergence with Hilbert's Space Filling Curve", *Journal of Computer and System Sciences* 3, 128-146.

A. R. Butz [1971]. "Alternate Algorithm for Hilbert's Space-Filling Curve", *IEEE Transactions on Computers* (April), 424-426.

J. J. F. Cavanagh [1984]. *Digital Computer Arithmetic: Design and Implementation*, McGraw-Hill, New York, NY.

G. J. Chaitin [1966]. "On the Length of Programs for Computing Finite Binary Sequences", *Journal of the ACM* 13:4, 547-569.

G. J. Chaitin [1969]. "On the Length of Programs for Computing Finite Binary Sequences; Statistical Considerations", *Journal of the ACM* 16:1, 145-159.

G. J. Chaitin [1969b]. "On the Simplicity and Speed for Computing Infinite Sets of Natural Numbers", *Journal of the ACM* 16:3, 407-422.

G. J. Chaitin [1975]. "A Theory of Program Size Formally Identical to Information Theory", *Journal of the ACM* 22:3, 329-340.

G. J. Chaitin [1975b]. "Randomness and Mathematical Proof", *Scientific American*, May, 47-52.

G. J. Chaitin [1976]. "Information-Theoretic Characterizations of Recursive Infinite Strings", *Theoretical Computer Science* 2, 45-48.

G. J. Chaitin [1987]. *Algorithmic Information Theory*, Cambridge University Press, New York, NY.

M. T. Chen and J. Seiferas [1985]. "Efficient and Elegant Subword-Tree Construction", *Combinatorial Algorithms on Words*, Springer-Verlag (A. Apostolico and Z. Galil, editors), 97-110.

W. Chou [1983]. *Computer Communications*, Prentice-Hall, Englewood Cliffs, NJ.

Y. Choueka, A. S. Fraenkel, and Y. Perl [1982]. "Polynomial Construction of Optimal Prefix Tables for Text Compression", draft, Technion University, Haifa, Israel.

J. G. Cleary and I. H. Witten [1984]. "Data Compression Using Adaptive Coding and Partial String Matching", *IEEE Transactions on*

Communications 32:4, 396-402.

M. Cohn [1986]. "Performance of LZ Compressors with Deferred Innovation", *Technical Report CS-86-127*, Computer Science Department, Brandeis University, Waltham, MA.

M. Cohn [1987]. Private communication, Computer Science Department, Brandeis University, Waltham, MA.

S. N. Cole [1969]. "Real-Time Computation by n-Dimensional Iterative Arrays of Finite State Machines", *IEEE Transactions on Computers* 18, 349-365.

D. Comer, R. Sethi [1977]. "The Complexity of Trie Index Construction", *Journal of the ACM* 24:3, 428-440.

S. A. Cook [1971]. "The Complexity of Theorem Proving Procedures", *Proceedings Third Annual ACM Symposium on Theory of Computing*, Shaker Heights, Ohio, 151-158.

D. Cooper and M. F. Lynch [1982]. "Text Compression Using Variable- to Fixed-Length Encodings", *Journal of the American Society for Information Science* (January), 18-31.

G. V. Cormack [1985]. "Data Compression on a Database System", *Communications of the ACM* 28:12, 1336-1342.

G. V. Cormack and R. Nigel Horspool [1984]. "Algorithms for Adaptive Huffman Codes", *Information Processing Letters* 18, 159-165.

N. Cot [1977]. "Characterization and Design of Optimal Prefix Codes", *Ph.D. Thesis*, Computer Science Dept. Stanford University, Stanford, CA.

T. M. Cover [1973]. "Enumerative Source Encoding", *IEEE Transactions on Information Theory* 19:1, 73-77.

K. Culik and I. Fris [1985]. "Topological Transformations as a Tool in the Design of Systolic Networks", *Theoretical Computer Science* 37, 183-216.

N. J. Cutland [1980]. *Computability: An Introduction to Recursive Function*

Theory, Cambridge University Press, New York, NY.

R. P. Daley [1973]. "An Example of Information and Computation Trade-Off", *Journal of the ACM* 20:4, 687-695.

R. P. Daley [1974]. "The Extent and Density of Sequences Within the Minimal-Program Complexity Hierarchies", *Journal of Computer and System Sciences* 9, 151-163.

R. P. Daley [1976]. "Noncomplex Sequences: Characterizations and Examples", *Journal of Symbolic Logic* 41:3, 626-638.

D. L. Dance and U. W. Pooch [1976]. "An Adaptive On Line Data Compression System", *Computer Journal* 19:3, 216-224.

M. D. Davis and E. J. Weyuker [1983]. *Computability, Complexity, and Languages*, Academic Press, New York, NY.

L. D. Davisson [1973]. "Universal Noiseless Coding", *IEEE Transactions on Information Theory* 19, 783-795.

L. D. Davisson [1983]. "Min-Max Noiseless Universal Coding for Markov Sources", *IEEE Transactions on Information theory*.

L. D. Davisson and R. M. Gray [1975]. "Advances in Data Compression", in *Advances in Communication Systems* 4, Academic Press, New York, 199-228.

L. D. Davisson and R. M. Gray, Eds. [1976]. *Data Compression*, Dowden, Hutchinson, and Ross, Stroudsburg, PA.

L. D. Davisson, McLiece, Pursley, and Wallace [1981]. "Efficient Universal Noiseless Source Codes", *IEEE Transactions on Information Theory*.

P. A. D. De Maine, T. Rotwitt, Jr. [1971]. "Storage Optimization of Tree Structured Files Representing Descriptor Sets", *Proceedings ACM SIGFIDET Workshop on Data Description, Access and Control*, November 1971, 207-217.

P. Denyer and D. Renshaw [1985]. *VLSI Signal Processing: A Bit-Serial Approach*, Addison-Wesley, Reading, MA.

V. L. Doucette, K. M. Harrison, and E. J. Schuagref [1977]. "A Comparative
    Evaluation of Fragment Dictionaries for the Compression of
    French, English, and German Bibliographic Data Bases",
    *Proceedings Third International Conference in the Humani-
    ties* (S. Lusignan and J. S. North, eds.), University of Water-
    loo Press, Waterloo, Ontario, Canada, 297-305.

Y. P. Drobyshev, V. V. Pukhov [1979]. "Analysis of the Influence of a Sys-
    tem on Objects as a Problem of Transformation of Data
    Tables", in *Modeling and Optimization of Complex Systems*
    (Proceedings IFIP-TC 7 Working Conference, Novosibirisk,
    1978), Lecture Notes in Control and Information Science, 18,
    Springer-Verlag, New York, NY, 187-197.

A. E. Dunlop [1980]. "SLIM - The Translation of Symbolic Layouts into
    Mask Data", *Proceedings Seventeenth Design Automation
    Conference*, Minneapolis.

E. B. Eichelberger, W. C. Rodgers, E. W. Stacy [1968]. "Method for Estima-
    tion and Optimization of Printer Speed Based on Character
    Usage Statistics", *IBM Journal of Research and Development*
    12:2, March 1968, 130-139.

P. Elias [1975]. "Universal Codeword Sets and Representations of the In-
    tegers", *IEEE Transactions on Information Theory* 21:2,
    194-203.

P. Elias [1987]. "Interval and Recency Rank Source Coding: Two On-Line
    Adaptive Variable Length Schemes", *IEEE Transactions on
    Information Theory* 33:1, 3-10.

S. Even and M. Rodeh [1978]. "Economical Encoding of Commas Between
    Strings", *Communications of the ACM* 21:4, 315-317.

S. Even, D. Lichtenstein, and Y. Perl [1979]. "Remarks on Ziegler's Method
    for Matrix Compression", draft, Technion University, Haifa,
    Israel.

N. Faller [1973]. "An Adaptive System for Data Compression", *Conference
    Record of the Seventh IEEE Asilomar Conference on Circuits
    and Systems*, 593-597.

R. M. Fano [1949]. *Ph.D. Thesis*, Massachusetts Institute of Technology, Cambridge, MA.

R. M. Fano [1952]. "Class Notes for Transmission of Information", *Course 6.574*, Massachusetts Institute of Technology, Cambridge, MA.

R. M. Fano [1961]. *Transmission of Information*, MIT Press, Cambridge, MA; and Wiley, NY.

B. J. Flehinger [1966]. *American Mathematical Monthly* 73, 1056-1061.

M. J. Fischer [1980]. "Optimal Tree Layout", *Proceedings Twelfth Annual ACM Symposium on the Theory of Computing*, 177-189.

A. S. Fraenkel and S. T. Klein [1985]. "Novel Compression of Sparse Bit-Strings - Preliminary Report", *Combinatorial Algorithms on Words*, Springer-Verlag (A. Apostolico and Z. Galil, editors), 169-183.

A. S. Fraenkel and M. Mor [1983]. "Combinatorial compression and partitioning of large dictionaries", *The Computer Journal* 26:4, 336-344.

A. S. Fraenkel, M. Mor, and Y. Perl [1983]. "Is Text Compression by Prefixes and Suffixes Practical?", *Acta Informatica* 20:4, 371-375.

P. A. Franasek and T. J. Wagner [1974]. "Some Distribution-Free Aspects of Paging Algorithm Performance", *JACM*, 31-39.

W. D. Frazer [1972]. "Compression parsing of computer file data", *Proceedings First USA-Japan Computer Conference*, October 1972, Session 19-1, 609-615.

H. Fujiwara, K. Kinoshita [1978]. "On Testing Schemes for Test Data Compression", *Systems-Comput.-Controls* 9:3 72-78 (appeared 1980?).

H. Fujiwara, K. Kinoshita [1979]. "Testing Logic Circuits with Compressed Data", *J. Design Automation and Fault-Tolerant Computing*, 3:3-4, 211-225.

W. H. Furry and H. Hurwitz [1945]. *Nature* 155, 52-53.

R. G. Gallager [1968]. *Information Theory and Reliable Communication*, Wiley, New York, NY.

R. G. Gallager [1978]. "Variations on a Theme by Huffman", *IEEE Transactions on Information Theory* 24:6, 668-674.

R. G. Gallager and D. C. Van Voorhis [1975]. "Optimal Source Codes for Geometrically Distributed Integer Alphabets", *IEEE Transactions on Information Theory*, 228-230.

J. Gallant [1982]. "String Compression Algorithms", *Ph.D. Thesis*, Dept. EECS, Princeton University.

J. Gallant, D. Maier, and J. A. Storer [1980]. "On Finding Minimal Length Superstrings", *Journal of Computer and System Sciences* 20, 50-58.

A. Gamal and A. Orlitsky [1984]. "Interactive Data Compression", *Proceedings Twenty-Fifth Annual IEEE Symposium on the Foundations of Computer Science*, Singer Island, FL, 100-108.

M. Gardner [1976]. "Mathematical Games: Monster Curves", *Scientific American*, 124-133.

M. R. Garey [1972]. "Optimal Binary Identification Procedures", *SIAM Journal on Applied Mathematics* 23:2, 173-186.

M. R. Garey [1974]. "Optimal Binary Search Trees with Restricted Maximum Depth", *SIAM Journal on Computing* 3, 101-110.

M. R. Garey and D. S. Johnson [1979]. *Computers and Intractability: A Guide to the Theory of NP-Completeness*, W. H. Freeman, Salt Lake City, Utah.

M. R. Garey, D. S. Johnson, and L. Stockmeyer [1976]. "Some Simplified NP-Complete Problems", *Theoretical Computer Science* 1, 237-267.

I. Gargantini [1982]. "An Effictive Way to Represent Quadtrees", *Communications of the ACM* 25:12, 905-910.

E. N. Gilbert [1971]. "Codes Based on Inaccurate Source Probabilities", *IEEE Transactions on Information Theory* 17:3, 304-314.

L. A. Glasser and D. W. Dobberpuhl [1985]. *The Design and Analysis of VLSI Circuits*, Addison-Wesley, Reading, MA.

A. V Goldberg and M. Sipser [1985]. "Compression and Ranking", *Proceedings Seventeenth Annual ACM Symposium on the Theory of Computing*, Providence, RI, 440-448.

S. W. Golomb [1966]. "Run-Length Encodings", *IEEE Transactions on Information Theory* 12, 399-401.

R. C. Gonzalez and P. Wintz [1977]. *Digital Image Processing*, Addison-Wesley, Reading, MA.

M. Gonzalez and J. A. Storer [1985]. "Parallel Algorithms for Data Compression", *Journal of the ACM* 32:2, 344-373.

D. Gordon [1987]. "Efficient Embeddings of Binary Trees in VLSI Arrays", *IEEE Transactions on Computers* 36:9, 1009-1018.

D. Gordon, I. Koren, and G. Silberman [1984]. "Embedding Tree Structures in VLSI Hexagonal Arrays", *IEEE Transactions on Computers* 33:1, 104-107.

D. Gotlieb, S. A. Hagerth, P. G. H. Lehot, H. S. Rabinowitz [1975]. "A Classification of Compression Methods and their Usefulness for a Large Data Processing Center", *National Computer Conference 44*, 453-458.

R. M. Gray [1984]. "Vector Quantization", *IEEE ASSP Magazine*, 4-29.

M. Guazzo [1980]. "A General Minimum-Redundancy Source-Coding Algorithm", *IEEE Transactions on Information Theory* 26, 15-25.

L. Guibas [1985]. "Periodicities in Strings", *Combinatorial Algorithms on Words*, Springer-Verlag, (A. Apostolico and Z. Galil, editors), 257-270.

L. Guibas and A. M. Odlyzko [1978]. "Maximal Prefix-Synchronized Codes", *SIAM Journal on Applied Mathematics* 35, 401-418.

W. D. Hagamen, D. J. Linden, H. S. Long, and J. C. Weber [1972]. "Encoding Verbal Information as Unique Numbers", *IBM Systems Journal* 11.

B. Hahn [1974]. "A New Technique for Compression and Storage of Data", *Communications of the ACM* 17:8, 434-436.

F. Halsall [1985]. *Introdcution to Data Communications and Computer Networks*, Addison-Wesley, Reading, MA.

R. W. Hamming [1980]. *Coding and Information Theory*, Prentice-Hall, Englewood Cliffs, NJ.

F. Harary [1972]. *Graph Theory*, Addison-Wesley, Reading, MA.

D. Harel and R. E. Tarjan [1984]. "Fast Algorithms for Finding Nearest Common Ancestors", *SIAM Journal on Computing* 13, 338-355.

A. Hartman and M. Rodeh [1985]. "Optimal Parsing of Strings", *Combinatorial Algorithms on Words*, Springer-Verlag (A. Apostolico and Z. Galil, editors), 155-167.

J. Hartmanis [1973]. "Generalized Kolmogorov Complexity and the Structure of Feasible Computations", *Proceedings Twenty-Fourth IEEE Annual Symposium on the Foundations of Computer Science*, 439-445.

J. Hartmanis [1974]. "Computational Complexity of Formal Translations", *Mathematical Systems Theory* 8:2, 156-166.

J. Hartmanis and J. E. Hopcroft [1971]. "An Overview of the Theory of Computational Complexity", *Journal of the ACM* 18:3, 444-475.

J. Hartmanis and T. P. Baker [1975]. "On Simple Gödel Numberings and Translations", *SIAM Journal on Computing* 4:1, 1-11.

J. P Hayes [1976]. "Check Sum Methods for Test Data Compression", *J. Design Automat. Fault-Tolerant Comput.* 1:1, 3-17.

K. A. Hazboun, M. A. Bassiouni [1982]. "A Multi-Group Technique for Data

Compression", *Proceedings 1982 ACM SIGMOD International Conference on Management of Data*, June 1982, 284-292.

G. Held [1983]. *Data Compression: Techniques and Applications, Hardware and Software Considerations*, John Wiley and Sons, New York, NY.

W. J. Hendricks [1972]. "The Stationary Distribution of an Interseting Markov Chain", *Journal of Applied Probability* 9, 231-233.

W. J. Hendricks [1973]. "An Extension of a Theorem Concerning an Interseting Markov Chain", *Journal of Applied Probability* 10, 886-890.

F. Henie [1961]. *Iterative Arrays of Logical Circuits*, MIT Press, Cambridge, MA.

F. Henie [1977]. *Introduction to Computability*, Addison Wesley, Reading, MA, 226-236.

H. Hermes [1969]. *Enumerability, Decidability, and Computability: An Introduction to the Theory of Recursive Functions*, Springer-Verlag, New York, NY.

E. E. Hilbert [1977]. "Cluster Compression Algorithm: A Joint Clustering / Data Compression Concept", *Ph.D. Thesis*, University of Southern California.

K. Hoffman and R. Kunze [1971]. *Linear Algebra*, Prentice Hall, Englewood Cliffs, NJ.

J. E. Hopcroft and J. D. Ullman [1979]. *Introduction to Automata Theory, Languages, and Computation*, Addison-Wesley, Reading, MA.

R. N. Horspool and G. V. Cormack [1984]. "A General Purpose Data Compression Technique with Practical Applications", *Proceedings of the CIPS*, Session 84, Calgary, Canada, 138-141.

R. N. Horspool and G. V. Cormack [1986]. "Dynamic Markov Modelling - A Prediction Technique", *Proceedings of the* Nineteenth Hawaii International Conference on System Sciences, Honolulu, 700-

707.

T. C. Hu [1982]. *Combinatorial Algorithms,* Addison-Wesley, Reading, MA.

T. C. Hu and K. C. Tan [1972]. "Path Length of Binary Search Trees", *SIAM Journal on Applied Mathematics* 22, 225-234.

T. C. Hu and C. Tucker [1971]. "Optimal Computer Search Trees and Variable-Length Alphabetical Codes", *SIAM Journal on Applied Mathematics* 21:4, 514-532.

D. A. Huffman [1952]. "A Method for the Construction of Minimum-Redundancy Codes", *Proceedings of the IRE* 40, 1098-1101.

S. E. Hutchins [1971]. "Data compression in context-free languages", *Proceedings IFIP Conference Ljubljana,* v.1: Foundations and Systems, North-Holland, 104-109.

D. T. Huynh [1986]. "Resource-Bounded Kolmogorov Complexity of Hard Languages", *Structure in Complexity Theory Conference, Lecture Notes in Computer Science* 223, 184-195.

IEEE Computer, December 1987, issue devoted to integrated optical computing.

IEEE Transactions on Information Theory 28:2, special two volume issue on quantization.

F. M. Ingels [1971]. *Information Theory and Coding Theory,* Intext, Scranton, PA.

M. Jacobsson [1978]. "Huffman coding in Bit-Vector Compression", *Information Processing Letters* 7:6, 304-307.

N. S. Jayant and P. Noll [1984]. *Digital Coding of Waveforms: Principles and Applications to Speech and Video,* Prentice-Hall, Englewood Cliffs, NJ.

F. Jelinek [1968]. *Probabilistic Information Theory,* McGraw-Hill, New York, NY.

O. Johnsen [1980]. "On the Redundancy of Binary Huffman Codes", *IEEE*

Transactions on Information Theory 26:2, 220-222.

C. B. Jones [1981]. "An Efficient Coding System for Long Source Sequences", *IEEE Transactions on Information Theory* 27:3, 280-291.

H. Jurgensen and M. Kunze [1984]. Redundance-Free Codes as Cryptocodes, *Technical Report*, Computer Science Dept., University of Western Ontario, London, Canada.

H. Jurgensen and D. E. Matthews [1983]. Some Results on the Information Theoretic Analysis of Cryptosystems, *Technical Report*, Computer Science Dept., University of Western Ontario, London, Canada.

D. Kahn [1967]. *The Code-Breakers*, MacMillan, New York, NY.

T. Kamae [1973]. "On Kolmogorov's Complexity and Information", *Osaka Journal of Mathematics* 10, 305-307.

A. N. C. Kang, R. C. T. Lee, C. Chang, and S. Chang [1977]. "Storage Reduction through Minimal Spanning Trees and Spanning Forests", *IEEE Transactions on Computers* 26:5, 425-434.

R. M. Karp [1961]. "Minimum-Redundancy Coding for the Discrete Noisless Channel", *IRE Transactions on Information Theory* 7, 27-39.

R. M. Karp [1972]. "Reducibility Among Combinatorial Problems", *Complexity of Computations*, (Miller and Thatcher, editors), Plenum Press, New York, NY.

J. Karush [1961]. "A Simple Proof of an Inequality by MacMillian", *IRE Transactions on Information Theory* 7, 118.

E. Kasner and J. Newman [1940]. *Mathematics and the Imagination*, Simon and Schuster, New York.

J. Katajainen and T. Raita [1987]. "An Analysis of the Longest Match and the Greedy Heuristics for Text Encoding", Technical Report, Department of Computer Science, University of Turku, Turku, Finland.

H. P. Katseff and M. Sipser [1977]. "Several Results in Program Size Complexity", *Proceedings Eighteenth Annual IEEE Symposium on Foundations of Computer Science*, Providence, RI, 82-89.

V. H. Kautz [1965]. "Fibonacci Codes for Synchronization Control", *IEEE Transactions on Information Theory* 11, 284-292.

M. Kearns, M. Li, L. Pitt, and L. Valiant [1987]. "On the Learnability of Boolean Formulae", *Proceedings Nineteenth Annual ACM Symposium on the Theory of Computing*, New York, NY, 285-295.

S. C. Kleene [1952]. *Introduction to Metamathmatics*, D. Van Nostrand Co., Inc., Princeton, NJ.

D. E. Knuth [1982]. *The Art of Computer Programming*, Vol I, II, and III, Addison-Wesley, Reading, MA.

D. E. Knuth [1982]. "Huffman's Algorithm via Algebra", *Journal Combinatorial Theory Series A* 32, 216-224.

D. E. Knuth [1985]. "Dynamic Huffman Coding", *Journal of Algorithms* 6, 163-180.

D. E. Knuth, J. H. Morris, and V. R. Pratt [1977]. "Fast Pattern Matching in Strings", *SIAM Journal on Computing* 6:2, 323-349.

A. N. Kolmogorov [1965]. "Three approaches to the Quantitative Definition of Information", *Problems of Information Transmission* 1, 1-7.

A. N. Kolmogorov [1969]. "On the Logical Foundation of Information Theory", *Problems of Information Transmission* 5, 3-7.

A. G. Konheim [1965]. *Mathematical Computing* 19, 143-144.

L. T. Kou [1977]. "Polynomial Complete Consecutive Information Retrieval Problems", *SIAM Journal on Computing* 6, 67-75.

L. G. Kraft [1949]. "A Device for Quantizing, Grouping, and Coding Amplitude Modulated Pulses", M.S. Thesis, Dept. of Electrical Engineering, Massachusetts Institute of Technology, Cambridge, MA.

R. M. Krause [1962]. "Channels which Transmit Letters of Unequal Duration", *Information and Control* 5:1, 13-24.

J. B. Kruskal [1983]. "An Overview of Sequence Comparison: Time Warps, String Edits, and Macromolecules", *SIAM Review* 25:2, 201-237.

H. Kucera and W. N. Francis [1967]. *Computational Analysis of Present-Day American English*, Brown University Press, Providence, RI.

H. T. Kung [1982]. "Why Systolic Architectures?", *IEEE Computer* 15:1, 37-46.

H. T. Kung and C. E. Leiserson [1978]. "Systolic Arrays (for VLSI)", *Technical Report CMU-CS-79-103*, Dept. of Computer Science, Carnegie-Mellon University.

H. T. Kung, B. Sproull, and G. Steele [1981]. *VLSI Systems and Computations*, Computer Science Press, Rockville, MD.

R. P. Laeser, W. I. McLaughlin, and D. M. Wolff [1986]. "Engineering Voyager2's Encounter with Uranus", *Scientific American* 255:5, 36-45.

K. B. Lakshmanan [1981]. "On Universal Codeword Sets", *IEEE Transactions on Information Theory* 27, 659-662.

G. M. Landau and U. Vishkin [1985]. "Efficient String Matching in the Presence of Errors", *Proceedings Twenty-Sixth Symposium on the Foundations of Computer Science*, Portland, OR, 126-136.

G. M. Landau and U. Vishkin [1986]. "Introducing Efficient Parallelism into Approximate String Matching and a New Serial Algorithm", *Proceedings Eighteenth Annual ACM Symposium on the Theory of Computing*, Berkeley, CA, 220-230.

G. M. Landau, B. Schieber, and U. Vishkin [1987]. "Parallel Construction of a Suffix Tree", *Proc. Fourteenth ICALP, Lecture Notes in Computer Science 267*, Springer-Verlag, New York, NY, 314-325.

L. L. Larmore [1987]. "Height-Restricted Optimal Binary Search Trees",

SIAM Journal on Computing (December).

L. L. Larmore and D. S. Hirschberg [1987]. "A Fast Algorithm for Optimal Length-Limited Codes", *Technical Report,* Dept. of Information and Computer Science, University of California, Irvine, CA.

R. H. Lathrop, T. A. Webster, and T. F. Smith [1987]. "Ariadne: Pattern-Directed Inference and Hierarchical Abstraction in Protein Structure Recognition", *CACM* 30:11, 909-921.

D. A. Lelewer and D. S. Hirschberg [1987]. "Data Compression", *Technical Report No. 87-10,* Dept. of Information and Computer Science, University of California, Irvine, CA.

Lewis and Papadimitriou [1981]. *Elements of the Theory of Computation,* Prentice-Hall, Englewood Cliffs, NJ.

S. Li and M. H. Loew [1987]. "The Quadcode and its Arithmetic", *Communications of the ACM* 30:7, 621-626.

S. Li and M. H. Loew [1987b]. "Adjacency Detection Using Quadcodes", *Communications of the ACM* 30:7, 627-631.

R. A. Lindsay and D. M. Chabries [1986]. "Data Compression of Color Images Using Vector Quantization", *Technical Report,* The Unisys Corporation, Salt Lake City, Utah.

J. A. Llewellyn [1987]. "Data Compression for a Source with Markov Characteristics", *The Computer Journal* 30:2, 149-156.

G. G. Langdon [1981]. "A Note on the Lempel-Ziv Model for Compressing Individual Sequences", *Technical Report RJ3318,* IBM Research Lab., San Jose, CA.

G. G. Langdon [1981b]. "Tutorial on Arithmetic Coding", *Technical Report RJ3128,* IBM Research Lab., San Jose, CA.

R. M. Lea [1978]. "Text Compression with an Associative Parallel Processor", *Computer Journal* 21:1, 45-56.

F. T. Leighton [1982]. Personal communication.

F. T. Leighton [1983]. *Complexity Issues in VLSI*, MIT Press, Cambridge, MA.

C. E. Leiserson [1980]. "Area-Efficient Graph Layouts (for VLSI)", *Proceedings Twenty-First Annual IEEE Symposium on Foundations of Computer Science*, Syracuse, NY, 270-281.

C. E. Leiserson [1982]. *Area-Efficient VLSI Computation*, MIT Press, Cambridge, MA.

A. Lempel, S. Even, and M. Cohn [1973]. "An Algorithm for Optimal Prefix Parsing of a Noiseless and Memoryless Channel", *IEEE Transactions on Infromation Theory* 19:2, 208-214.

A. Lempel and J. Ziv [1976]. "On the Complexity of Finite Sequences", *IEEE Transactions on Information Theory* 22:1, 75-81.

A. Lempel and J. Ziv [1985]. "Compression of Two-Dimensional Images", *Combinatorial Algorithms on Words*, Springer-Verlag (A. Apostolico and Z. Galil, editors), 141-154.

M. E. Lesk [1970]. "Compressed Text Storage", *Technical Report*, Bell Laboratories, Murray Hill, NJ.

V. E. Levenshtein [1968]. "On the Redundancy and Delay of Separable Codes for the Natural Numbers", *Problems of Cybernetics* 20, 173-179.

B. Leverett and T.G. Szymanski [1979]. "Chaining Span-Dependent Jump Instructions", *Technical Report*, Bell Laboratories, Murray Hill, NJ.

M. Li [1985]. "Lower Bounds by Kolmogorov-Complexity", Technical Report TR85-666, Computer Science Dept., Cornell University, Ithaca, NY.

H. H. J. Liao [1977]. "Upper Bound, Lower Bound, and Run-Length Substitution Coding", *National Telecommunications Conference*, 1-6.

R. J. Lipton and D. Lopresti [1985]. "A Systolic Array for Rapid String Comparison", *Proceedings Chapel Hill Conference on VLSI*.

Luc Longpre [1986]. "Resource Bounded Kolmogorov Complexity, a Link Between Computational Complexity and Information Theory", *Ph.D. Thesis*, Cornell University, Ithaca, NY.

D. W. Loveland [1969]. "A Variant of the Kolmogorov Concept of Complexity", *Information and Control* 15, 510-526.

D. W. Loveland [1969b]. "On Minimal-Program Complexity Measures", *Proceedings First Annual ACM Symposium on Theory of Computing*, Marina Del Rey, California, 61-65.

T. J. Lynch [1985]. *Data Compression: Techniques and Applications*, Lifetime Publications, Belmont, CA.

M. Machtey and P. Young [1976]. "Simple Gödel Numberings, Translations, and the P-Hierarchy: Preliminary Report", *Proceedings Eighth Annual ACM Symposium on Theory of Computing*, Hershey, Penn., 236-243.

B. MacMillian [1956]. "Two Inequalities Implied by Unique Decipherability", *IRE Transactions on Information Theory* 2, 115-116.

F. J. MacWilliams and N. J. A. Sloane [1978]. *The Theory of Error-Correcting Codes*, North-Holland, New York, NY.

M. Machtey and P. Young [1978]. *An Introduction to the General Theory of Algorithms*, North Holland, New York, NY.

S. Mahaney [1985]. Technical Report, Bell Laboratories, Murray Hill, NJ.

J. Makoul, S. Roucos, and H. Gish [1985]. "Vector Quantization in Speech Coding", *Proceedings of the IEEE* 73:11, 1551-1588.

K. V. Mardia [1972]. *Statistics of Directional Data*, Academic Press, New York, NY.

D. Maier [1978]. "The Complexity of Some Problems on Subsequences and Supersequences", *Journal of the ACM* 25:2, 322-336.

D. Maier [1982]. Personal communication.

D. Maier [1983]. *The Theory of Relational Databases*, Computer Science

Press, Rockville, MD.

D. Maier and J. A. Storer [1978]. "A Note Concerning the Superstring Problem", *Proceedings Twelfth Annual Conference on Information Sciences and Systems*, The Johns Hopkins University, Baltimore, MD, 52-56.

M. E. Majster [1979]. "Efficient On-Line Construction and Correction of Position Trees", *Technical Report TR79-393*, Dept. of Computer Science, Cornell University, Ithaca, NY.

G. Mandelbrot [1982]. *Fractal Geometry of Nature*, W. H. Freeman, Salt Lake City, Utah.

B. A. Marron and P.A.D. De Maine [1967]. "Automatic Data Compression", *Communications of the ACM* 10:11, 711-715.

P. Martin-Löf [1966]. "The Definition of Random Sequences", *Information and Control* 9, 602-619.

W. D. Maurer [1969]. "File compression using Huffman coding", In *Computing Methods in Optimization Problems 2*, Academic Press, 247-256. See also *Computing Reviews* 11:10, October 1970, 944.

J. Mavor, M. A. Jack, and P. B. Denyer [1983]. *Introduction to MOS LSI Design*, Addison-Wesley, Reading, MA.

A. Mayne and E. B. James [1975]. "Information Compression by Factorizing Common Strings", *The Computer Journal* 18:2, 157-160.

J. McCabe [1965]. "On Serial Files with Relocatable Records", *Operations Research* 12, 609-618.

J. P. McCarthy [1973]. "Automatic File Compression", International Computing Symposium (North Holland).

E. M. McCreight [1976]. "A Space-Economical Suffix Tree Construction Algorithm", *Journal of the ACM* 23:2, 262-272.

R. J. McEliece [1977]. *The Theory of Information and Coding*, Addison-Wesley, Reading, MA.

D. R. McIntyre and M. A. Pechura [1985]. "Data Compression Using Static Huffman Code-Decode Tables", *Journal of the ACM* 28:6, 612-616.

C. Mead and L. Conway [1982]. *Introduction to VLSI Systems*, Addison-Wesley, Reading, MA.

C. Mead and M. Rem [1979]. "Cost and Performance of VLSI Computing Structures", *IEEE Journal of Solid State Circuits* 14:2, 455-462.

K. Mehlhorn [1980]. "An Efficient Algorithm for Constructing Nearly Optimal Prefix Codes", *IEEE Transactions on Information Theory* 26:5, 513-517.

Miller [1961]. *Language and Computation*, McGraw Hill, New York, NY.

V. S. Miller and M. N. Wegman [1985]. "Variations on a Theme by Lempel and Ziv", *Combinatorial Algorithms on Words*, Springer-Verlag (A. Apostolico and Z. Galil, editors), 131-140.

J. H. Mommers, J. Raviv [1974]. "Coding for data compaction", IBM Watson Res. Report RC5150, November 1974.

R. Morris and K. Thompson [1974]. "Webster's Second on the Head of a Pin", *Technical Report*, Bell Laboratories, Murray Hill, NJ.

D. R. Morrison [1968]. "PATRICIA - A Practical Algorithm to Retrieve Information Coded in Alphanumeric", *Journal of the ACM* 15:4, 514-534.

A. Mukherjee and M. A. Bassiouni [1987]. "On-the-Fly Algorithms for Data Compression", *Proceedings ACM/IEEE Fall Joint Computer Conference*.

J. B. Mulford, R. K. Ridell [1971] "Data Compression Techniques for Economic Processing of Large Commercial Data Files", *ACM Symposium on Information Storage and Retrieval 1971*, 207-215.

B. K. Natarajan [1987]. "On Learning Boolean Formulaes", *Proceedings Nineteenth Annual ACM Symposium on the Theory of Com-*

puting, New York, NY, 296-304.

S. Newcomb [1881]. *American Journal of Mathematics* 4, 39-40.

J. von Neumann [1951]. "The General Logical Theory of Automata", in *Cerebral Mechananisms in Behaviour - The Hixon Symposium*, L. A. Jeffries, Ed.

W. P. Niedringhaus [1979]. "Scheduling Without Queuing, the Space Factory Problem", *Technical Report 253*, Dept. of Electrical Engineering and Computer Science, Princeton University, Princeton, NJ.

B. Noble and J. W. Daniel [1977]. *Applied Linear Algebra*, Prentice Hall, Englewood Cliffs, NJ.

N. D. Nonobashvili [1976]. "Some Questions on the Optimality of Representing Information by a Four-Letter Alphabet on a Transposition Scheme for Entering and Compressing Discrete Information", *Sakharth. SSR. Mecn. Akad. Moambe* 83:2, 317-320.

N. D. Nonobashvili [1977]. "An algorithm for compressing discrete information in a four-valued coding system", *Sakharth. SSR. Mecn. Akad. Moambe* 85:3, 565-568.

A. M. Odlyzko [1985]. "Enumeration of Strings", *Combinatorial Algorithms on Words*, Springer-Verlag, (A. Apostolico and Z. Galil, editors), 205-228.

D. S. Parker [1978]. "Combinatorial Merging and Huffman's Algorithm", *Technical Report*, Dept. of Computer Science, University of Illinois at Urbana-Champaign, Urbana, Ill.

D. S. Parker [1978b]. "On when Huffman's Algorithm is Optimal", Technical Report, Dept. of Computer Science, University of Illinois at Urbana-Champaign, Urbana, Ill.

M. S. Paterson, W. L. Ruzzo, and L. Snyder [1981]. "Bounds on Minimax Edge Length for Complete Binary Trees", *Proceedings Thirteenth Annual ACM Symposium on Theory of Computing*, Milwaukee, Wisconsin, 293-299.

E. A. Patrick, D. R. Anderson, and F. K. Bechtel [1968]. "Mapping Multidimensional Space to One Dimension for Computer Output Display", *IEEE Transactions on Computers* 17:10, 949-953.

T. Pavlidis [1982]. *Algorithms for Graphics and Image Processing*, Addison-Wesley, Reading, MA.

M. Pechura [1982]. "File Archival Techniques Using Data Compression", *Communications of the ACM* 25:9, 605-609.

Y. Perl, M. R. Garey, and S. Even [1975]. "Efficient Generation of Optimal Prefix Code: Equiprobable Words Using Unequal Cost Letters", *Journal of the ACM* 22:2, 202-214.

G. Peterson [1980]. "Succinct Representations, Random Strings, and Complexity Classes", *Proceedings Twenty-First Annual IEEE Symposium on the Foundations of Computer Science*, Syracuse, NY, 86-95.

W. W. Peterson and E. J. Weldon [1972]. *Error-Correcting Codes*, MIT Press, Cambridge, MA.

J. Pike [1981]. "Text Compression Using a 4-Bit Coding Scheme", *The Computer Journal* 24:4, 324-330.

R. S. Pinkham [1961]. "On the Distribution of First Significant Digits", *The Annals of Mathematical Statistics* 32:4, 1223-1230.

R. Y. Pinter [1982]. "On Routing Two-Point Nets Across a Channel", *Proceedings Nineteenth Design Automation Conference*, Las Vegas, NV.

L. Pitt and L. G. Valiant [1986]. "Computational Limitations on Learning from Examples", Technical Report TR-05-86, Aiken Computation Laboratory, Harvard University, Cambridge, MA.

E. C. Posner, E. R. Rodemich [1971]. "Epsilon Entropy and Data Compression", *Ann. Math. Statist.* 42, 2079-2125.

V. R. Pratt [1975]. "Improvements and Applications for the Weiner Repetition Finder", lecture notes (third revision).

W. K. Pratt [1978]. *Digital Image Processing*, John Wiley, New York, NY.

K. Preston, Jr. and M. J. B. Duff [1984]. *Modern Cellular Automata*, Plenum Press, New York, NY.

J. G. Proakis [1983]. *Digital Communications*, McGraw-Hill, New York, NY.

D. A. Pucknell and K. Eshraghian [1985]. *Basic VLSI Design: Principles and Applications*, Prentice-Hall, Englewood Cliffs, NJ.

R. A. Raimi [1969]. "On the Distribution of First Significant Figures", *American Mathematical Monthly 76*, 342-348.

R. A. Raimi [1969b]. "On the Peculiar Distribution of First Digits", *Scientific American* 221 (December), 109-120.

R. A. Raimi [1976]. "The First Digit Problem", *American Mathematical Monthly*, 521-538.

H. K. Ramapriyan, J. C. Tilton, and E. J. Seiler [1985]. "Impact of Data Compression on Spectral / Spatial Classification of Remotely Sensed Data", in *Advances in Remote Sensing Retrieval Methods*, H. E. Fleming and M. T. Chahine, Eds., Deepak Publishing.

J. H. Reif and J. A. Storer [1987]. "Minimizing Turns for Discrete Movement in the Interior of a Polygon", *IEEE Journal of Robotics and Automation* 3:3, 182-193.

J. Rissanen [1976]. "Generalized Kraft Inequality and Arithmetic Coding", *IBM Journal of Research and Development* 20, 198-203.

J. Rissanen [1982]. "Optimum Block Models with Fixed-Length Coding", Technical Report, IBM Research Center, San Jose, CA.

J. Rissanen [1983]. "A Universal Data Compression System", *IEEE Transactions on Information Theory* 29:5, 656-664.

J. Rissanen and G. G. Langdon [1981]. "Universal Modeling and Coding", *IEEE Transactions on Information Theory* 27:1, 12-23.

R. L. Rivest [1986]. "Learning Decision Lists", *Technical Report*, Massachusetts Institute of Technology, Cambridge, MA.

R. L. Rivest, A. Shamir, and L. Adleman [1977]. "A Method for Obtaining Digital Signatures and Public-Key Cryptosystems", *Technical Report MIT/LCS/TM-82*, MIT Laboratory for Computer Science, Cambridge, MA.

E. L. Robertson [1977]. "Code Generation for Short/Long Adress Machines", Technical Report 1779, Mathematics Research Center, University of Wisconsin, Madison, Wisconsin.

M. Rodeh, V. R. Pratt, and S. Even [1980]. "Linear Algorithms for Compression Via String Matching", *Journal of the ACM* 28:1, 16-24.

H. Rogers, Jr. [1958]. "Gödel Numberings of Partial Recursive Functions", *Journal of Symbolic Logic* 23, 331-341.

H. Rogers, Jr. [1967]. Theory of Recursive Functions and Effective Computability, McGraw-Hill, New York, NY.

A. Rosen [1987]. "Colormap: A Color Image Quantizer", *Technical Report 87-845*, Dept. of Computer Science, Cornell University, Ithaca, NY.

I. Rubin [1976]. "Data compression for Communication Networks: The Delay-Distortion Function", *IEEE Transactions on Information Theory* 22:6, 655-665.

F. Rubin [1976]. "Experiments in Text File Compression", *Communications of the ACM* 19:11, 617-623.

R. Rubinstein [1986]. "A Note on Sets with Small Generalized Kolmogorov Complexity", *Technical Report TR86-4*, Iowa State University.

S. S. Ruth and P. J. Kreutzer [1972]. "Data Compression for Large Business Files", *Datamation* 18:9, 62-66.

W. Ruzzo and L. Snyder [1981]. "Minimum Edge Length Embeddings of Trees", Conference on VLSI Systems and Computations, Carnegie-Mellon University, 119-123.

H. Samet [1983]. "A Quadtree Medial Axis Transform", *Communications of the ACM* 26:9, 680-693.

H. Samet [1984]. "The Quadtree and Related Hierarchical Data Structures", *ACM Computing Surveys* 16:2, 187-260.

H. Samet [1985]. "Data Structures for Quadtree Approximation and Compression", *Communications of the ACM* 28:9, 973-1004.

D. Sankoff and J. B. Kruskal, eds. [1983]. *An Overview of Sequence Comparison: Time Warps, String Edits, and Macromolecules,* Addison-Wesley, Reading, MA.

J. P. M. Schalwijk [1972]. "An Algorithm for Source Coding", *IEEE Transactions on Information Theory* 18, 395-399.

G. Schay Jr. and F. W. Dauer [1957]. "A Probabilistic Model of a Self-Organizing File System", *SIAM Journal on Applied Mathematics* 15, 874-888.

R. W. Scheifler [1977]. "An Analysis of In-Line Substitution for a Structured Programming Language", *Communications of the ACM* 20:9, 647-654.

B. Schieber and U. Vishkin [1987]. "On Finding Lowest Common Ancestors: Simplification and Parallelization", *Ultracomputer Note 118,* Courant Institute of Mathematical Sciences, New York University, New York, NY.

C. P. Schnorr [1974]. "Optimal Enumerations and Optimal Gödel Numberings", *Mathematical Systems Theory* 8:2, 182-190.

E. J. Schuegraf and H. S. Heaps [1974]. "A Comparison of Algorithms for Data Compression by Use of Fragements as Language Elements", *Information Storage and Retrieval* 10, 309-319.

E. S. Schwartz [1963]. "A Dictionary for Minimum Redundancy Encoding", *Journal of the ACM* 10, 413-439.

E. S. Schwartz [1964]. "An Optimum Encoding with Minimum Longest Code and Total Number of Digits", *Information and Control* 7, 37-44.

E. S. Schwartz and B. Kallick [1964]. "Generating a Canonical Prefix Encoding", *Communications of the ACM* 7:3, 166-169.

Schwartz, A. J. Kleiboemer [1967]. "A Language Element for Compression Coding", *Information and Control* 10, 315-333.

R. Sedgewick [1983]. *Algorithms*, Addison-Wesley, Reading, MA.

J. B. Seery and J. Ziv [1977]. "A Universal Data Compression Algorithm: Description and Preliminary Results", *Technical Memorandum 77-1212-6*, Bell Laboratories, Murray Hill, N.J.

J. B. Seery and J. Ziv [1978]. "Further Results on Universal Data Compression", *Technical Memorandum 78-1212-8*, Bell Laboratories, Murray Hill, N.J.

J. Seiferas [1977]. "Subword Trees", lecture notes, Pennsylvania State University, University Park, PA.

S. C. Seth [1976]. "Data Compression Techniques in Logic Testing: An Extension of Transition Counts", *Journal of Design Automation and Fault-Tolerant Computing* 1:2, 317-320.

D. G. Severance [1983]. "A Practitioner's Guide to Database Compression", *Information Systems* 8:1, 51-62.

C. E. Shannon [1951]. "Prediction of Entropy of Printed English Text", *Bell System Technical Journal* 30, 50-64 (reprinted in Slepian [1973]).

C. E. Shannon [1959]. "Coding Theorems for a Discrete Source with a Fidelity Criterion", *Proceedings IRE National Conference*, 142-163 (reprinted in Slepian [1973]).

C. E. Shannon and W. Weaver [1949]. *The Mathematical Theory of Communication*, University of Illinois Press, Urbana, IL.

M. Sipser [1983]. "A Complexity Theoretic Approach to Randomness", Proceedings Fifteenth Annual ACM Symposium on the Theory of Computing, 330-335.

D. Slepian, Ed. [1973]. *Key Papers in the Development of Information*

Theory, IEEE Press, New York, NY.

D. L. Slotnick, W. C. Bork, and R. C. McReynolds [1962]. "The Solomon Computer", *Proc. AFIPS Fall Joint Computer Conference*, Spartan Books, Washington, DC, 97-107.

L. Snyder [1982]. "Introduction to the Configurable, Highly Parallel Computer", *IEEE Computer* 15:1, 47-64.

M. Snyderman and B. Hunt [1970]. "The Myriad Virtues of Text Compaction", *Datamation*, 36-40.

R. I. Soare [1987]. *Recursively Enumerable Sets and Degrees*, Springer-Verlag, New York, NY.

W. Stallings [1985]. *Data and Computer Communications*, MacMillian Publishing Co., New York, NY.

K. Steiglitz, I. Kamal, and A. Watson [1988]. "Embedding Computation in One-Dimensional Automata by Phase Coding Solitons", *IEEE Transactions on Computers* 37:2, 138-145.

R. J. Stevens, A. F. Lehar, and F. H. Preston [1983]. "Manipulation and Presentation of Multidimensional Image Data Using the Peano Scan", *IEEE Transactions on Pattern Analysis and Machine Intelligence* 5:5, 520-526.

J. J. Stiffler [1971]. *Theory of Synchronous Communications*, Prentice-Hall, Englewood Cliffs, NJ.

J. A. Storer [1977]. "NP-Completeness Results Concerning Data Compression", *Technical Report 234*, Dept. of Electrical Engineering and Computer Science, Princeton University.

J. A. Storer [1977b]. "PLCC: A Compiler-Compiler for PL1 and PLC Users", *Technical Report 236*, Dept. of Electrical Engineering and Computer Science, Princeton University.

J. A. Storer [1979]. "Data Compression: Methods and Complexity Issues", *Ph. D. Thesis*, Dept. of Electrical Engineering and Computer Science, Princeton University, Princeton, NJ.

J. A. Storer [1982]. "Combining Pipes and Trees in VLSI", *Technical Report CS-82-107*, Dept. of Computer Science, Brandeis University.

J. A. Storer [1983]. "Toward an Abstract Theory of Data Compression", *Theoretical Computer Science* 24, 221-237.

J. A. Storer [1984]. "On Minimal Node-Cost Planar Embeddings", *Networks* 14, 181-212.

J. A. Storer [1985]. "Textual Substitution Techniques for Data Compression", *Combinatorial Algorithms on Words*, Springer-Verlag (A. Apostolico and Z. Galil, editors), 1985, 111-129.

J. A. Storer [1987]. "DCC-1 System for Dynamically Compressing and Decompressing Electronic Data", U.S. Patent pending (applied for 9/87).

J. A. Storer and T. G. Szymanski [1978]. "The Macro Model for Data Compression", *Proceedings Tenth Annual ACM Symposium on Theory of Computing*, San Diego, CA, 928-951.

J. A. Storer and T. G. Szymanski [1982]. "Data Compression Via Textual Substitution", *Journal of the ACM* 29:4, 928-951.

J. A. Storer and S. K. Tsang [1984]. "Data Compression Experiments Using Static and Dynamic Dictionaries", *Technical Report CS-84-118*, Computer Science Dept., Brandeis University, Waltham, MA.

C. Y. Suen [1979]. "N-Gram Statistics for Natural Language Understanding and Text Processing", *IEEE Transactions on Pattern Analysis and Machine Intelligence* 1:2, 164-172.

R. M. Sze [1983]. *VLSI Technology*, McGraw Hill, New York, NY.

T. G. Szymanski [1976]. "Assembling Code for Machines with Span Dependent Instructions", *Technical Report 224*, Dept. of Electrical Engineering and Computer Science, Princeton University, Princeton, NJ.

R. Tamassia [1987]. "On Embedding a Graph in the Planar Grid with the Minimum Number of Bends", *SIAM Journal on Computing*.

R. Techo [1980]. *Data Communications*, Plenum Press, New York, NY.

S. H. Teng [1987]. "The Construction of Huffman-Equivalent Prefix Code in NC", *ACM SIGACT News* 18:4, 54-61.

C. Tomborson [1987]. Computer Science Dept., University of Minnesota, Duluth, MN, private communication.

G. J. Tourlakis [1984]. *Computability*, Prentice-Hall, Englewood Cliffs, NJ.

B. A. Trakhtenbrot [1963]. *Algorithms and Automatic Computing Machines*, D. C. Heath and Company, Lexington, MA.

R. Tropper [1982]. "Binary-Coded Text: A Text-Compression Method", *Byte Magazine* April issue.

B. P. Tunstall [1968]. "Synthesis of Noiseless Compression Codes", *Ph.D. Thesis*, Georgia Institute of Technology.

J. S. Turner [1986]. "The Complexity of the Shortest Common String Matching Problem", *Proceedings Allerton Conference*, Monicello, Il. See also: *Technical Report WUCS-86-9*, Department of Computer Science, Washington University, Saint Louis, MO.

J. S. Turner [1986b]. "Approximation Algorithms for the Shortest Common Superstring Problem", *Technical Report WUCS-86-16*, Department of Computer Science, Washington University, Saint Louis, MO.

E. Ukkonen [1985]. "Finding Approximate Patterns in Strings", *Journal of Algorithms* 6, 132-137.

J. D. Ullman [1982]. *Principles of Database Systems*, Computer Science Press, Rockville, MD.

H. Urrows and E. Urrows [1984]. "Laser Data and other Data Disks: The Race to Store and Retrieve with Optics", *Videodisc and Optical Disk* 4:2, 130.

L. G. Valiant [1979]. "Universality Considerations in VLSI Circuits", *Proceedings IEEE International Conference in Information Theory*, Grigano, Italy.

L. G. Valiant [1979]. "A Theory of the Learnable", *Communactions of the ACM* 27:11, 1134-1142.

B. Varn [1971]. "Optimal Variable Length Codes (Arbitrary Symbol Costs and Equal Code Word Probability)", *Information and Control 19*, 289-301.

N. D. Vasyukova [1977]. "On the Compact Representation of Information", *Mathematika i Kibernetika* 4, 90-93.

U. Vishkin [1985]. "Optimal Parallel Pattern Matching in Strings", *Proceedings Twelfth ICALP, Lecture Notes in Computer Science* 194, Springer-Verlag, 497-508 (also to appear in *Information and Control*).

M. Visvalingam [1976]. "Indexing with Coded Deltas: A Data Compaction Technique", *Software Practice and Experience* 6, 397-403.

J. S. Vitter [1987]. "Design and Analysis of Dynamic Huffman Coding", *JACM* 34:4, 825-845.

V. A. Vittikh [1973]. "Synthesis of Algorithms for Data Compression", *Problems of Control and Information Theory* 2:3-4, 235-241.

R. A. Wagner [1973]. "Common Phrases and Minimum-Space Text Storage", *Communications of the ACM* 16:3, 148-152.

O. Watanable [1986]. "Generalized Kolmogorov Complexity of Computations", manuscript.

P. Weiner [1973]. "Linear Pattern Matching Algorithms", *Proceedings Fourteenth Annual Symposium on Switching and Automata Theory*, 1-11.

T. A. Welch [1984]. "A Technique for High-Performance Data Compression", *IEEE Computer* 17:6, 8-19.

M Wells [1972]. "File Compression Using Variable Length Encodings", *The Computer Journal 15:4*, 308-313.

M. N. Wegman [1987]. Manuscript, IBM Watson Research Center, Yorktown Heights, NY.

R. L. Wessner [1976]. "Optimal Alphabetic Search Trees with Restricted Maximal Height", *Information Processing Letters* 4, 90-94.

N. Weste and K. Eshraghian [1985]. *Principles of CMOS VLSI Design*, Addison-Wesley, Reading, MA.

S. A. Weyer and A. H. Borning [1985]. "A Prototype El,ectronic Encyclopedia", *ACM Transactions on Office Information Systems* 3:1, 63-88.

N. Weyland and E. Puckett [1986]. "Optimal Binary Models for the Gaussian Source of Fixed Precision Numbers", *Technical Report*, Mitre Corporation, Bedford, MA.

R. Williams [1987]. "Predictive Data Compression", *Technical Report*, Dept. of Computer Science, University of Adelaide, Adelaide, South Australia.

I. H. Witten, R. M. Neal, and J. G. Cleary [1987]. "Arithmetic Coding for Data Compression", *Communications of the ACM* 30:6, 520-540.

J. Wolfowitz [1960]. "On Channels in Which the Distribution of Error is Known Only to the Receiver or Only to the Sender", *Information and Decison Processes*, (R. E. Machol, Editor), 178-182.

E. J. Yannakoudakis, P. Goyal, and J. A. Huggil [1982]. "The Generation and Use of Text Fragments for Data Compression", *Information Processing and Management* 18:1, 15-21.

M. Yau and S. N. Srihari [1983]. "A Hierarchical Data Structure for Multidimensional Digital Images", *Communications of the ACM* 26:7, 504-515.

J. F. Young [1971]. *Information Theory*, Wiley Interscience, New York, NY.

T. Y. Young and P. S. Liu [1980]. "Overhead Storage Considerations and a Multilinear Method for Data File Compression", *IEEE Transactions on Software Engineering* 6:4, 340-347.

G. K. Zipf [1935]. *The Psycho-Biology of Language*, Houghton, Boston, MA.

G. K. Zipf [1949]. *Human Behaviour and the Principle of Least Effort*, Addison-Wesley, Reading, MA.

J. Ziv [1978]. "Coding Theorems for Individual Sequences", *IEEE Transactions on Information Theory* 24:4, 405-412.

J. Ziv [1985]. "On Universal Quantization", *IEEE Transactions on Information Theory* 31:3, 344-347.

J. Ziv and A. Lempel [1977]. "A Universal Algorithm for Sequential Data Compression", *IEEE Transactions on Information Theory* 23:3, 337-343.

J. Ziv and A. Lempel [1978]. "Compression of Individual Sequences Via Variable-Rate Coding", *IEEE Transactions on Information Theory* 24:5, 530-536.

INDEX